ASPECTS OF
EARLY VISNUISM

J. GONDA

MOTILAL BANARSIDASS PUBLISHERS
PRIVATE LIMITED • DELHI

First Edition : Leiden, 1954
Reprint: Delhi, 1969, 1993

ISBN : 81-208-1087-2

Also available at :

MOTILAL BANARSIDASS
41 U.A., Bungalow Road, Jawahar Nagar, Delhi 110 007
120 Royapettah High Road, Mylapore, Madras 600 004
16 St. Mark's Road, Bangalore 560 001
Ashok Rajpath, Patna 800 004
Chowk, Varanasi 221 001

PRINTED IN INDIA

BY JAINENDRA PRAKASH JAIN AT SHRI JAINENDRA PRESS,
A-45 NARAINA, PHASE I, NEW DELHI 110 028 AND PUBLISHED BY
NARENDRA PRAKASH JAIN FOR MOTILAL BANARSIDASS PUBLISHERS
PRIVATE LIMITED, BUNGALOW ROAD, DELHI 110 007

Prefatory Note

In this mechanical reproduction of a book published in 1954 what has been written in recent years on the problems discussed could not be taken into account. The author wishes however to confess that in the course of time his own ideas of some questions have considerably evolved. For a brief resume the reader may be referred to 'Die Religionen Indiens', I, Stuttgart 1960, especially p. 89 ff.; for an evaluation and incorporation of recent publications and a longer and up-to-date exposition of the author's own opinions to chapters I and II of a book 'Viṣṇuism and Śivaism' which is to appear before long. With regard to the much-discussed problem of the so-called origin of the Viṣṇu conception—we had better speak of the core and essence of the god's nature as understood by Vedic man—the author is still inclined to assume that there is much truth in the time-honoured Indian interpretation of Viṣṇu's character as representing pervasiveness and spatial extensiveness, and especially that pervasiveness and omnipresence which is essential to the establishment and maintenance of our cosmos and beneficial to the interests of gods and men. He would however hesitate to emphasize that "the general idea originally underlying this central mythical act seems to have been the phenomenon of the mighty and blessing stream of celestial light" (p. 172), and at the moment attach more value to Viṣṇu's relations with the cosmic axis (see p. 81 f.) and to textual evidence pointing to pervasiveness as such which was believed to manifest itself in a great variety of phenomena.

UTRECHT
12-4-1969

—J. Gonda

CONTENTS

ABBREVIATIONS[1])

AiĀ., AiĀr.:	Aitareya-āraṇyaka
AiB.:	Aitareya-brāhmaṇa
ĀpŚS., ĀpŚrS.:	Āpastamba-śrautasūtra
AS.:	Atri-saṃhitā
ĀśvGS.:	Āśvalāyana-gṛhyasūtra
ĀŚS., ĀśvŚS.:	Āśvalāyana-śrautasūtra
AV., AthV.:	Atharvaveda-saṃhitā
AVPar.:	Atharvaveda-pariśiṣṭa
BārUp.:	Bṛhadāraṇyaka-upaniṣad
BaudhDhŚ.:	Baudhāyana-dharmaśāstra
BaudhŚS.:	Baudhāyana-śrautasūtra
BD.:	Bṛhaddevatā
BḍPur.:	Brahmāṇḍa-purāṇa
BhG.:	Bhagavadgītā
BhāgPur.:	Bhāgavata-purāṇa
BhavPur.:	Bhaviṣya-purāṇa
BJābUp.:	Bṛhajjābāla-upaniṣad
BrPur.:	Brahma-purāṇa
DŚS.:	Drāhyāyaṇa-śrautasūtra
GarPur.:	Garuḍa-purāṇa
GB.:	Gopatha-brāhmaṇa
GGS., GobhGS.:	Gobhila-gṛhyasūtra
Har.:	Harivaṃśa
HirGS.:	Hiraṇyakeśi-gṛhyasūtra
ĪUp.:	Īśa-upaniṣad
JB., JaimB.:	Jaiminīya-brāhmaṇa (C.: Caland's Auswahl)
JaiUB., JaiUpB., JUB.:	Jaiminīya-upaniṣad-brāhmaṇa
Kāl.:	Kālidāsa
KālPur.:	Kālikā-purāṇa
Kāl. Ragh.:	Raghuvaṃśa by Kālidāsa
KāṭhGS., KGS.:	Kāṭhaka-gṛhyasūtra
KāṭhS., Kāṭh., KS.:	Kāṭhaka-saṃhitā

[1]) For particulars, editions, translations, etc. see: L. Renou, Bibliographie védique, Paris 1931; R. N. Dandekar, Vedic bibliography (since 1930), Bombay 1946; L. Renou, Littérature sanskrite, Paris-Neuchatel 1946.

Kaṭhop.:	Kaṭha-upaniṣad
Kauś., KauśS.:	Kauśika-sūtra
KauṣB., KB.:	Kauṣītaki-brāhmaṇa
KauṣUp.:	Kauṣītakī-upaniṣad
Kauṭ. Arth.:	Arthaśāstra by Kauṭilya
KūPur.:	Kūrma-purāṇa
KS. (in ch. III):	Kāśyapa-saṃhitā
LiPur.:	Liṅga-purāṇa
MahUp.:	Mahā-upaniṣad
MahānāUp.:	Mahānārāyaṇa-upaniṣad
MaiUp., MaitrUp.	Maitrī or Maitrāyaṇīya-upaniṣad
Manu:	Manusmṛti or Mānava-dharmaśāstra
MārkPur.:	Mārkaṇḍeya-purāṇa
MB.:	Mantra-brāhmaṇa
Mbh.:	Mahābhārata
MGS., MānGS.:	Mānava-gṛhyasūtra
MS., MaitrS.:	Maitrāyaṇī-saṃhitā
MśS.:	Mānava-śrautasūtra
MtPur.:	Matsya-purāṇa
Paipp.:	Paippalāda (recension of the AV saṃhitā)
PārGS.:	Pāraskara-gṛhyasūtra
PB., PañcB.:	Pañcaviṃśa-brāhmaṇa
Rām.:	Rāmāyaṇa
ṚV.:	Ṛgveda-saṃhitā
ṚVidh., Ṛgvidh.	Ṛgvidhāna
śāB., śāṅkhB.:	Śāṅkhāyana- (= Kauṣītaki-) brāhmaṇa
śāṅkhGS.:	Śāṅkhāyana-gṛhyasūtra
Śaun.:	Śaunaka (recension of the AV saṃhitā)
ŚB., ŚBr.:	Śatapatha-brāhmaṇa
ṢB.:	Ṣaḍviṃśa-brāhmaṇa
Ś ŚS., ŚS.:	Śāṅkhāyana-śrautasūtra
SV.:	Sāmaveda-saṃhitā
SVB.:	Sāmavidhāna-brāhmaṇa
ŚvUp.:	Śvetāśvatara-upaniṣad
TĀ., TaittĀr.:	Taittirīya-āraṇyaka
TB., TaittBr.:	Taittirīya-brāhmaṇa
TS.:	Taittirīya-saṃhitā
TUp.:	Taittirīya-upaniṣad
VaitS.:	Vaitāna-sūtra
Vāj.Saṃh., VS.:	Vājasaneyi-saṃhitā
Vāl.:	Vālakhilya (ṚV. 8, 49-59, sometimes num bered separately)

VāPur., VāP.:	Vāyu-purāṇa
Varāh. BS.:	Bṛhatsaṃhitā by Varāhamihira
VidhPur.:	Viṣṇudharmottara-purāṇa
ViPur.:	Viṣṇu-purāṇa
ViS.:	Viṣṇu-smṛti
VSK.:	Vājasaneyi-saṃhitā Kāṇva-recension

BEFEO.:	Bulletin de l'Ecole française de l'Extrême-Orient, Hanoi
BSO(A)S.:	Bulletin of the School of Oriental (and African) Studies, London
IA.:	Indian Antiquary, Bombay
IF., Indog. Forsch.:	Indogermanische Forschungen, Strassburg, Berlin
IHQ.:	The Indian Historical Quarterly, Calcutta
JAS.:	Journal asiatique, Paris
JAOS:	Journal of the American Oriental Society, New Haven
JRAS.:	Journal of the Royal Asiatic Society, London
Petr. Dict.:	Petrograd Dictionary, i.e. O. Böhtlingk und R. Roth, Sanskrit-Wörterbuch herausgegeben v.d. kais. Akad. d. Wiss., St. Petersburg
RGVV.:	Religionsgeschichtliche Versuche und Vorarbeiten, Giessen
SBE.:	Sacred Books of the East, ed. by F. Max Müller, Oxford
ZDMG.:	Zeitschrift der Deutschen Morgenländischen Gesellschaft, Leipzig, Wiesbaden
Zs.:	Zeitschrift

Other titles, if not quoted in full, will easily be identified.

CHAPTER ONE: VIṢṆU.

I. INTRODUCTION.

It is a matter of common knowledge that Viṣṇu, who in Hinduism is a divinity of the highest rank and who had already in the mythology of the brāhmaṇas assumed a considerable importance, occupied but a subordinate position in the Ṛgveda. In many books and papers on Indian religion this fact is emphasized, but the comment added by the authors in order to elucidate the early historical development of Viṣṇuism does not always seem to give an adequate idea of the complex character of the problem arising from it. Thus Sten Konow [1]) in a cautious discussion of the question was right in expressing the opinion that Viṣṇu must have been, in ancient times, an important divinity, and that in his Vedic appearance "schon die Keime vorhanden waren, aus denen sich ein grosser Gott entwickeln konnte", but he does not explain in what respect he was a great god. Nor does he sufficiently account for his assuming the character of the Supreme Being by observing that he could take the place of other gods and adopt their functions because he originally had a "weite Tätigkeitssphäre".

Other authors too inconsiderately took for granted that the Viṣṇu who appears in the Ṛgveda was representative of the Viṣṇu figure of that early period in its entirety [2]). They were inclined to pose the problem in this way: how has the comparatively subordinate Vedic deity become the Supreme Being and the Lord of gods? They, too, endeavoured to give the answer by pointing to the syncretistic character of the Hinduistic Viṣṇu. They are of course right in adopting the latter course of reasoning, but, as far as I am able to see, mistaken in neglecting those traits of the ancient god's nature which linked him with the Hinduistic God and which made it more understandable that it was this divine figure who could amalgamate with other potencies and deities. It would, indeed, appear to be a legitimate aim to examine,

---

[1]) S. Konow, Die Inder, in A. Bertholet und E. Lehmann, Lehrbuch der Religionsgeschichte, Tübingen 1925, II, p. 27; 29; 63. — Other scholars, for instance A. Bergaigne, La religion védique, II, Paris 1883, p. 414 ff. left the problem undiscussed. — One might be tempted to attach some importance to such stray references as ṚV. 1, 156, 3, where Viṣṇu is called *pūrvyam* ... *ṛtasya garbham* — whatever its exact meaning may have been.

[2]) Compare e.g. M. Monier Williams, Hinduism, London 1890, p. 87 ff.; 100 ff.; H. von Glasenapp, Die Religionen Indiens, Stuttgart 1943, p. 141; 143.

on the one hand, whether there were some elements in the nature of the god as described by the poets of the Ṛgveda and other very ancient documents, which may be considered as predisposing him to becoming an important central figure and, on the other hand, whether some traits of his character were perhaps suppressed by the ancient authors whose works have been preserved to us.

Yet the attempts made in this direction, though throwing light on part of the problem under consideration, have failed to give the impression of a final solution. Hopkins [3]), arguing that Viṣṇu's later popularity lay in the importance of his "highest place or step", the home of the departed spirits where he himself is said to dwell (ṚV. 1, 154, 5; 10, 15, 3) [4]), seems to have left out of consideration the comparatively unimportant rôle played by Viṣṇu's highest place as the 'heaven' of the emancipated in the oldest texts in which the god himself usually, or often, figures as the Infinite Spirit and the Highest Being. In the Mahābhārata it is no central conception: it is a place of virtue and sacrificial ceremonies, often locally defined and reflected in, or represented by tīrthas called Viṣṇupadas which are sometimes described as Viṣṇu's perpetual residence and as an entrance to his world [5]). It is true that side by side with "being adored in Viṣṇu's world" as the result of bathing, and "obtaining the fruit of the aśvamedha and going to the Viṣṇuloka" the phrase "attaining to the same world or heaven with Viṣṇu (*viṣṇor yāti salokatām*) is incidentally found (Mbh. 18, 6, 49). Nevertheless I am under the impression that the conception of final beatitude in Viṣṇu's highest place, that is in Heaven, was no more than one of a plurality of ideas and beliefs connected with this god and determining his future greatness.

The explanation proposed by Von Schroeder [6]) was not free from

---

[3]) E. Washburn Hopkins, JAOS. 16 (1896), p. CXLVII; the same, The religions of India, Boston 1895, p. 56. In a similar way: R. G. Bhandarkar, Vaiṣṇavism, Çaivism..., Strassburg 1913, p. 33 f.; see also N. Macnicol, Indian theism, Oxford 1915, p. 33. P. N. U. Harting, Selections from the Baudhāyanagṛhyap. sūtra, Thesis Utrecht 1922, p. VII even holds that "the reverence for the mysterious highest place or step" led to Viṣṇu's gradual rising to the rank of the supreme spirit. I also refer to the able discussion by Miss M. Das Gupta, in the Indian Historical Quarterly 7 (1931), p. 93 ff.

[4]) For the textual evidence see A. A. Macdonell, Vedic Mythology, Strassburg 1897, p. 167 and 169. See also: A. Hohenberger, Die indische Flutsage und das Matsyapurāṇa, Leipsic 1930, p. 98 ff.

[5]) References may be found in S. Sørensen, An index to the names of the Mahabharata, London 1904, p. 742 ff., and in Hopkins, Epic Mythology, Strassburg 1915, p. 209. — It might be remembered that the term *viṣṇupada-* does not only refer to the 'heaven'; it can also stand for a lotus, the ocean, a footprint of the god etc.

[6]) L. von Schroeder, Arische Religion, I, Leipsic 1914, p. 121.

simplism and conjectural argumentation: among the 'Naturgötter' the ancient solar deity Viṣṇu ascended to the high position of a great and highly honoured divinity, and in a similar way Rudra soon arose above the other 'Seelengötter'. The secret of the victory and vitality of the triad Brahmā Viṣṇu Śiva consists, he holds, in their representing the three main roots of religion and in the harmonious way in which they supplement each other. Without textual evidence casual references to "uralte und tiefgewurzelte Volkstümlichkeit" and doubtful "Elemente der Sinnlichkeit und Erotik" in the character of the Vedic Viṣṇu [7]) are no conclusive arguments to establish this view.

Keith [8]) is no doubt right in observing that denying to Viṣṇu the position of a great god in the period of the Ṛgveda would be to forget that the comparative prominence of the gods is not necessarily fully brought out in that collection, the range of interests of which was not very wide. But he leaves us in the dark as to the factors contributing to Viṣṇu's ascendancy over the other gods in later times and he, too, holds too simplistic views about the interrelation of the god's various aspects and activities in the ancient period. Even in the most ancient documents Viṣṇu had already several aspects, and it does not appear hazardous to suppose a priori that the authors of the Vedic sūktas borrowed at least some of their conceptions from the belief of a greater public which certainly did not always revere the god as Rāma or Kṛṣṇa [9]). Part of our efforts should be directed towards detecting the undercurrents which make their presence felt in the more or less rounded representations found in those documents which are of greater importance.

Like Keith, Ruben [10]) gave the verdict that Viṣṇu became a great god in post-Vedic times because he — for this pronoun I would, for the sake of prudence, read: a deity of his character and functions — was already important in pre-Aryan — I would prefer: non-Aryan — India. Although this author seems to be right in emphasizing, in this connection, the god's relation with Indra, I do not feel completely convinced by the argumentation following these remarks. It is for one

---

7) Von Schroeder, Mysterium und Mimus im Rigveda, Leipsic 1908, p. 56.

8) A. Berriedale Keith, The religion and philosophy of the Veda and Upanishads, Harvard 1925, p. 109.

9) For Kṛṣṇaism see also Hemchandra Raychaudhuri, Materials for the study of the early history of the Vaishnava sect, Calcutta 1936; W. Ruben, Krishna, Istanbul 1943. — J. E. Carpenter, Theism in medieval India, London 1926, p. 236 is inclined to attach some value to "the emphasis on Viṣṇu's constancy and compassion" which might have awoken the trust and love of the believer (cf. e.g. ṚV. 7, 100, 2 *sumati-*). Cf. also Bh. Kumarappa, The Hindu conception of the deity, London 1934, p. 89.

10) Ruben, Eisenschmiede und Dämonen in Indien, Leyden 1939, p. 284.

thing not certain that Viṣṇu qua talis originally was exclusively non-Aryan, those etymological explanations of the god's name which are founded on associations with words supposed to derive from linguistic substrata being, to my mind, decidedly more improbable than those which derive it from Sanskrit [11]). Besides, the supposed [12]) transfer to Indra of myths originally belonging to Viṣṇu seems rather speculative: although the names of Arbuda [13]) and Śambara [14]) and some

---

11) The etymology of the name Viṣṇu has been a matter of considerable speculation among scholars. M. Bloomfield, Am. J. of Phil. 17, p. 427 f.; H. Oldenberg, Nachr. Gött. Ges. d. Wiss. 1915, p. 374 f.; the same, Die Religion des Veda⁴, Stuttgart-Berlin 1923, p. 230 ff. are much inclined to explain it as "Herr der weiten Flächen" (*vi- snu-*, cf. *sānu-*) or "crossing the back of the world or the earthly regions". The same etymology was defended by H. Güntert, Der arische Weltkönig und Heiland, Halle 1924, p. 306 f. who interpreted the name by "wer die Fläche auseinanderbreitet". Other authors (e.g. H. D. Griswold, The religion of the Ṛgveda, Oxford 1923, p. 285) were however right in having their doubts. Th. Bloch, in the Wörter und Sachen 1 (1909), p. 80 and other scholars believed the name to contain the suffix *-snu* (cf. *jiṣṇu*, see e.g. W. D. Whitney, A Sanskrit grammar, § 1194) and the element *vi-* "bird" which unlike *ji-* is, however, no verbal root. K. F. Johansson, Über die altindische Göttin Dhiṣáṇā..., Uppsala 1917, p. 48, n. 0, even goes so far as to consider *Viṣṇu-* almost identical with the Gr. οἰωνός "a large bird". In recent times an attempt was made by R. N. Dandekar, 'Festschrift' Kane, Poona 1941, p. 107, to defend Bloch's view: however, Johansson's opinion, on which he relies, viz. that Viṣṇu originally was the sun-bird is far from convincing. Hopkins, JAOS. 36, p. 264, focussing attention on Viṣṇu's being a god of movement, upholds the view that the name contains the root *vi-* or *vī-* "go, hasten, be active". Macdonell, Vedic Mythology, p. 39 gives serious consideration to the root *viṣ-* "to be active", interpreting Viṣṇu as the representative of solar motion. According to J. Przyluski, whose hazardous speculations appeared in the Actes du XVIIIe congrès international des Orientalistes, 1931, p. 154; in the Archiv Or. 4 (1932), p. 261 ff., and in the Quarterly Journal of the Mythic Soc. of Bangalore 25 (1934-5), the god, who has no counterpart in IE. mythology, is 'pre-Aryan'; his name should be connected with the non-Aryan *viṭh, vĕth* (compare the name of the *Veṭhadīpa,* a race living in the Deccan). The name may of course be an aryanisation of an originally 'indigenous' word but Przyluski's method is dangerous. F. W. Thomas, Actes XVIIIe congrès, l.c., was inclined to consider *viṣṇu-* as having arisen from **vistnu,* like *kṛṣṇa-* from *kistnā-*. Authors of purāṇas made the word mean "who enters or pervades (viz. the universe)", disregarding the phonetic difficulty, and emphasizing an important side of the character of their God: cf. e.g. BdPur. 2, 3, 120; VāPur. 66, 137 *yasmād viṣṭam idaṃ sarvaṃ vāmaneneha jāyatā | tasmāt sa vai smṛto viṣṇur viśer dhātoḥ praveśanāt* (W. Kirfel, Das Purāṇa pañcalakṣaṇa, Bonn 1927, p. 185; cf. also p. 57 e.a.; D. R. Patil, Cultural history from the Vāyu Purāṇa, Poona 1946, p. 65; see also Dandekar, o.c., p. 106, n. 15). For other attempts see M. Das Gupta, o.c., p. 103, n. 1 and Dandekar, p. 106 f. In this book the unsolved problem will not be made an element of the argumentation.

12) See also Konow, The Aryan gods, in the Publ. of the Ind. Inst., Univ. Oslo, I, 1921.

13) See also F. B. J. Kuiper, Proto-Munda words in Sanskrit, Amsterdam 1948, p. 146.

14) The reader might also be referred to my paper Tumura's en Çavara's, in the Bijdragen tot de Taal-, Land- en Volkenkunde, 90, The Hague 1933, p. 167 ff.

mythological particulars seem to point to their having belonged to the non-Aryan components of the ancient Indian population, it does not follow that they formed part of a Viṣṇu mythology. In Indra's combat with Arbuda, for instance, Viṣṇu takes no share. It might even be of some importance that Trita, whose deeds have often a close resemblance to those of Indra (and still more to those of the Avestan Thrita) is said (ṚV. 2, 11, 20) to have assisted Indra in overthrowing Arbuda. Śambara's name, on the other hand, besides being almost exclusively associated with Indra's, is ṚV. 2, 24, 2 mentioned in connection with Bṛhaspati. I can, moreover, not see that Śambara's thinking himself a little god (ṚV. 7, 18, 20) alone need induce us to consider him an element of a Viṣṇu myth. For reasons to be expounded in the following pages a reference to Indra's casual character as a sun-god can, further, not serve as a decisive argument to show that the Aryans could easily make him Viṣṇu's companion.

We shall not enlarge here upon the intricate question — the importance of which is however not denied — of how far non-Aryan components can be clearly recognized in the early stages of Viṣṇuism. There is no doubt ample room for the supposition that the ethnic substratum has much contributed to the divinity of the Vedic period known as Viṣṇu. We may even surmise his ascendancy to have constituted, if not a 'reaction' of proto-Hinduism to the religion of the Nordic invaders [15]), then a coming to the surface of the beliefs of those masses whose voice is but imperfectly heard in the Ṛgveda. Yet all that has been said on this point is of a more or less speculative character and any attempt to point out more than general outlines would appear to be premature. Any effort to represent mere possibilities as certainty or even as an hypothesis must be distrusted. Since the expression of natural or 'primitive' and 'semi-primitive' humanity, irrespective of racial connections and geographical environments, is fairly similar, it is, indeed, far from easy to decide whether definite myths or exploits attributed to a deity or ceremonies celebrated in his

[15]) This view was suggested by J. H. Hutton, Caste in India, Cambridge 1946, p. 200. — I for one would like to object to a too inconsiderate use of the term 'reaction' and to too rectilinear and onesidedly 'chronological' interpretations of the data found in those texts and documents which have been preserved to us. Authors who like P. Thieme — who for the rest in criticizing my views on the *bráhman* idea (see my 'Notes on brahman' Utrecht 1950; P. Thieme, Bráhman, Zs. d. deutschen morgenl. Ges. 102, 1952, p. 91 ff.) gives evidence of inaccurate reading — pay attention exclusively to the chronological succession of the sources are apt to disregard social and other factors: views, beliefs, customs, which are early superseded in some circles may be long retained elsewhere. A text which is chronologically speaking younger does not necessarily reflect a more developed stage in the history of the concepts under discussion or more advanced ideas or beliefs.

honour, are Aryan or non-Aryan as long as unambiguous philological and linguistic data are wanting. Besides, the processes of identification and amalgamation of religious figures and conceptions originally belonging to different peoples or milieus are usually complicated to such a degree that the respective contributions are almost always difficult to determine even if the scarcity of the historical material available is not so great an impediment to the progress of research.

We should be aware that the inhabitants of those parts of ancient India which were within the sphere of Aryan influence, like other countries in similar circumstances, varied from each other not only by different 'racial' origin and different tribal beliefs and customs, but to a degree also by social or occupational interests. Variations in the degree of civilization both ethnically and socially, both locally and temporally, must have been reflected in the forms of religion. It may be true that the Ṛgveda as compared with other documents exhibits a comparatively larger element of Aryan culture, it is none the less true that it is mainly representative of the interests, aspirations, and cultural sphere of the male half of mankind, of the warriors and the possessors of herds and grounds, and of their priests and eulogists. The interests, opinions and religious beliefs and observances of women, of those concerned with agriculture, commerce, arts and crafts, etc., of the subordinates, whether these components of the population were or were not non-Aryan by descent or culture, are as a rule only seldom and passingly touched upon [16]). In my opinion these considerations suffice to prevent us from nourishing too great hopes of reaching definite results by applying the argumentum e silentio, that is by denying the existence of one form of worship or other in the Aryan community because the Ṛgveda is silent on it and to infer from this silence that it probably was 'autochtonous'.

I am not able to see why we should for instance be sure that the worship of a mother goddess, which according to Hutton [17]) was "probably brought in by earlier invaders of Mediterranean or of Armenoid race, speaking no doubt a Dravidian language, whose religion must also be associated with fertility cults, phallic symbolism, the *devadāsī* cult, and probably human sacrifice", had been entirely foreign to other components of the population. Nor am I convinced either of the absolute correctness of such statements [18]) as are found in the same book with respect to an admitted Mediterranean or southern

16) Hence also the lack of information on this point in modern books (e.g. M. W. Pinkham, Woman in the sacred scriptures of Hinduism, N. York 1941).

17) Hutton, o.c., p. 197.

18) Hutton, o.c., p. 200.

character of other forms of religion, and with regard to the close or even exclusive association of definite forms of worship with definite foreign or at least non-Aryan peoples or cults [19]). Too often borrowings from Caucasian or other cultures have been assumed [20]) without bestowing sufficient consideration upon the above aspects of the problems concerned. Like Nehring, Przyluski discussing in too speculative a manner the data concerning the great goddess in India and Iran [21]), seems tacitly to admit that the mother goddess or earth goddess must per se, or always, be superior to masculine gods and therefore be explicable only by the hypothesis of matriarchal institutions. Arguing that it is not probable that Indoeuropean or Semitic peoples had from the beginning a social organization of this kind he sees himself forced to suppose that the cult of this deity was an heritage from an earlier civilization. But how are we to know for certain that, for instance, the figurines found at various archaeological sites and other objects of the same order always and everywhere represent a chief and superior goddess such as can only be conceived to exist in a society where the feminine element is preponderant? [22]) Would we overstep the bounds of possibility by assuming that at least in some regions these figures [23]) played a part in the rustic household shrines of smaller communities (families, villages), side by side with other gods worshipped by other parts of the contemporary population, that is to say that the historical co-existence of female grāmadevatās and other, mainly male, gods within the whole of Hinduism was already of pre-historic occurrence? [24]) It may be remembered that a similar problem presents

---

19) Similar critical remarks may, in my opinion, apply to several passages in Ruben's Eisenschmiede (see above, n. 10).

20) For instance by A. Nehring, in A. Koppers, Die Indogermanen- und Germanenfrage, Vienna 1936, p. 194.

21) Przyluski, in the Indian Hist. Quarterly 10 (1934), p. 405.

22) These remarks are of course not intended to deny the spread of matriarchal institutions in the south of Asia, for which the reader may be referred to K. Birket-Smith, Geschichte der Kultur, Zürich 1946, p. 276 ff. and the literature mentioned by this author on p. 548 ff.; G. Buschan, Die Völker Asiens, Australiens und der Südseeinseln, Berlin, passim. Cf. also O. Schrader-A. Nehring, Reallexikon der indogermanischen Altertumskunde, II, Berlin-Leipsic 1929, p. 86 ff.

23) For literature on this subject see H. Mode, Indische Frühkulturen und ihre Beziehungen zum Westen, Basel 1944, p. 143, and the relevant books and papers mentioned in the bibliographical notes contained in S. Piggott, Prehistoric India, Harmondsworth 1950. Cf. also W. Gampert, Arch. Orientální 20, p. 572 ff.

24) Mode, o.c., p. 15 in a more cautious way speaks of a goddess who always represents "das eine Grundprinzip der Weiblichkeit, das Frauentum schlechthin, in seiner grundsätzlichen Beziehung zum menschlichen Dasein". He seems to be right in adding: "In ihrer Grundfunktion als Gebärende, als Mutter, vertritt sie symbolisch auch die Fruchtbarkeit, die lebenspendende Kraft der Erde". Piggott,

itself to those interested in ancient Europe. The view held by former authors that the presence of a mother goddess or an earth goddess in the ancient German religion was a relic of a pre-Indoeuropean age characterized by an agrarian culture does not find general favour [25]). The Celtic world, the religion of which was far from being homogeneous in character, likewise revered female deities which were often of local importance and connected with the earth, with field or rivers [26]). The rôle played by Demeter-Kore and Ceres-Proserpina in the ancient religions of Greece and Italy is too well known to be in need of comment [27]). So, why should the cult of female divinities have been entirely foreign to the eastern Indoeuropeans before their coming into contact with the peoples meant by Przyluski, Hutton and Nehring?

The Atharvaveda and the gṛhyasūtras can teach us that in the domestic circle, in which women were more influential, many customs and beliefs were preserved which though not or scarcely alluded to in the Ṛgveda recur in the ancient religions and folklore of other Indoeuropean peoples. This does not mean that they were exclusively Indoeuropean, a conclusion too easily implied in many treatises on this subject.

What I would like to emphasize is this. The contributions of the pre- and non-Aryan elements to Indian religion have, for all we know, been important. The prehistoric influence of foreign peoples, though difficult to delimit, may in all probability not be disregarded. And the 'Aryan' beliefs and customs, taken as a whole, must have had much in common with those of the ethnic substratum. There appears to be no reason for assuming that the religion of the 'Aryan world' before coming into contact with Austric and Dravidian peoples, unlike e.g. the Celtic world which is archaeologically better known, should have been homogeneous to such a degree that both sexes, all classes, all occupational and other groups (tribes, clans etc.) revered, in the same way, the same divine powers. Forms of worship, magic, religious beliefs etc.

---

o.c., p. 201 f. is likewise guarded in his statements. See also H. Whitehead, The village gods of South India, 1916, ch. II etc.

25) For the German goddesses see for instance J. de Vries, Altgermanische Religionsgeschichte, I, Berlin 1935, p. 188 f.; V. Grønbech, Die Germanen, in A. Bertholet-E. Lehmann, (Chantepie de la Saussaye's) Lehrbuch der Religionsgeschichte, Tübingen 1925, II, p. 588 f.; E. Tonnelat, La religion des Germains, in A. Grenier, etc., Mana II, Les religions de l'Europe ancienne II, Paris 1948, p. 346 ff.

26) See e.g. E. Anwyl, Ancient Celtic goddesses, The Celtic review III (1906), p. 26 ff.; J. Vendryes, in Mana II (see above), III, p. 275 ff.

27) For the earth as a mother goddess see also A. Dieterich, Mutter Erde², Leipsic 1913; E. Kalinka, in the Neue Jahrb. f. d. klass. Alt. 45 (1920), p. 406 ff., and other works part of which will be mentioned in other sections of this book.

occurring among the Aryan immigrants may have been identified, assimilated, and indistinguishably united from the very moment at which in prehistoric times Aryans and non-Aryans came into contact. An Aryan, Austric, or Dravidian name does therefore not necessarily cover a cult or institution of purely Aryan, Austric, or Dravidian origin. The existence of a definite cult or divine character among the so-called primitive tribes which are regarded as the descendants of the non-Aryan components of the ancient population does not exclude the possibility of similar cults within the 'original' Aryan community.

The above observations are, however, not to be taken as intimating that the present author is convinced by the arguments adduced by some authors [28]) in favour of the hypothesis of an Indoeuropean origin of the god Viṣṇu. It would appear that any effort to attain a detailed, complete, and well-defined statement about the functions and sphere of activities of the ancient Indian divinities would be vain. Beings and powers figuring in so-called primitive or semi-primitive religions and mythology, never having undergone a logical specification and systematization, are not clearly definable in accordance with modern standards. In ancient countries other than India and in comparable societies in some parts of the modern world similar instances of gods are found whose mutual positions seem never to have been clearly defined. In some texts, myths, customs, and ceremonies the associations of a god like Viṣṇu with vegetative life may stand in the foreground, under other circumstances other sides of his character may come into prominence. We can never be sure that the functions and activities of the god as found, or rather as read, in the ancient documents exhaust all that belongs or relates to him in the minds of contemporaries. Besides, the mythopoeic mind always tends to express the incomprehensible processes in nature by admitting the validity of various interpretations at one and the same time. We cannot expect to find consistent theories and philosophic dogmas. In studying proto-historic religion and 'Weltanschauung' we are dealing, not with systematic cosmology, meteorology, biology and dogmatics, but with religious experience, with a living presence with which man was confronted and which scarcely admitted of conceptual definitions. It is the very plurality and vagueness of the images used by the poets and of the explanations proposed by the early thinkers which serve to do justice to the complexity of the phenomena. But the sage and intellectual devoted to the scrutiny of nature and the simplest man and woman of

---

[28]) See Güntert, o.c., p. 312 f.; Dandekar, o.c., p. 99; cf. also Von Schroeder, Arische Religion, II, p. 10.

the village could meet in a common sentiment of veneration for a god whose nature expressed the processes protecting and promoting those occurrences and phenomena which are essential to the very existence of human beings. Yet, a thorough consideration of the facts to be discussed in this book may lead us to the conviction that the Vedic poets, whose attention and energy were almost absorbed by the worship of other gods, the most important of whom was the great deity of the warrior-class, Indra, did not accept all aspects of Viṣṇu's personality. It may also induce us to subscribe to the opinion of those scholars [29]) who hold that Viṣṇu might have been a god of greater eminence among the masses of the Indian population in early Vedic times, whether these masses were Aryan or belonged to the so-called original inhabitants of the country. Making allowance for all this we may say that the ancient Indian views of the god Viṣṇu show a remarkable degree of consistency.

It has not been, in this book, the author's endeavour to aim at anything like completeness in dealing with the much discussed accretions to the Viṣṇu figure, the identifications of the avatāras, with local appearances as for instance Vithobā who was assimilated to Kṛṣṇa, with the Kṛṣṇa problem itself, or even to give the same attention to all points which come up for discussion. His effort has in the first instance been to write a supplement to the literature on the subject now in existence by laying emphasis on a few points the importance of which would appear to have escaped others and by drawing attention to some aspects of early Viṣṇuism which seem to have been neglected by most scholars in this particular field. Before proceeding to do so mention must be made of exceptions, that is to say, of some observations on these aspects made by predecessors. Güntert [30]) emphasized those traits in Viṣṇu's character which he would consider as solar and ithyphallic, and Dandekar [31]) ably discussed some connections between the Vedic Viṣṇu and fertility. The former scholar, whose views were in part endorsed by Hillebrandt [32]), however attached too much importance to a supposedly phallic character of the god and drew far-fetched conclusions from the epithet *śipiviṣṭa* — upon which he concentrated his attention without succeeding in settling the uncertain significance of this difficult word. The Indian author exclusively deals with some aspects of the Vedic Viṣṇu. Before them Johansson [33]) had

[29]) See Dandekar, o.c., p. 98.

[30]) Güntert, l.c. (see n. 11). For Viṣṇu's solar character see also G. A. Grierson, The monotheistic religion of ancient India, Asiatic Quart. Rev. 28 (1909), p. 115.

[31]) Dandekar, o.c. (see n. 11).

[32]) A. Hillebrandt, Vedische Mythologie [2], II, Breslau 1929, p. 325.

[33]) K. F. Johansson, Solfågeln i Indien, Upsala Univ. 1910.

already expressed the view that Viṣṇu originally was a soul-being and as such a bird, the sun-bird and a vegetation-bird. Other scholars were, however, right in observing that the Swedish author had too onesidedly relied on his speculative identification of the god with other beings, especially with Garuḍa, and laid too much emphasis on other doubtful connections.

This book, further, does not only attempt to meet the requirements of those students of Sanskrit and of the cultural history of India who want to have a résumé of the problems dealt with. It has also been written for a wider public which, if so minded, may be invited to disregard the linguistic and strictly philological parts of the text. The present author, though completely recognizing the merits of Sten Konow's contribution to the new edition of Chanṭepie's Lehrbuch [34]), Eliade's Traité [35]) and similar books, regrets that many authors on, and students of, the history of religions show a lasting tendency to neglect the inexhaustible mine of information on any aspect or province of this branch of knowledge that is India. He has for the sake of the latter category of readers done his utmost to express himself as intelligibly as possible, inserting many references to handbooks in the notes and translating almost all texts quoted [36]). Finally, the author must confess that in writing this book he could not refrain from making some suggestions of his own, from reconsidering disputible points which in the course of time seem to have become, in the view of many students, established facts, and from attempting to discover some of the underlying ideas which give unity in the various functions and manifestations of the god. In doing so he is aware that in dealing with ancient Indian gods any theory is necessarily based on some more or less subjective predilection for viewing things from a special angle and for emphasizing particular facts and connections.

II. VIṢṆU AND FERTILITY.

Beginning our discussions, rather arbitrarily, with Viṣṇu's connections with plants and food it may first be observed that TS. 5, 2, 8, 7 declares the trees, in general, to be associated with him. In other texts

---

[34]) See n. 1 and 25.

[35]) M. Eliade, Traité d'histoire des religions, Paris 1949.

[36]) I have neither been able to consult all books and papers on the subject — e.g. M. S. Gladstone, Viṣṇu in the Ṛgveda, Thesis Cambridge 1928, 'copy in Univ. Library' — nor willing to discuss all opinions of my predecessors from which I feel compelled to diverge.

he is, rather, identified with particular plants or trees. Thus Mbh. 13, 149, 101 where he is called, i.e. identified with, the *nyagrodha-*, the *uḍumbara-*, and the *aśvattha-* i.e. the banyan or Indian fig tree, the ficus glomerata, and the holy fig tree or ficus religiosa respectively. The first tree is a well-known representative of fertility and vegetative life, the *uḍumbara-* is a 'Zeugungsbaum', leaves of which are used in wedding ceremonies and which, like the aśvattha, was connected with the souls of the deceased. The last tree is believed to represent fertility, to give children, and to avert disasters; it, moreover, plays an important part in the cosmological speculations of the Indians [1]). While these fig trees, with the exception of the second, also appear in a similar epic enumeration of the thousand names of the god Śiva (Mbh. 13, 17, 54; 70) and both gods are also elsewhere represented by fig trees [2]) — we should, in addition to this, not forget that the Highest Being calls himself "the aśvattha among all trees" (BhG. 10, 26), this tree being clearly considered the first of its kind [3]) —, it is Viṣṇu who according to a purāṇical legend was cursed to become an aśvattha, Śiva who became a banyan [4]). — The statement found ŚB. 1, 2, 5, 10, that Viṣṇu hid himself among the roots of the plants may, too, be of some importance.

Of plants, some are especially dear to this god: according to the Saura Pur. 43, 40, for instance, the *bilva-*, *apāmārga-*, *śamī* and *dūrvā*. The bilva which is sacred to Śrī will concern us in another part of this book [5]). The apāmārga (achyranthes aspera) was of old in frequent ritual, magic and medical use, being believed, by virtue of its name, to wipe off or remove (*apa-mṛj-*) diseases and other evils [6]); the gods, for instance, were said to have wiped away the rakṣas with it (ŚB. 5, 2, 4, 14) [7]). The *śamī* (acacia suma [8])) was employed to kindle

[1]) The reader may for the sake of brevity be referred to J. J. Meyer, Trilogie altindischer Mächte und Feste der Vegetation, Zürich-Leipsic 1937, passim (see I, p. 50 f., and Register III, p. 295; 331; 332; 335). Many bibliographical references to this subject may be found in the somewhat hazardous and individual book by F. D. K. Bosch, De gouden kiem, Inleiding tot de Indische symboliek, Amsterdam-Brussels 1948, esp. p. 67, and in A. K. Coomaraswamy, Yaksas, Washington 1928-31 (see ch. II, § 1, n. 63). — See also Hohenberger, o.c., p. 147 ff., passim.

[2]) Cf. Meyer, o.c., I, p. 50 f.

[3]) The Highest Being is Kṛṣṇa who is soon to be identified with Viṣṇu.

[4]) See Meyer, l.c. Associations of other gods with trees are not wanting.

[5]) See ch. II, § 1, n. 71.

[6]) Cf., e.g., M. Bloomfield, The Atharva-veda, Strassburg 1899, p. 67 and 69; H. Oldenberg, Die Religion des Veda, Register, s.v.

[7]) Compare especially Caland's note on ĀpÇrS. 18, 9, 15 (W. Caland, Das Çrautasūtra des Āpastamba 16-24; 31, Amsterdam 1928, p. 129).

[8]) Or similar trees. For the *dasahrā* see e.g. B. A. Gupte, Hindu holidays and ceremonials, Calcutta-Simla 1919, p. 185 f.

the ritual fire; it also served as a means of appeasement (this process being denoted by the verb *śam-*), cf.e.g. ŚB. 9, 2, 3, 37. On the dasahrā day which, following the Navarātra ceremonies, is sacred to the great female deity, a *śamī* is among the objects worshipped: for the chief ceremonies on that occasion this tree is absolutely necessary.

The dūrvā grass (panic grass or panicum dactylum) which has a wonderful power of remaining green and succulent and is the sweetest and most nutritious pasture for cattle [9]), was, like e.g. *vetasa-* (calamus rotang), *avakā* or *śaivala-* (blyxa octandra), a grassy plant growing in marshy land, connected with water (TĀ. 5, 10, 6; cf. also ṚV. 10, 142, 8; AV. 6, 106, 1). "Spreading by many shoots" (ŚB. 7, 4, 2, 15) it was also identified with breath, vital sap (ibid. 12) and cattle (ibid. 10). ŚB. 4, 5, 10, 5 declares the dūrvā to be akin to the soma. It is symbolic of longevity and offspring. It might be of interest to make a collection of all magic or ritual applications of these plants. Whereas, for instance, in the complicated directions relative to the building of a house [10]) in Vedic times, the presence of certain trees in the vicinity of the chosen place is forbidden — the aśvattha, which here is held to be associated with the Aśvins, causes the danger from fire, the nyagrodha here belonging to Varuṇa the danger of fighting, the udumbara associated with Prajāpati, bad eyes — other plants, grains etc. are a necessity: the avakā is put in the holes of the posts when they are driven into the earth in order to prevent fire; water, rice, and barley are poured on the middle post whilst pronouncing a formula directed to the god of the earth (*bhaumāya svāhā*), a water-jar is placed on stones which are covered with dūrvā, an act accompanied by another formula relating to the earth (*pṛthivī*), twigs of the udumbara, a *śamī*-besom, and similar objects are other utensils. — Mbh. 3, 110, 17 the dūrvā is said to be like the *kuśa-*, the well-known sacred grass used at various ceremonies [11]).

At a Viṣṇuite festival, called the "feast of the six sesamum acts" this plant, the *tila-*, which is held to be holy by the worshippers, plays an important part. The sesame and its seed is also associated with Lakṣmī, the goddess of wealth and Viṣṇu's consort. Because it is believed to bring luck, people rub themselves with its oil at the bali festival in order to avert evil and to become fortunate. The souls of

---

[9]) See J. Eggeling, Sacred books of the East, 41, p. 187, n. 3.

[10]) For a summary of the relevant texts see A. Hillebrandt, Ritualliteratur, Strassburg 1897, p. 81; Keith, Religion and Philosophy, p. 363.

[11]) For folklore connected with the *dūrvā* (or, in Hindi, *dūb*), see e.g. B. A. Gupte, Hindu holidays and ceremonials, Calcutta-Simla 1919, p. XXXIII f.; G. M. Bolling and J. v. Negelein, The pariśiṣṭas of the Atharvaveda, Leipsic 1909, p. 595.

the dead ancestors, which are often closely connected with the spirits etc. presiding over fecundity, are likewise worshipped with the seed. So is the goddess Gaurī [12]). — The *tulasī* plant (ocimum sanctum) is an object of veneration for the worshippers of the god, who, for instance, make necklaces of bits of its stem. It is a great purifier of the atmosphere and is believed to destroy mosquitoes.

We shall not mention here the lotus, since this plant is so important in Viṣṇu's mythology and iconography that we shall have to study it in other connections [13]).

Passing mention may be made here of the rôle played by Viṣṇu in magic rites with the *damana-* plant (artemisia indica), which is sacred to Kāma [14]). To both the god and the plant we shall have to revert.

In a passage dealing with the significance of food — food, as the life, source, goal, and desire of all, is to be considered the highest form of the ātman [15]) — it reads as follows (Maitrī Up. 6, 13): "that form of the blessed Viṣṇu which is called the all-supporting is the same as food. Life is the essence of food etc." The ŚB. 7, 5, 1, 21, identifies Viṣṇu with food — and the Mbh. 12, 47, 71 agrees with this.

Mbh. 12, 346, 14 ff. gives evidence of a certain connection of the god with mud, which is a 'bearer' of fertility. Having assumed the form of a boar and shaken off three balls of mud he caused them to become the deceased ancestors (cf. also Mbh. 13, 126, 3 ff.).

Casual references to an association between Viṣṇu and water are not wanting. An interesting view of the god as representing this element and the earth as the all-producing mother is expressed by the Indian informant cited by Dubois [16]): "Que ferait la terre sans le secours de l'eau? Sans les rosées et les pluies qui viennent développer les germes de sa fertilité, elle demeurerait stérile.... C'est l'eau qui féconde, conserve et fait croître tout ce qui a vie, tout ce qui végète. Elle fut donc regardée comme le dieu conservateur. C'est Vichnou." It is not surprising that this water should be 'immortal'. Although we must

---

12) See J. J. Meyer, Trilogie altindischer Mächte und Feste der Vegetation, III, p. 319 f. The sesame, which is considered a great bearer of creative force, was (ÇB. 9, 1, 1, 3) considered the representative of "both kinds of food, the cultivated as well as the wild-growing". Apart from being used for other purposes the seed which ripens and contains much oil was, in ancient Greece, likewise considered a means of producing fertility or prosperity: sesame-cakes were presented on the occasion of a wedding etc.

13) See also ch. III, n. 74.

14) I refer to Meyer, o.c., I, p. 48, and Eliade, Traité, p. 257.

15) Food is an important topic in the speculations of the ancient upaniṣads: see e.g. W. Ruben, Die Philosophen der Upanishaden, Bern 1947, p. 332 and 335.

16) J. A. Dubois, Moeurs, institutions et cérémonies des peuples de l'Inde, nouv. éd., Pondichéry 1921, II, p. 273.

always be aware of the tendency to ascribe to an all-god all divine characteristics and to identify him with an endless variety of phenomena, such texts as Mbh. 3, 189, 7 which states the water to be Nārāyaṇa's sweat may be of some interest. *Ambonidhi-* "the ocean" and *Apāṃ nidhi-* "id." are among the god's thousand names (Mbh. 13, 149), *Toyātman-* "whose self or nature is water" is Mbh. 12, 47, 60 an epithet of Kṛṣṇa, "in the hair of whose head are the clouds, in the joints of his limbs the rivers, in whose stomach the ocean." We also find the belief that the human body composed of the five 'elements' is the abode of five deities: Brahman resides in the earthy portion, Rudra in the fiery, Viṣṇu in the watery etc. [17]).

In epic and purāṇic accounts Viṣṇu is commonly said to live in the ocean: Mbh. 13, 149, 68 *Mahodadhiśaya-* is one of his names; ViPur. 6, 4, 4; SauraPur. 53, 29 etc. The sea which forms his bed is called *amṛtodadhi-* "ocean of nectar" (VāPur. 97, 22). It was Nārāyaṇa, who in the great epic is often identified with the Supreme God Viṣṇu, to whom tradition ascribes the merit of having given the advice to churn the ocean in order to acquire the *amṛta-* contained in it (Mbh. 1, 17, 12); cf. 18, 4; 6).

This leads us to make mention of Viṣṇu's associations with some very potent and appreciated fluids. According to a large number of Vedic texts (AV. 7, 26, 3; TS. 1, 3, 4 d etc. [18])) Viṣṇu is *ghṛtayoni-* which, literally meaning "ghee-wombed", has been translated by "whose birthplace is in the ghee" or "homed in butter" [19]). As the compound, in the Ṛgveda, applies to the sacrifice (3, 4, 2) "in Schmalz ruhend" [20]), to Agni (5, 8, 6) "abiding in ghee", and to Mitra and Varuṇa (5, 68, 2) who in the same sūkta are requested to give wealth and stated to be bringers of the fertile rains — hence Sāyaṇa's interpretation *udakasyotpādakau* "producing water (rain)" [21]) — it may be considered an ancient epithet used to characterize those powers and divine beings who were thought to "have their residence" in the ghee (the clarified butter which was poured out into the sacrificial fire), who proceeded from ghee or whose activity originated in it. Ghee which is, in Vedic

---

[17]) K. K. Handiqui, Yaśastilaka and Indian culture, Sholapur 1949, p. 206.

[18]) See M. Bloomfield, A Vedic concordance, Harvard Univ. 1906, p. 358. For the ritual applications of the formula (*ghṛtáṃ ghṛtayone piba*) see A. B. Keith, The Veda of the Black Yajus school entitled Taittirīya Saṃhitā, Harvard Univ. 1914, p. 39.

[19]) By Keith, o.c., and R. T. H. Griffith, The texts of the White Yajurveda, Benares 1927, p. 49. Eggeling, ÇB. 13, 8, 4, 9: "ghee-born".

[20]) Cf. K. F. Geldner, Der Rig-veda... übersetzt, I (Harvard Univ. 1951), p. 339.

[21]) The compound is a bahuvrīhi!

texts, mentioned together with soma, milk, and honey [22]), is considered to be the life-sap of the universe, of waters and plants (ŚB. 7, 2, 3, 4), it is called seed (6, 3, 3, 18), and appears in the form of rain (ṚV. 3, 62, 16). AV. 7, 29, 1 and 2 Viṣṇu, together with Agni, is associated with ghee: "ye drink of the ghee which is called secret" [23]).

TS. 3, 2, 6 the ritual butter, in a series of formulas expressing the wish that prosperity may increase by means of curds and ghee, is called the heart of Viṣṇu; ĀpŚS. 2, 10, 4 the portions of ritual butter are called Viṣṇu and Viṣṇu's place.

Mention must also be made here of an association between Viṣṇu and honey or, at least, with the substances meant by *madhu-*. Honey, which was, in a natural manner, regarded as the essence of plants and saps [24]), is not only a gift of the earth and such divinities of fertility as the Roman Ceres, but also an offering to the chthonian powers and the souls of the deceased [25]). It is often considered a means of promoting fertility. In the ṚV. 1, 154, 4, Viṣṇu's three steps are said to be full of 'honey'; in his highest step is a well of 'honey' (5). GobhGS. 4, 10, 15 and SMB. 2, 8, 12 the *madhuparka-* (a honey-mixture) is addressed: "You are the drink of glory (or dignity), of greatness (or majesty), of *śrī* (*yaśaso bhakṣo 'si, mahaso bhakṣo 'si, śrībhakṣo 'si*). TS. 3, 1, 10, 2 a stanza, also found in ĀpŚS. 12, 18, 8 and MŚS. 2, 3, 6, 15, is addressed to him: "O Viṣṇu, being near (to us), o victorious one, grant us protection; the streams dripping 'honey' milk for thee an unfailing source." One of his names is Madhu (see e.g. Mbh. 13, 149, 31).

Now, Madhu and Mādhava — which is another name of his — are also designations of the two months of the season of spring, or, both of them, of spring itself, which as a divine power is Kāma's companion

---

22) I refer to A. A. Macdonell, Vedic Mythology, Strassburg 1897, p. 168.

23) Cf. also TS. 1, 8, 22 a and b; for particulars see W. D. Whitney-Ch. R. Lanman, Atharva-veda Saṃhitā, Harvard 1905, p. 408 f. In VaitS. 8, 1 this text accompanies an offering to both gods. — TS. 5, 5, 2, 5 the ghee is said to belong to Agni, the rice grains to Viṣṇu.

24) See e.g. Macdonell, o.c., p. 85 etc.; Hillebrandt, Ved. Myth. I², p. 192; Meyer, o.c., III, p. 301; Güntert, o.c., p. 256; J. de Vries, Altgermanische Religionsgeschichte, II, Berlin-Leipsic 1937, p. 135 f.; 406.

25) For beliefs with regard to honey in ancient Rome see Th. H. Gaster, in the Arch. Orient. 5, p. 123 (honey being symbolic of the new age, is often used in fertility rites and still eaten at the Jewish New Year); F. Altheim, Terra Mater, Religionsgeschichtliche Versuche u. Vorarbeiten 22 (1931), 2, p. 134; Ed. Hahn, in M. Ebert, Reallexikon der Vorgeschichte, V, Berlin 1926, p. 380 f.; F. Eckstein, in Hdwtb. d. de. Abergl. IV, p. 289 (with an abundance of references). For associations between honey and dew see Güntert (§ 1, n. 11). TS. 5, 2, 8, 6 honey is called the food of the wild, curds that of the village.

or even identical with this mighty god [26]). This season, Kṛṣṇa's brother Balarāma, and Viṣṇu's consort Padmā (Śrī) are, to mention only this instance of allusion to spring-time in Viṣṇuite passages, found together in the 1st stanza of Bhāsa's Vāsavadattā. Needless to observe that spring-time means renewal of life.

Now and then some relation or other turns up between Viṣṇu and the god of sexual love, who was also much interested in vegetation and fertility in general. In discussing the significance of the *damana-* "artemisia" and the rites in connection with the worship of Kāma Meyer drew attention to the fact that according to a purāṇic account (PadmP. Utt. 86) Viṣṇu Janārdana was revered together with Rati, Kāma's wife. As Kāma was sometimes identified with Śiva and the sun, a similar identification with Viṣṇu is not surprising [27]); Viṣṇu-Kṛṣṇa was indeed said to be Kāma: "there is no difference between Kāma and Viṣṇu" (MtPur. 70, 52), and the latter is to be worshipped (ibid. 70, 34 ff.) with the names of the former. Mbh. 13, 149, 45 Kāma is one of his thousand names [28]); ibid. 34 he is also called Damana, a name which of course admits of various interpretations.

It might be of some use here briefly to trace the history of the supposed descent of the god of love. In AV. 9, 2, 19 he is described as the first who was born [29]); in the ViPur. 1, 7, 26 he is the son of Dharma and Śraddhā (cf. Mbh. 1, 66, 33 where he is Dharma's son); other accounts represent him as being born from water, or from Brahmā's heart. In the Harivaṃśa ch. 200 he is Dharma's son by Lakṣmī. The same work however holds him to have been born again as Pradyumna, son of Kṛṣṇa and Rukmiṇī (ch. 161), who was already often mentioned in the Mahābhārata, being casually regarded as a form or representation of Kṛṣṇa himself [30]). The god of love could therefore be called Viṣṇu's son: a fine instance of incorporation of a divine figure with the complex of Viṣṇu mythology [31]).

Coming now to the god's relations to sexual life, it may first be noticed that according to the popular belief of part of the inhabitants of the Indian peninsula in modern times, e.g. the Mundas, Viṣṇu is an inaugurating god who taught, and teaches, mankind how to procreate

---

[26]) I refer to Meyer, o.c., III, p. 297.

[27]) The reader may, for the sake of brevity, be referred to Meyer, o.c., I, p. 36-49; 190; III, p. 304, and to Hohenberger, Flutsage, p. 106; 138; 145.

[28]) Çiva is, however, also called Kāma.

[29]) For particulars see Macdonell, Ved. Myth., p. 120.

[30]) For textual evidence see Sørensen's Index, p. 555.

[31]) We shall have to revert to this phenomenon in another part of this volume.

offspring, to plant rice, and to make drinks [32]). The Birhors consider him to be the originator of hunting and eating, who is able to give, or to withdraw, plenty of food. The obscenities, or so-called obscenities, signalized by European authors [33]) in the cult and iconography of Viṣṇuism relate well with these features in the god's character. In the enumerations of his 'thousand names' (e.g. Mbh. 13, 149) we come across such names as *Prāṇa-* "life" (which is also given to Śiva), *Prāṇada-* "giving or preserving life", *Prāṇabhṛt-* "supporting life", *Jīvana-* "life" or "the enlivening one".

References to his concern in the continuance of the human race are already found in very ancient texts. In ṚV. 10, 184, 1, which is called a *garbhārthāśīḥ* "a prayer for a child" by the Sarvānukramaṇī, the god is besought to prepare the womb. This text is ritually used (MānGS. 2, 18, 2; cf. also 4 and BārUp. 6, 4, 21) in ceremonies to be performed by a person who longs for sons; the AthV. (5, 25, 5) has it among other verses promotive of successful conception and quoted by KauśS. 35, 5 in a rite for male conception [34]). The complete text runs as follows: "Let Viṣṇu prepare the womb, let Tvaṣṭṛ (who is the divine shaper of forms) frame the shape (of the embryo); ....create offspring, O Sinīvālī and Sarasvatī (female deities implored to give children, which will concern us further on) etc." In the Ṛgvidhāna this text is prescribed in case of sterility of a woman: she shall, after touching her female organs, mutter this sūkta and the khila of three stanzas coming after it in the Kashmir collection of khilas (4, 13) and beginning with the Nejameṣa (ṚVidh. 4, 23, 2 f. [35])). The text mentioned last is addressed to the more or less enigmatic figure of Nejameṣa [36]), who is requested to "fly back with good sons, to make me (fem. gen.) who longs for a son conceive a male embryo, to be born in the tenth month", the third stanza running as follows: "In Viṣṇu's best shape create a male son in the canal(?) of this woman (*viṣṇoś śraiṣṭhyena rūpeṇāsyāṅ nāryāṅ gavīnyām*), to be born in the tenth month". This sūkta is, e.g. ĀśvGS. 1, 14, 3 prescribed, along with other stanzas, in the ritual during pregnancy [37]). — The last stanza (9) of ṚV. 7, 36, which is addressed

[32]) See e.g. W. Ruben, Eisenschmiede und Dämonen in Indien, Leyden 1935, p. 233 f.

[33]) See e.g. Dubois, o.c., p. 178 ff., and the editor's note "Les sculptures des temples de Vichnou sont parfois très obscènes".

[34]) See also Whitney-Lanman, Atharvaveda-saṃhitā..., p. 266.

[35]) See my translation and note: The Ṛgvidhāna, Utrecht 1951, p. 118 f.

[36]) See also M. J. Dresden, Mānavagṛhyasūtra, Thesis Utrecht 1941, p. 174.

[37]) See also Bṛhaddevatā 8, 84 f. and A. A. Macdonell, The Bṛhaddevatā... edited and translated, Harvard Univ., p. 316 f., and Scheftelowitz, o.c., p. 28; and A. F. Stenzler, Indische Hausregeln, I, II, Leipsic 1865, p. 36. — See also the stanza AV. 7, 17, 4; cf. TS. 1, 4, 44a, used ĀpÇS. 9, 19, 16 etc.

to a variety of gods, mentions the Maruts and Viṣṇu by name: "This hymn of praise must attain you, o Maruts, it must (attain) Viṣṇu who with acts of assistance protects the infused (semen); that they provide the invoker youthful strength in order to (procreate) offspring...." [38]). A similar rôle is apparently imparted to the god 7, 100, 4 where he is called *sujaniman-* "affording a good birth, or good offspring" [39]). As a protector of the seed he appears also 4, 3, 7: *kád víṣṇava urugāyâya réto brávaḥ.* 1, 155, 3 he is said to induce both parents to enjoy the 'delight of seed' (*ní mātárā nayati rétase bhujé*), a passage which certainly admits of Sāyaṇa's interpretation: *prāṇināṃ putrādyutpādanasāmarthyāya bhuje teṣāṃ bhogāya rakṣaṇāya vā,* although it may at the same time refer to the marriage of heaven and earth [40]).

There has been some uncertainty as to the interpretation of the *ἅπαξ sumajjāni-* 1, 156, 2 which is rendered by "together with his wife" [41]). As *jani-* can also mean "woman" (cf. e.g. ṚV. 1, 85, 1) the sense of "along with women" would not only be possible, but when compared with 3, 54, 15 even probable, provided that *jāni-* at the end of a compound can be synonymous with *jani-* in the sense of "woman" [42]). This is however very doubtful. 3, 54, 14 Viṣṇu is said to be the far-stepping eminent or great [43]) one, to whom belong many women (*urukramáḥ kakuhó yásya pūrvîr* "der weitschreitende Riese, dessen (Gefolge) viele Frauen sind" Geldner). The poet adds that "the young women, the mothers, are not remiss (I think, in conceiving and bringing forth, see also Geldner: "Nicht kommen die jungen Frauen, die Gebärerinnen zu kurz": *ná mardhanti yuvatáyo jánitrīḥ*). If this interpretation be right, there is no need of the hypothesis that the god's female train as described by later authors — compare e.g. Ziegenbalg's [44]) record: "Von Wischtnum werden sehr unflätige Historien erzehlet, wie er gemachet, dasz alle weiber nackigt hinter ihm hergehen müszen...." — has resulted from his being identified with Kṛṣṇa. It also reminds

---

38) Sāyaṇa's commentary explains the term *niṣiktapā-* by *camase niṣiktānāṃ somānāṃ pātāram.*

39) Cf. also Geldner, o.c., II, p. 270. According to Sāyaṇa the adjective means *śobhanāni janimāni kīrtanasmaraṇādinā sukhahetubhūtāni yasya tādṛśaḥ.*

40) Thus Geldner, o.c., I, p. 213. Cf. also Güntert, o.c., p. 307.

41) Cf. Grassmann, Petr. Dict., Monier-Williams. "Dem die Frauen gut sind" (Geldner, o.c. I, p. 214) is not clear to me. For the meaning of *smat, sumat* see my 'Reflections on the numerals "one" and "two" in ancient Indo-European languages', Utrecht 1953, p. 70. Güntert, o.c. suggested translating by "günstige Geburt bewirkend", cf. Petr. Dict. III, 29.

42) I refer to the Petr. Dict. III, 83, and especially to Pāṇini 5, 4, 134!

43) See also Geldner's note, o.c., I, p. 398.

44) Ziegenbalg's Malabarisches Heidenthum, herausgegeben von W. Caland, Amsterdam 1926, p. 50.

us of the part played by the god in the wedding ceremonies: he is involved in the indispensable act of the seven steps [45]), and also of the frequent theme in purāṇic tales and other narratives of his giving a son to devout and virtuous, but childless, couples: cf. e.g. BhāgPur. 10, 3, 40, and the story recorded by Philippus Baldaeus [46]). Allusions to this side of the god's activity are also made in the stanza AV. 7, 17, 4; TS. 1, 4, 44 (cf. VS. 8, 17; MS. 1, 3, 38) "Let Tvaṣṭar, Viṣṇu, giving liberally, together with offspring, assign wealth to the sacrificer". As far as may be seen from KauśS. 35, 16 the stanza probably formed part of a text which was used in a women's rite intended to procure the birth of a son. The deities addressed in the corresponding stanza VS. 8, 17, which is ritually used during the concluding ceremonies of the soma sacrifice (cf. e.g. ŚB. 4, 4, 4, 9) are, apart from the two mentioned, Dhātar, Savitar and Prajāpati, who, each in his particular way, were credited with vivifying, creative and generative faculties [47]). ṚV. 10, 15, 1 I; AV. 18, 1, 45 I; VS. 19, 56 I *âhám pitṝ́n suvidátrān avitsi nápātaṃ ca vikrámaṇaṃ ca víṣṇoḥ* is ambiguous; anyhow, "I have found (won) the.... fathers, offspring (a son) and the wide-striding of Viṣṇu" seems to be the satisfactory translation; if so, the stanza does not imply that the offspring is given by the god under discussion [48]). However obscure the line ṚV. 1, 164, 36 I *saptârdhagarbhâ bhúvanasya réto víṣṇos tiṣṭhanti pradíśā vídharmaṇi* which recurs in the AV., 9, 10, 17 I "seven half-embryos, remain engaged in distributing, under Viṣṇu's direction, the seed of the world (of existence)" seems likewise to allude to the god's activity for the sake of procreation, or for creation in general. Mbh. 3, 114, 27 mention is made of Viṣṇu's own seed (*retas*).

The god sometimes assumes the outward appearance of a woman. Mbh. 1, 18, 45 ff. etc. he disguised himself as a lovely maiden alluring

---

45) I refer to M. Winternitz, Das altindische Hochzeitsrituell nach dem Āpast.GS..., Denkschr. Akad. Wiss. Vienna 40 (1892) p. 51 ff.; 57 ff. and Hillebrandt, Ritualliteratur, Strassburg 1899, p. 66. We shall have to revert to this point (section VII).

46) Ph. Baldaeus, Afgoderye der Oost-Indische Heydenen, ed. by A. J. de Jong, The Hague 1917, p. 72. Even the god Brahmā is said to have enjoyed this favour: cf. the story narrated in the Portuguese account of Hinduism, edited by Caland, Amsterdam 1915 ("Drie oude Portugeesche Verhandelingen over het Hindoeïsme"), p. 93.

47) For the moment this comment must suffice; see e.g. Macdonell, o.c., p. 33; 115; 117 f. Cf. also ĀpÇS. 12, 6, 3.

48) Other interpretations were, to mention only a few scholars, given by Hillebrandt, Geldner (see Geldner, o.c., III, p. 145), and Griffith, o.c., p. 214 who translates: "gained a son and progeny from Viṣṇu". For the yajamāna's identification with the striding Viṣṇu see p. 55 f., 58 f., and 63 f.

the asuras in order to recover the amṛta from them. In the same form he is believed to have rescued Śiva from great peril [49]). He is also related to have transformed himself into Bhagavatī (= Durgā-Lakṣmī) [50]).

It would in this connection not be superfluous to recall the belief of other peoples that the divine embodied in such processes, phenomena, and 'conceptions' as are related to the transference of the solar atmospheric powers for good to the earth and its inhabitants are not only able to generate or regenerate the life of the vegetable world, but also to impregnate women [51]).

III. VIṢṆU AS A LIBERAL AND BENEFICENT GOD.

Viṣṇu is often conceived as a deity willing, or able, to bestow abundant riches upon his worshippers. An often quoted text which is very illustrative of this characteristic is AV. 7, 26, 8; VS. 5, 19; TS. 1, 2, 13, 2 etc. "From the sky, o Viṣṇu, or also from the earth, from the great wide atmosphere, o Viṣṇu, fill thy hands abundantly with good things; and bestow them from the right and from the left". Now, AV. 7, 26 forms part of a series of texts [1]) addressed, according to KauśS. 59, 19 to Prajāpati — a particular worthy of notice — by a man who desires various benefits. Other texts, however, have the stanzas of 7, 26 used in connection with the presenting of oblations to Viṣṇu and with other acts which form part of the ritual. The stanza under consideration, which is TS. 6, 2, 9, 3 called a blessing, is to accompany the supporting of the left-hand or northward soma-cart (cf. TS. 1, 2, 13, 2 [2]); ŚB. 3, 5, 3, 22; ĀpŚS. 11, 7, 3). ĀpŚS. 20, 4, 5 prescribes its use, together with that of TS. 1, 2, 13 and of TB. 2, 4, 3, 4, in the aśvamedha at the moment of the horse's coming out of the water in which it has been sprinkled. Both ritual acts are doubtless intended to promote, on behalf of the kingdom or community, the vegetative power of nature [3]). — AV. 7, 17, 4 [4]) in which Viṣṇu and Tvaṣṭar are invoked to give wealth (*draviṇam*) to the sacrificer forms part of the same set

[49]) I refer to E. Thurston, Castes and tribes of S. India, Madras 1909, 5, p. 76.

[50]) See Caland, Drie oude Portugeesche verh., p. 17 ff.

[51]) For the sun etc. see also H. Frankfort, Kingship and the gods, Chicago 1948, p. 148 ff. and passim. — Some particulars: J. G. Frazer, Golden Bough, 10, p. 74 ff.

[1]) See Whitney-Lanman, o.c., p. 399.

[2]) See Keith, Veda of the Bl. Yajus School, p. 32.

[3]) Cf. W. Kirfel, Der Aśvamedha und der Puruṣamedha, in Festschrift — W. Schubring, Hamburg 1951, p. 39 ff., esp. p. 40.

[4]) See above.

of Atharvanic texts. It is ritually used in the concluding ceremony of the animal sacrifice: TS. 1, 4, 44, 1; ŚB. 4, 4, 4, 9 [5]). For Tvaṣṭar's part in the invocation see ŚB. 4, 4, 4, 8: "....May Tvaṣṭar, who dispenses boons, grant us riches". — In an unambiguous wording the poet of ṚV. 7, 100, 2 asks the god to show his universal benevolence (*sumatiṃ viśvajanyām*) and attentive regard (to the society to which he, the poet, belongs), "in order to give us lavishly abundant prosperity and wealth consisting of horses and much resplendent (metal)". The sūktas 7, 99 and 100 — addressed to Viṣṇu according to BD. 6, 25, though 99, 4-6 should be regarded as addressed to Indra as well — which generally express the wish for welfare (*bhūti-*) are used in adoring these gods (see Ṛgvidh. 2, 29, 5), ṚV. 6, 49, 13 the poet expresses the wish to enjoy, together with his children, possessions under the protection Viṣṇu affords to them after having thrice traversed the earthly spaces for the sake of oppressed human beings. Attention may also be drawn to TS. 1, 6, 4, 3 (r) "by the sacrifice to the god Viṣṇu, by the sacrifice, may I attain health and wealth, and security": see also 1, 7, 4, 4 where the same words are quoted, and the observation is added that Viṣṇu is the sacrifice [6]). In the same text, 5, 7, 2, 2 Agni and Viṣṇu are identified with wealth: with a verse addressed to these gods "one offers the stream of wealth". AV. 7, 29, 1 and TS. 1, 8, 22 a Agni and Viṣṇu being described as rejoicing in ghee, are said to place in every house seven treasures [7]). ṚV. 6, 69, 1; TS. 3, 2, 11 d Indra and Viṣṇu are besought to rejoice in the sacrifice and to bestow wealth; stanzas of similar purport are ṚV. 6, 69, 3 and 6. ṚV. 10, 141, 5 Aryaman, Bṛhaspati, Indra, Vāta, Viṣṇu, Sarasvatī and Savitar should be requested to give gifts. ṚV. 1, 156, 3 the poet expresses the wish to participate in the god's goodwill (*sumati-*).

Benevolence and readiness to help man being unmistakable traits of his character the god who is the sacrifice is in ritual texts often described as concerned with redress and expiation: ĀpŚS. 3, 18, 8 when the brahman, during the ceremonies, through inadvertency speaks (utters 'profane' words) he has to recite the Viṣṇu stanza TS. 1, 2, 13 e. See also 9, 11, 24; 11, 9, 3; 14, 8, 4; 30, 6; 31, 1; GobhGS. 1, 6, 19 f. etc. Reference to the mighty striding, in the dust of which (all) is gathered obviously suffices to redress a wrong act.

It was also this same deity who by propping up the sky and by his

---

[5]) I refer to W. Caland-V. Henry, L'Agniṣṭoma, Paris 1906, p. 391 f.

[6]) For this identification see further on, section IX.

[7]) For particulars see Whitney-Lanman, o.c., p. 408. A section, beginning with "Agni and Viṣṇu" of the TB., 3, 11, 3 was used (ĀpÇS. 19, 13, 3 f.) in offering the "stream of wealth" (TS. 5, 4, 8, 1; cf. Āp.ÇS. 17, 17, 8 and TB. 3, 11, 9, 9).

striding activity maintained the cosmic order and the steadfast ordinances; hense he bears the title of "herdsman" or "protector" (ṚV. 1,22,18).

That Viṣṇu was conceived as a liberal and beneficent god can also appear from his names or epithets *vasuda-* "granting wealth or appreciated objects", *vasu-* "wealth, possessions", *vasuprada-* "giving *vasu-*"; *mahādhana-* "possessing much wealth" in Mbh. 13 a. 149, although we must take account of the fact that his identification with Vāsudeva is not foreign to the accumulation of epithets beginning with *vasu-* which are given to him e.g. Mbh. 13, 149, 87. In accordance with his wealth is the splendour of his chariot: Mbh. 6, 8, 16 it is described as having the colour of fire and being adorned with gold; in 15 it consists of that metal. A word for gold forms also part of some of his names: *suvarṇavarṇa-* "of golden colour" etc.; but here his well-known associations with the sun cannot be left out of consideration. It is therefore no matter of surprise to come across such statements as ViPur. 1, 8, 25 "Śrī is growth, abundance, prosperity (*ṛddhi-*), Viṣṇu is the lord of wealth". From the same passage it appears that the god, in all forms, is combined with the goddess of prosperity. "Ils (les Gentils) disent qu'il (Vichnou) est le premier principe et qu'il s'est marié à une femme nommée Lachymy, qu'ils assurent tout ensemble boeufs, chevaux, maisons, semence, argent et tout ce qu'on peut desirer dans ce monde" [8]).

Viṣṇu accordingly is *svastida-* "conferring happiness" (Mbh. 13, 149, 109), *svastikṛt-* "causing welfare" etc.; *sukhada-* "giving happiness" etc.; Mbh. 3, 201, 24 even the celestials are said to have obtained bliss and happiness by adoring him. 5, 107, 18 Garuḍa says that his exalted position has its rise in Vāsava's younger brother, i.e. Viṣṇu. This god is ever anxious for the world's welfare, achieving acts beneficial to mankind: 6, 65, 48 ff. He is *nanda-* "invigoration, delight", *nandi-* "the thriving, happy one", *nandin-* "invigorating, delighting", *nandana-* "invigorating, gladdening", *nandakin-* "possessed of delight": Mbh. 13, 149 [9]). Hence also such well-known invocations as Bhāsa, Dhūtav. 1 "May Viṣṇu's foot protect you — the foot which is a festival for the whole world" [10]) and Karṇa 1 where Śrīdhara i.e. Viṣṇu is besought to give *śrī-* "good fortune".

The fortune of almost any more or less wealthy man in ancient India

---

[8]) Relation des erreurs (one of the French treatises on Hinduism edited by Caland, Twee oude Fransche verhandelingen over het Hindoeïsme, Amsterdam 1923), p. 8.

[9]) See my paper 'The meaning of Skt. *nand-*', Acta Or. 21, p. 81 ff.

[10]) For *utsava-* festival, which in my opinion originally meant "the generating, rousing, setting in motion, stimulating of power", see my relevant paper in India Antiqua... presented to J. Ph. Vogel, Leyden 1947, p. 146 ff.

mainly consisting of cattle we may subjoin here the references to Viṣṇu's connection with cows and other domestic animals in ancient texts. The PañcBr. making mention of the bṛhat-sāman chanted on verses addressed to Viṣṇu Śipiviṣṭa, or, literally, "chanted on (verses) of Viṣṇu which contain (the word) *śipiviṣṭa-* — an epithet of the god to which we shall have to recur elsewhere [11]) —, observes that Ś. is Prajāpati's manifestation being in (resting on) cattle (*eṣā vai prajāpateḥ paśuṣṭhā tanūr yac chipiviṣṭaḥ* PB. 18, 6, 26), adding that the man who executes the ritual as taught in the relative texts shall become firmly established in the breath-of-life and in (the possession of) cattle (*prāṇa eva paśuṣu pratitiṣṭhati* [12])). Now, Caland [13]) already drew attention to the probability that this passage was borrowed from MaitrS. 1, 11, 9: 171, 8 (cf. also Kāṭh. 14, 10: 209, 8 ff.) where the same explanation of the epithet occurs. Sāyaṇa quoting TS. 2, 5, 5, 2 *yajño vai viṣṇuḥ paśavaḥ śipiḥ* comments: "since Viṣṇu is Prajāpati [14]) he is Ś." — According to another passage in the same brāhmaṇa, 20, 3, 2 Prajāpati, Agni, Indra and the Allgods were not able to take possession of the domestic animals (cattle) after they had left, but Viṣṇu, by ritual means, was. Apart from *gopati-* which is of various application ("lord of cattle, chief": Indra, the sun, Śiva, Kṛṣṇa, Viṣṇu etc.), *gohita-* "beneficial to cows" is one of his names. Mbh. 13, a. 149 he is also styled *govidāṃ patiḥ,* and the name *govinda-,* though preferably given to Kṛṣṇa and explained as *gāṃ vindat-,* is also given to him: see e.g. the enumeration of his names in the BaudhDhŚ. 2, 9, 10.

In purāṇic accounts Viṣṇu is sometimes associated with the vaiśyas, the third class whose business was farming and trade, and whose attention was, according to these texts, mainly focussed on wealth and profit: Brahmā was worshipped in the first *yuga-* or age of the world, Yajña ("Sacrifice") in the second, Viṣṇu in the third or *dvāpara-*period (see VāPur. 32, 21), which is also called *vaiśyayuga-* "the period of the vaiśyas" (78, 36). Yet, the first yuga is usually associated with the first class (the brahmins), the second with the kṣatriyas etc. [15]). Mbh. 3, 189, 9 f. Nārāyaṇa is stated to be revered by kṣatriyas and vaiśyas [16]).

---

[11]) See section XIV.

[12]) For this phrase see my paper '*Pratiṣṭhā*', which is to appear in the Studia Indol. Intern. of the Centre of Int. Indol. Res.

[13]) Caland, Pañcaviṃśa-brāhmaṇa, Calcutta 1931, p. 486.

[14]) See Bhandarkar, Vaiṣṇavism, Çaivism and minor religious systems, Strassburg 1913, p. 36.

[15]) See also D. R. Patil, Cultural history from the Vāyu Purāṇa, Poona 1946, p. 77.

[16]) For Viṣṇu's benevolence see also Miss Das Gupta, IHQ. 7, p. 105 ff. who is no doubt right in saying that this trait must have helped the process of his later elevation in popular religion.

IV. VIṢṆU AND THE SUN.

So far we have mainly, and intentionally, emphasized the fertility aspect of Viṣṇuism and some phenomena relating to it. Evidence other than that already mentioned, is not wanting. The author of the 'Gentilité du Bengala' [1]) was apparently so much impressed by this side of the god's character that he formulated his view on Viṣṇuism in the following way: "L'ordre de Visnou fut de faire prosperer toutes choses dans le monde et de conserver tout, soit par fertilité ou autrement". And Dubois, entering a little more into details [2]) said that the earth could not produce without the fecundating water, the "dieu conservateur", i.e. Viṣṇu.

Now, the question may arise whether it is not somewhat strange that other authors who dealt with the 'original character' of the god have so often endeavoured to show that he really and essentially was a sun-god, calling attention to many features in his nature which fit in with the idea of a solar deity rather than emphasizing his concern in generation, the continuance of life and welfare of mankind. There is no necessity to repeat their arguments which may be regarded as sufficiently known to those interested in the subject [3]). Also in post-Vedic literature connections between Viṣṇu and the sun are frequently alluded to: apart from such vague indications as Mbh. 1, 88, 9 *śakrārkaviṣṇupratimaprabhāva-* and such general identifications as e.g. "thou (the sun, Sūrya) art Indra, Viṣṇu, Brahmā, Prajāpati, Agni (Mbh. 3, 3, 60), etc. etc., epithets like *sahasrāṃśu-* "thousand-rayed, the sun" (13, 149, 64); *gabhastinemi-* "the felly of whose wheel consists of sunbeams" (65); *vihāyasagati-* "who moves through the sky or atmosphere" (107), and, especially, *ravi-, virocana-, sūrya-, savitar-, ravilocana-* (ibid.); such references to the sky as the god's special region or abode (see e.g. Kāl. Ragh. 13, 1) [4]); statements made by authors of purāṇas that

---

1) Caland, Twee oude Fransche verhandelingen..., p. 109.

2) See above, p. 14.

3) For Viṣṇu's solar character see e.g. Macdonell, o.c., p. 37 ff.; Keith, Religion and philosophy, p. 108 f.; Johansson, Solfågeln i Indien, esp. ch. II; G. A. Grierson, in the JA. 1908, p. 253 f., and in Hastings' Encycl. II, p. 540; cf. also Oldenberg, Religion des Veda³, p. 232; Hillebrandt, Vedische Mythologie, II, p. 319; Dandekar, o.c., esp. p. 98 f.; E. W. Hopkins, in JAOS. 16, p. CXLVII f. See, further, J. N. Banerjea, The worship of Sāmba among the early Pāncharātrins, Proc. Ind. Hist. Congress VII (1944), p. 82 ff.

4) See also M. Das Gupta, Ind. Hist. Quart. 7, p. 113 ff.; Bh. S. Upadhyaya, India in Kālidāsa, Allahabad 1947, p. 308. Viṣṇu-Nārāyaṇa should be meditated upon as being in the orb of the sun, in the lotus, etc. He is the lord of the suns (MtPur. 8, 4); cf. also MtPur. 166, 1.

Varuṇa was made supreme lord of the waters, Vaiśravaṇa (i.e. Kubera) of wealth, Viṣṇu of the representatives of the sun (*viṣṇuṃ ravīṇām adhipam,* e.g. MtPur. 8, 4 [5])); explanations of the origin of that luminary handed down by a Portuguese author [6]): when Viṣṇu, as a baby, raised his eyes, sun and fire came into being by their very effulgence — and similar random examples may be adduced as illustration.

I would answer the above question by observing that, on the contrary, the same god often represents the sun as well as fertility and vegetative life. The paramount importance of the sun as an initiator of earthly life, as the great generative power in the universe, as the mighty being which sends off its male power to fertilize the earth, has early and everywhere been understood to be the source of life, which "by rising thrusts away the fetters of death" (cf. AV. 17, 1, 30) [7]). Farmers and peasants, all over the world, almost instinctively know that the growth of grain and fruits is largely dependent on the favourable influence of the sunbeams, which being absorbed by the plants may be said to pervade them. Gods concerned with phenomena in the atmosphere are, in general, often associated with fertility and vegetation [8]). The highest deities of the ancient Mesopotamian peoples, for instance, often were sun-gods and fertility-gods at the same time [9]). In Greece, one of the characteristics of Helios was that he concerned himself with vegetation — like Zeus, he was called φύτιος "the generative one" —, and in Crete he was the husband of the Great Mother. It may be of some use to enlarge here upon this point, because many scholars of the West, living in modern towns and devoted to abstract thought, would seem apt to underestimate the importance of

---

[5]) I also refer to E. W. Hopkins, Epic mythology, Strassburg 1915, p. 203 etc. Cf. also ViPur. 1, 8, 21 where Viṣṇu-Keśava is said to be the same as the sun, the lotus-seated goddess being his radiance.

[6]) Caland, Portug. verhandelingen, Amsterdam 1915, p. 81.

[7]) See for instance. G. van der Leeuw, Religion in essence and manifestation, London 1938, ch. 7; M. Eliade, Traité d'histoire des religions, Paris 1949; § 30; 37; 41 ff.; A. Audin, Les fêtes solaires, Paris 1945, passim; Meyer, Trilogie (see above), Register III, p. 320 s.v. Sonne; O. R. Gurney, The Hittites, London 1952, p. 136 f. etc.; V. Stegemann, in the Handbuch des deutschen Aberglaubens VIII, 31 ff.; Frankfort, o.c. (Kingship). — In India the sun was often connected with the lotus; see e.g. L. A. Waddell, in J. Hastings, Encycl. of Religion and Ethics, VIII (1915), p. 144.

[8]) See e.g. also W. Koppers, Pferdeopfer und Pferdekult der Indogermanen, in Koppers, Die Indogermanen- und Germanenfrage, p. 378 (with bibliography).

[9]) See e.g. I. Engnell, Studies in divine kingship in the ancient Near East, Uppsala 1943, p. 21 f.; 54 f.; Eliade, l.c. (with biblographical references). For Indonesian data see e.g. J. A. J. Verheyen S.V.D., Het hoogste wezen bij de Manggaraiers [island of Flores], Studia instituti Anthropos, Wien-Mödling 1951, p. 10 etc. American instances of a 'sun-god' as rain-giver: H. K. Haeberlin, in the Memoirs of the Am. Anthrop. Ass. 3 (1916), p. 13.

the idea of fertility for rural life all over the world. This idea has been, and still is, far and wide the centre of a more or less 'primitive' world concept. Fertility was life, in plants, in animals, in man. In conformity with this widespread conviction the Indian sun-god was already early believed to give rain [10]), and also to maintain conjugal relations with the goddess Earth [11]).

In Vedic texts the sun is, indeed, inter alia engaged in sending various blessings from heaven, in causing rain and bestowing wealth. He is the lord of vivifying power [12]). In the Mahābhārata, 3, 3, 5 ff. it is explained how the sun, out of compassion for the hungry creatures draws up water — which is converted into clouds of rain by the lord of the plants, i.e. the moon —, and also enters the earth with his heat. Thus plants are produced from the combination of water and heat; the food of all creatures originates from the sun. When, in a purāṇa, Bhav., ch. 134, the sun is described as being attended by apsaras, yakṣas, snake-demons and other beings of this description which are usually associated with water and fertility [13]), it is again characterized as a deity concerned with the same phenomena. The Pongal festival of Southern India [14]) is a solar feast as well as a ceremony connected with cattle and, especially, with the first fruits of the soil. It is celebrated in honour of Indra and the sun, to whom the first rice of the harvest is offered. Viṣṇu or Viṣṇu-Kṛṣṇa was, however, also given a share [15]).

This is not to allege that the solar character of a deity in which both aspects combine is always original. Indra rather frequently is the sun — see e.g. ŚBr. 3, 4, 2, 15 "Indra verily is he who burns yonder (the sun)" (*indro ya eṣa tapati*); MS. 1, 10, 16 : 155, 19 *asau vā āditya indraḥ*; TS. 5, 7, 1 c *asau vā āditya indra eṣa prajāpatiḥ*; AV. 13, 3, 13 [16]) —, but he is, as far as I am able to see, not primarily a represen-

10) Now see H. Lüders, Varuṇa I, Göttingen 1951, p. 308 ff.; Hillebrandt, o.c., II, p. 226 ff.; Hopkins, Epic mythology, p. 84; Meyer, o.c., III, p. 152 ff.

11) I refer to Meyer, o.c., III, p. 320.

12) I refer to Macdonell, o.c., p. 32 f.

13) I also refer to J. N. Banerjea, Sūrya in brahmanical art, IA. 54 (1925), p. 161 ff.

14) See Ch. E. Gover, The Pongol festival, JRAS. NS. 5, p. 91 ff. For other bibliographical references see Meyer, o.c., III. p. 118 ff., who also discusses this feast. Cf. W. Filchner-D. S. Marāthe, Hindustan im Festgewand, Celle 1953, p. 184 ff.

15) Cf. also Meyer, o.c., p. 118 ff. According to Gover, o.c., p. 94 the god of the festival is Indra and, secondarily, Viṣṇu, See also the interesting account by Abraham Rogerius, De open-deure tot het verborgen heydendom, re-edited by W. Caland, The Hague 1915, p. 137 f. (ch. 13).

16) For other particulars see e.g. Hillebrandt, Ved. Myth. II, p. 192; J. J. Meyer, Gesetzbuch und Purāṇa, Breslau 1929, p. 28, n. 1; Trilogie, III, p. 151 f. and p. 317, s.v. Rot.

tative of that luminary. Yet this very fact once again shows the close connection between Indra and Viṣṇu who, accordingly, in AV. 17 are invoked conjointly: "Indra.... do I call.... Arise, o Sun.... Thine, o Viṣṇu, are heroisms manifold". The poet praises Indra as powerful and cattle-winning, and asks Viṣṇu "to fill us with cattle". Cattle, of course, means prosperity. In stanza 9, Indra is however invoked to "protect us with unharmed rays" [17]).

V. VIṢṆU AND INDRA.

These remarks induce us to discuss some aspects of Viṣṇu's relations with Indra. Although a detailed re-consideration of the facts showing the latter's concern with growth, vitality, vegetation and fertility can be omitted [1]), the importance of this point renders it worth while to devote a brief comment to some salient features. It may now be considered a matter of common knowledge that Indra, who in the belief of Vedic man represented force, energy, and vitality in nature, was already at an early period regarded as being intimately connected with atmospheric phenomena and with various forms of fertility and vegetative life. In the religious undercurrents this trait of his character persisted after he had lost the high position accorded to him in former times. He shows his fertilizing power in the human race as well as in the vegetable world, being also concerned with the bestowal of children. The first of the deities worshipped in order to ensure a good harvest was Indra; the others were his companions, the Maruts, Parjanya whose concerns likewise were meteorological, Aśani, the lightning-flash, and Bhaga, the divine power of "getting and begetting". In the Veda he is sometimes described as carrying an *aṅkuśa-* or hook — an implement used, inter alia, for plucking fruit off trees [2]) —, with which he is said, or asked, to give wealth (ṚV. 8, 17, 10), or a wife (AV. 6, 82, 3); see especially ṚV. 3, 45, 4; it sometimes serves this bountiful god as a weapon (ṚV. 10, 44, 9). All corn which springs up without

---

17) There is no use in repeating the arguments adduced by S. K. De, Bhāgavatism and Sun-worship, BSOS. 6, p. 669 ff., against Grierson's untenable thesis that Bhāgavatism originated in sun-worship. See also M. Das Gupta, l.c.

1) See Hopkins, The real Indra of the Rig-Veda, JAOS. 16 (1896), p. CCXXXVI ff.; the same, Indra as a god of fertility, JAOS. 36 (1917), p. 242 ff.; 37, p. 85 f.; H. Lommel, Der arische Kriegsgott, Frankfort 1939; Meyer, o.c., III, p. 302; Gonda, Ojas, p. 9 ff.

2) For other applications of the tools of this description see my paper on 'Indogerm. *ser-* "(spitziger) Ast usw."', in the Mnemosyne, III, 6 (Leyden 1938), p. 153 ff. (with bibliography).

cultivation was considered corn raised by Indra [3]). He was called the bull of the earth (AV. 12, 1, 6), which, as is well known, was very often regarded as a cow.

Indra was often associated with the goddess of the furrow, with the Furrow herself, Sītā [4]): when the ploughing is started Sītā has her share in the offerings mentioned above (GGS. 4, 4, 28 ff.). According to the PārGS. 2, 17, 9 Sītā is even his wife. Elsewhere he is the lord or husband of the *urvarā,* "the fertile field" (cf. ṚV. 8, 21, 3). In the Ṛgveda he is stated to win tilth, he is lord of tilth (2, 21, 1; 6, 20, 1), and as such he is besought to reduce, in co-operation with Pūṣan, the furrow to the right condition (4, 57, 7). Finally his name is also mentioned in connection with the ploughshare, the penis, and the impregnation of domestic animals.

Examples are not wanting that a god whose main concern is, or was, vitality, fertility, and force or energy in nature, is also credited with a warlike temperament, with a natural bent for the annihilation of evil powers, demons and the enemies of mankind. The Vedic Indra is a demon-slayer, but his chief exploit, "the great myth which is the basis of his nature" [5]) is his victory over the demon of obstruction and drought. By this exploit he renders signal services to mankind.

In the Ṛgveda the warlike character of Indra and, correlatively, the demoniac, negative character of the dragon who had power over the waters was much emphasized. Yet, there is a curious passage which strongly reminds us of the Chinese conception of the origin of the annual rain: the dragon, who is the giver of rain, sleeps during the winter, hidden sleep in the ground; the second day of the second month, the day of the first thunderstorm, he breaks the earth and ascends to heaven, producing that very thunderstorm. ṚV. 1, 103, 7 it reads: "Thou hast, Indra, performed that heroic deed that thou arousest the sleeping serpent with thy *vajra*-" (cf. also 4, 19, 3). Does Vṛtra who prevents the water from flowing for the benefit of gods and men represent an one-sidedly negative aspect of the dragon who controls the waters and causes the rain to fall and who, therefore, is believed to be able to keep it back? And was the "serpent of the deep", Ahi budhnya [6]) a sort of positive counterpart or aspect of this monster? (cf. e.g. 7, 34, 16). It may be of some interest to remember here that this being, which no doubt owed its existence to considerations similar

---

[3]) I refer to Hopkins, JAOS. 36, p. 242 f.

[4]) See also Hillebrandt, Ved. Myth.[2] II, p. 199; Meyer, o.c., III, p. 154 ff.

[5]) Macdonell, Ved. Myth., p. 58.

[6]) I refer to Macdonell, o.c., p. 72 f. — For the dragon as a rain-god see E. Ingersoll, Dragons and dragon lore, New York 1928, ch. VI.

to those underlying the figure of Śeṣa in Hinduistic Viṣṇuism, is mentioned together with the waters, the lord of the mountains, and Savitar (6, 49, 14), after a reference to Viṣṇu's striding (13) and immediately before an invocation addressed to Bhaga and Puraṃdhi [7]).

The point touched upon here, however, does not seem to bear upon more than one aspect of the Vṛtra myth, or, probably, upon more than one of its components. It cannot be part of our task here to reconsider the mythological complex centering in the Vṛtra combat. Suffice it to say that the ancient view that it was nothing but a myth explaining the phenomenon of the thunderstorm and describing the release of the water, fails to account for many particulars in the texts. After the studies devoted to the subject by Benveniste and Renou [8]), and by Lüders [9]) it seems clear that this central myth refers to a cosmic drama of paramount importance and that it probably was the product of a variety of influences and conceptions, the nucleus of which was the well-known and ever-changing, growing, blending motive of the dragon-killer, represented by or having fused with the divinity of victoriousness over obstruction, barring, and impediments. In the Vedic Vṛtra-combat the release of the waters was considered the central feature, and this occurrence meant the transformation of an inhabitable chaotic universe into a cosmos [10]). This great performance is repeatedly said to take place in the mountains, in atmospheric regions [11]). It was the assistant of the hero-god, to wit Viṣṇu who played the important rôle in this drama to which the next chapter will be devoted. The significance of the soma sacrifice before the battle and of Viṣṇu's share in it [12]) becomes at the same time clearer.

The Vedic Vṛtrahan being identical with the Iranian Vṛϑragna the question arises whether such a salient feature in the character of the latter as his ability to appear in various incarnations is historically related to similar embodiments of Indian gods. Vṛϑragna's incarn-

---

[7]) In the great epic Ahi budhnya reappears as one of the eleven Rudras (1, 66, 2) and as a name of the god Çiva (13, 17, 103); Mbh. 5, 114, 4 he is, like Kubera, a guardian of gold, a favourite occupation of snakes in folklore.

[8]) E. Benveniste et L. Renou, Vṛtra et Vṛϑagna, Paris 1934.

[9]) H. Lüders, Varuṇa, I, Göttingen 1951, p. 167 ff.

[10]) See especially the particulars collected by Lüders, o.c., p. 183 ff. When the serpent was conquered, the sun rose, earth and sky were established, earth and atmosphere were extended, etc. etc.

[11]) For variants of the dragon (or: snake, for Vṛtra was a snake) combat see also Ruben, Lit. vorar. Stämme Indiens, p. 40; 42. — It may incidentally be remarked that the ancient Egyptians on the same basis of a dramatic conception of nature which sees everywhere a strife between divine and demoniac, cosmic and chaotic powers, connected the serpent with darkness. See also B. Renz, Der orientalische Schlangendrache, Augsburg 1930.

[12]) I refer to Geldner's note, Rigveda übersetzt, III, p. 286 (on 8, 3, 8).

ations being ten in number, Charpentier [13]) too rashly connected the greater part of them with the avatāras of Viṣṇu. In a more cautious way Benveniste [14]) drew attention to Vṛϑragna's, Vṛtra's (ṚV. 1, 121, 11), Indra's, and Viṣṇu's appearance as a boar. Although the possibility that Viṣṇu, through the medium of Indra-Vṛtrahan, inherited a trait of character of ancient Indo-Iranian origin must be conceded, the history of the boar avatāra seems to be too complicated and the incarnations of the Avestan god are too different from anything attributed to an individual Indian god to attain to a reasonable degree of probability.

It would, in general, appear to be the most satisfactory view of those features which the characters of Viṣṇu and the dragon-killing Indra have in common to regard them as mainly conditioned by the community of their interest and by their co-operation. Such features are, apart from those mentioned in other sections of this volume, expressed by phrases like "fearful wild beast of the mountain" which is used to characterize Indra (ṚV. 10, 180, 2) as well as Viṣṇu (1, 154, 2). The phrase *urú krámiṣṭa jīváse* is, as Hopkins [15]) observed, used of both gods (1, 155, 4; 8, 63, 9), if we also take into consideration 6, 69, 5 where the act is attributed to both of them conjointly making the atmosphere broader, and extending the worlds, for man to live. Sometimes these gods are invoked in the same sūkta: ṚV. 6, 69, 1; 3 and 6 they are besought to bring wealth, 1 to escort the persons praying along a safe road. The poet of 1, 156, 4 even attributed to Viṣṇu, accompanied by his friend, the exploit of opening Vala's cow-pen [16]). Macdonell [17]) has already duly discussed the fact that in sūktas extolling Viṣṇu alone Indra is the only other deity incidentally associated with him. The relations between the weather-god and the divinity concerned with the pervasion of the celestial energy [18]) may mythologically be expressed in various ways. They represent related forces and processes and naturally co-operate [19]).

[13]) Charpentier, Kleine Beiträge zur indoiranischen Mythologie, Uppsala 1911, p. 25 ff.

[14]) Benveniste-Renou, o.c., p. 194 f.

[15]) Hopkins, JAOS. 36, p. 264, n. 21.

[16]) I refer to Macdonell, o.c., p. 159 f.; see also p. 127.

[17]) Macdonell, o.c., p. 39 f.

[18]) This feature in Viṣṇu's character will be discussed in section VII, etc.

[19]) It would perhaps be well to discuss here also the interesting passages ÇB. 13, 5, 4, 28; ÇāṅkhÇS. 16, 9, 25-32; ĀpÇS. 20, 23, 11 mentioning the animal sacrifices of the seasons. It stands to reason that e.g. in the rainy season the victims are sacred to Parjanya, or to the Maruts; it is likewise natural that the weathergod par excellence, Indra, is remembered in three or four of the six periods of the year. Is there a similar sense in the fact that Indra and Bṛhaspati, and the former and Viṣṇu had to receive the corresponding offerings in the winter and the cool

VI. VIṢṆU, INDRA, AND THE VAJRA.

It would be superfluous to dwell upon the well-known friendship, in ancient times, of the deity under discussion, acting as an assistant and playing a secondary part, for the mighty and central figure of the god who fights Vṛtra, or to draw, once again, attention to the fact that the latter is the only other deity who in Vedic hymns extolling Viṣṇu alone, is associated with him [1]). It would be equally needless to recall that in the epic period the relations between these two gods undergo a radical change [2]): after having been Indra's assistant and younger brother, Viṣṇu becomes the typical fighter for the gods, assuming a superior position and being called "(the god) who is over Indra" (*Atīndra-*) [2]). Let us therefore focus our attention on some interesting details connected with Indra's chief exploit.

It would appear to me that some outstanding features in Viṣṇu's character are especially obvious when, in the ancient documents, his relations with Indra are under discussion. It may, in my opinion, be said that Viṣṇu whilst remaining, in the descriptions of Indra's exploits, in the background, contributes by his presence or by his striding movement to Indra's success. He is more than a mere companion, he is a *yujyaḥ sakhā* (ṚV. 1, 22, 19): equal in rank or power, similar to Indra himself, well matched, and equal to discharging the obligations of that friendship. Sometimes we are even under the impression that it was he who made this success possible. Calling only attention to those points which seem to be relevant to our argument we first consider ṚV. 4, 18, 11. Whereas ṚV. 8, 12, 27 Viṣṇu is stated to have made his three steps by vital energy (*ojas*) [3]), 4, 18, 11 the latter when about to slay Vṛtra asks his companion to stride out rather widely. This request is repeated 8, 100, 12, where it is followed by the words:

---

season? Was it because the divine powers engaged in the 'Vṛtra-combat' and the other points under discussion were, in the months preceding the spring, in special need of stimulants? (For Bṛhaspati who finds the light, dispels darkness, is often said to be Indra's ally, called *vajrin-*, and described as an increaser of wealth and prosperity; see Hillebrandt, Ved. Myth., p. 102 f.).

1) I refer to Macdonell, o.c., p. 39 f.; Oldenberg, o.c., p. 136; Hillebrandt, o.c., II, p. 313 f.; Keith, o.c., p. 109.

2) See e.g. Hopkins, Epic mythology, p. 140; 204 etc.

3) For the sense of *ojas* see my relevant treatise 'Anc. Ind. *ojas* etc.', Utrecht 1952. The possession of this power is in most cases an attribute of Indra, very seldom of Viṣṇu: AV. 7, 25, 1 by the ojas of Viṣṇu and Varuṇa space (*rajāṃsi*) has been established, an activity within the god's special sphere; and ṚV. 10, 113, 2 (see further on). The ṚV. passage runs as follows: *yadâ te viṣṇur ójasā trîṇi padâ vicakramé...*, admitting of the translation: "by your (Indra's) *ojas*".

"We both will slay Vṛtra and release the streams " [4]). Sāyaṇa in commenting upon this sūkta appositely quoted Bṛhaddevatā 6, 121 ff.: "Having tormented these three worlds Vṛtra remained (unassailable) by his fury. Indra could not slay him. Going to Viṣṇu he said 'I wish to slay Vṛtra. Stride apart (*vikramya*) today and stand at my side. Dyaus (Sky) must make room (*antara-*) for my raised bolt'. Saying 'Yes', Viṣṇu did so, and Dyaus gave him an opening (*vivara-*)" (cf. also ṚV. 8, 100, 12).

It is illuminating to compare this episode with other passages in which Viṣṇu's activity is in some way or other helpful to his great friend. TS. 2, 4, 12, 3 tells that Vṛtra had enveloped these worlds and struck fear into Indra and Tvaṣṭar. Indra then addressed Viṣṇu: "Viṣṇu, come hither; we will grasp that by which he is this world". Viṣṇu deposited himself in three places (*tredhātmānaṃ vi ny adhatta*) a third on the earth, a third in the atmosphere, a third in the sky, for he was afraid of his growth. By means of these thirds Indra successively raised his bolt, aided (*anuṣṭhitaḥ*) by Viṣṇu, whom he afterwards addressed: "Thrice hast thou furthered me". TS. 6, 5, 1 Indra when raising his bolt to hurl at Vṛtra was supported by Viṣṇu; cf. ŚB. 5, 5, 5, 2 ff.; PB. 20, 15, 6; JB. Ausw. 148. Viṣṇu also figures as a helper of Indra against the asuras: AiB. 3, 50, where other gods, Varuṇa and Bṛhaspati, are also of the party. Other passages of interest are e.g. ṚV. 1, 156, 5 "The divine V. who as a greater doer of good has approached (joined) I., the doer of good, in order to be his companion, ...who has a triple seat, helped the Āryan...."; 1, 85, 7; 6, 20, 2; cf. also 8, 69, 16. ṚV. 7, 93, 8 I., V., and the Maruts are mentioned together; 10, 128, 2 the same divinities and Agni.

Viṣṇu by making flow the soma-stalk strengthened Indra's greatness with vital energy (*ojas*): ṚV. 10, 113, 2: this means that before the great combat V. prepared the soma-draught for I., a fact which is also mentioned ṚV. 2, 22, 1; see also 6, 17, 11 etc. In 8, 15, 9 V. praises, i.e. strengthens, I. with songs (*gṛṇāti*). Besides, I. is stated to have enhanced, in the intoxication of the soma, his own manly power, near V. (at V.'s? 8, 3, 8 *vāvṛdhe vṛ́ṣṇyaṃ śávo máde sutásya víṣṇavi*). From V.'s station or place (*sthānam*) I. wrought mighty deeds: TS. 1, 1, 12; KS. 1, 12; MS. 1, 1, 13; cf. also ŚB. 1, 4, 5, 3; the text as given in the KS. runs as follows: *viṣṇos sthāmna ita indro vīryam akṛṇot* [5]), and the ŚB. adds: "it was while standing in this place that I. drove off towards the south the evil spirits, the rakṣas". — We may perhaps

---

[4]) For the persons speaking in this sūkta see Geldner, o.c., III, p. 427 f.
[5]) See also Keith, Veda Black Yajus school, p. 14.

attach some importance to ṚV. 1, 22, 19 *víṣṇoḥ kármāṇi paśyata yáto vratâni paspaśe | índrasya yújyaḥ sákhā* "Behold the works of Viṣṇu — from where he watches his ordinances or, rather, sphere of action": watchful activity in the background after (st. 18) having made the three strides?

Mbh. 3, 101, 9 f. describing the Vṛtra combat narrates that I. invoking V.'s protection was favoured by the gift of a portion of the latter's energy (*tejas*) and strength (*balam*). In other epic passages too Viṣṇu is, speaking generally, often conceived as assisting or accompanying, or as being associated with, Indra. Cf. e.g. 1, 65, 1; 84, 9; 6, 50, 42; 59, 80; 7, 52, 34; 81, 25; 12, 64, 13 ff., and also such episodes as that narrated 3, 142, 22 ff., where I., mentally disturbed, concentrated upon V. who promised to kill Naraka for the good of I. Here we see V. from being an assistant and protector develop into the greater god, whose actual appearance and activity is needed to get Indra, the gods, and the world out of difficulties. In the epos he thus becomes the fighter for the gods. Viṣṇu-Kṛṣṇa even comes to use Indra as demiurge and, being *indrakarman-*, to work through him: Mbh. 13, 149, 97; Rām. 6, 120, 18. In the Rām., 7, 27, 14 f., I. even begs vainly for V.'s aid. Then Viṣṇu is said to be attended by his former greater brother. According to the Har., 50, 26, I. performs V.'s functions when the latter enjoys his annual sleep [6]). How much Indra sank in the estimation of a great many Indians may be apparent from one quotation: when, in the ancient story of Ambarīśa as told by Rāmānanda (Rāmalīla, XVIth cent.), V., in the guise of I, offers the king a boon, the latter refuses to accept it saying that he will have nothing to do with a gift of Indra [7]). When being represented as the creator himself and the Supreme Being Viṣṇu even carries the *vajra-*, the well-known weapon of the Vedic Indra: Hariv. 222 (= 3, 37), 2.

This remark leads us to discuss the other references to a close connection between Viṣṇu and the *vajra-*. Special attention may in the first place be drawn to those epic texts in which the god is described as entering Indra's bolt. Mbh. 3, 315, 10 ff. we are reminded of numerous cases in which gods in disguise conquered their enemies; amongst them Viṣṇu, having assumed the shape of the Horsenecked one, of the dwarf, etc., also, for the purpose of chastising his foes, entered Śakra's bolt and hid himself in it (st. 17). In the version of the Vṛtra-myth related Mbh. 5, a. 10 it is the Supreme Lord of the gods Viṣṇu himself who promises, through his influence, victory to

---

[6]) See section XII.

[7]) I refer to D. Sen, The Bengali Rāmāyaṇas, Calcutta 1920, p. 31.

Indra for the sake of the gods: being invisible he will enter the vajra (st. 12). Afterwards, after having mentally invoked Viṣṇu, Indra sees a mass of foam coming out of the sea, which, together with the vajra, he hurled at the enemy; Viṣṇu having entered the foam destroyed Vṛtra (st. 37 ff.). 12, 281, 31 the same god is said to have entered the vajra, bent upon protecting the universe, and by doing so enabling Indra to kill Vṛtra (cf. also 282, 10: *vajreṇa viṣṇuyuktena*). Special attention must, in this connection, be paid to Mbh. 1, 23, 16, where Garuḍa who is addressed with names and epithets otherwise due to Viṣṇu, is called *śara-* "arrow", that is, Sāyaṇa adds, *mahādevasya tripuravadhe bāṇabhūto viṣṇuḥ,* "Viṣṇu acting as Śiva's arrow, when the latter destroyed the city of the asuras" (cf. 7, 202, 77). In the Tripura battle as described in the MtPur. a. 129 ff. Viṣṇu, Agni, and Soma constitute the arrow of Śiva who acts as the champion of the gods (133, 41 f.: *ānanaṃ hy agnir abhavac chalyaṃ somas tamonudaḥ | tejasaḥ samavāyo 'tha ceṣos tejo rathāṅgadhṛk* (= Viṣṇu)); Viṣṇu coming out of the arrow and assuming the form of a bull destroys the army of the asuras (136, 58 ff.). It may be remembered that according to the conception which seems to have been in the mind of the author of TS. 6, 1, 3, 5 Indra's bolt (*vajra-*) contained arrows within it, which became śara grass or reeds, used for arrows ("the thunderbolt", it is added, "is śara grass"). — On another occasion a bolt was made of the bones of a brāhmaṇa; it was irresistible and permeated by V. (*viṣṇupraviṣṭena*) and used by Indra to strike Viśvarūpa, the son of Tvaṣṭar (12, 342, 41).

Now the first question which may arise concerns the relation of the representation given in these texts to the share Viṣṇu has, according to a passage in a brāhmaṇa, in the construction of the vajra. By offering to Agni, Soma, and Viṣṇu, the ŚB. states (3, 4, 4, 14), one constructs the bolt: one makes Agni the *anīka-* "point", Soma the *śalya-* "shaft or socket" and Viṣṇu the *kulmala-* "that part of the implement by which the point is attached to the shaft" [8]). In a similar text, AiB. 1, 25, 2 it reads as follows: "In the upasads the gods fashioned an arrow. Of it Agni was the point, Soma the socket (*śalya-*), Viṣṇu the shaft (*tejana-*), and Varuṇa the feathers". Now Agni is, according to the same ŚB. [9]) which in this is in harmony with other Vedic authorities, fiery energy, and identical with the sun; being instrumental in destroying the rakṣas he is a conqueror engaged in

[8]) The commentary has: *anīkaṃ vajrasya mukhapradeśaḥ, kalpaṃ* (sic) *tataḥ pūrvo bhāgaḥ kulmalaṃ tatpucchabhāgaḥ*. Cf. also Eggeling, SBE. 26, p. 108, n. 2, and Mbh. 7, 202, 77.

[9]) For references see Eggeling, SBE. 44, p. 513 ff. and 572.

burning up the enemies of the gods. Soma is light, truth, and life-sap, and Indra's faithful companion, as well as identical with the moon. Both of them are said to be in water and plants. Being so closely connected with these divinities and forming, with them, the weapon of Indra — who is the highest, mightiest, and strongest of the gods, the great conqueror of the most dreaded enemy, Vṛtra, who is energy, vital power, and generative capacity itself, the drinker of soma, and in destroying rakṣas and asuras Agni's ally, and, like him, light and immortal life [10]) —, must Viṣṇu, in this connection, not have been credited with similar functions and qualities? Another interesting passage is Mbh. 7, 202, 77 where Śiva constructing a chariot in order to vanquish the same asuras makes the Mandara mountain his bow, the snake Vāsuki its string, Viṣṇu the arrow, Agni the point of the arrow, Vāyu the wings on both sides. Since the other divinities are charged with functions which suit them very well, we may infer from this passage that it was Viṣṇu's character that made him fit to serve as an arrow. There can be no doubt: the pervader was believed to make an excellent missile weapon. — The sun — and Viṣṇu is connected with that luminary — is, on the other hand the highest among the lightning-flashes (*vidyut-*; ŚŚS. 4, 21, 2; ĀśvGS. 1, 24, 8) [11]).

Now, Indra is in the same brāhmaṇa explicitly called "thunder": 11, 6, 3, 9 *stanayitnur evendraḥ* [12]), and "thunder" is explained as "lightning, thunderbolt": *aśani-* [13]). Lightning and thunder were often regarded as an indication of rain and a 'symbol', or preferably representation, of fertility, rather than a sign of danger [14]). The thun-

---

[10]) For Indra, ibidem, p. 541 f.

[11]) If Bloomfield (JAOS. 13, p. CXIII ff.; Amer. J. of Phil. 7, 469 ff.) was right in considering the text AV. 1, 12 to be addressed to lightning, conceived as the cause of various diseases, the words "he who, one force (*ekam ojas*), has stridden out threefold" (st. 1) are very remarkable, the three strides being a characteristic of Viṣṇu.

[12]) Sāyaṇa takes *stanayitnu-* in the sense of "thunder-cloud".

[13]) For Indra's associations with thunder and lightning see: Hopkins, JAOS. 16, p. CCXXXVI ff.; the same, JAOS. 36, p. 242 ff.; Oldenberg, Religion des Veda, p. 138 f.; H. Lommel, Die alten Arier, Frankfurt a.M. 1935, p. 111 and elsewhere, etc.

[14]) See e.g. W. Eberhard, Chinese festivals, New York 1952, p. 88; H. H. Diephuis, Naturkräfte und ihre Verehrung in der altrömischen Religion, Thesis Utrecht 1941, p. 140, who inter alia observes: "Von diesem Standpunkt aus ist es alsdann gar nicht befremdend, dass der Blitzgott eng mit der Göttin der Vegetation verbunden ist". "Vor allem im Sommer entfaltet der Gott (Donar-Thor), wenn lange Dürre die Menschen gequält hat, seine Kraft in Blitzen und Wetterleuchten; er spendet als segnender Himmelsherr das von Riesen und Drachen, die er im Kampfe besiegt, zurückgehaltene Naß" (V. Stegemann, Hdwtb. de. Abergl. I, 1402, cf. also 1407). — ÇB. 1, 1, 1, 17: both water and vajra produce a hollow in the ground.

derbolt, though it may, under certain circumstances be feared, is at the same time held to be a fertilizing phenomenon and an offensive or destructive weapon of war. In the mythology of the original inhabitants of America there are numerous deities of thunder and lightning who also function as fertility gods. This may even be said to be the normal rôle of such deities; the god of the yellow grain at the same time was a god of war [15]). "In the myths the war-gods receive.... the bow and arrows or lightning bolts as real weapons of war, to be used in their fight against enemies and monsters. In the ceremonies, however.... lightning is.... the rain-bringing, fertilizing phenomenon" [16]). In Peru the fertilizing stones belonging to these deities are found all over the country [17]). In India, with the Sema Nagas, celts are called toad axes and are believed to be thunderbolts that have fallen in a flash of lightning. The toad is the friend of the spirit of fruitfulness, but he is also associated with thunderstorms. The Semas and other peoples in their neighbourhood when finding a celt keep it, believing that it will cause fertility to their crops [18]). In Tibet the life-creating thunderbolt it considered the image of the male organ of generation as well as a means of destruction; besides, it is instrumental in creating deliverance from death [19]). Thus the power which promotes the fertilization of the soil is at the same time represented as a warrior annihilating the demon of drought and evil. There is a well-known type of seasonal festival, the primitive purpose of which was to reinvigorate the earth after the stagnation of winter, or after a period of drought; a ritual combat representing the triumph of life over death or of good over evil repeats the mythical combat between the god and powers under consideration and his antagonist who is often conceived as a dragon. Thus the fight between the Hittite weather-god and the dragon Illuyankaš [20]). The Babylonian goddess Ištar had already the

---

15) See e.g. Hopkins, Indra and other gods of war and fertility compared, JAOS. 37, p. 85 f.; H. K. Haeberlin, The idea of fertilization in the culture of the Pueblo Indians, in the Memoirs of the American Anthropological Association, 3 (1916), p. 1 ff., passim; cf. also L. Malten, in the Jahrbuch d. de. archaeol. Inst. 43 (1928), p. 90 ff.; Eliade, Traité, p. 113.

16) Haeberlin, o.c., p. 37; p. 48 (lightning striking in the corn-field is an event regarded as the acme of fertilization).

17) Hopkins, l.c.

18) See J. H. Hutton, The Sema Nagas, London 1921, p. 196; 256 f.; cf. also R. E. Enthoven, The folklore of Bombay, Oxford 1924, p. 76 f.; N. E. Parry, The Lakhers, London 1932, p. 498 f.; J. P. Mills, The Lhota Nagas, London 1922, p. 165.

19) Some particulars may e.g. be found in S. Hummel, Geheimnisse tibetischer Malereien, Leipsic 1949, p. 3 ff. In tantric Buddhism the vajra = the liṅga (phallos), see e.g. Eliade, Techniques du yoga, Paris 1948, p. 206 f.

20) I refer to A. Götze, Kleinasien, in 'Kulturgeschichte des alten Orients', Handbuch der Altertumswissenschaft von I. v. Müller-W. Otto, III, 1, 3, 3, 1,

double character combining, like the Iranian Anaïtis (Anāhitā), fecundity and warlike courage [21]). A 'Donnerkeil' is often the weapon or attribute of the weathergod, the deity concerned with fecundation who displays his activity in the atmosphere, a 'Donnerkeil' whether it is represented as axe or as lightning [22]).

So we might feel inclined to ask ourselves whether the above passages in the epos and the ŚB. perhaps reflect an old conception of a fertilizing power connected with the sun and called Viṣṇu, being within, or being at least able to enter, the thunderbolt for the sake of destroying the demon of drought and fecundating the earth, the bolt being wielded by a power called Indra who was mainly conceived as concerning himself with all power and activity for good in nature, and especially in the atmosphere, with the weather and the phenomena dependent on it, and who periodically released the waters after destroying the dragon possessing or withholding them.

There are, indeed, various references to a similar belief in ancient India regarding the functions of thunder and lightning [23]). We are told (ŚB. 9, 3, 3, 15) that as to "this shower of wealth, the body (from which it flows) is the sky, the udder the cloud, the teat the lightning, and the shower (of ghee) is the (rain-) shower; from the sky it comes to the cow" (*tasyai vā etasyai vasor dhārāyai, dyaur evātmābhram ūdho vidyut stano dhāraiva dhārā divo 'dhi gāṃ āgachati*). In AV. 10,10

München 1933, p. 131; O. R. Gurney, The Hittites, London 1952, p. 152. This weather-god was assisted by his sons, one of whom was the god of vegetation.

21) G. Contenau, La déesse nue babylonienne, Paris 1914, p. 120 f.; E. Benveniste, The Persian religion according to the chief Greek texts, Paris 1929, p. 27 f. ..." Anāhita, who in Iranian beliefs was an incarnation of warlike valour as well as wisdom and fecundity..."; p. 61 ff.

22) See Chr. Blinkenberg, The thunderweapon in religion and folklore, Cambridge 1911; K. Birket-Smith, Geschichte der Kultur, Zürich 1946, p. 392, who rightly observes that the axe is lightning itself, recalling the fact that this conception is always connected with prehistoric stone-axes found in many parts of Asia and Africa. It may be remembered that this tool was used as a weapon and as an instrument for clearing forests and reclaiming land. Some remarks on axes and hammers in connection with deities presiding over fertility are also made by Güntert, Weltkönig, p. 15; 47; and by H. Lommel, Der arische Kriegsgott, Frankfurt a. M. 1939, p. 63 ff. — See also De Vries, o.c., II, p. 213 ff.

23) For lightning in general see Hillebrandt, Vedische Mythologie, I, p. 137 ff.; ancient folklore in connection with it: J. J. Meyer, Das altindische Buch vom Welt- und Staatsleben, Leipsic 1926, p. 897; D. J. Kohlbrugge, Atharvavedapariśiṣṭa über Omina, Thesis Utrecht 1938, p. 53 ff. — The idea of the immanence of a higher being in the lightning was on the other hand known to ancient Indian authors: see JUB. 1, 26, 8 *ya evaiṣa vidyuti puruṣaḥ*... Compare also the observations made by M. Falk, Nāma-rūpa and dharma-rūpa, Calcutta 1943, p. 206; cf. e.g. ChUp. 5, 10, 2.

which praises the cow [24]) the same idea recurs: after the interesting statement that the gods Agni and Soma entered her, the cow is addressed as follows (st. 7) "Thine udder, o excellent one, is Parjanya, the lightnings are thy teats, o cow". In these texts lightning is in an unambiguous manner represented as an instrument for showering rain upon the earth [25]). Apart from such general indications of a connection between thunder or lightning and rain as, for instance, AV. 4, 15, 6 ff., where both phenomena, like rain, clouds, water and the great serpents are invoked to show favour to the earth, we also come across such statements as AV. 11, 4, 2 f. "Homage, O breath [26]), to thy lightning, homage to thy raining. When breath with thunder roar at the herbs, they are impregnated; they conceive...."; 4, 15, 11 f. "May Prajāpati from the sea, the ocean, sending waters, excite the water-holder.... come hither with that thunder, pouring down waters, our asura father". ṚV. 5, 83, 6 the same words occur in a hymn to Parjanya; in st. 2 this deity is said to be in possession of a great weapon, obviously the thunderbolt; cf. also 4 the winds begin to blow, flashes of lightning fall down, the herbs rise up....". If I was right in taking the verb *ābhuṣati* in the sense of "causing to thrive, invigorating" [27]), AV. 7, 11, 1 is another assertion of the fecundating and propitious influence of thunder. Other texts which might be of interest in this connection are AV. 9, 1, 21 [28]); 7, 3: by identifying lightning with the tongue of the mighty ox the poet seems to emphasize its being instrumental in transferring a very potent and propitious liquid [29]). ŚB. 12, 8, 3, 11 lightning and hail are called the two terrible forms of rain; 1, 5, 2, 19 "Should the sacrificer be desirous of rain.... he may also say to the adhvaryu "Ponder thou in thy mind the east wind and lightning!" "; 8, 6, 1, 20 the stanza VS. 15, 19 is explained in such a way that "this one above, the wealth-giver" refers to Parjanya ("because from there wealth, i.e. rain, food for creatures, is bestowed hitherwards"), and the following words "thundering is his striking weapon, lightning his missile" (*sphūrjan hetir vidyut prahetiḥ*) are explicitly affirmed [30]).

---

24) The reader might be referred to M. A. Muusses, Koecultus bij de Hindoes, Thesis Utrecht 1920, p. 11 ff.

25) For the process of raining according to the ancient Vedic documents see H. Lüders, Varuṇa, I, Göttingen 1951, p. 115 ff., and also H. Reichelt, Der steinerne Himmel, Indog. Forsch. 32, p. 23 ff.

26) The breath of life, in whose control is this All (st. 1).

27) J. Gonda, The meaning of Vedic *bhūṣati,* Wageningen 1939, p. 20 f.

28) Cf. ṚV. 1, 22, 3; AV. 10, 7, 19.

29) For the invigorating and protecting properties attributed to saliva see my paper on *bhūṣati* (above, n. 27), p. 14 f., and p. 15, n. 2.

30) Other instances may be found in Kohlbrugge, o.c.; cf. also such texts as Varāhamihira BS., 28, 12; 16; 46, 84 f.

From ṚV. 9, 76, 3 it appears that the lightning was believed to cause the clouds to swell, compare also 10, 65, 13; 66, 11.

It may not be out of place to remark here that many names of apsaras — who, as is well known, were closely connected with trees, rivers, and water, and are considered 'deities' of fecundation and fortune [31]) — contain a word for lightning: *Vidyutā, Vidyutparṇā, Vidyutprabhā, Saudāmanī,* etc. As other heavenly damsels are called [32]) after hail (*Puñjikasthalā*), snow (*Himā*), fertile soil (*Urvarā*), etc. these names may, at least originally, have been indicative of their function rather than their beauty.

If we are right in considering the above texts as illustrative of one of the ancient Indian beliefs regarding the function of lightning and of one of the explanations of the process of raining, we must now discuss the vajra more closely. Although there is no general agreement as to its original substratum, there appears to be no doubt that thunderstorm and thunderbolt were important factors in the creation of this mythological concept [33]). What, then, were for the Vedic Indians the implications involved in the vajra concept? Granting that arguments based on an incomplete collection of the almost innumerable identifications as found in the brāhmaṇas can sometimes easily be weakened by evidence to the contrary derived from the same source, granting, too, that the unsystematic and speculative thought of the early thinkers often led them to combine the most heterogeneous concepts and to identify, if there was any need to do so, a diversity of entities which elsewhere formed part of other combinations, I am, however, not prepared to reject the results of an investigation of this sort, if they are sufficiently consistent and in the main in harmony with other well-established facts. The study of the identifications can, at least, contribute to finding an answer to the question as to what the concept under consideration meant for the authors of the brāhmaṇas, what they felt to be its essence and nature, and what properties they attributed to it.

A survey of a random collection of the objects and concepts identified with the vajra shows that the criteria were, in the main threefold: concurrence as to function, similarity of outward appearance,

---

31) See G. Borsani, Contributo allo studio sulla concezione e sullo sviluppo storico dell' apsaras, Milan 1938.

32) For the names of the apsaras see Borsani, o.c., p. 36 ff.

33) The vajra is said to roar like a bull (e.g. ṚV. 1, 100, 13; 2, 11, 10), or to be a bull (2, 16, 6): these texts and other passages are not in commendation of Meyer's view (Trilogie, III, p. 149 ff.) that the original and ṛgvedic significance of the vajra was "Lichtkeil", i.e. the power inherent in the sunbeams. Compare also Lommel's criticism, o.c., p. 40 f.

or a certain association. Often more than one of these motives concurred to call an object a vajra. Curiously enough, the vajra itself is in the texts examined never identified with another object or phenomenon. The sun, water, rain, ghee, butter, the sacrifice, a knife or butcher's axe, the wooden sword used in sacrificing, the press-stones are called a *vajra-*, and so are the *yūpa-* (sacrificial post), a spade, a club, an axe, a staff, reed, and, further, cattle, the triṣṭubh-metre, the *vaṣaṭ*-call, seed, *ojas,* speech, praise, the year, the moon, brightness, and some other entities. ŚB. 7, 5, 2, 24 the *vajra-* is *vīrya-* "strength, manly vigour"; 8, 4, 1, 20 it is synonymous with *ojas.* On a closer examination of some selected texts we see that water is considered a vajra because it produces a hollow in the ground (ŚB. 1, 1, 1. 17), that water is a vajra, for both of them destroy the evil of a place (7, 5, 2, 41), that the yūpa is a vajra: it stands erect as a weapon against the enemy (AiB. 2, 1, 4). What strikes us most is that various objects or entities which exert a favourable influence upon vegetation or which are instrumental in producing what is good and useful for man in a more general sense, or also objects and phenomena which are regarded as active for the sake of the annihilation of evil, are, throughout the brāhmaṇas, called vajras. As a rule such vajras serve as a means of repelling evil spirits, destroying demons, driving away all sorts of evil and misfortune, but they are also instrumental in gaining what is good and desirable; "with butter, a vajra, the gods gained the seasons and the year, and deprived their rivals of these" (ŚB. 1, 5, 3, 4); "the clarified butter being a vajra, he now delivers the cow by means of it, and by delivering her he makes her his own" (3, 3, 1, 3); "by that vajra, the ghee, the gods clove the strongholds and conquered these worlds" (3, 4, 4, 6); see also ŚB. 5, 3, 4, 24; 3, 7, 1, 14 and other passages. A fine instance of the double character of the vajra is found ŚB. 3, 6, 4, 15 after having cut a tree for a sacrificial post one has to offer ghee upon the stump, "lest the evil spirits should rise from it": ghee being a vajra one thus repels these spirits by means of the vajra.... Ghee being also seed (*retas*), one thus endows the trees with that seed, and trees grow up again from that stump. Compare also 3, 4, 4, 8 "with that vajra.... he cleaves these worlds and conquers these worlds", and 7, 3, 2, 10 (see further on).

Special attention may be drawn to those passages where the vajra is a means of obtaining those entities which are to be elsewhere the concern of the god Viṣṇu and the deities associated with him. PB. 12, 13, 18, e.g., it reads: "The man who wishes food should hold the *ṣoḍaśin*-laud on the *virāj*-verses; the *ṣ.* is a vajra, food is *virāj*-like; by means of a vajra he grants him (the sacrificer) food; he becomes an eater of food" (*vajreṇaivāsmai annaṃ spṛṇoty annādo bhavati*). 19, 6, 3 cattle is said to be "enclosed" or "obtained" (*parigrah-*) by means of the same vajra. ŚB. 13, 4, 4, 1; 7, 1, 10 and elsewhere the vajra is stated to win lordship or political power (*kṣatra-*). Positive and negative influence: 7, 3, 2, 10 a white horse = the sun = a vajra, "having driven off the rakṣas, the fiends by that vajra, they obtained well-being in a place free from danger and destruction" (*abhaye 'nāṣṭre svasti samāśnuvata*). In this connection a text like ŚB. 7, 3, 1, 19 is worthy of mention: "He takes them with the sacrificial wooden sword (*sphya-*); now, the sword is a vajra, and the vajra means vigour (*vīrya-*), and this (earth) means acquisition (*vitti-*); by vigour he thus obtains *vitti-*".

The vajra is, indeed, very often expressly stated to mean, or to be, (manly) vigour or strength: ŚB. 1, 3, 5, 7 *vīryaṃ vajraḥ*; 7, 5, 2, 24; 13, 4, 1, 13; 6, 1, 4; 5; 2, 4; 6; 15; 17; 14, 1, 2, 3. With the *vajra-*, which is *vīrya-*, the sacrificer beats off evil (*pāpmānam*): 13, 5, 1, 17. It separates from evil and destruction: 7, 2, 1, 17; repels evil and corruption: 7, 2, 4, 12 etc.; smites misfortune: ŚāB. 3, 2; 10, 1; prevents a wicked enemy from laying hold of a man; ŚB. 13, 1, 2, 9; it is considered a protector (*abhigoptar-*): 6, 3, 3, 10; 18; 24; it defends the sacrifice: 1, 2, 5, 20 [34]).

It may be of some use to recall that the authors of the Ṛgveda very often mention the flowing or release of the waters in close connection with Indra's hurling the vajra. It evidently was the very aim of the god's warlike activity: cf. e.g. 1, 85, 9 "When the skilful Tvaṣṭar had produced, with his turning-lathe, the well-made, golden, thousand-edged bolt, Indra took it to perform manly deeds: he slew Vṛtra, and drove out the flood of waters"; 1, 57, 6; 61, 12; 80, 5; 85, 9; 103, 2; 2, 15, 3; 4, 17, 7; 5, 29, 2. The vajra, moreover, often occurs in passages dealing with water, vegetative life, or the powers, beings, or entities representing or bringing about fertility: ṚV. 1, 80, 8 (navigable) rivers; 84, 11 the soma-cows; 8, 7, 22 waters and sun; 70, 2 sun; 9, 47, 3 soma; 72, 7 the navel of the earth, waters, and streams; 77, 1 cows and milk; 106, 3 waters; 111, 3 sunbeams, songs of praise. AV. 2, 3, 6 "Weal be to us the waters, propitious the herbs; let Indra's thunderbolt smite away the demoniacs...."; ṚV. 10, 84, 6 ∾ AV. 4, 31, 6 "Born together with success (*ābhūti-* [35])), O missile thunderbolt, thou bearest superior power (*sahas*), O superior power; be thou

[34]) For such texts as ÇāB. 3, 3 see D. J. Hoens, Çānti, Thesis Utrecht 1951, p. 8.

[35]) This translation, which is also Geldner's ("Erfolg"), seems to be preferable to "efficacy" (Whitney-Lanman). The word might also express the idea of "place of growth or origin", which seems most probable AiB. 7, 13, 10. Cf. also G. Liebert, Das Nominalsuffix *-ti-* im altindischen, Lund 1949, p. 41.

allied with our (or: your?) resoluteness (*kratu-*), O fury, much-invoked one, in the mingling of great riches"; ṚV. 10, 83, 1 ∾ AV. 4, 32, 1 "He who honoured thee, o fury, missile thunderbolt, prospers as to superior power, vital energy...." (in this sūkta and in the foregoing Fury, *Manyu-* is addressed); AV. 6, 125, 2 "to the force of the waters...., to Indra's bolt"; 6, 2 Soma is associated with the vajra; this divine power is even given the epithet *Vṛtrahan-*; 97, 3 Indra is called "....a kine-conqueror, thunderbolt-armed"; ṚV. 9, 72, 7 (cf. 106, 3) the *vajra-* is styled "a bull of all-pervading or mighty wealth" (*vibhūvasu-*). And similar texts may also be quoted in illustration of the significance of the vajra for these priests and poets.

The use of the term *vazra-* in the Avesta, and the function of the 'object' meant by it, is fairly consistent with the above. The *vazra-* is the main weapon of the god Mithra who is not only the god of the heavenly light, the lord of the vast luminous space and of the wide pastures, and especially, the deity of truth and faith; he is also a god of war and a punishing lord [36]). Besides, he is explicitly stated to be the god who gives plenty of water, who causes the rain to fall down and the plants to grow (Yt. 10, 61); he is the god who provides men with herds, political power, sons, life; who gives abundance, wealth, power, victory, renown, and welfare (Yt. 10, 65; 33). His *vazra-*, which is described Yt. 10, 132, cleaves the skulls of the daēvas. There is, in my opinion, room for the assumption that *vazra-* when associated with arrows, spears and similar weapons (e.g. Yt. 13, 72) is used in a secondary sense. The many different meanings of the Sanskrit word represent more serious deviations from the original use.

In view of the above considerations it is worth discussing the etymology of the word. Whereas the authors of books on the history of Indian religions, generally speaking, paid no special attention to the prehistory of the name of the bolt [37]), comparative linguists agree in connecting it with the Lat. *vegeo* "to be brisk, to set in motion", *vigeo* "to be in the prime of life etc.", *vigil* "wakeful, brisk", and with OHG. *wackar, wachar,* Germ. *wacker,* Dutch *wakker* "brisk, alert,

[36]) I refer to H. S. Nyberg, Die Religionen des alten Iran, Leipsic 1938, p. 59 ff.; J. Hertel, Die Sonne und Mithra im Awesta, Leipsic 1927, esp. p. 214 ff.; the same, Mithra und Erexša, ibidem 1931; G. Messina, Mitra e la sua religione solare e guerriera, Rome 1941; E. Herzfeld, Zoroaster and his world, Princeton 1947, p. 422 (each of these books containing one-sided views and disputable suggestions). See also Dandekar, Ann. Bhand. Or. Res. Inst. 31, p. 7 f.

[37]) See e.g. Oldenberg, Die Religion des Veda, p. 138 f.; Keith, o.c., p. 127; Macdonell, o.c., p. 55; Lommel, o.c., p. 40 ff. In a similar way Bergaigne, o.c., II, p. 272; E. Benveniste et L. Renou, Vṛtra et Vṛthragna, Paris 1934, p. 128 ff.; Reichelt, o.c., p. 44 f. (See also Hertel, Mithra und Erexša, p. 200; Sonne und Mithra, l.c.).

vigilant, awake" [38]). They are no doubt right in doing so as far as the outward form of the words is concerned, AI. *vájra-*, Av. *vazra-* and the Germ. *wackar* etc. even admitting of the hypothesis of a common IE. *-ro-* derivation. Yet the question may arise, if the semantic aspect of the etymology has been sufficiently commented upon. Is Walde-Pokorny's: root *ṷeg*¹- "frisch, rege, kräftig sein" (or Walde's *ṷeg*¹- "rege, munter, wach"): AInd. *vájra-* "Donnerkeil (des Indra)", Av. *vazra-* "Haukeule (des Mithra)" a satisfactory explanation? To my mind, Kluge-Götze's basal [39]) meaning "lebenskräftig sein" would seem to come nearer to the point. Wagenvoort [40]), in presenting us with a rapid survey of the meanings of the Latin *vigor, vigēre, vegēre, vegetus,* is quite right in qualifying the general sense of the element *veg-* [41]) which they have in common by observing that they express the idea of a moving, energetic power inherent in them (cf. e.g. Cic. Tusc. 5, 37), and, further, that they also relate to fertility, the vegetative power of nature, particularly of the vegetable kingdom. The very word *vegetation* is a derivative of the same root. Still more than such German connotations as: (*wacker* in the sense of) "munter, rüstig, rüstig tätig" or (of *wacker* when almost a synonym of) "mutig" or "fröhlich", can the cognate Indian words contribute to the assumption that already the IE. root expressed the same shades of meaning.

It may be convenient to dwell here for a moment, by way of digression, upon the meaning of the other Vedic terms derived from the root under discussion. In explaining the sense of *vājayati* scholars usually resort to a profusion of modern terms each of them being considered a partial equivalent: "(rege sein, kräftig sein;) zur Eile antreiben, anregen; zu Thaten kräftigen; wirksam machen; anspornen, anregen zu; eilen" (Grassmann, Wörterbuch); "wettlaufen, wettfahren, kämpfen, eilen; zur Eile treiben, anregen, zur Kraftäusserung bringen" (Petr. Dict.); "Sieg —, Siegerpreis (Beute) —, reichen Gewinn erstreben, kämpfen, wettkämpfen.... wetteifern; anspornen, ermutigen, wecken" (Geldner, Glossar [42])); "to race, speed, hasten, run, contend,

---

[38]) Cf. e.g. A. Walde, Lat. etym. Wtb.², Heidelberg 1910, p. 812; A. Walde-J. Pokorny, Vergl. Wtb. d. Indogerm. Spr. I, Berlin-Leipsic 1930, p. 246 f.; F. Kluge-A. Götze, Etym. Wtb. d. deutschen Sprache¹⁵, Berlin 1951, p. 847; Franck-Van Wijk, Etym. Wdb. d. Nederl. Taal², The Hague 1929, p. 771.

[39]) Reserving the term 'original' for a meaning testified to by historical evidence; see my 'Ancient-Indian *ojas*...', Utrecht 1952, p. 74.

[40]) H. Wagenvoort, Imperium, Amsterdam 1941, p. 126 f.; in the English edition ('Roman dynamism, Studies in ancient Roman thought, language and custom', Oxford 1947), p. 128 f.

[41]) For *vig-* in *vigil* etc. see M. Leumann-J. B. Hofmann, Lateinische Grammatik, Munich 1928, p. 96.

[42]) Geldner, Der Rigveda in Auswahl, I, Stuttgart 1907, p. 159.

the rural gods, in order to revive vegetation [55]), to restore the productive power of the earth, to renew the world. The magico-religious game puts the player or runner into possession of vigour and energy, which both add to the divine and favourable energy in the universe and enable the man engaged in it to draw down blessings on himself. An insight into the character of these forms of activity — which, no doubt, were at the same time engaged in as 'recreation' in our sense of the word, or, rather, served to satisfy the human desire of emulation and competition — is greatly helpful in interpreting such passages as ṚV. 7, 24, 5 *átyo na vājáyan* "like a steed which stimulates or produces (the above) power" (*balaṃ kurvan* Sāyaṇa; less correctly "das um den Siegerpreis läuft" Geldner); 2, 11, 7 *hárī.... vājáyantā* "(Indra's) two bay steeds who stimulate (that) power" (*vegaṃ kurvantau* S.), an action attended by the sound of sprinkled ghee (*ghṛtaścútaṃ svārám*), which according to Sāyaṇa refers to thunder and falling rain; 6, 75, 7 [56]) where the horses of a king are said to be *vājáyantaḥ*: Geldner's translation "die kampflustigen" lacks precision; Keith's (TS. 4, 66 g) "show their strength" is, in my opinion, not correct, although we must allow for the possibility of a loss of the original connotations expressed by the verb *vājáy-*.

Now, 7, 24, 5 the steed is introduced by way of illustrating the efficacy of the *stoma-* or hymn of praise of which this stanza forms part. 6, 24, 6 the same simile is used to emphasize the idea that Indra, who is to be invited or brought near by hymns, is approached with 'this eulogium' by men who, like steeds (running) a race, are said to be *vājayantaḥ* "generating, or adding to, (the above) power" (*balinaṃ kurvantaḥ*). The well-known fact that songs of praise, solemn formulas confirming a god's power, charms, and words pronounced by mighty, inspired and competent men, are instruments producing the desired results, throws light on these stanzas and on the idea implied in the verb *vājáy-* [57]). In a similar way, 2, 19, 7 *evâ ta indrocátham ahema śravasyâ ná tmánā vājayantaḥ;* here Geldner's translation ".... recht wie Preiskämpfer (die Rennpferde) um dem Ruhmespreis zu gewinnen"

---

[55]) See e.g. A. Piganiol, Recherches sur les jeux romains, Public. de la faculté des lettres... Strassbourg 13, 1923, p. 137 ff.; G. van der Leeuw, Religion in essence and manifestation, p. 373 ff.; the same, Wegen en grenzen², Amsterdam 1948, p. 107 ff.; M. Eliade, Traité d'histoire des religions, Paris 1949, p. 275 ff.; Meyer, o.c., I, p. 224; II, p. 200; Gonda, *Bhūṣati*, p. 22 f.

[56]) This stanza is, in the aśvamedha, used to address the horses of the warriors who were to guard the sacrificial horse from any danger. See e.g. ĀpÇrS. 20, 16, 10 where Caland translated the word under discussion by "Gewinn erstrebend". Elsewhere (ĀśvGS. 3, 12) the stanza forms part of a text used in blessing the king's armour etc.

[57]) I refer to my treatise on *bhūṣati*, p. 10.

would appear to lead to misunderstanding (*annecchayā tvām̥ balinam̥ kurvantaḥ*). The other passages (ṚV. 3, 14, 3; 4, 42, 5; 7, 32, 11; 10, 160, 5; AV. 7, 50, 3) are similar [58]). In particular cases the power which was believed to be stimulated or generated may of course have been conceived as materializing, as being represented by definite phenomena or concrete entities. From what has been said it may be seen that the meaning handed down in the Nighaṇṭu 3, 14: *vājayati*, like *pūjayati* and many other words in the sense of "honouring, praising, worshipping" (*arcitakarman-*) is completely understandable.

The meaning of the substantive *vāja-* is in perfect harmony with that of the verb. Formed like *kāma-* [59]), which stands for "desire" as well as "the object of desire or of pleasure" — the traditional distinction between 'concreta' and 'abstracta' being, with regard to ancient IE. terms of this description, inappropriate [60]) —, *vāja-* generally speaking expresses, not a concept in the modern sense of the word, but a group or complex of ideas, beliefs, conceptions, experiences converging in a 'Daseinsmacht' [61]), a power usually conceived of as substantial in character and, hence, very apt to materialize, a power manifesting in animal and vegetative life, strength, potency, in the capacity for life, to grow, to last, in vigour, — the last word being an approximately correct English 'equivalent'. The ten or more 'different meanings' enumerated in Grassmann's Wörterbuch and other dictionaries are chiefly references to various aspects or manifestations of *vāja-* [62]). Thus *vāja-* [63]) can be considered the opposite of death: AV. 11, 7, 3 *sán .... ásam̥ś cobhaú mr̥tyúr vâjaḥ prajâpatiḥ* "the being one and the non-being one, both, death, vigour, Prajāpati"; it is a 'quality' attributed to a horse, a mule, a ram, a bull, and a he-goat (AV. 4, 4, 8; 6, 38, 3 f.); it is believed to be present in the water(s) (AV. 13, 1, 2 in a text extolling the might and the qualities of the sun [64])), in great divinities like Agni, who is (ṚV. 3, 25, 3) said to be *kṣáyan vâjaiḥ* (: *balaiḥ* Sāyaṇa) "ruling over, or a master of, vājas", Soma who is (9, 31, 2) styled *vâjānām pátiḥ* "lord of the vājas" [65]) — 10, 26, 7 and 9 the same

[58]) Compare, e.g., also PB. 14, 8, 6; 15, 2, 7; ÇāB. 23, 2.

[59]) Cf. W. D. Whitney, A Sanskrit grammar⁵, Leipsic 1924, § 1148 f.

[60]) I refer to my 'AI. *ojas*, Lat. **augos* and the I-E. nouns in *-es- / -os'*, Utrecht 1952, p. 53, and passim.

[61]) Ibidem, p. 46 f.

[62]) We should never forget that many 'meanings' appearing in our dictionaries owe their existence only to the fact that the English language is not able to express the Indian 'concept' by one word.

[63]) For reasons of space I must desist from going over all passages in which the word occurs, many of them being very similar.

[64]) Remarkably enough, Whitney-Lanman here and elsewhere put a questionmark after the translation ("power" e.a.).

[65]) For this idea of lordship see my 'Notes on *brahman*', Utrecht 1950, p. 67 f.

epithet and *vājānāṃ vṛdháḥ* "promoter of *v.*" are applied to Pūṣan — and often attributed to Indra (cf. e.g. 4, 22, 3 *mahó vâjebhir mahádbhiś ca śúṣmaiḥ* "great in vājas, i.e. in the possession and display of v. in various manifestations [66]), and in great deeds of courage or of energy"). These gods like other divinities interested in man's welfare and engaged in supplying food and wealth, fertility and favourable atmospheric conditions — e.g. Sarasvatī 7, 95, 6 — are very often invoked to confer their favours, consisting in *vāja-* [67]) which is often attended by such much desired entities as wealth, possessions, refreshing drinks, plenty of food, sons, cattle, welfare: see e.g. ṚV. 1, 53, 5 *sám indra rāyâ sám iṣâ rabhemahi sáṃ vâjebhiḥ....* | *sáṃ devyâ prámatyā vīráśuṣmayā góagrayâśvāvatyā rabhemahi*; 30, 22; 48, 16; 92, 7 (Uṣas); 116, 19 (Aśvins); 6, 1, 11; 8, 102, 9 (Agni); 9, 90, 2 (Soma), etc. etc. It is always worth while to examine the opposites if there are any mentioned in the same passages: AV. 19, 31, 11, forming part of a text to be used by a man desiring wealth, or in the case of loss of wealth, with an amulet which is addressed as follows: "Thou art the virile (*vṛṣan*) lord of amulets (*maṇi-*), in thee the lord of prosperity (*puṣṭapati-*) generated prosperity; in thee are these vājas, all possessions; ... do thou suppress the niggard, misery (indigence), and hunger, (keep them) far away". ṚV. 10, 53, 8 (cf. AV. 12, 2, 26; VS. 35, 10; TĀ. 6, 3, 2) "Here let us leave those who are pernicious (*aśevāḥ*; *durevāḥ* "malignant" AV.), and cross the flood to vājas which are auspicious (*śivān*; *anamīvān* "free from disease" AV.)" [68]). From such texts as AV. 13, 1, 22 it appears, not only that man is supposed to be able to gain *vāja-*, but also that this achievement is regarded as a victory: *táya* (to wit. by the ruddy one, which doubtless refers to dawn) *vâjān viśvárūpāṃ jayema táyā víśvāḥ pṛ́tanā abhí ṣyāma.* Other passages of interest are, inter alia, ṚV. 10, 11, 5 ∾ AV. 18, 1, 22: Agni is said to have won the *v.* of the *vipra-* "the inspired one" which may mean: "on behalf of the poet" [69]), and especially those in which the *vāja-* is stated to be generated or set in motion. AV. 7, 6, 4 *vâjasya nú prasavé mātáraṃ mahîm áditiṃ nâma*

---

[66]) In translating "groß an Siegen" (this substantive, like "Siegergewinn" is often preferred by the author of the important modern translation of the Ṛgveda) Geldner calls attention only to one of the many ideas implied in or manifestations of, *vāja-*.

[67]) In this case the German translator resorts to the 'partial equivalent' "Belohnung".

[68]) Here again, Geldner's interpretation ("Wir wollen zu günstigem Gewinn ans Ufer steigen") is not very satisfactory; although *vāja-* may, of course, be considered a sort of 'Gewinn', the connotations of the German word might lead us astray. The same remark may apply to Whitney-Lanman's "booty" in the next passage.

[69]) The rather obscure line however admits also of other interpretations.

vácasā karāmahe should, in my opinion [70]), be translated as follows: "Now, in the generation of v., will we commemorate (?) with speech the great mother, Aditi by name". The same phrase occurs in three successive stanzas which form part of a series of verses incorporated in the Vāj.Saṃh. (9, 21 ff.) and other texts, and used as an accompaniment of the oblations, one for each season, which are a component of the *vājapeya*-rite. This "Drink-of-vigour" [71]) was no doubt connected with the desire to attain, by ritual means, to high prosperity. "The nature of the rites is clearly on the one hand that of the attainment of victory and power by the symbolic [72]) acts of winning, of being hailed as victor, and anointing: references to fertility are obvious also, and the sun spell of the wheel is noteworthy" [73]). The above oblations are the so-called *vājaprasavīyāni* (see e.g. ŚB. 5, 2, 2, 4). Being known to the ritualists of the Black Yajurveda as *annahomāḥ* ("food-oblations") (see TB. 1, 3, 8, 1), they are intended to "promote, stimulate, generate, produce" (*pra-sū-* [74])) the vigour (*vāja-*). The root *sū-*, other derivatives of which are *savitar-* i.e. (besides Bhaga, Dhātar, Bṛhaspati) the sun when regarded as a stimulating, vivifying or arousing, generating divine power — the sun is the lord of generation or stimulation (ṚV. 5, 81, 5), and, according to Yāska, Nir. 10, 31 the stimulator or generator of everything (*sarvasya prasavitā*) [75]) — and *prasavitar* — the use of which may be illustrated by ŚB. 5, 1, 1, 4 —, expresses such ideas as generating and stimulating a power for good (so as to place it at a person's disposal): ŚB., l.c., Bṛhaspati asked Savitar: "Stimulate this for me, (so that) stimulated by thee, I may win this" [76]).

Now, the stanzas accompanying the *vājaprasavanīya*-oblations consist of invocations addressed to a number of gods which (cf. ŚB. 5, 2, 2, 4)

---

70) See India Antiqua, A volume of Oriental studies presented... to J. Ph. Vogel, Leyden 1947, p. 149 f.

71) For particulars see especially A. Weber, Über den Vājapeya, Sitz. Ber. Akad. Berlin 1892, p. 765 ff.; Keith, Religion and Philosophy, p. 339 f.; the same, The Veda of the Black Yajus School (Taitt.S.), p. CVIII ff.

72) I would object to the term 'symbolic': these acts are not outward signs or imitations, but on the strength of their supposed identity, or at least connection, with the processes to be started, continued, or promoted, essential factors in their mechanism.

73) Keith, Rel. and Phil. p. 340 repeating also Hillebrandt's supposition that this rite was intended to be offered only by one who was in the technical sense a *gataśri-* "who had attained prosperity, and so could aspire to highest things" (cf. also Hillebrandt, Ritualliteratur, p. 143).

74) See my above (n. 70) paper on *utsava-* in the Festschrift-Vogel, and Eggeling, SBE. 41, p. 2, n. 1.

75) For particulars see Macdonell, Ved. Myth. p. 34; Hillebrandt, Ved. Myth. II, p. 100 ff.

76) Compare also ṚV. 4, 54, 2; 6 and many other passages.

are supposed to effect a stimulation or generation for the sacrificer, so that he, being *prasūta-* by them, wins. These are Soma, Agni, the Ādityas, Viṣṇu, Sūrya, Bṛhaspati, Aryaman, Indra, Vāc, Sarasvatī, Savitar, and Pūṣan. The stanzas containing the invocations proper are also found in the Ṛgveda, 10, 141, where instead of Vāc and Pūṣan, Vāta, Bhaga, and Sūnṛtā make their appearance. These divinities, which are, generally speaking, much celebrated for their interest in man's welfare, bestowing light, life, offspring, welfare, prosperity, and protection, dispelling evil, demons, and diseases, and concerning themselves with water, plants and the supply of food [77]), are requested to give the persons praying plenty, strength, welfare, and blessings. These invocations are preceded by the three stanzas beginning with *vājasya . . . prasavaḥ:* "In the beginning (*agre* [78])) the generation (stimulation) of vigour generated (roused: *suṣuve*) this king Soma in the plants, in the water. May they be rich in honey [79]) for us. . . . The generation of vigour extended over this sky and over all these worlds, the sovereign. Knowing it causes him to give gifts who does not wish to do so. It must grant us wealth with a complete number of heroes (descendants). Surely the generation of vigour pervaded all these worlds, on every side. From olden time the king goes about, knowing, increasing the people (or: our offspring), and the well-being amongst us" [80]).

Reverting now, for a moment, to the term *vāja-*, we draw special attention to those texts in which it appears in a passage commemorating Indra's Vṛtra-battle: ṚV. 3, 37, 6 Indra is addressed as follows: "Be victorious in the vājas, i.e. in those actions, occasions etc. in which *vāja-* is produced or stimulated, we approach thee with the prayer to kill Vṛtra", cf. also 1, 81, 1; and to those in which mention is also made of the vajra, e.g. 8, 2, 31 *evéd eṣá tuvikūrmír vâjāṅ éko vájrahastaḥ | sanâd ámṛkto dayate* "Surely this (god) alone who is powerful in working, who wields the thunderbolt, has the disposal of the vājas. . . ."; 9, 76, 3 Soma is requested to cause, on behalf of those speaking, heaven and earth to swell just like lightning impregnating the clouds, and to allot them vājas; and, in addition to these allusions to the vajra such texts as 9, 91, 4 *rujâ dṛḷhâ cid rakṣásaḥ sádāṃsi punānâ*

---

[77]) For Vāc, Speech, in this connection see Macdonell, o.c., p. 124, and B. Essers, Vāc, Thesis Groningen 1952, esp. p. 65 ff. Vāc, being enumerated among the deities of the atmosphere, can appear as "the voice of the middle region", i.e. thunder. Cf. also ṚV. 8, 89, 10 f.

[78]) For the sense of this term, which refers to the mythical example existing 'before' chronological time, but making its influence felt in time, see J. Gonda, Inleiding tot het Indische denken, Antwerp-Nimeguen 1948, p. 40.

[79]) For the sense attached to "honey" (*madhu*) see p. 16.

[80]) In this connection AV. 3, 20 (see especially st. 8 I) is also worth mentioning.

inda ūrṇuhi ví vâjān "Destroy even the strong abodes of the demon, purifying yourself, o Soma, make the vājas accessible". There is also important evidence of a connection between vāja and those weather conditions which are favourable to the vegetation: 1, 63, 6 *tvâṃ ha tyád indrārṇasātau sùarmīḷhe nára ājâ havante | táva svadhāva iyám â samaryá ūtír vâjeṣv atasâyyā bhūt* "Thou, indeed, art invoked by men in battle (fighting-match), when the issue is the conquest of water-streams, a contest for the light of the sun. This aid of thine, O self-dependent one, should be within our reach in the contest, in the occasions for rousing vegetative power". Compare also 1, 85, 5 (rain); 7, 57, 5 (increase in prosperity: *prá vâjebhis tirata* (viz. the Maruts) *puṣyáse naḥ*); 1, 91, 18 (refreshing draught), etc. etc.

The word also serves as a designation of one of the three lower deities known as Ṛbhus (cf. also ṚV. 3, 60, 7). It would be out of place to discuss here the character of these beings, which is a matter of great difficulty [81]). They are closely connected with Indra, famous for their skill and, inter alia, said to have made a cow which yields nectar, a horseless car which traverses space and, for Indra, two bay steeds; besides, they proved able to rejuvenate their parents. It is therefore not surprising to come across the name of Vāja in stanzas invoking other gods (Mitra, Varuṇa, Aditi, Earth, Sky, Bhaga, the Aśvins, Mother Bṛhaddivā [82])) for aid and favour (1, 111, 5; 5, 42, 5; 8, 90, 10; 10, 93, 7). 6, 50, 12 Rudra, Sarasvatī, Viṣṇu, and Vāyu are addressed together with this divinity, and Parjanya and Vāta, Rain and Wind, are requested to augment the supply of refreshing nourishment.

It might therefore be an attractive hypothesis to consider the word *vajra-* to have been: the instrument by means of which the active fighter and energetic champion of the welfare of mankind, the weather-god, rouses, generates, or makes accessible, the powers and substances which mean food and life [83]). It would be superfluous to add that other aspects of the same tool, or other weapons of the same god, or of similar gods, could be denoted by other terms.

We can, however, not conclude these digressive remarks on the meaning of the root *vaj- vāj-* in Vedic [84]) without drawing attention

---

[81]) See, inter alia, Macdonell, o.c., p. 131 ff.; Hillebrandt, Ved. Myth. II, p. 120 ff.; Keith, o.c., p. 176 ff.; A. W. Ryder, Die Ṛbhu's im Ṛgveda, Thesis Leipsic 1901; R. Shamasastri, The Ṛbhus and the four soma cups, The Poona Orientalist, 7 (1942-3), p. 177 ff.

[82]) This goddess is mentioned with Iḷā, Rākā, and Sarasvatī.

[83]) For the sense of the nouns in *-ra-* see my 'Anc. Ind. *ojas*...', p. 82; for the accentuation: Macdonell, Vedic grammar, p. 129 f.

[84]) Space forbids dwelling on the adj. *vājin-* and other related words. Suffice it to refer to such instructive passages as AV. 1, 4, 4; 4, 4, 2; 7, 80, 2; 13, 1, 1;

to the very frequent phrase *vājaṃ san-*. Like the compounds *vājasani-*, *vājasā-*, and *vājasāti-*, the last of which is likewise of constant recurrence, it expresses the idea of winning or securing the special power meant by the term *vāja-*. Men as well as gods (Indra, Pūṣan, Soma) are said, or (in the latter case) requested, to do so. The gods, then, secure the *vāja-* which is sometimes accompanied by wealth, rain, manly strength, vitality etc.), on man's behalf. I am under the impression that such meanings as "bestowing, giving" to be found in our dictionaries have no reasonable ground, the sense being "gaining, securing (for oneself or for another)". The verb *san-* is, further, mostly used in connection with those 'concepts' or entities which are essential for the continuation of human life on earth. ṚV. 3, 34, 8 and 9 Indra is stated to have secured the sun, the divine water, the earth, the sky, the steeds, the cow, and gold (*tattallokavāsibhyo dadau* Sāyaṇa); 9, 76, 2 Soma wins the sun; 90, 4 water, dawn, the sun, cows; 74, 1. Cows, water, sons, herbs, wealth, thriving often occur in the same context. Plants can appear as the subject of the verb: AV. 6, 21, 3; man's life may be the object (19, 32, 7; ṚV. 10, 97, 5). In the wedding-stanzas AV. 14, 2, 70; 72 the bride is asked to win (*āsan-*) *vāja-*, and matrimony regarded as being conducive to the same end. ṚV. 4, 17, 8 Indra appears as the slayer of Vṛtra and the winner of *vāja-* [85]). 9, 2, 10 Soma is called *goṣā.... nṛṣā.... aśvasā vājasā.*

Now the name of the god Viṣṇu, which might be expected to turn up in connection with the verb *san-*, is in the ancient documents conspicuous by its absence, although the term *vājasana-* (: *annaprada-* Nīlakantha) is Mbh. 12, 43, 9 applied to him, and *vājasani-* 13, 149, 98 a name of his (ṚV. 3, 51, 2 it qualifies Indra, 9, 110, 11 Soma). This fact does not appear to result merely from the god's subordinate position in the most ancient texts. It would constitute a serious objection to the suggestion to explain the word *viṣṇu-* by deriving it from *vi-* and *snu-* beside *san-*, like *kṣu-* "food(?)" beside *ghas-* "to eat", *-tatnu-* from *tan-* [86]). From *san-* itself we have *siṣṇu-* "securing" (Agni ṚV.

19, 27, 1. For the denominative *vājayát-* see e.g. ṚV. 4, 41, 8 (*vāja*-generating literary compositions desirous of the assistance of Indra and Varuṇa, are compared to those engaging in a contest); 5, 60, 1; 1, 109, 1; 130, 5; 8, 3, 15. Notice also interpretations as: *vājinam annavantam* (Sāyaṇa, e.g. ṚV. 1, 106, 4).

[85]) Other instances may be found in Grassmann's dictionary.

[86]) Compare also Macdonell, Vedic grammar, § 138. The first word (cf. AV. 5, 27, 10 *purukṣū-*) in *-u* is not certain (see also Renou, Grammaire de la langue védique, §§ 78 and 161), since M. Bloomfield ('On some disguised forms of Skt. *paśu* "cattle"', IF. 25, p. 185) would have it come from *paśu*. The meaning "food" is already given Naigh. 2, 7. See also W. Neisser, Zum Wörterbuch des Ṛgveda, Leipsic 1930, II, p. 76. For *-tatnu-* (see also Renou, o.c., § 191, n. 1) see AV. 1, 34, 5: *paritatnú-* "encompassing, surrounding". For similar words

8, 19, 31) and *sasni-* "gaining, securing, procuring" [87]). Another defect of this etymology, which from the morphological point of view would have more to recommend it than many other conjectures regarding the origin of this name, would lie in the total absence of the compound *vi-ṣan-* in Indo-Iranian [88]). Yet, the Greek *διανύω* [89]) which would correspond to **vi-ṣan-* is a verb of considerable occurrence, expressing such ideas as "accomplishing, finishing (also of a journey), traversing (e.g. a distance), arriving at (+ *εἰς*)" — it also means "finish doing or continue doing", and "live" —, the simplex *ἀνύω* standing for "to accomplish, to effect; to finish a journey", but also for "to make one's way, to reach, win, obtain, get". In consideration of the cognate words in Indo-Iranian we may suppose the idea of "accomplishing, winning, securing, reaching" to have been the basal meaning of the root *sen-*, a preverb like the Gr. *δια-* "through, in different directions, asunder, to the end, thoroughly etc." qualifying it by adding the connotation of "reaching etc. by pervading or traversing". Taking into account, on one hand, the character of the god Viṣṇu as it would appear to have been on the strength of the facts and interpretations set forth in this volume, and on the other hand the predilection for the preverb *vi-* in words connected with Viṣṇu's activity, such an original sense of the name as "who by pervading, traversing etc. wins or secures powers or influences (for good)" would in itself be a quite reasonable assumption. It would also be in harmony with the epithets *vyāpaka-*, *vyāpanaśīla-* which are often given to the god in later times and are clearly regarded as expressing an important aspect of his character: in commentaries (e.g. Sāyaṇa ṚV. 1, 61, 7; 90, 5) they are substituted for the name itself (see also such texts as Kāl. Kum. 6, 71). It would, moreover, account for the 'orthodox etymologies' which, though of a pre-scientific character, likewise show that the Indians themselves often agreed in assigning this pervading character or ability to the god: *viṣṇur viśater vā, vyaśnoter vā* (Nir. 12, 18), i.e. *viṣṇu-* derives from *viś-* "to enter",

---

compare also Whitney, Sanskrit grammar, § 1178. — An analysis *vi- snu-* was suggested in India: *viśeṣeṇa snauti prasravate gacchatīti viṣṇuḥ* (Nīlakaṇṭha, Mbh. 5, 70, 13).

[87]) See also Oldenberg, Ṛgveda. Textkrit. u. exeget. Noten, II, Berlin 1912, p. 353. V. K. Rajwade, in the Annals of the Bhandarkar Inst. I, Poona 1919, p. 56 f. The word *sasni-* applies to Soma, Indra, Indra and Agni, a chariot; cf. especially ṚV. 9, 61, 20 killing Soma and securing *vāja-* (*sasnir vājam*).

[88]) The Avestan *han-* apart from being often connected with the word *mīzda-* "reward, advantage" is similar in meaning (see e.g. Y. 46, 19; Yt. 13, 88).

[89]) Cf. A. Walde-J. Pokorny, Vergleichendes Wörterbuch der indogermanischen Sprachen, II, Berlin-Leipsic 1927, p. 493 f.; the opinion defended by these authors and other scholars regarding the etymology of Gr. *ἔναρα* "arms and trappings of a slain foe" are, to my mind, very questionable.

or from *vi-aś-* "to reach, attain, fill, penetrate"; a similar interpretation is: *viṣṇu-* from *viṣ-* III in the sense of *vyāpti-* "pervasion" (Dhātup. 3, 13): *vyāptaṃ tvayaiva viśatā trailokyaṃ sacarācaram* (MtPur. 248, 41). The fourth ancient etymology: *atha yad viṣito bhavati, tad viṣṇur,* i.e. *viṣṇu-: vi-si-* "to let loose, set free, release, cause to flow" is interesting in consideration of other functions of the god [90]). As it would have been easy to invent other etymologies, the preference given to those which convey the meanings under discussion, does not seem to be without significance [91]).

VII. THE THREE STRIDES.

Let us now pass to the essential feature in the character of the Vedic Viṣṇu, his taking three strides. With these steps he is described as traversing the earth, the terrestrial spaces, or these worlds (e.g. AiB. 6, 15, 11). In later texts this fact is not forgotten: Mbh. 5, 10, 6 *trayo lokās tvayā krāntās tribhir vikramaṇaiḥ purā;* Mṛcch. 5, 2; Harṣac. u. 3. In considering these famous three steps we should not omit pointing out that they are very often stated to cover and to conquer the whole universe [1]): compare e.g. Mbh. 3, 126, 35 *dharmeṇa vyajayal lokāṃs trīn viṣṇur iva vikramaiḥ* [2]), and such comments upon the significance of the Viṣṇu-strides in the Vedic ritual as are e.g. given in the Śat.Br. 1, 9, 3, 8 ff [3]). We also find texts identifying Viṣṇu's *krama-, krānta-,* and *vikrānta-,* or *vikramaṇa-, vikrānta-, krānta-* with these three worlds: by making the Visnu-steps one ascends these worlds and is high above everything here (ŚB. 5, 4, 2, 6). The god deposited himself in three places, a third on the earth, a third in the atmosphere, a third in the sky (TS. 2, 4, 12, 3). He pervades the whole universe in three steps (VS. 23, 49; VaiS. 37, 1). In that he strides the god's strides, the sacrificer becoming Viṣṇu wins *(abhi jayati)* these worlds (TS. 5, 2, 1, 1; 7; cf. also 1, 7, 5, 4; ĀpŚS. 4, 14, 6; 10 etc.; 13, 18, 8; cf. further, VS. 23, 50). For the sacrificer in per-

---

90) For the sibilants: H. Sköld, The Nirukta, Lund 1926, p. 129.

91) For the significance of Indian etymologies I refer to a paper which is to appear in the JRAS. — We should do well to remember also such passages as Matsyapur. 2, 30 where the Primeval Being by entering the cosmic egg, and by the very act of *vyāpti-* becomes Viṣṇu (... *prabhāvād api tadvyāptyā viṣṇutvam agamat punaḥ*).

1) For references see Macdonell, Vedic Mythology, p. 37 f.; Hillebrandt, Vedische Mythologie II, p. 313 ff.

2) See e.g. also Bhāsa, Dhūtav. 1, 46 + *tricaraṇātikrāntatriloko nārāyaṇaḥ* ...

3) See further on.

forming the ceremony of the strides is nothing else than Viṣṇu in very presence conquering the worlds [4]). The number three is often characteristic of the god: TS. 1, 7, 11, 1; VS. 9, 31 Agni with one syllable won speech (vital breath), the Aśvins with two syllables expiration and inspiration (the bipeds), Viṣṇu with three syllables won (*udajayat*) the three worlds...."; cf. also TS. 1, 8, 8, 1; 1, 8, 17, 1; 5, 6, 5, 2. He is said to be threefold one (*tridhātu-*, Mbh. [5])) or the god with the three abodes (*tridhāman-*, Mbh.); he is described as roaming about in the three worlds (*kramatā.... trilokavikrame*); cf. e.g. also Mbh. 12, 227, 8. In the dwarf incarnation, to which we shall refer again further on, the god likewise extends his striding activity to the three parts of the universe. The number three indicates, in a way, the god's universal character. The universe is tripartite, eleven gods belong to the upper regions, eleven to the earth, eleven to the waters (ṚV. 1, 139, 11); they are three times eleven; but Viṣṇu belongs to all three regions, he alone supports the *tridhātu-* universe (1, 154, 4).

Now, all beings are believed to abide in these three strides (ṚV. 1, 154, 2 *yásyorúṣu triṣú vikrámaṇeṣv adhikṣiyánti bhúvanāni víśvā*, etc.). All is gathered in the dust of his feet (TS. 1, 2, 13, 1; see also ṚV. 1, 22, 17 [6]). In the latter period of Indian history purāṇas (e.g. Saura 62, 47) and similar texts declare the whole of the world to be in his three strides; his feet and foot-prints are often referred to [7]). The ideas of wealth and abundance seem to have been associated with them: ṚV. 1, 154, 4 they are said to be full of honey [8]); 6, 49, 13. "Under the.... protection of V. who thrice traversed the terrestrial spaces for the sake of oppressed mankind, we will with our children enjoy the delight of plentiful supply". We may connect this thought with the succession

---

[4]) See also S. Lévi, La doctrine du sacrifice dans les brāhmaṇas, Paris 1898, p. 89 f.

[5]) See also Hopkins, Epic Mythology, p. 205.

[6]) I refer to Geldner, Der Rig-veda I, p. 21.

[7]) See e.g. Mbh. 12, 29, 36; cf. also Sørensen, Index, p. 750; Bhāsa, Dhūtav. 1; Veṇisaṃh. 1, 1, etc. etc. Güntert, Weltkönig, p. 296 ff. discussed the signification of foot-prints, for which see e.g. E. Stemplinger, Hdwb. d. de. Abergl. III, (1930), 240: "In der Fußspur bleibt die Wesenheit einer göttlichen, menschlichen oder dämonischen Person". Legends concerning 'Herrgottstritte' are widespread. — We may recall the belief that persons are restored to life by the touch of the foot of a mighty being: thus Ahalyā by Rāma's foot. I also refer to the observations made by De Vries, Altgermanische Religionsgeschichte, I, p. 130, who supposes the idea of transmission of power to underlie the sanctity of foot-prints attributed to deities: by treading on these spots a man could be filled with the god's power and be enabled to transfer it to the fields. See also W. Kirfel, Bilderatlas zur Rel. gesch. Hind., p. XXIX and R. B. Onians, The origins of European thought, Cambridge 1954, p. 524 ff.

[8]) See also A. Bergaigne, La religion védique, Paris 1883, II, p. 416; Geldner, o.c., I, p. 212.

of requests expressed TS. 1, 3, 4d; VS. 5, 38 [9]) "Step widely, o Viṣṇu; give us broad space for dwelling in", (*uru viṣṇo vi kramasva, uru kṣayāya nas kṛdhi*); cf. also ŚB. 3, 6, 4, 3; 4, 5, 1, 16 etc. According to 3, 6, 3, 15 the man who recites this text in sacrificing takes a firm stand in that *pratiṣṭhā* or firm abode which is the sky (heaven) [10]), by offering with that formula he gains that world [11]). It is recited at the beginning of the animal sacrifice which enables the sacrificer to conquer all spaces or worlds (ĀpŚS. 7, 1, 1) [12]). We already know [13]) that even Indra was in need of Viṣṇu's striding activity which was no doubt considered a source of helpful energy. It engendered power for the great god when he was about to slay Vṛtra and asked his companion "to stride more widely" (ṚV. 4, 18, 11). By means of Viṣṇu's third step on earth Indra raised his bolt, aided by Viṣṇu (TS. 2, 4, 12, 3).

The strides are, indeed, made for man in distress (ṚV. 6, 49, 13), in order to give him the earth as a dwelling-place (7, 100, 4), or to enable him to live (6, 69, 6). They are conducive to life (1, 155, 4) [14]). In the last stanza life is brought into relation with "scope for movement" of "wide space" (*urugāya-*): "...This deed of manly strength... of the protector, the inoffensive one, the bountiful, who widely traversed the terrestrial (space) with only three strides in order (to secure) scope for movement and life" (*urugātavyāya lokatrayarakṣaṇāya* Sāyaṇa). Other passages and other phrases besides the three strides likewise show that the idea of motion is characteristic of the god. He is said to be "swift": *evayā-*, *evayāvan-*, epithets elsewhere connected with the Maruts, or *eṣa-* [15]). In the Mahābhārata Viṣṇu is regarded as the deity who presided over motion (14, 42, 25; cf. Manu 12, 121).

These strides are also conducive to the annihilation of evil influences: they overcome hostility (TS. 1, 6, 5, 2; 7, 5, 4; 4, 2, 1, 1; 5, 2, 1, 1 etc. [16]): *viṣṇoḥ kramo 'sy abhimātihā*); "slay rivals (*sapatnahā*), destroy enemies (*śatrūyato hantā*), kill the malignant or envious one (*arātīyato hantā*)". VS. 12, 5; ŚB. 6, 7, 2, 13 ff. these formulas form

---

[9]) For particulars see Keith, Veda of the Black Yajus School, I, p. 38 f.

[10]) See my paper 'Pratiṣṭhā' (see ch. I, s. 3, n. 12).

[11]) For other ritual use of this formula see Whitney-Lanman, AthV. Saṃh., p. 405 f.

[12]) I.e. "Er erreicht z.B. die Welt (den Raum) der Väter, oder den Himmelsraum" (Caland, Das Çrautasūtra des Āpastamba, I, Göttingen-Leipzig 1921, p. 222).

[13]) See above. I am inclined to question the correctness of Hillebrandt's views, o.c., II, p. 313.

[14]) Mention may also be made of the well-known prayer for protection, addressed, in the benedictory stanza of a stage-play, to Viṣṇu's feet.

[15]) Cf. Oldenberg, in ZDMG. 62, p. 473. See also Macdonell, o.c., p. 38; cf. e.g. ṚV. 7, 40, 5; 8, 20, 3.

[16]) I refer to Bloomfield, A Vedic concordance, Cambridge Mass. 1906, p. 893.

part of the rite of the Viṣṇu-strides, by means of which the sacrificer is held to create offspring (ŚB. 6, 7, 2, 12; cf. e.g. ĀpŚS. 4, 14, 6) in making the steps he strides along the earth, the air, the sky, looks along the quarters and destroys his enemies. With the series of similar formulas handed down in the Atharvaveda 10, 5, 25—35 one made Viṣṇu-strides against one's enemies (KauśS. 49, 14): "Viṣṇu's stride art thou, rival-slaying, earth- (atmosphere- etc.) sharpened, possessed of Agni's (Vāyu's etc.) bright energy (*agnítejāḥ*); along the earth (etc.). I stride out (*vi krame*); from earth (etc.) we exclude him who hates us, whom we hate; let him not live, let breath go away from him". It may be observed that these formulas form part of a text used in preparing and employing so-called water-thunderbolts which probably were handfuls of water magically prepared and hurled at an enemy [17]). Elsewhere a formula of the same purport is introduced by recalling the fact that the gods headed by Viṣṇu won (*abhy ajayan*) these worlds by the metres so as to be irrecoverable; hence, the sacrificer in taking the god's steps and thus becoming Viṣṇu wins these worlds (TS. 1, 7, 5, 4).

Passing mention may also be made of the formula "Thou art the stepping of V., thou art the step of V., thou art the stride of V." which is, inter alia, prescribed in the ritual of the Vājapeya [18]) at the moment of the sacrificer's approach to the chariot with which he shall gain the victory in a formal race (see e.g. TS. 1, 7, 7 g; cf. TB. 1, 3, 5, 4; ĀpŚS. 18, 4, 15); in the Rājasūya to accompany the three Viṣṇu-strides to be made towards the east (TS. 1, 8, 10 g; TB. 1, 7, 4, 4; ĀpŚS. 18, 12, 10), which are part of the so-called *devasū* oblations (those intended for the "divine quickeners", the gods who have the power of quickening, to wit Savitar of true impulse, Agni the house-lord, Soma the lord of the forest, Bṛhaspati speech, Indra the most excellent, Rudra the lord of cattle, Mitra the true, Varuṇa the lord of dharma, who "quicken" the king for lordship over their respective domains, for control over similar powers, for kingship, energy etc. etc. [19])), and also to accompany, in the section of the king's triumphant career in his chariot, his mounting (TS. 1, 8, 15, 1; TB. 1, 7, 9, 2; ĀpŚS. 18, 17,2; in the preceding paragraph the chariot is called "Indra's thunderbolt"). In the ŚB., 5, 4, 2, 6, the rite of the strides is also performed — and the formula pronounced — on the tiger's skin, as a part of the elaborate

---

[17]) For particulars see Caland, Altindisches Zauberritual, Amsterdam 1900, p. 171 ff.; Whitney-Lanman, o.c., p. 579 ff. — Cf. also K. Rönnow, Trita Āptya, Upsala 1927, p. 61, n. 2.

[18]) See above, p. 50.

[19]) See e.g. ÇB. 5, 3, 3, 1 ff.; ĀpÇS. 18, 12, 6.

ritual of the consecration proper [20]) the purport of which is the endowment of the sacrificer with the variety of powers and energies inherent in kingship. By making the steps, the text adds, he rises high above everything here [21]); he becomes Viṣṇu and gains these worlds (TB.: *viṣṇukramān kramate: viṣṇur eva bhūtvemāṃl lokān abhijayati*).

It seems, further, important to remember that Viṣṇu's strides were, in a sense, included in the marriage ceremonies, an ever-recurring part of which was the seven steps [22]): the bridegroom causes the bride to take seven strides in the north-eastern direction [23]) with the formulas: "One for sap. Two for juice. Three for offspring. Four for prosperity. Five for welfare. Six for the seasons. Be a friend of the seven steps; be very gracious, o Sarasvatī [24])...." or a similar text, each time subjoining the word: "May Viṣṇu lead you up". Here the god seems to be invoked as presiding over ritual striding as well as over the powers mentioned [25]). One gets the impression that Güntert [26]) was wrong in contending that "die im Veda durchaus herrschende Dreizahl der Viṣṇu-Schritte später durch die Siebenzahl ersetzt (wurde)", because these seven strides were already known to the authors of ṚV. 10, 8, 4 [27]) and AV. 5, 11, 10, where they have nothing to do with Viṣṇu [28]). The rite appears to have been used to effect a durable alliance for the sake of obtaining strength or productivity. According to ŚB. 12, 9, 2, 5 the step means "briskness, impulse" (*jūti-*) in man: *etāvati vai manuṣye jūtir yāvān vikramaḥ*. By going two steps the man who betakes himself to

---

20) See e.g. Keith, Religion and Philosophy, p. 341; Eggeling, SBE. 41, p. XXVI; Hillebrandt, p. 145.

21) We shall not discuss here Viṣṇu's highest step or *paramaṃ padam* (Macdonell, Ved. Myth., p. 38; see also VS. 6, 3; ÇB. 3, 7, 1, 15; 18; and such texts as ViPur. 1, 2, 16; 6, 38).

22) For particulars see M. Winternitz, Das altindische Hochzeitsritual..., Denkschriften Akad. d. Wiss. Vienna 40 (1892), p. 51 ff.; 57 ff.; M. J. Dresden, Mānavagṛhyasūtra, Thesis Utrecht 1941, p. 58 ff.

23) This is the quarter of gods and men, where the gate of heaven is. In this direction libations are offered, various ritual acts performed, and the Viṣṇu-strides made (cf. e.g. ÇB. 6, 7, 2, 12). Standing turned towards the north-east Prajāpati creates the creatures.

24) For Sarasvatī see ch. II and H. de Willman-Grabowska, Rocznik Or. 17, p. 250 ff.

25) Remember also the details of the rite as described by Hillebrandt, Ritualliteratur, p. 66, and P. V. Kane, History of Dharmaśāstra II, 1, Poona 1941, p. 534: there are seven small heaps of rice and the young man makes the bride step on each of these. I ask myself whether Güntert's expatiations with respect to this ceremony are altogether relevant (Weltkönig, p. 296 ff.).

26) Güntert, l.c.

27) Cf. also Geldner's note: Rig-veda III, p. 130.

28) For the number seven see e.g. W. Schmidt, Der Ursprung der Gottesidee, IX, Münster, p. 91 f.; 423; M. Eliade, Le chamanisme, Paris 1951, p. 248 ff.; Th. Zachariae, Kleine Schriften, Bonn-Leipsic 1920, p. 39 ff. (with bibliography).

the purificatory bath leaves evil behind him with the briskness which is in him [29]). A pair or coupling means strength (see e.g. ŚB. 5, 3, 3, 14) or productivity (4, 3, 1, 3) [30]). Moreover, by reproducing the god's mighty act the power inherent in it is actualized; by performing it together a bond between the persons concerned is established and power is supposed to be transmitted [31]).

The general idea underlying the three strides of the god is in all probability — as was suggested already by Śākapuṇi, cited by Yāska, Nir. 12, 19 [32]) — the diurnal course of the sun through the tripartite cosmos in his ascent from the horizon through the atmosphere to the zenith, which might, at least occasionally, have been considered a sort of heaven (cf. e.g. ṚV. 1, 154, 5; 8, 29, 7) [33]). Instead of "the sun" I am, however, inclined to read "sunbeams" or "sunlight", or, what is perhaps still more adequate, "the sun's energy", because the pervading, omnipresent, and fecundating stream of light and energy seems to fit in better with the character of the divinity as far as it appears from the textual evidence than the solar orb itself. If Viṣṇu's three steps refer to the diffusion of light by the sun rather than the luminary proper there is no need of the supposition that all three steps are said to be full of honey (ṚV. 1, 154, 4) because the highest and most important is full of it [34]). Nor does any contradiction exist between those passages according to which the strides are made on earth (ṚV. 1, 154, 1; 155, 4; 7, 100, 3) and the texts emphasizing the god's cosmic activity. At the same time the references to Viṣṇu as a denizen of various parts of the universe — the highest abode is his favourite dwelling-place (ṚV. 1, 154, 5), he dwells in the mountains (1, 154, 2; 3), stands on the summit of the mountains (1, 155, 1) — as well as the frequent emphasis laid on his greatness (7, 99, 1 ff.), and on the length, width, and extent of his striding activity may become more clear in meaning. Then also Viṣṇu's acting as Indra's companion or assistant in fighting Vṛtra may be interpreted as reflecting ancient ideas with regard to help given by the power inhering in sunlight to the weather-god when the

---

[29]) Güntert, l.c., rightly calls attention to the belief regarding the residence of power in steps or foot-prints.

[30]) For other particulars see my 'Reflections on the numerals "one" and "two"...', Utrecht 1953, p. 10 etc.

[31]) This point would be worth investigating more closely.

[32]) *tredhâ ni dadhe padám* (ṚV. 1, 22, 17): *tridhā nidhatte padam, pṛthivyām antarikṣe divīti śākapūṇiḥ*. For particulars see Macdonell, Ved. Myth., p. 38; Keith, o.c., p. 108. — Cf. also ÇB. 1, 9, 3, 9.

[33]) Hopkins's views on this point are, in my opinion, far-fetched (Proc. Amer. Or. Soc., JAOS. 16, p. CXLVIII).

[34]) Macdonell, o.c., p. 38; Geldner, o.c., I, p. 212.

latter is about to destroy the demon who precludes the waters from fertilizing the soil [35]).

The interpretation suggested here implies that the god's activity was to a great extent atmospheric. Other considerations would appear to lead to the same conclusion. First ṚV. 7, 99, 3: *írāvatī dhenumátī hí bhūtáṃ sūyavasínī mánuṣe daśasyâ | vì astabhnā ródasī viṣṇav eté dādhártha pṛthivîm abhíto mayûkhaiḥ* " "Be ye two rich in refreshing food, rich in milch-kine, with good pastures through benevolence to man", (with these words) hast thou, O Viṣṇu, propped asunder heaven and earth, and firmly fixed the earth with beams of light on all sides" [36]). A divinity described as holding apart heaven and earth and as supporting both of them — for 1, 154,1 Viṣṇu *áskhabhāyad úttaraṃ sadhásthaṃ* — can scarcely have been conceived otherwise than as active in the regions surrounding the earth. The god is also called "lord of the spaces, or of the quarters of the sky" (*āśānām pati-* TB. 3, 11, 4, 1).

There are, however, other passages which have a greater claim to a thorough examination [37]). One of the most interesting linguistic particulars in connection with early Viṣṇuism is the unmistakable predilection for compounds beginning with *vi-* [38]). Though sometimes forming, together with the name of the god, alliterative phrases (cf. ṚV. 4, 18, 11; 8, 100, 12 *viṣṇo vitaráṃ ví kramasva*), the ideas expressed by the indeclinable *vi-*: "being etc. apart, asunder, division, distribution, being or going between or through etc." may be regarded as the main factor in the spread of these words. Viṣṇu's striding itself is, to begin with, generally denoted by the compound *vi-kram-* and its derivative *vikramaṇa-*, which according to Mbh. 5, 70, 13 accounts for the very name of the god: *viṣṇur vikramaṇat.* ṚV. 4, 18, 11; 8, 100, 12; MS. 4, 12, 5d etc. Indra urges his companion by addressing him with the abovementioned words; cf. also 8, 12, 27; 52, 3, where Viṣṇu performs the act for Indra. AV. 12, 1, 10 describing the earth says that the Aśvins measured her, that Viṣṇu strode out on her, that Indra made her free

---

35) I am highly sceptical with regard to Güntert's (o.c., p. 312 f.) identification of the three jumps of joy which the sun is, in Germany, Denmark, England, believed to make on Easter Day, with Viṣṇu's strides. Nor am I able to see the germ of the later avatāra-conception in the Vedic representation of the stride.

36) Cf. also TS. 1, 2, 13 f.; VS. 5, 16; ÇB. 3, 5, 3, 14 etc.

37) As other gods or mythical beings are also named "Ray" no particular importance can be attached to Viṣṇu's names *Marīci-, Dhāman-, Bhānu-* occurring in Mbh. 13, a. 149. — How could ÇB. 3, 4, 4, 15 "the day is Agni, the night Soma, and what is between the two, that is Viṣṇu" have anything to do with the conception under consideration? — The identification of the rays with the Viśve devāḥ (ÇB. 12, 4, 4, 7) cannot be made an objection to the above hypothesis.

38) See also K. F. Johansson, Über die altindische Göttin Dhiṣáṇā und verwandtes, Uppsala-Leipsic 1917, p. 47, n. 2.

from enemies. It is intimated that the process *vi-kram-* is of world-wide character, covering enormous distances: ṚV. 1, 22, 16f.[39]); 154, 1; 7, 100, 3; 8, 29, 7. There are many explicit references to the width, extent or spaciousness of the striding: SV. 5, 38; 41 etc. [40]). "O Viṣṇu, stride thou widely out, make ample room for our abode" (*uru viṣṇo vi kramasva, uru kṣayāya nas kṛdhi*). By pronouncing this stanza the sacrificer, according to ŚB. 3, 6, 3, 15, takes a firm stand in the sky and gains that world [41]). That Viṣṇu's great performance was believed to create ample room appears also from ṚV. 7, 100, 4 *ví cakrame pṛthivîm eṣá etâṃ kṣétrāya víṣṇur mánuṣe daśasyán | dhruvâso asya kīráyo jánāsa urukṣitíṃ sujánimā cakāra* "This Viṣṇu has traversed the earth for the sake of a portion of space (landed property) for man (or: for Manu, the father of men), doing favour to him. *Indigent* (?) [42]) people came into possession of a firm abode. He whose creatures are well-made created spacious room for dwelling". 6, 69, 5 Indra and Viṣṇu are stated to have covered a great distance (*urú cakramāthe*); (in doing so) they caused the atmosphere to become wider, they extended the 'spheres' (or: divisions of the world) (for man) to live [43]). Following are some examples of the use of the verb in connection with other grammatical subjects: ṚV. 5, 47, 3 (TS. 4, 6, 3 1 etc.) the sun, compared to a stone placed in the midst of the sky, is in a significant way said to have "stridden apart and to guard the two ends of space". In describing the puruṣa ṚV. 10, 90, 4 after stating that a fourth of that primaeval man out of whom the universe was created, is in all beings, coming into being here, adds: "Thence he strode out asunder in all directions to animate and inanimate objects (*vi akrāmat.... abhí*)": the sense must be: "he extended, distributed himself to, spread over, developed into" [44]). A similar passage is AV. 9, 5, 20 *ajó vâ idám ágre vì akramata....*" The goat strode out here in the beginning" [45]): its breast became the earth, its back the sky, its middle the atmosphere, its two sides the quarters, etc. etc. (cf. also 8). From these instances it will be seen that 'striding widely' could imply the ideas of covering, pervading, being identical with, residing in the expanses traversed. In a text accompanying the consecration of a king (KauśS. 17, 1 ff.; Vait. 36, 7) it reads: "A tiger, upon the tiger's

---

39) I refer to Geldner, o.c., I, p. 21.

40) See Bloomfield, Vedic concordance, p. 275 f.

41) See also Caland on ĀpÇrS. 11, 17, 6, and Whitney-Lanman, o.c., p. 405 f.

42) Cf. Geldner, o.c., II, p. 39; R. Pischel, in R. P. und K. F. Geldner, Vedische Studien I, Stuttgart 1889, p. 221 ff.; Bloomfield, JAOS. 31, p. 51 f.

43) Compare also such occurrences as AiB. 1, 1, 7 etc.

44) For parallel passages etc. see also Whitney-Lanman, o.c., p. 902 ff.

45) For *agre* see p. 51.

(skin), do thou stride out unto the great quarters" (AV. 4, 8, 4, cf. KS. 37, 9 b); the next line which I would not disconnect from this implies the 'universal character' of him who has performed the act of striding: "Let all the people want thee, the water of heaven...." The rather obscure stanza AV. 1, 12, 1 [46]) may perhaps be regarded as containing a reference to the co-operation of the weather-god and the power residing in the sunlight which fills the atmosphere: an allusion is made to the ruddy bull, born of wind and cloud (?) which goes thundering with rain and which, being "one vital power" (*ekám ójas*), has stridden out threefold.

There are good reasons for supposing that these two ideas, that of making ample room and that of pervading, of passing into all parts of the expanse traversed, were present to the minds of those who believed a divine power or person to have stridden widely. ṚV. 1, 154, 2 all beings (*bhuvanāni,* the word implies the worlds and places of residence) are said to live in Viṣṇu's wide steps (*urúṣu triṣú vikrámaṇeṣu*) [47]); Mbh. 3, 12, 26 "Being a child, o Kṛṣṇa, thou hast covered by three steps (*vikramaṇa-*) heaven, sky, and earth by your energy (*tejasā*)". 3, 201, 19 ff. Viṣṇu is addressed in this way: "All beings are pervaded (*vyāptāni,* see further on) by thee....; when thou art pleased, the universe enjoys peace.... Thou art the cause of happiness for both celestials and human beings. By thy three steps thou conqueredst (came into possession of: *hṛta-*) all the three worlds. It was thou who hast destroyed the asuras...." Mbh. 5, 10, 7 the two last-mentioned facts are more closely connected, and 12, 207, 27 the potency and creative function of the act is perfectly clear: *tasya vikramaṇāc cāpi devānāṃ śrīr vyavardhata* "By his traversing and pervading activity the prosperity of the gods increased".

By striding Viṣṇu in fact obtained for the gods the all-pervading power which they now possess, called *vikrānti-* [48]): ŚB. 1, 9, 3, 9 f. whilst explaining the significance of the Viṣṇu-strides observes that Viṣṇu, being the sacrifice, obtained this *vikrānti-;* by his first step he gained the earth, by the second the aerial expanse, by the last the sky. This same pervading power, the text adds, is acquired by the god, as the sacrifice, for the sacrificer (*etām v evaiṣa etasmai viṣṇur yajño vikrāntiṃ vikramate*). Here we see again that the god gains a particular power or energy for men. By imitating the god's striding activity, the author continues his observations (10), one ascends the above-

---

[46]) I refer to Whitney-Lanman, o.c., p. 12 f.

[47]) See also 10, 15, 3; in connection with the Aśvins: 8, 9, 12; in a stanza forming part of funeral verses: ṚV. 10, 15, 3 = AV. 18, 1, 45 etc.

[48]) For similar services see Macdonell, o.c., p. 41. — Cf. also Hariv. 263, 26 ff.

mentioned worlds, the goal, the safe refuge (*pratiṣṭhā*) being the highest light, Prajāpati or the heavenly world [49]). "The light of heaven is man's salvation" [50]), and here Viṣṇu is already, what he is to become on a much larger scale in later times, the saviour. Compare also 1, 1, 2, 13 and 3, 6, 3, 3 [51]). Mbh. 12, 47, 88 Viṣṇu as the eternal origin of the worlds, the invincible, is saluted in this way: "Thou hast pervaded (*vyāpta-*) the sky (heaven) with thine head, earth with thine feet, and the three worlds with thy *vikrama-*....; the directions are thine arms, the sun is thine eye....". Hence, the same epic 3, 271, 68 ff. remarks, the earth is called *vaiṣṇavī* "belonging to, pervaded by, Viṣṇu". From various passages it appears that this particular striding-power, this pervading energy was believed to be so overpowering in character, that it was held a means of gaining prosperity and victory: Mbh. 12, 207, 27 by Viṣṇu-Vāmana's striding (*vikramaṇa-*) the prosperity (*śrī-*) of the gods increased; 13, 6, 16 the kṣatriya acquires *ṣrī-* by *vikrama-*; Varāh. BS. 69, 11 it leads to wealth, 68, 92 to victory (*jaya-*); Kāl. Ragh. 12, 93 to the fortune of victory (*jayaśrī-*) [52]). In this more general sense of „prowess, heroic valour, heroism" it is also ascribed to Indra, great kings etc.

In addition to the instances of *vy-āp-* already mentioned we may briefly touch upon some connotations of this verb and its derivatives which are of interest for the history of early Viṣṇuism. BhG. 11, 20 the space between heaven and earth is stated to be *vyāpta-* "pervaded" by God, and 10, 16 his *vibhūtayaḥ* "formative principles constituting manifestations" enable him to pervade the universe and to abide in it. Cf. also Mbh. 3, 201, 19 *tvayā vyāptāni sarvāṇi bhūtāni*. The verb, which applied to a personal God already in the ŚvUp. 4, 10, was used in the brāhmaṇas in connection with the attainment of heaven by gods or, in imitation of these, by sacrificing men: PB. 7, 4, 2; 16, 11, 9; 14, 4; 21, 1, 9 *sahasrayājī vā imān lokān vyāpnoti*; JB. 1, 120; 136. AV. 17, 1, 13 Indra is addressed as follows: "with what body (*tanū-*) thou didst permeate (*vyāpitha*) the atmosphere, with that bestow thou protection (*śarman-*) upon us". Id. 13, 2, 30 the sun is said to have penetrated (*vy-āp-*) the two oceans with his light (*rúci-*). Cf. also 8, 9, 20; 9, 5, 12; 11, 7, 22; 12, 3, 5. The verb can also apply to evil powers: Mbh. 14, 11, 7 ff. relates that formerly the earth was pervaded or

---

49) See also the next paragraphs.

50) G. van der Leeuw, Religion in essence and manifestation, London 1938, p. 68.

51) Passing mention may be made of TS. 2, 5, 6, 2 where the new and the full moon are the *vikrānti-* "striding" (etc.) of the gods. — In an act based on the principle of analogy JB. no. 156 C.; cf. also ÇB. 1, 7, 3, 23.

52) We may perhaps also call attention to (TB. 1, 2, 1, 23); ĀpÇS. 5, 14, 5 *vi kramasva mahāṅ asi... triṣu lokeṣu jāgṛhi prajayā ca dhanena ca.*

encompassed by Vṛtra (*vṛtreṇa.... vyāptā, ātmatvena gṛhītam* Nīlakaṇṭha). The adj. *vyāpta-* can be used in the sense of "successful, complete": AiB. 4, 4, 5 *sa yo vyāpto gataśrīr iva manyeta* [53]).

In this connection, it may be remembered that, according to Hinduistic opinions, the name of the god derives from the root *viś-* "to enter, to pervade": LiPur. 70, 97; BdPur. 1, 4, 25; VāPur. 5, 36 *viṣṇuḥ sarvapraveśanāt* "because he penetrates into all (existing beings and objects)". With reference to the Vāmana avatāra [54]) ViPur. 3, 1, 46 and KūPur. 51, 36 [55]) give the following explanation: *yasmād viṣṭam idaṃ sarvaṃ vāmanena mahātmanā | tasmāt sa vai smṛto viṣṇur viśer dhātoḥ praveśanāt.* Sometimes the term *vyāpti-* is used in that connection: MtPur. 2, 30 in describing how the universe was created by Nārāyaṇa furnishes us with the following information: *praviśyāntar mahātejāḥ svayam evātmasaṃbhavaḥ | prabhāvād api tadvyāptyā viṣṇutvam agamat punaḥ.* Allusions to this interpretation, which is in perfect harmony with the assured beliefs that Viṣṇu is the personal aspect of brahman, that his 'world' is the best goal, that even the gods are pervaded by his essence (*viṣṇumaya-*), are already found in earlier documents. Mbh. 12, 341, 42 f. the god says: *vyāptā me rodasī.... kramaṇāc cāpy aham.... viṣṇur ity abhisaṃjñitaḥ*; here Nīlakaṇṭha gives, inter alia, the following linguistic comment: the root *viṣ-* in the sense of *vyāpti-*, *viś-* in the sense of "entering, penetrating" (*praveśane*), *ṣṇu-* in the sense of "effusion" (*prasravaṇe*), *eteṣām anyatamasya rūpaṃ viṣṇur ity abhipretyāha: vicchanti gacchanti līyante 'smin vicchanty asmāl lokā iti vā veveṣṭi vyāpnotīti vā vicchyati dīpyata iti vā,* quoting in addition to this some lines from the śruti (sacred tradition) *gacchanty asminn āgacchanti ca yasmāt prajāḥ yenāvṛtaṃ khaṃ ca divaṃ mahīṃ ca yasya bhāsā sarvam idaṃ vibhāti yad icchanto brahmacaryaṃ caranti* etc. Perhaps VS. 1, 30; ŚB. 1, 3, 1, 17 is, in this connection, not devoid of significance: when the sacrificer's wife is girded with a triple cord, the words are spoken: "A zone art thou for Aditi (i.e. the earth, represented by the sacrificer's wife); .... the pervader (headband?) [56]) of Viṣṇu art thou" (*viṣṇor veṣyo 'si*). Eggeling [57]) may be right in considering the word *veṣya-* a paronomasia and in

---

[53]) Mark the association with *gataśrī-* for which see Caland, on ĀpÇS. 1, 14. 9. Cf. also ÇB. 10, 4, 2, 4 ff. and other connotations of this family of words found in texts belonging to the Hinduistic period.

[54]) See chapter XX.

[55]) See also D. R. Patil, Cultural history from the Vāyu Purāṇa, Poona 1946, p. 65; W. Kirfel, Das Pūraṇa pañcalakṣaṇa, Bonn 1927, p. 280. — Cf. such passages as BrPur. 7, 75, VāPur. 88, 49 etc.: *tam āviśat tadā viṣṇus tejasā...*

[56]) *veṣya-*: *vyāpaka-* Mahīdhara.

[57]) Eggeling, SBE. 12, p. 73, n. 3.

supposing the pervading rays of Viṣṇu to be alluded to [58]), but we cannot be sure that the above interpretation (: *vyāpaka-*) was already meant by the author [59]).

It is however easily conceivable that in a 'ritual question' put by the brahman to the udgātar (VS. 23, 49) this point should have been made the theme: "Has Viṣṇu pervaded (*āviveśa*) this whole universe in the three strides in which the god is worshipped?"

According to philosophers of a later period God (i.e. Viṣṇu) pervades (*vyāpnoti*) the spiritual and non-spiritual entities of this world by being their internal ruler (cf. Rāmānuja, Gītābh. 9, 4). Viṣṇu is the *vyāpin-, sarvavyāpin-*. The words *tvayā tataṃ viśvam* (BhG. 11, 38) are explained by the same verb (ibid. 11, 38; cf. 24). Rāmānuja's predecessor Yāmuna argued that BhG. a. 15 describes God's *vyāpana-, bharaṇa-,* and *svāmya-* "pervasion, maintenance, and sovereignty (of the universe)" (Gītārthas.). And the Bhagavadgītā itself already taught that the Supreme Being by his divine manifestations (*vibhūti-*) pervades these worlds and abides in them (*vyāpya tiṣṭhasi* 10, 16). Thus, *Vyāpin-, Vyāpaka-* (e.g. Nīlakaṇṭha Mbh. 1, 23, 17) are names of the god. Following this tradition Sāyaṇa's commentary very often explained the god's nature by such terms as *vyāpanaśīla-* (ṚV. 1, 90, 5; 5, 3, 3; 8, 12, 27 etc.), *sarvasya jagato vyāpaka-* (1, 61, 7); *vyāpin-* (10, 15, 3); *vyāpaka-* (2, 34, 11), *sarvajagadvyāpin-* (9, 65, 20), *sarvavyāpin- deva-* (6, 21, 9), *svamahattvena sarvavyāpaka-* (8, 25, 12) etc.

Attention must also be drawn to the fact that other gods, especially those whose interests are not widely divergent from Viṣṇu's, are also characterized by nouns beginning with *vi-* in the sense of "in different directions, asunder": apart from *vicakṣaṇa-* "seeing widely, — in various directions" (Sun, Agni, Soma, Indra etc.), *vibhāvan-* "beaming, shining (widely)" (Agni, Dawn) etc., we come across, in the Ṛgveda, *vibhu-* and *vibhū-* which express such ideas as "far-extending or all-pervading might, sovereignty, effectiveness" (Agni, Brahmaṇaspati, Indra, the Maruts, but also used in connection with the *vajra-*, the waters, *ojas*); the disposition of the Maruts is called *vidharman-*, Indra and Agni are *vibhaktṛ-s* etc. The idea expressed by *vi-* could no doubt serve to characterize a side of the nature of these divinities or an aspect of their activities. It seems to have been especially connected with Viṣṇu, who in the Mbh. and later texts is very often called *vibhu-*, a term applied in the MuṇḍUp. 1, 1, 6 to the imperishable

58) The southern end of the cord is addressed which is drawn through the girdle (Mahīdhara).

59) For the idea of "entering, pervading etc." in general see e.g. BhG. 7, 7; Mbh. 12, 47, 21 ff.

source of all existence, the substantive *vibhūti-* coming into use for Viṣṇu's divine and universal power and dignity (cf. e.g. ViPur. 4, 1, 27, where the commentary observes: *vibhūter* (sc. *Viṣṇoḥ*) *avatārarūpāyāḥ pariṇāmasya sadbhāvavikārasya*) [60]).

Another term which in the course of time came to serve as an epithet of Viṣṇu is *virāj-*. Apart from the well-known Vedic metre which plays so important a rôle in the mystical speculations of the ancient thinkers [61]), the term expresses the idea of "ruling far and wide"; besides, it occurs in the cosmogonic theory set forth in ṚV. 10, 190. From the original Puruṣa, st. 5 says, Virāj — an intermediate between the primaeval Puruṣa and the evolved Puruṣa — was born, from Virāj Puruṣa. The function ascribed to this being was that of a creator who at the same time was the first-born one. We find the same idea Mbh. 7, 201, 57 ff., where Nārāyaṇa who is older than the oldest ones is at the same time said to have taken his birth as the son of Dharma and to be the creator of the universe. Similar ideas occurred in connection with Hiraṇyagarbha, a figure likewise destined to fuse with the Supreme God of the later period (cf. Mbh. 12, 43, 15; ViPur. 1, 2, 2) [62]). Virāj is the all, the totality, the sum of all existence, the hypostatization of the conception of the universe as a whole: he whose illustrious, eminent, governing activities, whose universal sovereignty has a wide scope in all directions [63]). From various identifications and mythological associations which at first sight make a fantastic impression, it appears how much the ancient thinkers wrestled with the problem of defining this idea and giving it its place in a cosmological and philosophical system. Sometimes Virāj is identified with Prajāpati (TB. 1, 4, 9, 5), or created by him (ŚB. 13, 2, 5, 3); or identified with Agni (TB. 1, 1, 5, 10). Sometimes Virāj is the earth (ŚB. 12, 6, 1, 40; Mbh. 7, 69, 24 and elsewhere V. = Pṛthivī), or conceived as a cow, the daughter of Kāma and identical with Vāc (AV. 9, 2, 5; cf. ChUp. 1, 13, 2); here two calves rose out of the sea (AV. 8, 9, 1), the sun is her calf (13, 1, 33). Then again, though having 'calves' Virāj is called the father of bráhman (8, 9, 7). But the poet of the Atharvan text devoted to this figure (AV. 8, 9 and 10) is quite sure that "it was this (universe) in the beginning" (8, 10, 1); it touches everything (8, 9, 9); in a stanza —

60) Space forbids the discussion of these important terms at length. — Other words worth mentioning are *vibhūtadyumna-* "abounding in glory" (ṚV., Viṣṇu, Indra), and *vigāman-* "stride" (of V.).

61) This sense will be studied in ch. II, § 1.

62) See also S. Radhakrishnan, Indian philosophy, London (1927; 1948), I, p. 170 ff.

63) Cf. also ṚV. 10, 90, 5 "When born he (Puruṣa) reached beyond the earth behind and before (to west and east)".

which has also found other application [64]) — Virāj is said to be "she who first shone forth (*vyaucchat*), who goes about among these other ones (fem.), having entered (*praviṣṭā*)"; she is, in addition to this, stated to be intrinsically mighty and to have conquered (8, 9, 11). She, moreover, resembles Viṣṇu in "striding asunder" (*vikrāntā*, 8, 10, 8) [65]).

Reverting now to the idea of spatial extensiveness, expressed by the element *vi-* which suits the character of the god Viṣṇu — as it appears to have been in Vedic times — remarkably well, we must now dwell on another term of similar sense. Authors [66]) have no doubt been right in saying that the god's Vedic epithets *urugāya-* "wide-going, making strides over a wide area" and *urukrama-* "wide-striding" allude to the action which is essential to him. It would, however, be important to grasp the full meaning, and all the implications, of the concept expressed by *uru-*.

In the Ṛgveda *uru-* is often used to denote the characteristic vastness of the expanses of atmosphere, sky and earth: *uru antarikṣam* for instance is a well-known phrase. Agni is said to extend with his "brilliance-energy" (*varcas*) sky, earth, plants, water and the vast atmosphere (3, 22, 2). The light of the sun, the desirable good, and the light space, the *u. a.* combine 10, 124, 6. 4, 52, 7 Uṣas (Dawn) extends over it. 6, 70, 1 sky and earth are called vast, broad (*urvī pṛthvī*), abounding in ghee, yielding 'honey', rich in seed (cf. 4); 7, 12, 1 (*rodasī*), 18, 24 Indra's renown spread over the space between both halves of the universe. The gods, and especially those whose name is often mentioned in this book, are stated to be active in one of these vast spaces: Indra spread out the broad earth, i.e. moulded it in the vast form which she has (*paprātha kṣām. . . . vy urvīm*; 6, 17, 7); cf. 2, 13, 7, where Indra himself is called bright (cf. 6, 19, 1); the same god spread the broad atmosphere (7, 98, 3). Not only his strides are broad (1, 121, 1), but also his belly (8, 1, 23), his intoxication (8, 16, 4), his horses (6, 21, 12), his chariot (8, 98, 9); cf. 8, 36, 1. Broad is the seat of the Maruts (1, 8, 5), light (2, 27, 14 etc., cf. 1, 136, 2); Soma is asked to give a broad path (9, 85, 4), Bhaga to show the broad way to heaven (8, 31, 11), etc. etc.

These frequent references to "broadness" not only point to the possession of vastness, unlimited and extensive nature, boundlessness, 'Unermeßlichkeit' of the sphere of action, free scope for activities,

---

64) See Whitney-Lanman, o.c., p. 100.

65) See also the long note by Wilson: Wilson-Hall, Viṣṇu Purāṇa, I, p. 104 ff. — Passing mention may also be made of Viṣṇu's 'manifestations' called *vibhava-* (Ahirbudhnya Saṃh. 5, 50 f.) and *vyūha-* (ibid. 51).

66) E.g. Macdonell, o.c., p. 37 f.

absence of obstruction etc., but not seldom also express the idea of being a cause of room or a source of welfare. ṚV. 5, 44, 6 refers to a vast space or expanse, the earth which secures (procures), for our sake, room (space) [67]): *mahîm asmábhyam uruṣâm urú jráyaḥ*; 6, 23, 7 Indra is implored to grant his devotees room (*urúm.... lokám*); 7, 84, 2; 10, 180,3 the same god is said to have driven away and given room (the same phrase) to the gods (cf. also 7, 33, 5; 60, 9); cf. also 10, 128, 5; AV. 14, 1, 58 "I release thee from Varuṇa's fetter.... I make for you wide space (*urúṃ lokám*), an easy road". As *loka-* implies such ideas as "free or open space, free motion, space, room, or world in which to exist" we are probably right in supposing these and similar texts to express the desire for "living-space" (Lebensraum). AV. 12, 1, 1 the earth itself is requested to make "wide room" for the persons speaking; 18, 3, 22 divine beings, who "increased Indra" have "made for us a spacious assembly (circle: *pariṣad-*), rich in kine". So, when we view AV. 7, 26, 3; TS. 1, 3, 4 d in the light of these texts it seems to be evident that Viṣṇu's striding action was supposed to be favourable to man's 'living-space': "(Viṣṇu), upon whose three wide out-stridings dwell all beings. Widely, O V., stride out, make us to dwell widely...." [68]). It was, no doubt, one of Viṣṇu's functions to put in order expanses of space to make them usable for human habitation.

From the use of the word *uru-* in some passages we may conclude that the idea expressed by it was, or could be, opposed to that of *aṃhas* [69]) "serious trouble, distress, oppression". The etymology points to a basal sense of "closeness, narrowness", which is perhaps still apparent in ṚV. 6, 2, 4 (*āhananaśīlaṃ pāpam* Sāyaṇa): Av. *ązah* also "captivity"; *ąz-* "to tie, to constrict"; Lat. *angor* "strangling, oppression, fright"; *angustus* „narrow"; *ango* "to strangle, frighten"; Gr. *ἄγχω* "to strangle, throttle, squeeze, embrace"; *ἄγχι* "near"; Irish *ing* „straitened circumstances"; Germ. *Angst, Enge* etc. etc. [70]). AV. 8, 7, 13 *mṛtyu-* and *aṃhas* are two evils occurring side by side; the word is also associated with *enas* "sin" (TS. 3, 1, 4, 3). The adjective *uru-* and *aṃhas* (or *aṃh-* in general) occur in the same context, e.g. ṚV. 1, 105,

---

[67]) Rather than "granting much, producing abundantly" (Monier-Williams).

[68]) For the text see Whitney-Lanman, o.c., p. 406. ĀpŚS. 11, 7, 6 the formula TS. 1, 3, 4d is used in a rite performed in order to gain entrance to the world of heaven.

[69]) See especially S. Rodhe, Deliver us from evil, Lund-Copenhagen 1946, p. 40 ff.

[70]) It is easily conceivable that words for "narrow" often rest on the idea of "tight, pressed, constricted", and on the other hand, developed into terms for "difficulty, trouble, distress": see e.g. C. D. Buck, A dictionary of selected synonyms..., Chicago 1949, p. 886.

17 Trita buried in a well was released by Bṛhaspati from his confinement (*kṛṇvánn aṃhūraṇâd urú,* "Befreiung aus der Enge" Geldner); 5, 65, 4 *mitró aṃhóś cid âd urú kṣáyāya gātúṃ vanate* "Mitra gewinnt selbst aus Bedrängnis einen Ausweg, freie Bahn zu einem Wohnsitz" (Geldner); cf. also 5, 42, 17 *uraú devā anibādhé syāma* "Wir möchten in weiter Unbeschränktheit leben, ihr Götter"; 3, 1, 11; 2, 26, 4; AV. 14, 1, 58. We may therefore suppose a passage like 5, 87, 7 to imply the idea of creating or procuring freedom from narrowness, from lack of living-space: *dīrghám pṛthú paprathe sádma pârthivam* (through Viṣṇu's Maruts). This room and "extensiveness" is, indeed, sometimes explicitly associated with the ideas of dwelling at ease and of living: ṚV. 8, 68, 12 *urú ṇas tanve tána urú kṣáyāya nas kṛdhi | urú ṇo yandhi jīváse.* In this connection mention must be made of 8, 63, 9 where the god (Viṣṇu) is said to have stridden widely (*vy.... uru kramiṣṭa*) "for the sake of the bull (Indra) in order to live". Viṣṇu's striding gives full scope to life by creating room for it. Where it is *uru-*, there is also freedom: 7, 98, 3 Indra has extended the vast atmosphere, by combating he made freedom (but at the same time "width, room, free scope, comfort": *varivas*) for the gods. 7, 77, 4 Uṣas is requested to grant a broad place of residence (piece of pasture) and safety or security (*abhayam*); 9, 78, 5 the same prayer is addressed to Soma. AV. 6, 4, 3 (a text addressed to various divinities, for protection) the "wide-goer" is asked to make wide for those speaking, heaven (sky), to repel any misfortune. ṚV. 6, 28, 4 (AV. 4, 21, 4) makes mention of *urugāyám ábhayam* "auf gefahrloser weiter Trift" (Geldner). AV. 6, 40, 1 is intended for securing safety: "be the wide atmosphere safety for us". Cf. AV. 16, 3, 6. Wealth, comfort, and prosperity are often said to attend the prevalence of that which is called *uru-*: ṚV. 8, 75, 11 Agni is implored to give wealth and to make room; 5, 38, 1 the favours of Indra's 'broad' (extensive, generous) gifts are said to be *vibhu-* "abundant (far-extending, omnipresent)", cf. also 5, 15, 5; 10, 47, 3; 147, 5 "make room (Indra), grant (us) wealth"; AV. 9, 2, 11 "Kāma has slain my rivals; he has made for me wide space and prosperity" [71]). ṚV. 6, 47, 8 Indra is implored to lead the persons speaking to vast room, celestial light, security, welfare (*svasti*) [72]).

The compound *urugāyá-* (see above) which ṚV. 1, 155, 4 combines with *jīvas* "life", is elsewhere (e.g. 1, 154, 6) an epithet of Viṣṇu. The question arises whether it also refers to this god or to his 'heaven' when another interpretation would be possible: ṚV. 10, 109, 7 *uru-*

---

71) Cf. also AV. 6, 33, 3; 11, 1, 19; 11, 2, 11 etc.

72) Attention may also be drawn to ÇB. 1, 2, 2, 8; 3, 9, 4, 12 (VS. 6, 33).

gāyám upāsate may mean "they occupy broad space" (thus Whitney-Lanman AV. 5, 17, 11, or "enjoy wide scope, freedom") and "approach (the god) who makes large strides" (Geldner). In favour of the latter view one might adduce ṚV. 1, 154, 5 *tád asya priyám abhí pâtho aśyāṃ náro yátra devayávo mádanti | urukramásya sá hí bándhuḥ....*; in Viṣṇu's dear abode, where men who are devoted to the god revel, is the association with the wide-striding one. Cf. also st. 6 and 8, 29, 7. Or may the two above renderings be supposed to be essentially identical? According to the Viṣṇupurāṇa 1, 8, 22 śrī is identical with *dyaus*, "Viṣṇu who is one with the universe (*sarvātmaka-*) is wide-extended space". It would, however, be difficult to interpret 7, 35, 15; 10, 65, 15 in a 'Viṣṇuitic' sense.

A few passages remain to be discussed here. Whereas ṚV. 10, 121, 5 — addressed to the Unknown God who has created the universe — and AV. Ppp. 4, 1, 4 use the verb *stabh-* "fixing firmly, supporting, propping" to indicate the act of establishing sky (heaven) and earth, sun and firmament, AV. śaun. 4, 2, 4 calls this process *vi-tan-* "extending": the wide heaven, the great earth etc. are extended by the greatness of the Unknown God. The same idea occurs elsewhere: AV. 12, 1, 2 "Let the earth be spread out (*prathatām*) for us, be prosperous for us", clearly indicating that "spreading out the earth" means "giving prosperity to man" [73]). Cf. also st. 55, and ṚV. 1, 159, 2 where the earth is made broad (*uru-*) for the offspring of the creating divinities and free from the power of death over the whole of its expanse (*urú prajâyā amṛ́taṃ várīmabhiḥ*). We must remember the well-known fact that, etymologically speaking, the earth is in Sanskrit called the great, wide, or broad one, an idea also familiar to modern Indian tribes: according to a Birhor tradition the primaeval waters produced a lotus, through the stalk of which the lord of the sun ascended; having taken his seat on the lotus he caused earth to be brought to him by a tortoise and other animals of terrestrial relations; he spread it out, and it became the earth [74]). The broadness and extensiveness of the components of the universe, which is essential to the continuation of life and human welfare is ṚV. 6, 69, 5 ascribed to Indra and Viṣṇu: after having taken strides, or in doing so, they extended the atmosphere and spread the spheres of the universe "for us to live". A similar idea is expressed by the verb *viṣṭambh-* "to keep apart, to fix in such a way that the entities fixed are kept widely apart": ṚV. 7, 86, 1 (Varuṇa established, in this way, heaven and earth, which are *uru-*); cf. 6, 70, 1;

---

[73]) Cf. also Eliade, Traité, p. 216; Hertel, Himmelstore, p. 23 ff.
[74]) See Ruben, Eisenschmiede, p. 238.

6, 8, 3 (Agni); 5, 29, 4; 6, 44, 24; 10, 44, 8 (Indra). ṚV. 1, 154, 1 the act of establishing the celestial abode is ascribed to Viṣṇu, the wide-striding one; he performed it "while going or traversing threefold". This performance, this very "supporting asunder" of sky and earth is a creative act of outstanding importance [75]). It means, or entails, that the fecundating sky and atmosphere and the producing earth can, each of them, and in co-operation, accomplish their task in the proper manner. In this process Viṣṇu has a share: cf. also ṚV. 8, 100, 12; 1, 154, 4; and especially 7, 99, 3 *vì astabhnā ródasī viṣṇo* (and, in later texts, e.g. MtPur. 248, 39). The first passage is interesting, because here the act is attributed to the lightning, the share of which in the processes under discussion has already been commented upon: Indra, who is speaking here, asks his friend Viṣṇu to "stride asunder" (as) widely (as possible), and Dyaus (Sky) to make room for the *vajra-* to perform the process of *viṣkabh-;* then he himself and Viṣṇu will kill Vṛtra and release the waters. Here lightning is instrumental in procuring what is essential: room. Only when there is room and extensiveness the power of obstruction, whose very name, *Vṛtra-* "barring", indicates his most characteristic feature, can be annihilated [76]).

It is, further, worthy of attention that in contradistinction to sky and earth the atmosphere is 'boundless': it is co-extensive with space [77]). It is the natural and inalienable sphere of action of those powers which are engaged in transmitting to mankind the blessings from above. Viṣṇu, who is among them, fills his hands abundantly with valuable objects "from the sky, from the earth, and from the great wide atmosphere", bestowing them upon man "from the right, and from the left" (AV. 7, 26, 8). The idea expressed AV. 7, 6, 4 is consistent with this: the generative organs (*upastha-*) of the great mother, Aditi, are the broad atmosphere. The lap of Aditi "on whom this universe of life has settled" (VS. 9, 5), the place of universal creation, must continually be protected from narrowness and obstruction. It is Viṣṇu, who by his striding activity, is instrumental in making that essential good: room [78]).

---

75) See Van der Leeuw, De godsdienst van het oude Aegypte, The Hague 1944, p. 52 and elsewhere. — Cf. also Hohenberger, o.c., p. 105.

76) Indra and Viṣṇu also ṚV. 6, 69, 5. — ṚV. 1, 103, 2 Indra spread the earth and killed Vṛtra. — AV. 7, 11, 1 the thundering is called *pṛthu-*.

77) I refer to Geldner, o.c., III, p. 348.

78) We cannot enter here into details concerning the relations between other gods and *varas* "width, room, expanse" (cf. e.g. ṚV. 1, 190, 2 Bṛhaspati; 6, 62, 1 Aśvins). 8, 75, 11 Agni is in a significant manner called *urukṛt-*. — In the Avesta the epithet *vourugavyaoti-* "having or procuring wide pastures" is often given to the aiding and protecting god Mithra who "comes to man for freedom" (Yt. 10, 5; 46); see also Nyberg, Rel. d. alten Iran, p. 60. — ṚV. 7, 99, 4 Indra and Viṣṇu are stated to have made room or free scope (*urum ... lokam*) for the

VIII. VIṢṆU AND THE MOUNTAINS.

Some importance may also be attached to the fact that the god was sometimes believed to have dwelt in the mountains: cf. ṚV. 1, 154, 2 f. *girikṣit-* "mountain-dwelling", and *giriṣṭhā-* "mountain-abiding"; cf. also 1, 155, 1. TS. 3, 4, 5, 1 Viṣṇu is even called the overlord of the mountains, the same passage attributing, in a natural way, the rule over the waters to Varuṇa, plants to Soma, cattle to Rudra, etc. Other gods incidentally associated with the mountains are Soma, Indra, and the Maruts [1]). It is no matter of mere chance that it is just this group of gods who have this peculiarity in common. Mountains are not only conceived as the abode or playground of pastoral deities, nymphs etc., but also considered an important source of rain and, of course, of water in general. See for instance ṚV. 5, 32, 2; 59, 7; and 1,85, 4 and 10 [2]). The original religion of the Munda peoples probably included the worship of hill- and mountain spirits [3]). In the Chota Nagpur region the god of earth or vegetation often appears as a mountain deity, being second to, or also identical with, the Sun-god. Mountain spirits are, moreover, credited with the power to transform themselves into lions and other animals [4]): now, one of the above Ṛgveda texts, 1, 154, 2, explicitly describes Viṣṇu as roaming about like a terrible animal [5]). Sāyaṇa thinks in the first place of a lion. According to the Harivaṃśa, a. 217 the mountains which came into existence on the surface of the newly arisen earth were Viṣṇu's tejas. Being unable to bear them the earth sank away. In one of the succeeding chapters (a. 222) it is told that the god after having assumed the shape of a mountain, the Varāha-parvata ("Boar mountain") [6]), killed the demon

---

sacrifice; I doubt whether Geldner (o.c., I, p. 120) is correct in explaining the similar passage in 1, 93, 6 (referring to Agni and Soma) as follows: "sie haben den arischen Kult ausgebreitet". — For the value of "space" see also such texts as PB. 21, 1, 9. — Mention may be made here of such texts as TS. 1, 1, 12 f and g where Agni and Viṣṇu are called "place-makers" and requested to make place; see also ĀpÇS. 2, 13, 7 f.

1) See Lüders, Varuṇa, I, p. 190, and n. 2.

2) Cf. also Meyer, o.c., III, p. 226.

3) S. Ch. Roy and R. Ch. Roy, The Khāṛiās, Ranchi 1937, p. 310 ff.; R. Rahmann, Gottheiten der Primitivstämme im nordöstlichen Vorderindien, Anthropos 31 (1936), p. 93.

4) Crooke, Popular religion², I, p. 62; 260; Meyer, o.c. III, p. 125.

5) ṚV. 10, 180, 2 the same phrase applies to Indra. The term translated by "roaming about" (*kucara-*) is TB. 3, 8, 2, 3 used in connection with the sacrificial horse.

6) For other relations between Viṣṇu (or his avatāras) and mountains see Ruben, Eisenschmiede, p. 271 f.; cf. also p. 245.

Hiranyākṣa: according to a. 218, 33 he had created the selfsame mountain "after his own form" or "resembling himself". This tradition no doubt refers to Viṣṇu as a mountain deity.

Other peoples likewise believe in deities residing in, ruling over, or representing, mountains and concerning themselves with agriculture or maintaining relations with definite animals, e.g. with the horse [7]). Had one or the other of Viṣṇu's animal avatāras anything to do with this?

In discussing the components constituting the figure of the High God Viṣṇu Ruben [8]) is no doubt right in devoting some pericopes to mountain-deities. However, the question may arise if his way of looking on the contribution furnished by divine mountains to the god's character will stand all criticism. "In eben jenem ethnologischem Gebiet in Chota-Nagpur", the said scholar writes, "ist ein Vegetations- oder Erdgott in der Form eines Berggottes häufig, der nach Hinterindien weist und als eine andere Komponente des Viṣṇu aufzufassen ist. Er ist der zweite Gott, steht etwas unter der Sonne; er heisst Marang buru; das ist ein Berg in Chota Nagpur; ....er ist der Gott des Ahnenhügels, des Djangels, des Regens....; er ist Schützer, Ahnherr und Kulturheros; manchmal auch gleich dem Sonnengott..." Although it must be confessed that we have no reason for denying any such influence of the 'aborigines', the general impression we obtain from the Vedic texts and from parallels found outside India seems to be that Ṛgvedic Indians already had 'crystallized views' (as far as this term admits of application) regarding a relation between mountains and the power called Viṣṇu, and, further, that these views were consistent with the character of the most ancient Viṣṇu knowable.

We saw already that in the Ṛgveda the god is called "mountain-dwelling" (*girikṣit-*) and "mountain-abiding". 5, 87, 1 he is mountain-born. There is, in my opinion, no necessity to connect [9]) these epithets immediately with the range of ideas expressed by the god's "highest step". In the sūkta 1, 154 (cf. AV. 7, 26, 2) Viṣṇu is said to dwell in the mountains, while roaming about like a terrible forest animal; in 1, 155, 1 he and Indra are conjointly called "the two undeceivable ones who have stood on the summit (*sānuni*) of the mountains, as it were

[7]) See e.g. Nehring, in Koppers, Die Indogerm. u. Germ. Frage, p. 687 ff.; L. Weiser, in Hdwtb. d. deutschen Abergl. I (1927), 1043 ff. (In Iceland and Scandinavia the cult of mountain deities was intended to obtain fertility. They are also concerned with the weather (e.g. in Germany, England etc.)); J. A. MacCulloch, in Hastings' Encycl. 8 (1915), p. 863 ff. (many instances of gods associated with, or dwelling on, mountains; Indian ceremonies on mountains for rain and a fruitful season; sun-gods supposed to dwell there etc.).

[8]) Ruben, Eisenschmiede, p. 235, etc.

[9]) With Macdonell, o.c., p. 39.

(horsemen?) with an excellent steed". TS. 3, 4, 5, 1 Indra is stated to be the lord of what is most excellent or strongest (*jyeṣṭhānām*), Yama of the earth, Vāyu of the atmosphere, Sūrya of the sky.... Soma of plants.... Viṣṇu of the mountains. The last passage in which a considerable number of spheres are appositely attributed to a group of well-known divinities cannot be disregarded: this author believed in a relation between this god and the mountains [10]). Viṣṇu is, further, like Pārvatī in later times, called "mountain-born" (*girija-*) and as such he is allied with the Maruts (ṚV. 5, 87, 1), atmospheric deities and intimate associates of Indra, one of the main functions of whom is to shed rain.

It is, further, worthy of attention that in the Ṛgveda Viṣṇu repeatedly occurs in the same stanza as the divine mountains: 8, 31, 10 the protection is implored of the mountains, the rivers and of Viṣṇu, the companion; 5, 46, 3 and 6, 21, 9 Viṣṇu and the mountains find themselves in the company of many divinities (Indra, Agni, Aditi, Sun, Earth, Maruts, Pūṣan, Purandhi, plants etc.), most of them are, in some way or other, connected with the range of ideas which also form constituent elements in the Viṣṇu conception. The *parvatāḥ* "mountains" when invoked as divine powers never appear alone, but only with waters, rivers, trees, earth, sky, Indra, Savitar, Maruts: cf. e.g. ṚV. 4, 34, 8; 6, 49, 14; 7, 34, 23; 35, 8; 10, 36, 1; 64, 8; 8, 54 (Vāl. 6), 4; AV. 11, 6, 10; 19, 10, 8 [11]). ṚV. 7, 37, 8 the person speaking wishes to obtain the wealth of the mountain; 5, 41, 9 the favour of the mountains is implored with a view to the continuation of the family; 4, 55, 5 their aid is invoked; cf. 5, 46, 6 (mountains and rivers); 6, 52, 4 (dawns, rivers, mountains, ancestors); 10, 35, 2. 3, 54, 2 they are called *vṛṣaṇaḥ* "vigorous, impregnating like bulls". 3, 57, 6 Agni's carefulness or protection (*pramati-*) is compared to the streams of the mountain; AV. 9, 1, 18 their honey is mentioned; 6, 12, 3 they are honey; 4, 9, 8 they are the father of an ointment-amulet. They are the abodes of the gods: ṚV. 4, 54, 5; herbs grow on them: AV. 8, 7, 17; the soma: 3, 3, 3; ṚV. 5, 85, 2; the sun rising from them slays the unseen (evils): AV. 6, 52, 1. Indra splits their bellies, penetrating to the waters: 2, 5, 5. In a series of formulas to be recited with a view to successful conception the semen is said "to have been brought together" from the

[10]) It should however be noticed that in a similar passage, AV. 5, 24, 6, the Maruts are called the overlords of the mountains. The Paipp. rec. of the AV. agrees with the TS. The Çaun. AV. differs from the other texts which contain this subject-matter including the Paipp. also in other particulars: cf. st. 9; 13 (see Whitney-Lanman, o.c., p. 263 ff.); it gives the impression of a text that has been recast. — Cf. also ÇÇS. 4, 10, 1.

[11]) We even find the compound *indrāparvatā*, cf. e.g. 3, 53, 1.

parvata-, from the womb of the sky (or: "from the sky as womb") 5, 25, 1. The gifts of the greatly nourishing Indra are compared to the juices of the mountain (*giri-*): ṚV. 8, 49, 2 (Vāl. 1, 1).

The ancient Indians as far as they lived in mountainous regions were, no doubt, as interested in the amounts of snow (cf. AV. 12, 1, 11) on, and in the water and the herbs of, the mountains as their descendants and other peoples living in dry climates or on rocky or sandy soil are to this day. "The waters are founded on the mountains" (*giribudhnā u vā āpaḥ*, ŚB. 7, 5, 2, 18) is a statement understood in modern times as well. There is Parjanya's dwelling: ṚV. 9, 82, 3. The ocean, the Himālaya and Indra are givers of wealth: Mbh. 12, 59, 118. Their wells and other waters are often mentioned: see e.g. ṚV. 1, 85, 10; 5, 32, 2; 59, 7; 85, 4. Clouds resembling hills are supposed to give water in a short time just like those having the form of waves, fishes, crocodiles etc. (Varāh.BS. 28, 14). In case of drought one should revere Indra, the mighty river Ganges, the mountains and Mahākaccha, i.e. Varuṇa (Kauṭ. Arth. 4, 3, (78), 16) [12]). Post-Vedic texts speak of mountains, both mythical and actual, as favourite resorts of gandharvas and apsaras [13]), deities who are closely associated with fecundity. The famous Mandara, for instance, is praised because of its springs, small rivers (Mbh. 3, 42, 25), and apsaras (28). Garuḍa dwells on the Himālaya which is frequented by the same nymphs and other divine beings (3, 108, 10), and abounds in rivers and lotus-flowers. There Viṣṇu performed austerities (12, 328, 8). The sides of a high mountain are described as being sprinkled with drops of rain from the clouds (3, 108, 5), which according to the well-known mythical tale were believed to have been the wings of the mountains. The last-mentioned term can also apply to the clouds [14]).

From what has been said here we may conclude that the ancient association between the god Viṣṇu, who was concerned with the sunlight in the atmosphere as well as fecundation, and the mountains, which are stores of water, the abode of beneficial plants and which, often inaccessible to man, rise high in the clouds and the atmosphere, is only natural and intelligible [15]).

---

[12]) I refer to Meyer, Das altindische Buch vom Welt- und Staatsleben, Leipsic 1926, p. 326 f. and 815 f. — For worship of mountains etc., see also the same, Trilogie II, p. 176 ff.; III, p. 126 ff.; cf. also III, p. 291. — The dragon has resorted to the mountain: AV. 2, 5, 6.

[13]) Macdonell, Vedic Myth., p. 135.

[14]) See the same book, p. 10.

[15]) For this rôle of mountains in popular belief see e.g. W. Mannhardt, Wald- und Feldkulte, I, Berlin 1875, p. 99 ff.

IX. THE SACRIFICE.

We shall now consider a very important point, to wit the constant identification of Viṣṇu with the sacrifice in the brāhmaṇas. We may take for granted that he must have been a god of considerable notability, for both the people and the brahmans, or to express ourselves otherwise, that he must already have represented an important idea, before he was declared to be identical with so great and powerful an institution as this device for ensuring the operation of all powers for good and this instrument for warding off evil[1]). The sacrifice is, indeed, according to the brāhmaṇas, the universal principle of life[2]): cf. e.g. ŚB. 14, 3, 2, 1 "Now, this — to wit, the sacrifice — is the self (*ātmā*) of all beings, of all gods; after its successful consummation the sacrificer prospers in offspring and cattle....". It leads to heaven, has a nutritive function, is happiness itself[3]). The sacrifice resembles the virāj metre (ŚB. 1, 1, 1, 22), the frequent identification of which with *śrī*- "prosperity etc." is examined in another part of this book[4]). It is the navel of the earth (VS. 23, 62), a conception to which we shall also have to revert[5]). Viṣṇu is not only constantly declared to be the sacrifice (cf. e.g. ŚB. 5, 2, 3, 6; 4, 5, 1), he is also the protector of the oblations (e.g. VS. 1, 4; 7, 20); besides, the sacrificer is identified with him (cf. VS. 4, 10; ŚB. 3, 2, 1, 17)[6]). We already saw that in performing the Viṣṇu-strides the sacrificer is nothing else but the god in very presence conquering the worlds: cf. e.g. TS. 5, 2, 1, 1 ff.[7]).

In the history of Indian religious thought the tendency to proclaim the identity of any great god and the most essential and important entities or phenomena was often evident. In comparatively early times "the lord of creation and offspring", Prajāpati, came to be involved in this process. This god, who in the great epic is called the presiding deity of the organ of generation (Mbh. 12, 313, 3[8]); 14, 42, 27), is according to the brāhmaṇas the great divine progenitor (ŚB. 8, 4, 3, 20), the most vigorous of gods, whose very function consists in creating, the god who is productiveness itself (ŚB. 5, 1, 3, 9). All beings and

[1]) In this I agree with Konow in Bertholet-Lehmann, Lehrbuch der Religionsgeschichte, II, p. 62.

[2]) I refer to Lévi, La doctrine du sacrifice, p. 81; Meyer, Trilogie, II, p. 54 f.

[3]) See Lévi, o.c., p. 87 f.; 95; 89; 141; 154.

[4]) See chapter II.

[5]) See p. 84 ff.

[6]) However, the sacrificer is also identified with Indra, Agni, Prajāpati, and other powerful beings.

[7]) Cf. also BhG. 4, 24.

[8]) In the same section Viṣṇu is regarded as the divinity presiding over the feet and walking (st. 1); 14, 42, 25 the same god is said to preside over motion.

objects owe their existence to him (10, 4, 2, 2). He is the chief of deities (13, 1, 8, 2) [9]). It was Prajāpati who has created the sacrifice as a counterpart of himself: ŚB. 11, 1, 8, 3 "The sacrifice is Prajāpati, for he created it as a counterpart of himself" [10]). To him the speculations of the brāhmaṇas attribute such qualities as in later times are given to Viṣṇu: immortality (6, 3, 1, 17); identity with brahman (7, 3, 1, 42); he is the one god above all gods [11]), the highest lord; he is the final goal of those who seek union with the divine after death (PB. 4, 8, 9) [12]); man is nearest to him (ŚB. 5, 1, 3, 8); he is both the defined and undefined (7,2,4,30); without him there would be no firm foundation (7, 1, 2, 1). Prajāpati, further, is the same as the sun [13]), which was created out of his head (PB. 6, 5, 1), as it is in another text (ŚB. 14, 1, 1, 10) Viṣṇu's head. He is also Savitar's well-winged eagle (ŚB. 10, 2, 2, 4). The goddess Śrī is said to have issued from him (11, 4, 3, 1). Now, Prajāpati is in these texts not only associated with the sacrifice, but expressly identified with it (see e.g. MS. 3, 6, 5; ŚB. 1, 1, 1, 13; 3, 2, 2, 4; 11, 1, 1, 1; AiB. 7, 7, 2 etc.) [14]).

Although Prajāpati in the brāhmaṇas thus occupies the position of the creator god and the supreme divinity of the world, efforts to substitute for him new, or other, conceptions and divine beings are not long in manifesting themselves. Not only was the 'impersonal' brahman-'concept' put in his place, the personal Brahmā was, in the Mahābhārata, very often identified or identifiable with him, and other personal figures took over part of his rôle. Among them Viṣṇu was not the least. Already in the Ṛgveda Prajāpati is associated with Viṣṇu [15]); they are besought to grant offspring (cf. ṚV. 10, 184, 1). Ritual connections between them are not wanting (TS. 5, 6, 9; Maitr Up. 6, 16). Both of them are believed to maintain relations with the earth (ŚB. 6, 2, 3, 1), of which Prajāpati is the begetter (7, 3, 1, 20) and lord or husband (14, 1, 2, 11; 3, 25), and which he is said to have entered (10, 1, 3, 2). Prajāpati, like Viṣṇu in later times, appears as boar and tortoise [16]). That is to say: the central figure of a boar and

---

[9]) See also Meyer, o.c., III, p. 315.

[10]) See also the observations made by Lévi, o.c., p. 28 f., and p. 15.

[11]) I refer to Eggeling, SBE. 43, p. XX.

[12]) These remarks are not to deny that other deities are involved in similar speculations, see e.g. ÇB. 11, 4, 4, 2 ff. (brahman); PB. 20, 16, 9 (the sun); ÇāB. 8, 3 (all the deities); Agni and Viṣṇu ÇB. 12, 1, 3, 1.

[13]) That is to say: the same as Savitar: ÇB. 12, 3, 5, 1; see also Macdonell, o.c., p. 33.

[14]) The reader might be referred to Lévi, o.c., p. 28 f.; Keith, Religion and Philosophy, p. 442 f.; Eggeling, SBE. 44, p. 556 ff.

[15]) See Macdonell, o.c., p. 118.

[16]) See section XVIII and XIX. Compare also Hopkins, Epic Mythology, p. 210.

a tortoise myth, which was borrowed from popular belief, was successively identified with Prajāpati and Viṣṇu. In the Mahābhārata Prajāpati is often the same as Viṣṇu or Kṛṣṇa; in other passages he is, of course, identified with Śiva [17]).

One might perhaps venture the hypothesis that Viṣṇu was, in a sense, also Prajāpati's successor in being the sacrifice.

Yet a variety of facts might, on the other hand, induce us to suppose him to have been at the same time the creator-god's competitor. There is indeed, in addition to what has been said regarding the close association and identity of both gods with the sacrifice [18]), first the special concern on Viṣṇu's part with this institution itself and with the sacrificer, a concern which is in harmony with certain features in his character manifesting themselves under other circumstances. He is not only the sacrifice or its life (cf. ŚB. 4, 2, 3, 10), he is also its guardian and protector: TS. 1, 1, 3 n; 1, 1, 11 s, t; ŚB. 4, 2, 2, 10; AiB. 7, 5, 4 Viṣṇu guards that of the sacrifice which is badly sacrificed. He is even believed to be accessible to feelings of love towards requisites for a sacrifice, as may for instance appear from the formulas to be recited in erecting the udumbara post in the priest's shed (VS. 5, 25): "I scatter you whom Viṣṇu loves (*vaiṣṇavān*), killers of fiends and wicked charms" (blades of darbha grass are meant). Emphasis is on the other hand laid on the necessity to guard Viṣṇu, the sacrifice: cf. e.g. VS. 7, 20. VS. 2, 8 has the officiant stepping to the south side of the altar and pronouncing the words: "Let me not with my foot offend thee, Viṣṇu"; c.f. e.g. also ŚB. 1, 4, 5, 2. By reciting stanzas addressed to Viṣṇu one drives away the rākṣasas from the sacrifice (TS. 6, 2, 9, 2). The identity of Viṣṇu and the sacrifice also implies that what is not brought about in sacrificing can be brought about through the god (PB. 13, 5, 5). Numerous consequences of this identity and its application in actual practice are discussed in the brāhmaṇas. When one, for instance, offers to Viṣṇu "one visibly obtains the sacrifice and makes it one's own" (ŚB. 5, 4, 5, 18). By muttering a formula addressed to the god one gets hold of the sacrifice (1, 7, 4, 20; 3, 2, 1, 38). It should be remembered that in the view of the authors of these works all beings are settled in, or have entered (*viṣṭāni*), the sacrifice (8, 7, 3, 21); that this institution is deemed all-sustaining (9, 2, 3, 27), that it is a means of gaining union with, and participation in the world of brahman (cf. e.g. 11, 4, 4, 2 ff.). By sacrificing to the god Viṣṇu, by the sacrifice one desires to attain 'health, wealth, and security' (TS.

---

17) For particulars see Sørensen's Index, p. 556 ff.

18) See also Lévi, o.c., p. 15, esp. n. 3; p. 48; 89; 141.

1, 7, 4, 4). By the gods and the sacrifice, respectively representing Agni and Viṣṇu, the man who is ill is healed; even if his life is gone he yet lives (2, 3, 11, 2). It has already been observed that the sacrifice even ensures entrance to heaven (cf. ŚB. 12, 6, 1, 39; 8, 1, 2). From such texts as ŚB. 1, 1, 2, 13; 9, 3, 9, reference to which has already been made in chapter VII, the paramount power of the striding god, who is the sacrifice, and his 'universal character' are perfectly clear: by striding he obtained *vikrānti-* for the gods, gaining the earth, the aerial expanse, and the sky; and this same *vikrānti-*, this all-pervading power, is won by the god, as sacrifice, for the sacrificer. For this reason the latter makes the god's strides, i.e. imitates his great mythical action. When he is consecrated, the sacrificer is Viṣṇu (3, 2, 1, 17).

The sacrifice, similarly, is often said to be a winning or securing power. Compare such texts as ŚB. 3, 2, 2, 4 and, especially, the cases in which the authors of the Ṛgveda use a term for sacrificing in combination with the verb *san-*, the use of which has already been commented upon. ṚV. 8, 53, 7 — the sūkta is addressed to Indra — *vayáṃ hótrābhir utá deváhūtibhiḥ sasavâṃso manāmahe* would appear to mean [19]): "We believe ourselves to have secured (thine aid or, in general, the success aimed at) through our offerings and invocations"; in a similar way: 54, 6. If Grassmann [20]) is right in translating *vājasāti-* 5, 33, 7 by "Opferwerk u.s.w. zur Erlangung von Gütern", this stanza and 7, 35, 1 [21]) may be regarded as supplementary evidence. Attention may also be drawn to 9, 79, 1 where *dhiyaḥ* "formulated religious thoughts" is the subject of the same verb. Compare also 6, 17, 15; 2, 32, 1 etc.

The parallelism between the objects and presumed effects of the all-important ritual, the mighty means of securing the fulfilment of any desire on the one hand, and the activity of a god who was believed to obtain, for men and other beings, control of those powers which were considered to be of vital importance, and to prepare the way for the representatives of fertility and productivity on the other, might have led to an early identification of that divine power and activity which was denoted by the name of Viṣṇu and the mighty instrument in the hands of the priests [22]) [23]).

---

[19]) I cannot agree with Geldner (o.c., III, p. 376): "Wir glauben durch (unsere) Opfer und Götteranrufungen (das Spiel) gewonnen zu haben". In the same way: 54, 6.

[20]) H. Grassmann, Wörterbuch zum Rig-veda, 1254. I am inclined to prefer it to Geldner's (o.c., II, p. 33) "Auslohnung".

[21]) *yuddhe annalābhe nimitte vā* Sāyaṇa.

[22]) Two notes by Sāyaṇa may be quoted here: ṚV. 10, 15, 3 Viṣṇu: *vyāpin-yajña-*, and 10, 113, 2 Viṣṇu: *vyāpto yajño vā.*

[23]) For Viṣṇu and the sacrifice cf. also TS. 3, 2, 6a; ĀpÇS. 10, 30, 8; 13.

X. THE SACRIFICIAL POST.

The conceptions regarding the sacrificial post or *yūpa-* seem to be of special importance, because Viṣṇu maintained relations with it. This indispensable implement which may be regarded as representing, inter alia, the phallos and which was believed to play a rôle in the process of raining [1]), and to bring wealth and esteem to those concerned with sacrificing (ṚV. 3, 8, 1; 3), is expressly stated to belong to Viṣṇu: TS. 1, 3, 5, c; 6, 3, 3, 1; ŚB. 3, 6, 4, 1; 9. When about to cut this stake one has to sacrifice with a stanza addressed to this god. The explanation added in the ŚB., § 2 — "because Viṣṇu is the sacrifice" — may have resulted from the speculations of the brahmans. The primary connection between the god and this stake which is a "thunderbolt" (ṢB. 4, 4, 11; ŚB. 3, 7, 1, 17: who has set up the *yūpa-* has hurled the *vajra-* [2])) may have been a more direct one as alluded to by the author of TS. 6, 3, 3, 1: the post has Viṣṇu for its deity; 'it is of Viṣṇu' (cf. 1, 3, 5). ViPur. 1, 8, 19 Viṣṇu is the *yūpa-*. When it was set up the sacrificer had to touch it pronouncing VS. 6, 4; ṚV. 1, 22, 19 "See the works of Viṣṇu, — from where he pays attention to his *vratāṇi* (ŚB. ibid.)". "The works of V.", this means, the author observes, "see Viṣṇu's conquest (*viṣṇor vijitiṃ paśyata*)". Then, looking up at the top-ring he had to pronounce VS. 6, 5; ṚV. 1, 22, 20 "The patrons ever see that highest step of Viṣṇu, laid as it were an eye in heaven" [3]). Cf. also such texts as ĀpŚS. 9, 20,1; 7, 11, 4.

The yūpa like the Indra tree — ṚV. 3, 8, 8 the yūpa is called the *ketu-* or "banner" of the sacrifice — and similar stakes [4]) may be considered a representative of the great cosmic tree, and of the axis mundi. Being an intermediary between the divine world and earthly life [5]), such an axis, and also the yūpa, fills a place or space which is sacred par excellence. The yūpa is essentially identical with the *skambha-* described in Atharvaveda 10, 7 [6]). This fulcrum or pillar

---

1) I refer to Meyer, o.c., III, p. 313; Keith, Rel. and phil., p. 325. The yūpa is, however, more than this.

2) Cf. also KauṣB. 10, 1: where it is said to smite away the evil of the sacrificer; ÇB. 3, 7, 3, 2.

3) See Geldner, o.c., I, p. 21 f. — Cf. also ÇB. 3, 6, 4, 3; 7, 1, 15.

4) For the bodhi tree see Auboyer, Trône, (cf. p. 86, n. 11), p. 73.

5) The reader might also be referred to P. Mus, Bārābudur, Esquisse d'une histoire du bouddhisme fondée sur la critique archéologique des textes, I, Hanoï-Paris 1935, p. 253 ff.

6) Cf. Whitney-Lanman, o.c., p. 589 ff.; Auboyer, o.c., p. 77 ff.; Gonda, Brahman, p. 43 f. — For similar beliefs in connection with the Meru, see Hohenberger, o.c., p. 147 ff.

likewise represents the vertical axis which forms the centre of the universe linking heaven and earth: cf. e.g. AV. 10, 7, 35 etc.: it sustains the components of the universe; all existence has entered it; being the frame of creation, it enters the thousandfold aspects and components of the universe (cf. st. 9), sun and moon stand fixed in it (12), all the gods are "set together" in it (13). Like other conceptions of this description the yūpa is associated with the altar [7]). The Buddhist *vajrāsana-*[8]) which was described in an illustrative manner by Hiuen-Tsang [9]) was considered the navel of the universe. Here we are confronted with a difficulty similar to that discussed in connection with the term *vajranābha-*: what was the original sense of the term "diamond seat"? If relations really could exist between the vajra and the 'navel', the seat representing that most important centre could originally have been called a "thunderbolt-seat". The idea of a god seated in that place, — or perhaps a divinity traversing the universe by the axis occasionally represented by the thunderbolt which renders sacred the spot where it strikes the earth, the idea of a power temporarily residing in lightning and coming down in it — would be in harmony with the well-known belief of the ancient Greeks and other peoples that in this phenomenon a divine power descends from the heavens. Places which had been struck by lightning were enclosed and regarded as tabu [10]).

---

7) See Auboyer, o.c., p. 49-104, and especially p. 51.

8) Auboyer, p. 74 ff.

9) See St. Julien, Hiouen-Thsang, Mémoires sur les contrées occidentales, Paris 1857-8, I, p. 458 ff.

10) See, inter alia, Blinkenberg, Thunderweapon, p. 14 and 110 f. — The question arises whether the diamond was called *vajra-* because it was, in popular belief, regarded as identical with it, or, at least, as resulting from it. In many parts of the world flint stones, believed to be 'thunder-stones' were, and are, kept by peasants because they were supposed to protect the house against lightning and other disasters, sometimes including those arising from evil spirits. These objects were often regarded as great treasures. In the island of Falster (Denmark) these so-called 'thunder-arrows' were not only supposed to fall down in a thunderstorm but also to contain a diamond (Blinkenberg, p. 77). From a short note in Funk and Wagnalls Stand. Dict. of Folklore, mythology and legend, N. York 1949, 312 we may infer that the belief that diamonds were thunderbolts was rather wide-spread. Mr. Bonser, honorary librarian, Folk-lore society, London, kindly drew my attention to G. F. Kunz, The curious lore of precious stones, 1913, p. 70 f. who makes mention of a similar statement made in an anonymous Italian manuscript of the XIVth century. In some countries rock-crystal, which according to a Swiss belief arises from thunder and lightning, goes by the name of thunderbolt (see Blinkenberg, p. 88 and 97). In German folklore it could rain diamonds (K. Olbrich, in the Hdwtb. d. deutschen Abergl. II, 194 f.). The ancients regarded them as a concentration of the purest and finest particles of gold, as 'Goldknoten' (Blümner, in Pauly-Wissowa's Realenc., 5 (1905), 322 f.). The discovery of small diamonds in certain meteorites, both stone and iron is an established fact; the Indian diamantiferous beds contain pebbles of quartzite, jasper, slate, etc. (Encycl.

Even if one is not inclined to subscribe to any particular conclusion drawn by the authoress one may learn from the recent study by Miss Auboyer that altar and throne or seat of authority are intimately connected. Both of them are a support on which the sacred, the 'holy being' (god, Buddha, *cakravartin-* i.e. the god's substitute) is placed or believed to take his seat. The axis mundi is also closely related to the *padma-* and the *cakra-* which in fact are equivalent [11]). The yūpa, on the other hand, is the substitute of the sacrificer, who is also identified with Indra (see ŚB. 5, 1, 3, 4; 4, 2), and who is intended to be born in the heavenly world (7, 3, 1, 12), and believed to be carried to it (cf. 6, 1, 2, 36; 12, 5, 2, 8; 8, 1, 2). The yūpa is also a means of attaining the abode of the gods. The sacrificer and his wife ascend into the higher regions by it. Touching the top-piece (which is made of wheat, ŚB. 5, 2, 1, 6) he pronounces such formulas as: "We have reached the light, the gods; we have become 'immortal', etc." 5, 2, 1, 9 ff.; Sāyaṇa on TS. 1, 7, 9 [12]). Rising by the measure of his head over the post, the sacrificer, next, exclaims: "We have attained life" (*amṛtā abhūma,* 14); by doing so he wins the world of the gods [13]). It seems to be in perfect harmony with the character of the god Viṣṇu as it appears to have been under other circumstances, that the yūpa should belong to him. Traversing the parts of the universe and linking these, and especially the sun and the earth, forming the mystic centre of the cosmos, being the path which leads to the upper regions, the sacrificial stake and the other objects equivalent to, or connected with, it [14]), belong to the god, who pervades the universe, is concerned with the transmission of light and of the celestial blessings to the earth and who causes them to penetrate into all parts

---

Brit. ed. 1945, 7, 319). Have the ancient imitations of stone-age axes in semi-precious stones (cornelian, agate, amethyst; see Blinkenberg, p. 108) anything to do with a belief in the fulminous origin of diamonds? Anyhow, the ancient Germans considered similar stones 'Thor's hammers' and amulets making the bearers victorious (Olbrich, ibid. 7, 1708 f.).

[11]) See Auboyer, o.c., p. 93.

[12]) By touching that wheat, ÇB. 5, 2, 1, 13 explains, he puts himself in contact with food.

[13]) See also the subsequent paragraphs of the ÇB.; TS. 6, 3, 3 and 4. — It seems warranted to connect these acts with the well-known mystic voyage to the celestial worlds by means of a 'sacred post' or axis mundi. Cf. also Coomaraswamy, Elements of Buddhist iconography, Harvard Univ. 1935, p. 82; Mus, o.c., p. 117 f.; Eliade, Traité, p. 259; the same, Le chamanisme, Paris 1951, p. 237 f. and elsewhere. It may also be noted here that the sun, which is believed to stand over the navel of the earth and to be touched by the upper end of the axis, is (Mbh. 13, 16, 44) said to be the gate of the path leading to the gods. — For the ancient view regarding the *yūpa-* see also ṚV. 3, 8. ṚV. 1, 13, 11 it is explicitly addressed as *vanaspate deva.* — According to MtPur. 248, 67 the yūpa is (are) Viṣṇu-varāha's tusk(s).

[14]) I refer to Auboyer, p. 83 ff.

of the atmosphere and the terrestrial world (or, rather, who represents that very penetration or penetrative power), the god who comes to be the path to heaven for millions, and who in the course of time is to develop his character so as to be represented by the king who is brought into contact with the sun and the solar energy by the yūpa-throne. The erection of the yūpa means Viṣṇu's victory which pierces all darkness and destroys all evil, like the thunderbolt, like lightning with which it is put on a par.

XI. VIṢṆU'S NAVEL.

In passing now to the consideration of some other beliefs connected with Viṣṇu we shall first note the importance attached to his navel. The great epic and many other works represent Brahmā as born from Viṣṇu's navel or from a lotus which grew out of it: Mbh. 3, 12, 37; 203, 15 etc.; compare also 12, 47, 58: from his navel sprang a lotus, on which this universe is situated. Thus this central part of God's body is considered the centre of the world, the source of existence.

As is well known the navel often plays a prominent part in semi-primitive speculations with respect to the origin of life in general. This part of the body being commonly considered its central point, the idea of "navel" was easily associated with that of the central and most important point of various things without, however, giving up its original sense. Several scholars [1]) drew attention to the fact that the tree of life, the source of paradise, and the stone representing the "omphalos of the earth" are often believed to be in the centre of the earth. It has, in the second place, been observed that a female deity of fertility, a so-called 'mother-goddess', the mother of the created world is not seldom associated with this 'navel', this centre of the earth [2]). The magna mater who at the same time presides over fertility was not only revered under a tree or supposed to make her appearance from it, she was also the goddess of "the earth's navel"[3]). The ancient Greeks used to establish conical or pyramidal sacred navel-stones to mark this central point. The most famous of these was that which was set up in Apollo's temple at Delphi. The primary connection of these

---

[1]) I refer to U. Holmberg, Der Baum des Lebens, Ann. Acad. Scient. Fenn. B, 16, 3, Helsinki 1922 f., p. 95; H. Bergema, De boom des levens in schrift en historie, Thesis Amsterdam V.U. 1938, p. 466, n. 112.

[2]) See e.g. Holmberg and Bergema, l.l.c.c. Cf. also Eliade, Traité, p. 247 f.; the same, Images et symboles^2, Paris 1952, p. 33 ff.

[3]) See also Bergema, o.c., p. 467; 556.

stones was with the primitive deity of the earth and the spirits of the deceased who were also in some mysterious way the source of life and fertility for their living relatives on earth. The navel is, moreover, often also considered the centre or source of creation, in general because it is the source of life, of energy, of reality. Hence also the association of Asklepios, the Greek physician-god, with the navel of the earth: being originally a snake-demon and a deity of fertility he was thought to turn round the omphalos of Gè [4]).

In the Ṛgveda, the word *nābhi-* "navel" likewise serves to express such ideas as "central spot"; "source, (place of) origin"; "source of creation or of origin". Cf. 1, 139, 9. Drawing special attention to those occurrences which may have a bearing upon the questions discussed in this volume we recall such passages as 9, 82, 3 stating that Parjanya, the god concerned with the shedding of rain [5]), has established himself in the navel of the earth (*nābhā pṛthivyāḥ*); 72, 7 (addressed to Soma) saying that "the supporter of the great sky [6]), Indra's thunderbolt, the bull of abundant wealth, Soma, was sprinkled in the navel of the earth...." (cf. also 86, 8). The conception of the omphalos and its associations with powers connected with fertility was, indeed, well-known to the authors of the Ṛgveda. Not seldom Agni is mentioned together with this navel of the earth: whereas 1, 59, 1 calls him the navel of the settlements or nations (*nabhir asi kṣitīnām*), comparing him to a pillar which sustains mankind, st. 2 regards him as the "head of the sky, the navel of the earth". ṚV. 1, 143, 4 he is said to have been established in that very navel, which is explained as the piece of ground serving for the sacrificial altar; see also 10, 1, 6. Connections between Agni who is kindled on the earth's navel and wealth and great prosperity are expressed VS. 11, 76: "while he is kindled on the omphalos, we call for considerable increase of property"; cf. ŚB. 6, 6, 3, 9 [7]). The sacrificial ground is called the navel of the earth; ṚV. 2, 3, 7; compare also 1, 164, 35 (VS. 23, 62; AV. 9, 10, 14), where the altar is the extreme limit of the earth, the sacrifice the navel of (all) existence

---

[4]) I refer to W. J. Woodhouse, in Hastings' Encycl. of Rel. and Ethics, 9 (1917), p. 492; J. E. Harrison, Themis, Cambridge 1912, p. 384; C. W. Vollgraff, in the Bulletin de correspondance hellénique 1903, p. 271 f.; Nilsson, o.c. I, p. 189; Eliade, Traité, p. 323; A. J. Wensinck, The ideas of the western Semites concerning the Navel of the Earth, Amsterdam 1916, p. 19; W. Gaerte, Kosmische Vorstellungen, Anthropos 9 (1914), p. 956 ff.

[5]) The reader might be referred to Macdonell, Vedic Mythology, p. 83 ff., and to the concise remarks in L. Renou et J. Filliozat, L'Inde classique, I, Paris 1947, p. 325.

[6]) See Macdonell. o.c., p. 110.

[7]) Cf. also TS. 4, 1, 10 d., MS. 2, 7, 7 : 83, 13; 3, 1, 9 : 12, 13; K.S. 16, 7: 19, 10.

(*bhuvanasya nābhiḥ*), soma the seed of the male horse (i.e. the fertilizing rain which impregnates the earth). In the other Vedic texts the same idea recurs: the place where Agni is kindled is the omphalos: "The sky's head art thou, the earth's navel, the essence of waters and plants, protection of all life, extending" (TS. 4, 7, 13, 2; VS. 18, 54 etc.; cf. ŚB. 9, 4, 4, 13). I would suggest interpreting the conception at issue in the following way: the sacrifice which is the universal principle of life [8]), which is "the food of immortality" itself [9]), is, like the mother-goddess and the snake of fertility in other countries, localized in that very place which with respect to the earth is the source of life, the mystic centre and point of contact with the high and indispensable powers. Thus AiB. 1, 28, 23 in commenting upon ṚV. 3, 29, 4 declares the station of Iḷā "Nourishment" [10]) to be identical with the navel of the *uttaravedi-* (northern altar); according to the ṚV. this station is situated in the navel of the earth. "The navel means the centre, and the centre is safe from danger", the ŚB. 1, 1, 2, 23 states [11]). It is in harmony with the tenor of these speculations that the sun is also thought to stand over the navel of the earth: cf. ŚB. 6, 7, 1, 8; and also AV. 13, 1, 14 "The ruddy one (the sun) disposed the sacrifice for Viśvakarman.... may I say: thy navel on the greatness (extension) of existence (*vocéyaṃ te nâbhiṃ bhúvanasyâdhi majmáni* [12]))"; cf. also st. 37. We further find that the lightning is believed to have been placed as navel within the ocean (i.e. the cloud-ocean): AV. 1, 13, 3; this would mean that lightning is the creative centre of the atmospheric waters. The atmosphere can also contain a navel: the navel of the horse which is addressed in the agnicayana rite is in the atmosphere, its place of origin (womb) on earth (VS. 11, 12; TS. 4, 1, 2, 1 etc.). The atmosphere itself is, further, said to have arisen from the navel of the Puruṣa (ṚV. 10, 90, 14; AV. 19, 6, 8 etc.), his head being the origin of the sky, his feet that of the earth; this clearly indicates the central position of the atmosphere and its essentiality for the world's productiveness. Hence also the lofty idea expressed by the author of ṚV. 1, 185, 5: the navel is the centre of the universe, the birthplace

---

[8]) Lévi, Doctrine du sacrifice, p. 81.

[9]) Ibidem, p. 95.

[10]) See Macdonell, o.c., p. 124.

[11]) From these and similar conceptions such texts as ÇB. 12, 8, 3, 8 become clear: Placing the throne-seat one addresses it with "Thou art the womb (birthplace) of royal power, thou art the centre of royal power" (VS. 20, 1 etc.). Compare J. Auboyer, Le trône et son symbolisme dans l'Inde ancienne, Paris 1949, p. 177 ff., and such texts as ÇB. 12, 9, 1, 3.

[12]) For *majman-* see p. 68 ff.; cf. ṚV. 1, 143, 4; 7, 82, 5.

of all existence where heaven and earth meet and kiss each other [13]). In the more or less mystic speculations found in certain parts of the oldest literature even the sky, "our father and generator", could be styled a *nābhi-* (ṚV. 1, 164, 33; AV. 9, 10, 12): in the latter half of the stanza the embryo is, however, said to have been placed in the space between sky and earth.

Mention may finally be made of special associations. ṚV. 6, 7, 2 we find a navel of the sacrifices, a seat of properties (or riches), that is to say: Agni as the mouth and drinking-vessel of the gods. 8, 12, 32 the (ritual) "milking" takes place *nābhā yajñasya*. ṚV. 10, 13, 3; AV. 18, 3, 40 the navel of *ṛta-* "truth" [14]) is mentioned. Elsewhere we come across the navel of *amṛta-*: ṚV. 5, 47, 2 (the horses), which may be those of the sun, *ātasthivâṃso amṛ'tasya nâbhim* [15]); 4, 58, 1 this phrase clearly applies to the soma [16]); AV. 6, 44, 3 it combines with Rudra's urine to qualify a self-shed cow-horn duly prepared to serve in a particular remedial rite (KauśS. 31, 6); 9, 1, 4 the same phrase recurs to denote another, and better known, article, the honey-whip [17]), which is also called "breath of creatures" and "dripping with ghee": these objects must of necessity have been considered highly potent and fecundating instruments. This is also apparent from AV. 12, 3, 41: "streams of good, fattened with honey, mixed with ghee, navels of *amṛta-*", no doubt referring to the very essence, the summum, of vital power, life, fecundity, abundance. 4, 11, 6 the gods are said to have ascended to heaven, to that particular navel, i.e. to the very birthplace of 'immortality', that is life, itself. ṚV. 8, 101, 15 the cow, Aditi, is qualified by the same epithet, foreboding the almost absolute sanctity of this animal in later times [18]). 2, 40, 1 Soma and Pūṣan [19]), the creators of wealth and of sky and earth, the guardians (or herdsmen) of all existence are made by the gods navel of *amṛta-*, i.e. source of

---

[13]) One might feel tempted to take *svasārā* in this stanza to stand for "brother and sister" ((elliptic dual, see e.g. B. Delbrück, Altindische Syntax, Halle a. S. 1888, p. 98), *rodasī* being feminine; cf. st. 4 *ródasī devấputre*; 3, 54, 7.

[14]) For *ṛta-* now see H. Lüders, Varuṇa, I, Göttingen 1951, p. 13 ff.

[15]) "Der Mittelpunkt des Himmels oder Bezeichnung der Vedi", Geldner, o.c., II, p. 53.

[16]) For the interpretation of this stanza see Geldner, o.c., I, p. 488. — For the soma see also ṚV. 9, 74, 4 *ṛtásya nâbhir amṛ'tam*.

[17]) Cf. ṚV. 1, 22, 3; 9, 69, 2 etc.; Macdonell, o.c., p. 49 and 54; Oldenberg, Religion des Veda[4], p. 208, n. 1 and p. 51, n. 1; H. S. Vodskov, Sjaeledyrkelse og Naturdyrkelse, I, Copenhagen 1897, p. 519 ff.

[18]) See e.g. Macdonell, o.c., p. 151 f.; M. A. Muusses, Koecultus by de Hindoes, Thesis Utrecht 1920, p. 8 f.

[19]) See S. D. Atkins, Pūṣan in the Rig-veda, Princeton 1941.

life[20]): compare the succeeding stanzas of this sūkta. The same predicate is 3, 17, 4 found in connection with Agni (cf. also 10, 5, 3). Reference must further be made to the passages dealing with the navel of Varuṇa: TS. 4, 2, 10 c; VS. 13, 42 etc. "The rush of the wind, the navel of Varuṇa, the horse born in the midst of the flood": the horse is Varuṇa (ŚB. 7, 5, 2, 18); cf. also ŚB. 7, 5, 2, 20; 35. ṚV. 6, 47, 28 occurring in a blessing of the war-chariot, this vehicle is addressed: "You are Indra's *vajra-*, the front (or array) of the army of the Maruts, the child of Mitra, the navel of Varuṇa" (cf. also AV. 6, 125, 3; VS. 29, 54 etc.[21])): although Mahīdhara may be right in explaining the term by *priyam apatyam* it is worth noticing that it occurs in the same context as Indra's bolt and the Maruts.

In two sūktas of the 10th maṇḍala of the Ṛgveda, 81 and 82, the highest position among divine powers is granted to Viśvakarman, "the All-maker"[22]). He is described as the creator and maker of the world, as the all-seeing and all-knowing god, as a ṛṣi, a priest, our father, as the lord of speech, swift as thought, beneficent and the source of all prosperity (*viśváśambhur.... sādhúkarmā*); he alone gives names to the gods, he is an establisher (*dhātar-*) and a disposer (*vidhātar-*) and the highest apparition. In having a face, arms, and feet, on every side he resembles the Brahmā of a later period who is four-faced. He is beyond the comprehension of mortals. Now, this god is (10, 82, 6) said to have been the first embryo of the primaeval waters, in which all gods came together or united; upon the navel of the Unborn One is fixed the One (the First principle, the source of all nature), on which all existence is established (*ajásya nâbhāv ádhy ékam árpitaṃ yásmin víśvāni bhúvanāni tasthúḥ*). As Viśvakarman clearly represents an ancient effort to express the idea of a unique god, the conception of whom was at this period tentatively evolved, and as this figure, moreover, not only possesses attributes to be given, in later times, to Brahmā or Viṣṇu, but also tends to fuse with Prajāpati (ŚB. 8, 2, 1, 10; 3, 13; AiB. 4, 22, 9), as, further, Viśvakarman is associated with the sun (e.g. GB. 2, 1, 23 *asau vai viśvakarmā yo 'sau tapati*; ṚV. 10, 170, 4) and Viṣṇu is, for a considerable part, the heir of Prajāpati-Viśvakarman's functions, this text is not without importance. It clearly forebodes the well-known conception of later times: Brahman, the creator-god and representative of the One on which all existence

---

20) I would not prefer Geldner's "Mittelpunkt der Unsterblichkeit", o.c., I, p. 328.

21) I refer to Whitney-Lanman, o.c., p. 374.

22) See e.g. Macdonell, o.c., p. 118; S. Radhakrishnan, Indian Philosophy, I, London 1927; 1948, p. 91 f.

depends and from which it arises, is born from the lotus, the representative par excellence of vegetation, which springs from the navel, the centre of creation, of Viṣṇu who in Vedic times was the sacrifice — believed to be the navel of all existence (ṚV. 1, 164, 35; see above) and the universal principle of life —, of Viṣṇu, the successor of Indra and Prajāpati, from whom as the Supreme Being, all life and all mundane existence proceed [23]). It may have become sufficiently evident from the texts discussed in this section that the term *nābhi-* was almost exclusively used in connection with very potent conceptions, powers, or divinities associated with the same sphere of interests and activities as Viṣṇu and the gods or goddesses connected with him. It is a remarkable fact that, in post-Vedic times, the navel-concept should have been preferably transferred to one deity. It is the more interesting, but perfectly understandable, that this deity should have been Viṣṇu, who, moreover, as Kṛṣṇa, was called the navel of the world, as it were (the nave,) the point of support for the spokes (ViPur. 5, 7, 35 *tvam asya jagato nābhir arāṇām iva saṃśrayaḥ; tvaṃ asya jagataḥ saṃśrayaḥ ādhāraḥ ārāṇāṃ nābhir iva* Comm.).

XII. SOME OTHER BELIEFS IN CONNECTION WITH VIṢṆU.

A. *His sleep.*

Another point of considerable interest is Viṣṇu's periodic sleep. As the Highest Being the god is said to fall asleep at the end of every yuga or age of the world. According to the account given in the Mbh., 3, a. 263, Viṣṇu is the *pradhānapuruṣa-* or Supreme Soul, who at the termination of such a long period not only burns the world but, as the earth becomes flooded with water, also sleeps upon the serpent Śeṣa [1]). When, finally, his creative function is stirred, he awakes. Then, being engaged in meditation for the re-creation of the universe, a lotus springs from his navel and from this the four-faced Brahmā comes out. The Supreme Being is, thereupon, said to continue creating in the form of Brahmā. This conception has no doubt arisen from the ancient belief of the One or Primordial Being resting on or emanating from the primaeval waters: ṚV. 10, 121, where Hiraṇyagarbha, identified with Prajāpati and, in later times, with Brahmā, is said to have arisen

---

[23]) See e.g. Mbh. 3, 12, 20; 203, 15; 12, 182, 15 etc. As is well known Brahman is called "the one who originates from the lotus" (Padmaja) and Viṣṇu: **Padmanābha** "the lotus-naveled one".

[1]) For Çeṣa see s. XXI.

in the beginning from the great water which pervaded the universe (cf. also 10, 129; 82, 6) [2]). Forming part of the later elaborate and periodic system of chronology, the destruction and re-creation of the world caused by Brahmā's falling asleep and re-awakening — for Viṣṇu here represents Brahmā — is but a phase of eternal life. Yet, the very idea of the periodic existence and non-existence of creation, the very idea of periodicity, must, to a certain extent, have been inspired by the life of nature, by vegetation, itself. — References to Viṣṇu reclining on his ocean-bed frequently occur in purāṇas and contemporaneous kāvya-works [3]).

However, Viṣṇu's annual sleep seems to be of more immediate relevance to our subject. According to the Indian belief the god goes to sleep, for a period of four months on the 11th of the bright half of Āṣādha (i.e. June-July) [4]). As long as Viṣṇu sleeps, that is as long as the annual rains, it is said, the world sleeps. It is almost a matter of common knowledge that a "Wachstumsgeist" is supposed to enjoy a periodical sleep, or even to suffer a periodical death: hence the ceremonies of rousing the spring or summer [5]). The recurrent change of the seasons and the eternal periodicity of life are reflected in the customary practices attributed to the divine person representing the life of nature in general, and vegetation in particular. This trait of Viṣṇu's character may therefore be considered another indication of his close relations with these phenomena.

When, during the god's annual sleep. his functions, like those of man when he is asleep (ŚB. 10, 5, 2, 15) cease, that is: during the four months of the Indian monsoon following the summer — a period known for various magical and demoniac dangers — many ceremonies are observed [6]), among which is a pūjā of the earth. If a woman in these months worships the goddess Earth she will be happy, have children, wealth, and all objects she wants. It is, however, considered unlucky to marry. Immediately after the Bali-festival and other festivities, which we have reserved for another section, are celebrated. Now, Viṣṇu has gained the victory over Bali. The spirits of vegetation

[2]) See e.g. Macdonell, o.c., p. 11 ff.; Keith, Religion and Philosophy, p. 437; 537; Radhakrishnan, o.c., p. 99 ff.

[3]) See e.g. Wilson-Hall, o.c., II, p. 211 ff.; Hohenberger, o.c., p. 112; Hariv. a. 152; 218; Patil, o.c., p. 64; Kālidāsa, Ragh. 10, 7 ff. Viṣṇu's sleep also gave rise to more or less mystic speculations, see e.g. Hariv. a. 50, to which a short discussion is devoted by Ruben, Krishna, p. 147 f.

[4]) For considerations of space I refer to the texts mentioned by Meyer, o.c., II, p. 94.

[5]) See e.g. W. Mannhardt, Wald- u. Feldk. I, p. 253; 420; 434 ff. etc.; Meyer, o.c., I, p. 228; II, p. 94 f.; 98; Eliade, Traité, p. 255; 277 f.

[6]) I refer to Gupte, o.c., p. 27 ff.

are powerful [7]), the crops are ripe. Hence the name of these festivals: "new rice" (*navānnam*). The god's rising also marks the beginning of the sugarcane harvest; the cane-mill is adorned with red lead and lamps [8]). The owner of the crops worships in his field. On a wooden board two figures of Viṣṇu and his consort are drawn with butter and cow-dung. The whole village is a scene of almost delirious festivity [9]).

One interesting detail remains to be noticed: according to the Harivaṃśa, 50, 26, the lord of the clouds, i.e. Indra, performs, as long as Viṣṇu sleeps, his duties, causing the wheel of rains (or: wheel of the year, *vārṣikaṃ cakram*) to operate. Another, and comparatively late, indicium of the co-operation of these two gods, and of their division of labour [10]).

B. *Viṣṇu and the thumb.*

There was a curious custom to be observed by a person performing the rites in honour of his deceased ancestors: he had to push the thumb of the priest into the food intended for them [1]). In doing so a well-known and much used Viṣṇu mantra was recited: ṚV. 1, 22, 17 "Viṣṇu has traversed this (all); in three places he has set down his foot. It is brought together in this dusty (foot-print) of his" [2]), which in part of the relevant texts was followed by: "Viṣṇu must protect this food of the gods" (or "of the manes" respectively) [3]). Caland [4]) at the time suggested explaining this ritual act by pointing to Viṣṇu's dwarf-avatāra, in which the god after having traversed the universe with three strides defeated Bali. By pushing the thumb into the food the evil spirits were obviously chased away, defeated by the mighty example of the god's victory. Yama quoted by Hemādri, ed. Bibl. Ind. III, 1, p. 1378, likewise recalled Viṣṇu's successful fight against the rākṣasas: as big as a thumb the lord Viṣṇu goes about combating the demons...., adding that a śrāddha performed without observing this special custom

7) See Meyer, o.c., II, p. 20; G. A. Grierson, Bihar peasant life, Patna 1926, p. 400.

8) For the ritual use of red lead (it has an 'erotic' function) see e.g. Meyer, o.c., III, p. 310. For light and lamps: ibidem, p. 307 f.

9) Other particulars may for instance be found in W. Crooke, An introduction to the popular religion and folklore of Northern India, Allahabad 1894, p. 378. For the use of butter see Meyer, o.c., III, p. 319.

10) For Viṣṇu's sleep also Ruben, Krishna, p. 146 f. I am not convinced that this author is right in suggesting special connections with ancient Turkish myths.

1) I refer to Caland, Altindischer Ahnenkult, Leyden 1893, p. 57; 86 f.; 141, etc.

2) For the ritual applications of this text see also Whitney-Lanman, o.c., p. 405 f.

3) For particulars see Caland, o.c.

4) Caland, o.c., p. 187 f.

would fall to the asuras. Oldenberg [5]), however, was inclined to take the thumb — a limb not often mentioned in the ritual texts — for the phallos. It may be objected that the thumb was pushed into the food with the exception of the nail [6]): in this position it could scarcely be thought to represent the penis. It would, further appear to me that Johannson's supposition [7]) is likewise open to doubt: the Swedish scholar would take Viṣṇu to appear here as the thumb-soul. Admitting the occurrence of the thumblike soul in other texts [8]) — the soul has, among various peoples, indeed often been thought of as a being like the phallos or as great as a thumb [9]) — I fail to see how this interpretation can be founded on the relative passages themselves. From the thumblike soul in other texts it does not follow that every thumb or thumblike being represents the soul. Taking everything into account it seems reasonable to recall the significance attached to the extended thumb by other peoples: the thumb, often considered to be the powerful finger, not seldom played an important rôle in combating demons and witches, in averting the evil eye, and in communicating its supranormal, or at least special, power to other beings and objects [10]). We should, moreover, consider the interpretation given by the Indians themselves: RVidh. 1, 17, 4 ff. "By plunging, during a śrāddha, the thumb into food with ṚV. 1, 22, 17 ff. one removes the rakṣas. Having the length of a thumb Viṣṇu.... kills the rākṣasas; that is why he will strike at a śrāddha.... The food will be imperishable" [11]). Compare also BaudhDhŚ. 2, 15, 2 *niraṅguṣṭhaṃ tu yad dattaṃ na tat prīṇāti vai pitṝn* [12]) and the favourable influence supposed to be exerted by the *chotika-* "snapping the thumb and forefinger" and similar motions of the hand made by the spectators at a dramatic performance [13]). So the

---

5) Oldenberg, Religion des Veda, p. 232, n. 1.

6) Cf. the paddhati on KāṭhGS. quoted by Caland ("the nail is a dead object, not to be brought into contact with the food").

7) Johansson, Solfågeln i Indien, p. 8 f.

8) Let it suffice to refer to R. E. Hume, The thirteen principal Upanishads, Oxford 1934, p. 585.

9) E. Monseur, L'âme poucet, Revue de l'histoire des religions 26 (Paris 1905), p. 361 ff.

10) See e.g. E. Stemplinger, in the Handwörterbuch d. deutschen Aberglaubens, II (1929-130), 174 ff.; the same, Antike und moderne Volksmedizin, Leipsic 1925, p. 174 ff.; X. F. M. G. Wolters, Notes on antique folklore, Thesis Utrecht 1935, p. 69 ff.

11) See my Ṛgvidhāna, Utrecht 1951, p. 22 f. (st. 4 read: five, instead of: fine).

12) And the ritual according to the Baudhāyanīyas: Caland, o.c., p. 26 f.

13) See my 'Ursprung und Wesen des indischen Dramas' (Acta Orientalia 19, Leyden 1943), p. 438 f. — Charpentier, Ups. Univ. Arsskr. 1911, p. 52 f. and p. 52, n. 3 expresses the view that the sacrifice represents the earth and the thumb Viṣṇu's penetrating into it.

conclusion might perhaps be that an old custom based on the evil-averting power of the thumb was re-interpreted under the influence of the conception of Viṣṇu's demon-destroying dwarf-incarnation.

C. *Viṣṇu, the doorkeeper.*

The AiB. 1, 30, 19, in quoting ṚV. 1, 156, 4 where "Viṣṇu accompanied by his friend opens the cattle-shed", states that Viṣṇu is the doorkeeper of the gods. It does not seem to be justifiable to assume with Dandekar [1]) that this isolated qualification, which may have been inferred from the mantra, proves the god to be in the ascendant. Yet, mention may be made of an Indian belief in connection with door guardians: Nāgas (snake-demons) are said to perform this important function [2]). As such they are supposed to assume an attitude of bhakti, with regard to the god whose precincts they attend. Did the note of the author of the AiB. result from similar considerations with respect to Viṣṇu? Or from a belief concerning a certain similarity to the behaviour of other mighty beings who by their very presence protect a place or entrance? [3])

D. *The god's abode.*

It is convenient here to say a few words on the contact which the earthly beings may have with 'Viṣṇu's world'. Viṣṇu's highest step, ṚV. 1, 154, 5 states, is his beloved resort; it is the abode of the devout deceased; there, in the highest heavens, is a spring of honey (cf. 1, 22, 20). Viṣṇu himself is, according to 3, 55, 10, the guardian watching over (or: ruling) this highest place [1]). This abode, which 1, 22, 20 is called the eye in the sky, is in the Kaṭhop. 3, 9 the end of the journey of the man who knows how to control his soul in order to obtain final emancipation. The access to it is, MaitrUp. 6, 30 says, through the disk of the sun which is pierced (*bhittvā sūryamaṇḍalam,* a phrase found also in other texts [2])) by those who ascend from this world by a special ray of the sun. In a similar passage in the BārUp. (5, 10, 1) a person departing from this world is said to go to the wind which opens for him like the hole or hub of a chariot-wheel. Mounting higher, he gains access to the sun through an opening like the hole in a drum [3]).

[1]) Dandekar, 'Festschrift' Kane, p. 105. Miss Das Gupta seems to be of the opposite opinion: Ind. Hist. Qu. 7, p. 107.

[2]) For nāgas as guardians see J. Ph. Vogel, Indian Serpent-lore, London 1926, p. 306; Zimmer, o.c., p. 63.

[3]) See e.g. Auboyer, Trône, p. 73.

[1]) Macdonell, Ved. Myth. p. 10; 38 f.; Hohenberger, o.c., p. 98 ff.

[2]) Hertel, Himmelstore, p. 44 ff.

[3]) See Auboyer, o.c., p. 8 ff.

According to JUpB. 1, 3, 5 "one escapes through the midst of the sun, which is a fissure in the sky: as is the (axle-)hole of a cart or of a chariot, even so is this fissure in the sky". 1, 18, 10 the same text speaks of "the immortality which burns yonder", and 20, 3 it maintains that heaven and earth are firmly fixed and kept asunder by the atmosphere in the same manner as two wheels are connected by the axle. So the centre of a disk or the hub of a wheel was apparently considered a place of particular importance, a gateway through which one could enter the space behind the disk, or from which a substance could proceed. In this connection it may be of interest to observe that the centre of a wheel sometimes had the shape of a lotus [4]). According to a well-known dhyānaśloka Viṣṇu resides in the midst of the sun's orb [5]).

In accordance with the above passage in the MaitrUp. the Mbh. 3, 261, 37 locates Viṣṇu's abode above the seat of Brahman. Other conceptions regarding this 'place' were closely bound up with the various ideas current with regard to the abode of the emancipated, or the structure of the universe: SB. 4, 4, 17 one turns the yūpa towards the east: this (*prācīnasaṃnamanaṃ* comm.) is the highest place of Viṣṇu. Cf. also Mbh. 5, 111, 7; ViPur. 1, 2, 51 f.

In view of what has been said on the god's relations with the sacrifice and the central place of the latter a text like PB. 1, 6, 5 is perfectly understandable: *ṛtasya tvā deva stoma pade viṣṇor dhāmani vimuñcāmi* etc. "On the place of truth, O divine Stoma, in Viṣṇu's abode I unyoke thee" (*ṛ. p.: yajñasya sthāne; dh.: tejasi* Sāyaṇa).

E. *The śālagrāma.*

As is well known, Viṣṇu is also believed to be represented by the śālagrāma stone [1]). The sacredness of this black stone containing fossil ammonite seems to be comparatively ancient. A motive for it seems to be that several interior spiral grooves visible in the stone are considered by the people to be representations of Viṣṇu's discus. Another interpretation, mention of which was made by Sonnerat [2]), may, however, possibly be more original: a śālagrāma can be of nine colours, and then

---

[4]) I refer to S. Kramrisch, The Indian temple, Calcutta 1946, p. 403.

[5]) According to the Matsyapur. (and probably also to other descriptions) Viṣṇu is represented on the hub of the wheel which 'symbolizes' the universe; the god is seated on a lotus-flower (285, 2 ff.).

[1]) The reader may for want of space be referred to H. Krishna Sastri, S. Indian images of gods and goddesses, Madras 1910, p. 70 ff.; (G. Thibaut), SBE. 34, p. 126; 178; Kane, Hist. of Dharmaś. II, p. 715 f.; Ruben, Eisenschmiede, p. 232 f.; the same, Krishna, p. 82; 136; Rao, o.c. I, 1, p. 9 ff.

[2]) M. Sonnerat, Voyage aux indes orientales et à la Chine, Paris 1782, I, p. 307.

represent the nine 'historic' avatāras of the god. These colours are also said to belong respectively to Narasiṃha, Vāmana, Vāsudeva etc. [3]). Now, the number 9, i.e. 3 square, often occurs in connection with powers concerned with vegetation. Festivals in honour of these are not seldom celebrated for nine days [4]). Periods of nine days were, inter alia, well-known in the soma ritual. Kubera is in possession of nine treasures. Durgā appears in nine forms. In texts belonging to a later period Viṣṇu and Śiva are called *navaśakti-* "having nine faculties". Viṣṇu is also *navavyūha-* "of ninefold appearance or manifestation". We should however remember that the number 9 also played a part in mystic speculations in various folkloristic undercurrents.

F. *The soma.*

It is interesting to state that Viṣṇu is sometimes also unmistakably associated with the soma plant and sap [1]). His name occurs among the deities on behalf of whom the soma is pressed out: ṚV. 9, 33, 3; 34, 2 Indra, Vāyu, Varuṇa, Maruts, Viṣṇu; 56, 4 Indra and Viṣṇu; 63, 3 the same and Vāyu; 100, 6. Elsewhere it is, in accordance with Viṣṇu's task to assist Indra, the former who prepares the soma-draught for the latter: ṚV. 2, 22, 1. 6, 17, 11 it is stated that Pūṣan and Viṣṇu poured out three lakes of soma for him. VS. 8, 1; TS. 3, 2, 10 g etc. Viṣṇu is requested to guard the soma: "O far-striding Viṣṇu, this is thy soma; guard it; let not the evil-eyed one espy this of thine". Cf. also ĀpŚS. 12, 21, 12. When the gandharva Viśvāvasu had stolen the divine plant (cf. also ŚB. 3, 2, 4, 1 ff.) and entered the water with it, the gods went in search of it; then Viṣṇu perceived it and announced to the others that he had found it: PB. 6, 9, 22. The soma-cart belongs to him: ŚB. 3, 5, 3, 22.

When the guest-offering to Soma arriving at the sacrificial hall is performed a series of mantras is pronounced (see e.g. VS. 5, 1; TS. 1, 2, 10), the first of which is to accompany five oblations: "Thou (i.e. the sacred food) art the meals of hospitality of Agni. For Viṣṇu (sc. I take) thee!" etc. According to Mahīdhara, a renowned commentator on the White Yajurveda, Viṣṇu stands here for Soma, the pervader of the sacrifice: we know that the former is often considered a pervader. ŚB. 3, 6, 3, 19 he is, indeed, explicitly identified with Soma:

---

[3]) Rao, o.c., p. 11.

[4]) See e.g. De Vries, Altgerm. Relig. II, p. 451. For the occurrence of the number 9 in various magical practices see also H. Marzell, Hdwtb. de. Abergl. VI, 1056 ff. For India see e.g. Gupte, Hindu holidays, p. 181 ff.; and for the 'sacredness' of this number in general A. B. Keith, in Hastings' Encycl. of Rel. and Eth. IX, p. 407 f.

[1]) See Rönnow, Trita Āptya, p. 94.

"Viṣṇu is no other than Soma". A similar interesting identification is given ibid. 3, 2, 4, 12. Mbh. 13, 149, 67 Soma is among his thousand names, this appellation implying such connotations as "drink of life", "healing power", "king of the vegetable kingdom", "stimulating power", "bestower of strength, wealth and prosperity" and brings to mind rain, water and fertility.

XIII. EMBLEMS AND ATTRIBUTES.

An insight into the significance of a god's emblems and attributes is useful, nay indispensable, for an understanding of his character. Viṣṇu is described as being in possession of various objects, usually called his weapons and ornaments, and of a bird serving as his vehicle; he is represented as reclining on a snake, this being believed his couch. On a somewhat closer examination, these objects and animals appear to be consistent with the main features in the nature of their owner as far as they are apparent from his deeds and from the myths and rites connected with him. A study of these 'attributes' is therefore greatly helpful in checking the conclusions and suppositions arrived at in other sections of this book.

The god carries, to begin with, in uplifted hand a sharp-rimmed battle-discus, the famous cakra Sudarśana of the epic tales. According to Mbh. 1, 225, 23 it was given to (Viṣṇu-) Kṛṣṇa by Agni: it was a fiery weapon (*āgneyam astram*), through which its owner should be superior in battle to any creature, and which would always return into his hands. Another story is told in the same epic, 13, 14, 74 ff.: it was given to Kṛṣṇa by Mahādeva (Śiva), when the latter had killed a daitya who lived in the water. It was also created by Śiva [1]). There is some uncertainty as to its original shape. It has been held to be a circular disk with a small opening in the middle. Like Buddha's *dharmacakra*- it is represented as a disk with spokes and rays [2]). It may be noticed that a *cakra*- or disk does not appear to have ever become a favourite weapon in India [3]). The use of this particular mythical disk is, more-

---

[1]) For particulars see Hopkins, Epic Mythology, p. 206.

[2]) I refer to Hopkins, in the JAOS. 13 (1889), p. 298 f.; Hohenberger, o.c., p. 120 f.; J. N. Banerjea, Sūrya in brahmanical art, IA. 54, p. 161 ff.; S. Kramrisch, The Hindu temple, Calcutta 1946, p. 221; 403; Patil, Cultural history from the Vāyu Purāṇa, p. 227 and Bulletin of the Deccan College Research Institute 5, p. 154; V. R. R. Dikshitar, Hindu administrative institutions, p. 109. For later forms of the disk see G. Jouveau-Dubreuil, Iconography of Southern India, Paris 1937, p. 59 ff.

[3]) P. C. Chakravarty, The Art of War in Ancient India, Dacca Univ. 1942, p. 171.

over, in puranic and similar accounts, mostly associated with Viṣṇu. It must therefore be studied as a traditional emblem in special connection with this god, who is also believed to be able to dig a well with it.

It has long since been identified with the widespread religious 'symbol', the sun disk: it is "effulgent as fire" or as the sun, and cannot be looked at on account of its blazing energy (*tejas*, cf. Mbh. 13, 14, 77; ṚV. 5, 63, 4). The *cakra-* or wheel was employed in various ritual performances as a representative of the sun [4]). The name of the disk may be puzzling. The Mbh., l.c., says that Bhava (Śiva) called it *sudarśana-* in consequence of the fact that nobody could look at it except himself. Is it a matter of chance that the name coincides with that of the jambu tree on the mount Meru, the fruit of which pours out a silvery juice which, when drunk, delivers from decrepitude? [5]) Connections between the sun and a tree of life are a familiar theme in books dealing with the origins of life and prosperity from the point of view of history of religions [6]). Be this as it may, it is small wonder that a society which sets much value on protection against the evil eye and various visible causes of misfortune, and which uses the same terms for "beautiful, splendid, handsome" and for "auspicious, beneficial, prosperous, fortunate" (*śubha-, bhadra-, kalyāṇa-*, cf. also *subhaga-*), should have given to some derivatives of *dṛś-* "to see, to look at" connotations verging on the latter group of meanings. The word *darśata-* "visible, striking the eye, conspicuous, beautiful" no doubt implied the idea of "auspicious" in AV. 4, 10, 6 where it applies to a 'pearl-shell amulet' used in a ceremony for longevity: "you are 'conspicuous' on the chariot" [7]). The same adjective occurs in AV. 7, 81, 4 which is addressed to the sun and moon and seemingly intended to promote prosperity. In the Ṛgveda *darśata-*, like *sudṛś-* and *sudṛśika-*, almost always applies to the sun, fire, the thunderbolt (*vajra-*), dawn, and, further, to such auspicious and beneficial entities as the soma, the sun-horse, and such gods as Mitra and Varuṇa. Sometimes a literal meaning "conspicuous" would even be less apposite: ṚV. 1, 2, 1, where

---

4) See Macdonell, o.c., p. 155.

5) For this tree see Mbh. 6, 7, 21 ff. (Sørensen, Index, p. 349). See also Ruben, Krishna, p. 138; F. S. Growse, Mathurā², 1880, p. 68.

6) See e.g. Holmberg, Baum des Lebens, p. 62 f.; Bergema, Boom des levens, p. 265; 363, etc.; Eliade, Traité, p. 238.

7) Pearls were valued as bearers of beneficial power; hence their use in medicine. See e.g. R. Garbe, Die indische Mineralien, Leipsic 1882, p. 74; L. Hilgenberg and W. Kirfel, Vāgbhaṭa's Aṣṭāṅgahṛdayasaṃhitā, Leyden 1941, p. 815; Eliade, Images et symboles, p. 190 ff.; M. Bloomfield, The Atharvaveda and the Gopathabrāhmaṇa, Strassburg 1899, p. 64. Cf. also Eliade, Traité, p. 373 ff.

it is said of Vāyu — translators gave "lovely, gerngesehen"; 4, 36, 7. Special attention may be drawn to 4, 16, 5 (*puṣṭi-*) and 10, 140, 4. The opposite adjective *durdṛśīka-* is 7, 50, 1 used in connection with an *ajakāva-* which seems to be either an illness or a species of venomous vermin. In the epos *durdṛśa-* etc. are often applied to rākṣasas, piśācas and other hostile beings, to the battle-field, decrepitude etc.

This disk is in the epics sometimes accompanied by the adjective *vajranābha-* which has been translated in various manners: "eine diamantene Nabe habend" (Petr. Dict.)[8]), "(with a) nave like thunder"[9]), or "with a piece of iron attached to its centre"[10]). It would be an attractive supposition to take the original sense of the compound to have been "in the navel (centre) of which is the 'lightning-bolt'" (cf. *vajrapāṇi-* "wielding a *vajra-*" and its Vedic synonyms *vajrabāhu-*, *vajrahasta-*, *vajradakṣiṇa-*). In view of the importance of the *vajra-* and the *nābhi-* concepts in ancient Indian religious thought this term would, then, be highly significant: the navel (place of origin, birthplace) or place of contact with life and higher powers contains the *vajra-*, the bolt instrumental in fertilizing and in promoting life. As the disk represents the sun such texts as ŚB. 6, 3, 1, 29; 7, 3, 2, 10 where that luminary is called a *vajra-* suggest themselves. It may also be noted that Indra's *vajra-* more than once occurs in the same passage with Viṣṇu's disk: Mbh. 8, 89, 45 f.; 13, 14, 75. — From archaeological evidence it may be concluded that the sun-disk and lightning could combine in various manners: in Roman Gaul the sun was placed, between two lightning-bolts, on an altar, and axes, representing lightning, were constructed in the form of a circle which imitated the sun. Axes were also arranged so as to form the radii of a circle. Axe and sun go further together in amulets, found in Croatia[11]). The ancient Lithuanians revered an iron hammer as an emblem of the sun-god. In the Hallstatt culture birds were at the same time connected with the wheel of the sun and with the axe of the skygod who sent the rain and

---

[8]) Similarly Stchoupak, Nitti, Renou; "having a hard nave" (Monier-Williams).

[9]) M. N. Dutt, A prose Engl. transl. of the Mbh. 8, 76, 32.

[10]) Ibidem, 1, 227, 23. Cf. also Nīlakaṇṭha on Mbh. 1, 225, 23: *vajraṃ varatrāsā nābhau yasya tat. sūtrabaddhaśakunivat punaḥ prayoktur hastam āyātīty arthaḥ. vajraṃ trapuvaratrayoḥ iti medinī.*

[11]) Dr. A. Vollgraff-Roes was so kind as to supply me with these data, referring to E. Espérandieu, Recueil général des bas-reliefs ... de la Gaule romaine, Paris, 1907 —, I, p. 336; J. Déchelette, Manuel d'archéologie préhistorique celtique ..., Paris 1908-1914, II, p. 483; Mitteilungen d. antiquar. Gesellschaft Zürich 1844, p. 24. See also Bergema, o.c., p. 522; De Vries, o.c. I, p. 120; A. Roes, Der Hallstattvogel, Jahrb. für prähist. und ethnogr. Kunst, Berlin 1940, p. 57 ff.; Haeberlin, Mem. Amer. Anthr. Ass. 3 (1916), p. 36 ff.

the vessel containing the water. Indian instances are not known to me[12]).

We now come to the god's *gadā*, mace or club. In contradistinction to Śiva who only incidentally wields a club, Viṣṇu is, according to an observation made by Ruben[13]), "der grosse Keulenträger". This is the more remarkable as this implement, practically speaking, does not play a rôle in the god's warlike activities. It does not seem impossible to co-ordinate this feature in Viṣṇu's equipment with the predilection for clubs and similar weapons or implements in agricultural societies[14]) and thus as a sort of reminiscence of his original milieu. This is not to deny that the club can be a representative of the penis erectus[15]): sticks and clubs with a phallic significance are far from unusual in fertility rites and similar ceremonies[16]). It is also worth mentioning that this weapon was given to Viṣṇu by Varuṇa, the lord of the waters: Mbh. 1, 225, 28, where it is, moreover, said to be capable of killing every daitya and to produce the sound of lightning (*aśani-*). Although its name, Kaumodakī, is not easy to explain in a satisfactory manner, it strongly reminds us of the word for the white water-lily, *kumuda-* (for *kumudinī* "an assemblage of these flowers" Hindī has *kamodinī* which also denotes the flower itself) and its derivative *kaumudī* "moonlight" (which is said to cause the kumadas to blossom), "the day of full moon in the month Kārttika (October-November)"[17]), and "the festival held on that day"; in Hindī we also find *kaumodī*. The identical *kaumodī* serves as a synonym of *kaumodakī*. The festival is, finally, in younger texts also called *kaumodinī*[18]). The question arises whether the name of the club is, in the regular way, a derivative of *kumodaka-* which is given as an epithet of Viṣṇu[19]). Or must the semantic affiliation be otherwise?[20])

Among the other weapons of the god we sometimes find the plough

---

12) It may be added that the *cakra-* is also described as an emblem of power (Rao, o.c., I, p. 293).

13) Ruben, Eisenschmiede, p. 213; see also p. 277.

14) See Ruben, Eisenschmiede, p. 213; the same, Krishna, p. 278 ff.; K. Birket-Smith, Geschichte der Kultur, Zürich 1946, p. 443.

15) Cf. Meyer, o.c., III, p. 321, and ch. V.

16) I refer to A. Slawik, in Koppers, Indogermanen- und Germanenfrage, p. 722. — In modern slang, e.g. in the Netherlands, words for "club" are used for "penis erectus".

17) According to an Indian explanation this day was so called because then the white water-lily flowered luxuriantly (Sumaṅgala Vilāsinī, Pāli Text Soc. 1, 139); see, however, also Meyer, o.c., II, p. 9 f. (and p. 10, n. 1).

18) I refer to Meyer, o.c., III, p. 333.

19) Hemacandra, Abhidh. 216.

20) The traditional explanation of *kaumudī* etc. (*kau*: "on the earth", *mudī* "joy") is a case of 'popular etymology'. — Viṣṇu's epithet *kustubha-* must be considered a 'derivative' of *kaustubha-*.

(cf. e.g. Mbh. 13, 149, 73), the implement typical of Kṛṣṇa's brother Balarāma (*haladhara-, halāyudha-, lāṅgalin-*), the import of which is shown in another section of this book [21]). In a curious stanza, Mbh. 12, 342, 79 the god describes himself as tilling the earth and consisting of black metal (iron): Nīlakaṇṭha will be right in explaining this detail by "taking the form of an iron ploughshare": *lāṅgalakīlarūpī*. Club and plough point to association with agriculture and with the fertility of the soil [22]).

As to Viṣṇu-Kṛṣṇa's brilliant breast-jewel, the Kaustubha, the *maṇiratnam* or *maṇir divyaḥ,* emerged from the milky ocean when it was churned [23]), Ruben [24]) seems to be right in regarding it as a miraculous and powerful gem, closely akin to the famous Syamantaka, which was a presentation of the Sun to Satrājit and, bestowing rain and fertility upon the country, the very picture of that luminary [25]). In an interesting manner Kālidāsa, Ragh. 10, 10, calls the Kaustubha "the essence of (oceanic) waters".

The Śrīvatsa, a particular curl of hair on the breast of Viṣṇu-Kṛṣṇa and other divine beings [26]), may be classified under the well-known outward tokens of the status of *cakravartin-* "universal sovereign" or *mahāpuruṣa-* "great man" [27]). To the explanation of the name given by Ruben [28]) ("Heilkalb") I would prefer that of "the favourite of Śrī", i.e. "Śrī's favourite abode" or something to that effect [29]). As an auspicious sign the Śrīvatsa has nine angles: this number often occurs in connection with precious or auspicious objects, powers and ceremonies related to welfare, etc.

Viṣṇu's conch-shell (*śaṅkha-*) is a famous specimen of a very great *maṅgala-* or auspicious object. Because of its aquatic origin and resem-

21) See p. 133 f.

22) For the iconography of Viṣṇu see Rao, o.c., passim; G. Jouveau-Dubreuil, Iconography of Southern India, Paris 1937, p. 59. — For other particulars regarding the weapons: Hohenberger, o.c., p. 120 f.

23) For particulars see e.g. Sørensen, Index, p. 403; cf. also H. H. Wilson-F. Hall, Viṣṇu Purāṇa, London 1864 ff., I, p. 147; 2, p. 94; Rao, o.c., I, p. 25 f.

24) Ruben, Krishna, p. 33.

25) For particulars see also Gupte, o.c., p. 61 ff.; Ruben, Eisenschmiede, p. 260 f.

26) See e.g. Hopkins, Epic Mythology, p. 184; 205. It is far from being typically Viṣṇuite, and for instance a characteristic of the Jinas.

27) For lists of these characteristics see e.g. E. Burnouf, Le Lotus de la bonne Loi, Paris 1852, App. VIII, p. 553 ff. and E. Senart, Essai sur la légende du Bouddha...², Paris 1882, p. 88 ff.

28) Ruben, Krishna, p. 63.

29) For some particulars see M. R. Kale, on Kāl. Ragh. 17, 29 (Bombay 1930). The name may, of course, have had its history, but I am not wholly convinced that the MInd. *sirivaccha* <AInd. *śrīvṛkṣa-* lies at the root of it (Charpentier, Die Suparṇasage, Uppsala-Leipsic 1920, p. 331, n. 1). See also Wilson-Hall, o.c., Index, p. 189 s.v.; Rao, o.c., p. 25 etc.

blance to the vulva the shell is often regarded as a representative of, or identical with, (female) fertility [30]). It is a means of warding off evil, of destroying demons, of strengthening and delighting the divine powers. It is believed to afford protection against the evil eye, and is often an object of veneration [31]). In ancient Greece pearls and shells had frequent and various associations with the Mother-goddesses, with sexual love and marriage [32]). According to the ViṣṇudhPur. 3, 73, 20 the image of Kāma has as 'ornaments' conch and lotus. It may be assumed that the *śaṅkha-* was very early brought into relation with deities of similar character. When Viṣṇu came to occupy a high position this object, being one of his main emblems, could not fail to become endowed with special religious importance in the circles of his devotees.

It may be remembered here that these 'emblems' of the aspects of divine power were conceived to represent parts and aspects of the god's faculties. They are occasionally ordered by him to assume individual existence and to be born among men.

There is no necessity to dwell at length on the Garuḍa, Viṣṇu's 'vehicle' and the emblem of his flag-staff. In a well-known section of the Mahābhārata (1, a. 27 ff.) it is told how this famous bird, after slaying nine yakṣas [33]) and two snakes which guarded the soma or amṛta took it away from the gods. After that he was immortal and free from diseases. He and Indra made friends with each other. He was the enemy of the snakes, feeding on these animals [34]). Johansson [35]), who was followed by Charpentier [36]), endeavoured to show that Viṣṇu originally was a soul-being concerned with generation, and a bird, the

---

30) Cf. Meyer, o.c. I, p. 233 and III, p. 311.

31) See e.g. J. Hornell, The Indian chank in folklore and religion, Folk-lore 53 (1942), p. 113 ff.; W. Crooke, Popular religion and folklore, Westminster 1897, I, p. 79 f.; Ruben, Krishna, p. 136; Eliade, Images et symboles, Paris 1952, p. 164 ff. According to Baldaeus, o.c., p. 45 the Veda was produced from a chank by Viṣṇu.

32) See e.g. W. Déonna, Aphrodite à la coquille, Revue archéologique 1917, p. 312 ff.

33) For these genii of fertility and vegetation, representatives of the force of the soil etc. see A. K. Coomaraswamy, Yakṣas; Hillebrandt, Vedisch *yakṣa-*, in Festgabe Garbe, Erlangen 1927, p. 17; Meyer, o.c., III, p. 329; J. Masson, La religion populaire dans le canon bouddhique pāli, Louvain 1942, p. 126 ff.

34) Other particulars can be found in Hopkins, Epic Mythology, passim (see Index, p. 243); Charpentier, Die Suparṇasage, p. 328 ff.; Masson, o.c., p. 124 f.; Ruben, Krishna, passim (see p. 323). — In later times and in Further India Garuḍa represents victoriousness, being often made to accompany the god who is represented by the king; see J. Boisselier, Garuḍa dans l'art khmer, BEFEO. 44 (Hanoi 1951), p. 55 ff.

35) Johansson, Solfågeln i Indien, p. 21 ff.; 28 ff.

36) Charpentier, Upsala Univ. Arsskrift 1911, p. 144; 153 f.

sun-bird [37]), and, as such, likewise engaged in fecundating the earth. The eagle which carries off the soma [38]) — and which in Vedic literature is not yet called Garuḍa [39]) — is, in the opinion of these Swedish scholars, no other than Viṣṇu himself. It would appear to me that the objections raised to this hypothesis [40]) by Oldenberg [41]) and Hillebrandt [42]) are reasonable. Referring to the interpretation of Indra's and Viṣṇu's co-operation proposed in other parts of this book, I cannot feel convinced by Johansson's argumentation with respect to ṚV. 4, 18; 8, 100; 10, 113 and similar texts. But though having my doubts about these speculative constructions I must admit that the close association existing in the epics between Viṣṇu and the Garuḍa cannot have appeared from nowhere. There seems to be less to say for the suggestion that the Garuḍa-figure originated in shamanism [43]) than for the theory which sees the sun-bird in him. The gods praising him (Mbh. 1, 23, 15 ff.) call him, inter alia, *tapana-* "burning, shining", and "the sun" (*sūrya-*), "fire" and *prabhāḥ* which is explained by Nīlakaṇṭha as the fiery energies of the sun etc. (*sūryādīnāṃ tejāṃsi*). His brother, moreover, is Aruṇa, the charioteer of the Sun (Sūrya), or the foregoer of this god, the 'personification' of dawn, and, in a striking and apposite manner, distinguished from his well-made younger brother by being not full-grown (Mbh. 1, 16, 16 ff.). His implacable enmity with the serpents [44]) — he is also called *Bhujagāri-* "the enemy of the snakes" — is as significant a feature in his character as his conquest of the "draught of immortality". Garuḍa is in the epic and subsequent literature identical with Tārkṣya [45]) who in the ṚV., 10, 178, 1 is described as a god-impelled *vājin-* i.e. a "bearer of the particular power

---

37) For the sun-bird in general see e.g. H. Bergema, De boom des levens, Thesis Amsterdam V.U. 1938, p. 378; A. Roes, Symbolen uit het oude Oosten, The Hague 1946, p. 33 ff.; in the Veda: Macdonell, Ved. Myth., p. 112; 152. For various aspects of the sun-god see also Hopkins, The religions of India, Boston 1895, p. 40 ff.; 56; S. Dasgupta, Obscure religious cults..., Calcutta Univ. 1946, p. 336 ff.

38) Cf. also Hopkins, Epic Mythology, p. 136.

39) The earliest occurrence seems to be TĀ. 10, 1, 6 (it is also found in the Suparṇādhyāya).

40) See also Charpentier, Die Suparṇasage, p. 328 ff.

41) Oldenberg, in the Nachrichten Göttingen (NGGW.) 1915, p. 374 ff.

42) Hillebrandt, Vedische Mythologie, II, p. 311 f. Cf. also Güntert, Weltheiland, p. 306.

43) Cf. Ruben, Krishna, p. 181; see also A. Ohlmarks, Studien zum Problem des Schamanismus, Lund-Copenhagen 1939, p. 127; U. Harva, Die religiösen Vorstellungen der altaischen Völker, Folkl. Fell. Communic. 125, Helsinki 1938, p. 84; 205; 547; M. Eliade, Le chamanisme, Paris 1951, p. 149 ff.

44) Cf. also Eliade, Traité, p. 119.

45) See e.g. Macdonell, Vedic Mythology, p. 149.

called *vāja-*" [46]). Though comparatively early referred to as a bird, he is, in all probability correctly, to be considered an equine representative of the powerful sunlight. If the main sphere of activity of the 'earliest Viṣṇu' really was the space surrounding the earth and if he performed his task in, or by means of, the sunbeams, a mighty bird moving in the air and exhibiting traits of character proper to the Sun and its rays, made an excellent 'duplicate-representative' of the energy and nature of the god (or divine power), — a function of many vehicles or animal attendants [47]). When the gods, Mbh. 1, 23, 17, call the bird Viṣṇu, this does not imply that he originally was that divine being, that Viṣṇu originally was a bird and that one being had split up into two. He is also addressed by the name of Indra (16), and this god is, in his turn, called Viṣṇu in a. 25, 13. It means that the figure of Garuḍa is for those speaking so similar to the power or being which by pervading wins life that they could, for the moment, be identified. Similarity was always apt to be interpreted as identity. As power which makes itself known in terrestrial and atmospheric nature was frequently perceived in animal form — the often superior animal being regarded by man as a bearer of power —, this is no matter for surprise [48]).

Highly conspicuous among Viṣṇu's emblems is the lotus. When depicted in sculpture one of his four hands holds a lotus-flower [49]). Out of the golden lotus which appeared on his forehead came Śrī, who is, in commemoration of this fact, called *kamalālayā* "who abides in a lotus": cf. Mbh. 12, 59, 131 f. This goddess is very closely connected with the *padma-* or nelumbium speciosum (which closes towards evening): she is called Padmā and praised as *padmasaṃbhavā* "lotus-born", *padme sthitā* "standing on the padma", lotus-eyed, lotus-coloured, *padmamālinī* "decked with lotus garlands", and other epithets containing this word. We have already seen how a lotus springs from Viṣṇu's navel when he awakes after his age-long periodical sleep and how from this flower the four-faced Brahmā comes into existence, who, sitting on it, starts creating. We can only mention in passing that *Padmin-* "possessing lotus-plants or flowers", *Padmanābha-* "lotus-naveled",

---

46) See section VI.

47) The reader may also be referred to H. Zimmer, Myths and symbols in Indian Art and civilisation, New York 1947, p. 69 ff.

48) I am not able to make out whether some importance must be attached to Mbh. 1, 33, 13, where the bird asks Viṣṇu to be allowed to stay above him. It may be said in justification of his usual position on the god's flag-staff.

49) See e.g. Rao, o.c., passim; J. N. Banerjea, IA. 54, p. 161 who, inter alia, discusses the relations between this flower and the sun. For the lotus in association with deities or other motifs related to fertility etc. see e.g. A. K. Coomaraswamy, Geschichte der indischen und indonesischen Kunst, Leipsic 1927, p. 319.

Padmapāṇi- "lotus-handed", *Aravindākṣa-* "lotus-eyed" (this name is also given to the sun) are among the many names and epithets of the god. In the Harivaṃśa 42 (41), 27 ff. (2225 ff.) the lotus is Viṣṇu's first avatāra: *pauṣkarako nāma prādurbhāvaḥ*. Mbh. 12, 43, 14 Kṛṣṇa is called *Śrīpadma-* "lotus of prosperity". As he was also believed to take the form of various fig-trees [50]), this embodiment of the god in the lotus-flower is perfectly understandable.

The lotus is, indeed, a representative of the force and energy inherent in the waters and of the humidity of the soil: of a great popularity and a large area of occurrence. Being the first product of the creative principle — this is the significance of the above myth of its origin from the Highest Being when awakening from his sleep on the cosmic waters — it was conceived as a sort of generative organ of these very waters [51]). Water being regarded as a female substance or 'concept', the lotus, identified or associated with similar creative entities of a female character (humidity, trees, the earth) could, in the wording of a myth which made this flower the birthplace of Śrī and of the Creator-god Brahmā himself, act as the womb of creation, the womb of the universe [52]).

These few notes may suffice with regard to a subject which has already often been discussed by my predecessors [53]).

---

50) Ch. I, s. II.

51) See also the details collected by Hohenberger, o.c., p. 111 f.

52) For the so-called symbolism of the lotus — this term is not correct, because the ancient Indians, like other peoples in their circumstances and of their cultural niveau, did not look on a lotus-flower as a mere outward sign of a principle or divine 'concept'; for them it was a visible representation, the very embodiment of the divine itself — see e.g. F. D. K. Bosch, De gouden kiem. Inleiding in de Indische symboliek, Amsterdam-Brussels 1948, p. 24 ff.; Zimmer, o.c., p. 90 ff.; cf. also Meyer, o.c., III, p. 308; R. Schmidt, Der Lotus in der Sanskrit Literatur, ZDMG. 67, p. 462 ff. A few lines may be quoted from S. Hummel, Geheimnisse tibetischer Malereien, Leipsic 1949, p. 5: "Der Donnerkeil hat im Ausdruck der Urdynamik als des geschlechtlich-vitalen als männliches Prädikat zum polaren weiblichen Gegenbild die Lotusblüte... Die Prägung der Glocken zeigt im Innern sehr oft die Blütenblätter des Lotus und stellt so einen Blütenkelch dar. Die Glocke ist wie der Blütenkelch des Lotus selbst ein Symbol des Weiblichen". — Hariv. a. 299 (3, a. 12) dealing with the origin of all existence from the Lotus (*puṣkara-*) describes it as golden — gold being also a token of an incorruptible nature —, as giving a seat in its flower to the goddess Earth, as containing the abodes of all the gods and the perfect and beatified beings. From its calyx or innermost part flows a fluid like the *amṛta-* of the gods... Thus the Supreme Being had made the lotus to contain the universe: he, the universal lord, of incomparable might, the origin of all light, the *bhagavān*, the *mahātmā*, *svayaṃbhūḥ* ("the self-existing" i.e. "the one who was not created by any other power") created or, rather, emanated from himself, on his couch in the great ocean, this lotus-treasure, which was the world. — The lotus also belongs to the eight maṅgalas or "signs of good luck" (see e.g. Monier-Williams, Dict., s.v.; H. von

XIV. THE GOD'S NAMES.

In a presentation of some conclusions derived from a study of part of Viṣṇu's names and epithets — a thousand of which are enumerated in Mbh. 13, a. 149 and PadmaPur. 6, 72, 113 ff. — R. Otto [1]) drew attention to the fact that some of them, Ojas, Tejas etc. [2]), are 'primitive'. It is, however, far from certain that these 'names' were given to this god at an early period. Tejas being a name of the sun, and also occurring for "Light" (when considered a 'person'), appears also in the list of the thousand names of the god Śiva, who, on the other hand, often borrowed such epithets and other particulars from his rival. Terms for important 'concepts' [3]) or epithets of other mighty beings or powers were obviously often transferred to these gods when they gained in importance. Thus Parjanya and Pavana, ancient names of 'the deities concerned with rain and wind' [4]) also appear in the list. The very application of these names to Viṣṇu shows that the powers and faculties denoted by them were, at a certain moment, considered as aspects of his character. It is, moreover, interesting to see that part of them (e.g. *ojas* and *tejas*) originally had associations with definite other deities.

That such names of trees and plants as Nyagrodha (also given to Śiva), Aśvattha, Kumuda etc. when applied to Viṣṇu show his frequent relations with the vegetable kingdom has already been mentioned in another section [5]). Otto may be right in explaining his name Sthāṇu — which is also given to Śiva, to a Rudra, a Prajāpati, and a serpent demon — from the cults of trunks and stakes [6]): the word literally means "stem, post". We cannot help remembering here Viṣṇu's relations with the sacrificial post. — However this may be, Taru and Vṛkṣa

---

Glasenapp, Buddhistische Mysterien, Stuttgart 1940, p. 102), being regarded as representing perfection.

[53]) A rather common epithet of the god is *Puṇḍarīkākṣa-* "The lotus-eyed One" (Mbh. 5, 70, 6 explained as *puṇḍarīka-* and *akṣa- na kṣīyate hanyate*). For worship of Viṣṇu under the name of Çrī- P. (Further India): L. Finot, BEFEO. 32, p. 1 ff.

[1]) R. Otto, Gottheit und Gottheiten der Arier, Gießen 1932, p. 84 ff.

[2]) Cf. also Ugra, Ūrjita, etc.

[3]) The term concept should, strictly speaking, be avoided; see my 'Ojas', p. 46 f.

[4]) See further on: s. XV.

[5]) Section II.

[6]) I refer to Eliade, Traité, ch. 8; Bergema, o.c., p. 459 ff.; G. A. Barton, Poles and posts in Hastings' Encycl. 10, 93 ff. See also W. Koppers, Monuments to the dead... in Central India, in the Annali Lateranensi, 6 (Rome 1942), p. 117 ff.

"Tree" as well as Sthāvara "Immovable, Tree or Plant" are among the names of the god. Otto [7]) seems right in recalling the nṛsiṃha-avatāra (Viṣṇu appearing from a pillar) and in referring to the Bṛhajjabālopaniṣad, 6, 1, where a *nṛsiṃha-* standing on the bank of the Bhavānī is considered a divinity able to protect or to injure men.

I would explain the epithet Kumbha — which is a word for "jar or pitcher" — by Viṣṇu's connection with vegetative life — with which the water-jar is often associated — rather than fetishism. Neither am I convinced that such names as Vyāla "Snake (or other beast of prey)" nd Kapi "Monkey" must be considered to be traces of animal fetishism. The god's essence was believed to be present in those animals which are connected with the same phenomena as he was himself. He could then be represented by them. That the title Kapīndra is given to Viṣṇu in Mbh. 13, a. 149, whereas it is elsewhere conferred upon Hanuman or Sugrīva is, to my mind, no argument in support of the thesis that the god originated in such a fetish.

We now come to the much discussed name Śipiviṣṭa [8]). Scholars often endeavoured to understand this obscure word as suggesting a phallic aspect of the god: Johansson made it "being or appearing in phallic form", Dandekar: "the changing phallus, the swelling and diminishing penis" joining Güntert [9]) in the assertion that the word cannot be separated from *śepa-* "penis" [10]). If this vocable has anything to do with it, which is very doubtful, a sense like "contained in the penis" (*viṣṭa-* "entered in, contained in", cf. e.g. ṚV. 7, 49, 4) would appear to my mind the least improbable guess, but I fail to find any unmistakable reference to a phallic character of the deity going under this name [11]). We already know that the god was believed to enter the lightning, a phenomenon of comparable function.

Nor does a name like Mukunda which Mbh. 13, a. 149 and in other texts is given to the god, and which may be of 'Munda' origin — other

---

[7]) Otto, o.c., p. 86. (I cannot subscribe to all etymologies and explanations proposed by this author).

[8]) For this term see K. Geldner, Vedische Studien, Stuttgart 1901, p. 81 n.; Eggeling, SBE. 44, p. 293, n. 2; Johansson, Solfågeln, p. 12 ff., followed by Charpentier VOJ. 25, p. 427; Keith, Veda Bl.Y.S., p. 194, n. 1; 622, n. 8; Dandekar, Festschrift Kane, p. 108 f., etc. See also section I. — According to TS. 3, 4, 1, 4 Viṣṇu Ç. is the redundancy of the sacrifice, the greatness of the victim, and prosperity; cf. also ĀpÇS. 5, 22, 6; 9, 4, 8; 19, 12; 14, 18, 14; 18, 15, 4: cf. also 20, 22, 6.

[9]) Güntert, o.c., p. 305 f.

[10]) Cf. also Grassmann, Wörterbuch, 1394.

[11]) See also Geldner, Rig-veda übersetzt, II, p. 270. — Viṣṇu Çipiviṣṭa is not always completely identical with Viṣṇu: VS. 22, 20. — Could *śipi-: hīnaroman-* refer, as a slang term, to the penis??

meanings of the word are "a kind of precious stone", "the resin of boswellia thurifera" etc. — constitute an argument in favour of Viṣṇu's 'Austric' origin: such names were often transferred, the very epithet Mukunda being for instance also given to Śiva.

The well-known name Hari seems to suit the god very well. *Hari-* "tawny, pale or reddish yellow, fallow etc." is in Vedic usage applied to fire, the sun, lightning, and serves as a substantive to indicate a tawny horse, Agni, Soma, the pressing stones, the sun, lightning. The adjective especially denotes the colour of the soma plant and juice. Indra's appearance is "tawny" (ṚV. 10, 96). ṚV. 3, 44, 3 the celestial orb as well as the earth are characterized as "tawny": *dyâm índro hári-dhāyasam pṛthivîm hárivarpasam* | *ádhārayad*.... (cf. Sāyaṇa: *harito haritavarṇā dhāyaso dhārakā raśmayo yasyāḥ sā,* and *oṣadhibhir hari-tavarṇām*). In other texts a lion, a monkey, a jackal, the *mudga-* (bean: phaseolus mungo), sandal, and *śaspa-* "young or sprouting grass" are, inter alia, said to have this colour. So are rays of light. Although as a divine name Hari also occurs in connection with Indra, Soma, and various other beings including demons, it especially belongs to Viṣṇu (see e.g. ViPur. 1, 2, 2) [12]). We cannot know for certain [13]) that the first god to whom this name was given was Indra, and that Viṣṇu borrowed it from him.

Yet it is interesting to notice that the name Vaikuṇṭha which in the Mbh. and in later texts is given to the latter figure, belongs to the former in the ŚB. and in the KauṣUp. 4, 2 and 7: "Indra V., the unconquered (*aparājita-*) missile (the vajra?)" [14]). See also ŚB. 14, 5, 1, 6 = BārUp. 2, 1, 6, where the commentary explains V. by *aprasahya-* "irresistible" and Indra by *parameśvara-* "supreme lord, supreme being". In both passages the persons speaking deal with the person (*puruṣa-*) in the air (*vāyau*) who is said to be regarded as brahman or, according to another thinker, to I.V., the text containing the additional remark that the man who adheres to the latter opinion is triumphant and unconquerable (*jiṣṇur hāparājiṣṇur bhavati*). One is almost tempted to consider the coincident occurrence of a number of terms which were to come into frequent use in post-Vedic Viṣṇuism as occasioned by the existence of a theory concerned with a highest being or power contained in the atmosphere and considered identical with brahman, a being going by the name of Indra, the wielder of the bolt which is free from

---

[12]) See also Von Schroeder, Arische Religion II, p. 10.

[13]) As is maintained by Bh. K. Shastri, The bhakti cult in ancient India, Calcutta 1922, p. 101.

[14]) Cf. TS. 2, 2, 8, 1. Or the word *senā* means "army": thus Renou, Kauṣītaki Upaniṣad, Paris 1948, p. 63.

bluntness (*vi-kuṇṭha-*, if this is the etymology of *vai-kuṇṭha-* [15])) or who was in some other way concerned with the idea of piercing sharpness, a theory which might, perhaps, have formed the foundations of the conception of Viṣṇu's heaven Vaikuṇṭha: in the epic Viṣṇu-Kṛṣṇa himself is called V., and his friend and adherent Arjuna bears the name of Jiṣṇu. If so we are again faced by the complex of ideas: penetration of space and universe by the powers wielded, or represented, by Indra and Viṣṇu and, in consequence of that, man's salvation. Some importance must also be attached to JUpBr. 4, 5, 1 (and cf. 10, 10), where the same power (the celestial light) which is called Savitar when it dawns, Viṣṇu when it is about to rise, Puruṣa when rising, Bṛhaspati when risen, Maghavan when ascending, is known under the name Indra Vaikuṇṭha at noon, etc.: in both passages the JUpBr. co-ordinates I.V. with the sun in the zenith. We have however refrained from making these considerations a point in our above argument [16]).

XV. VIṢṆU'S RELATIONS WITH OTHER GODS.

A consideration of Viṣṇu's relations with other gods and of the purport of those passages in which he occurs in their company will be greatly helpful in revealing the god's character. Confining ourselves mainly to an examination of the older documents and trying to escape repetitions, we may, to begin with, observe that the number of deities which whom Viṣṇu is more than incidentally associated is not very large. That is to say: if we do not mention the rather frequent enumerations of divinities, mostly occurring in sūktas addressed to many gods. In these Viṣṇu's name is several times mentioned together with Indra, Agni, Mitra, Varuṇa, Aditi, Maruts, Pūṣan, Brahmaṇaspati, Bhaga, Savitar, Sun, Earth, Sky, Sarasvatī (cf. e.g. 5, 46, 3; 7, 35, 9; 39, 5). In similar texts showing less names Viṣṇu is often joined with the Maruts, the Aśvins, Indra, Pūṣan, Vāta ("Wind"), Agni, Rudra. If any desire is expressed at all, these divine powers are implored for blessing, happiness, food, protection (cf. 5, 49, 3; 6, 50, 12; 7, 35, 9; AV. 6, 3, 1). These gods are, generally speaking, also those with whom Viṣṇu is especially allied in other passages.

Confining, for obvious reasons, our remarks on the joint occurrences

---

15) See also Renou, o.c. — For Indra compare also the remarks made by Ruben, Die Philosophen der Upanishaden, Bern 1947, p. 279 and elsewhere.

16) Section VI.

of the names of Indra and Viṣṇu to the following, we state here that these gods are, both of them, victorious (6, 69, 8); benevolent (1, 156, 5) *bṛhat-* i.e. "firm, reliable" [1]) and "strong" or "energetic" (*tavasā*), but 1, 61, 7 the latter is called *sahīyān.* They are friends: 1, 22, 19; 8, 52, 3; but Viṣṇu is at the same time Indra's assistant: 1, 85, 7; 6, 20, 2; 8, 3, 8; 10, 113, 2. Hence, no doubt, his epithet *Sacābhū-* "Fellow; Associate", which is also given to the Aśvins, Indra's *vajra-,* Heaven and Earth, the mother of the calf. In a long text, AV. 17, 1, which begins with a series of invocations addressed to the most powerful (*sah-*) Indra, the heroic Viṣṇu is implored to "fill" the person(s) speaking with cattle and to set him (sic) in the highest firmament.

Not infrequently Viṣṇu is mentioned in the same stanza with the Maruts. ṚV. 7, 36, 9 they are jointly invoked to give the person speaking *vayas* "youthful vigour, youth" in order to enable him to generate offspring (*prajāyai*) [2]). Being mountain-born, he is (5, 87, 1) accompanied by those deities which are constantly associated with lightning and thunder, wind, rain and sun-like brightness, who shine in the mountains (8, 7, 1), or have these high regions for their dwellings (8, 94, 12). It is worthy of attention that Viṣṇu in this sūkta 5, 87 which represents the Maruts (who as a rule are closely related to Indra) as Viṣṇu's satellites (cf. 1 *víṣṇave marútvate* and 4 d *nṛbhiḥ*), the god should have been given the epithet "the great" (*mah-*). He is (st. 4) said to have departed from their common great seat; driving on the summits of the mountains and attended by the Maruts Viṣṇu is a god who increases felicity. The same troop of deities is invoked at the offering of Viṣṇu (2, 34, 11, cf. 7, 40, 5). Like the god they are called *evayā-* "swift" [3]). ṚV. 8, 20, 3 they are the bountiful ones of the swift god [4]). 7, 93, 8 Viṣṇu and the Maruts are invoked together with Indra in a sūkta addressed to the last-mentioned and Agni. — In a sūkta (ṚV. 10, 128; AV. 5, 3; TS. 4, 7, 14, 1—4 [5])), which is often used at the beginning of a sacrifice (see e.g. ĀpŚS. 1, 1, 4; cf. 6, 16,7 b; VaitS. 1, 14), the Maruts with Indra, Viṣṇu, Agni are invoked conjointly, next the broad-spaced atmosphere and the wind (*vāta-*). — In the Mahābhārata Viṣṇu is in a similar way linked together with the Maruts: 12, 340, 103 he is called their lord; 65, 32 Nārāyaṇa, in the form of Indra, is accompanied by them.

---

1) For the sense of this adjective see my 'Notes on brahman', Utrecht 1950, p. 31 ff. and esp. p. 35 f.

2) For this aspect of Viṣṇu see section II.

3) I also refer to Geldner, Der Rig-veda I, p. 320.

4) Macdonell, o.c., p. 40 gives some other particulars. Compare also ṚV. 8, 15, 9.

5) See Geldner, o.c., III, p. 357 and Whitney-Lanman, o.c., p. 224 f.

Viṣṇu's relations with Tvaṣṭar, Prajāpati and procreation (cf. ṚV. 10, 184, 1; AV. 7, 17, 4; cf. MaiUp. 6, 16) being discussed elsewhere, we mention here a casual association with Rudra (ṚV. 7, 40, 5) who must be 'satisfied' on the occasion of a sacrifice to Viṣṇu. ṚV. 1, 156, 1 Viṣṇu, the swift and extensive (*saprathāḥ*) god, who abounds in splendour, is asked to be dear and kind like Mitra; Mbh. 12, 280, 28 he is identified with Mitra, Varuṇa and other gods. He is more often associated with Varuṇa. In AV. 7, 25, which constitutes a hymn of praise to both of them [6]), the spaces (*rajāṃsi*) are said to have been established by their vital force (*ojas*); whatever shines is in their direction, and also "what breathes and looks mightily" [7]). In a curious passage, ŚB. 5, 4, 5, 1 f., Varuṇa's lustre (*bhargas*), i.e. his vigour (*vīrya-*), that is to say Viṣṇu, the sacrifice, is related to have gone away when he was consecrated [8]). In the so-called dhruvāśvakalpa, a rite for obtaining reliable horses, described in the Mānavagṛhyasūtra 2, 6 [9]), an offering is presented to "the three principal deities", viz. Uccaiḥśravas, the mythical horse produced by the churning of the ocean, Varuṇa, and Viṣṇu. In the only parallel text, KGS. 57, Viṣṇu and Uccaiḥśravas are not mentioned. As the rite requires aśvattha and nyagrodha trees, jars filled with water, grains, pieces of gold, all kinds of herbs, juices and jewels and various other auspicious objects, and as, moreover, the *jaya-* oblations — which are intended to effect success — are offered, Viṣṇu may have been introduced here owing to his patronage of well-being.

The god's name is joined a few times with that of Pūṣan. Atkins [10]) discussing the relevant passages in the Ṛgveda arrives at the conclusion that the evidence is too meagre to determine any basis such as "solar likenesses" upon which the connection between these two gods was made. Now, Pūṣan is no doubt a deity with solar affiliations; besides being in a sense an ideal of herdsmen-worshippers, who protected herds and flocks, he was also interested in growth, wealth, and well-being in general. He has connections with Agni, Savitar, Soma, Bhaga, Saras-

---

[6]) For parallels and variants see Whitney-Lanman, o.c., p. 405.

[7]) Cf. ÇB. 4, 5, 7, 7 where the first stanza is quoted: "For Viṣṇu is the sacrifice... which now undergoes distress, and Varuṇa is the inflicter". See also TB. 2, 8, 4, 5 etc.

[8]) See Eggeling, in the SBE. 41, p. 113 f.

[9]) I refer to M. J. Dresden, Mānavagṛhyasūtra, Thesis Utrecht 1941, p. 128 ff.

[10]) S. D. Atkins, Pūṣan in the Rig-veda, Princeton 1941, p. 26. In this re-investigation of the much-discussed figure of Pūṣan (a good survey of other contributions to the solution of the problem is given in ch. I) too much emphasis is, again, laid on a supposed development of the conception called Pūṣan in the texts known to us. See also Dandekar, Pūṣan, N. Ind. Ant. 5, p. 49 ff.

vatī, and, especially, with Indra [11]). He is even called Indra's brother (ṚV. 6, 55, 5). Indra and Pūṣan are (6, 57, 1; cf. 7, 35, 1) invoked for friendship, for well-being, and *vājasātaye* "for the acquiring of wealth" [12]). Pūṣan accompanies Indra when the latter slays *vṛtrāṇi* (6, 56, 2). Thus their companionship is of a similar character to that of the great god and Viṣṇu. Unlike Atkins [13]) I would emphasize a certain similarity in concern in the above and some other respects rather than the absence of a common basis in the connections of these gods with natural phenomena. As to Pūṣan's relations with Viṣṇu the conclusion might, in a similar way, be that they were associates because of a certain similarity in functions and sphere of activities: ṚV. 1, 90, 5 they are invoked to make the prayer "cattle-crowned" and to give well-being; 6, 48, 14 Pūṣan is described as a god bringing an abundance of food like Viṣṇu. They poured out soma for Indra (6, 17, 11). 4, 3, 7 Pūṣan the bringer of a well-nourished condition (*puṣṭi-*), Viṣṇu and Rudra are associated, 8, 54, 4 P., V., Sarasvatī and the seven streams. Cf. also 8, 31, 10 f. Although their names occur, among those of many other gods, in close succession (5, 46, 3; 6, 21, 9; 7, 44, 1; 10, 66, 5; cf. also VS. 25, 5), their companionship seems to have been of a more or less occasional character. In the brāhmaṇas Pūṣan, a distributor of portions (ŚB. 1, 2, 4, 4), a representative of cattle and *puṣṭi-* "well-nourished condition, prosperity" (cf. 3, 1, 4, 9) and of productiveness (5, 2, 5, 8), who is even identified with the earth (6, 3, 2, 8), is said to have taken Śrī's wealth or happiness (*bhaga-*) when other gods took other possessions, or rather attributes, from her (11, 4, 3, 3). Of more immediate interest is MaiUp. 6, 35 where Brahman, the supreme object of worship which transcends all manifestation, is adored: the Real's face is said to be covered with a golden vessel and Pūṣan is requested to uncover that "unto him, i.e. Viṣṇu, whose practice or law is the real" (*satyadharmāya viṣṇave* [14])): here the knower of the paths conducts man to the Highest.

Being the sacrifice Viṣṇu is often allied with the two divinities [15]) who maintain close connections with this institution, to wit Agni and Soma. ṚV. 8, 12, 16 Indra is said to drink soma either with Viṣṇu, or with Trita, or the Maruts (*yát sómam indra víṣṇavi. . . . mándase*). According to Sāyaṇa this means: *viṣṇau pānārtham āgate saty anyadīye yāge. . . .*

---

11) I refer to Atkins, p. 22 f.

12) For this term see section VI.

13) Atkins, o.c., p. 24.

14) In the parallel texts BārUp. 5, 15, 1; IUp. 15; VSK. 40, 15 it reads *s. dṛṣṭaye.*

15) I also refer to Macdonell and Keith, Vedic index of names and subjects, London 1912, I, p. 81.

tena viṣṇunā sārdhaṃ pibasi. As, however, Trita is called a preparer of soma [16]) and the Maruts are (5, 30, 6) likewise engaged in pressing this drink, it seems more correct to put this text on a par with 2, 22, 1 (cf. also 8, 3, 8) where Viṣṇu is said to prepare soma [17]), a form of activity which is not out of tune with his character. The soma is, 9, 96, 5 inversely called a begetter or author of thoughts, i.e. 'hymns or prayers' of sky and earth, of Agni, Sūrya, Indra, and Viṣṇu. This no doubt means that the potent and inspiring draught sets those powers in motion which are known as 'hymns', Agni etc.,; cf. also Sāyaṇa: *somo hi devān āpyāyayati.* Thus Viṣṇu is once more linked together with those divine powers and entities with which he is usually allied or with which he has part of his sphere of activities in common. The soma is sometimes prepared for Indra, Vāyu, Varuṇa, the Maruts, and Viṣṇu: 9, 33, 3; 34, 2; 65, 20; or for Indra, Viṣṇu, Vāyu: 63, 3; for Indra, Viṣṇu and the gods: 100, 6; for I. and V.: 56, 4. — ŚB. 13, 4, 3, 8 (; AŚ. 10, 7, 4; ŚŚ. 16, 2, 10) mention is made of a *somo vaiṣṇavo rājā,* whose people are the apsaras, who are said "to be staying here: handsome maidens have come hither" (ŚŚ.: *tā imā āsata iti yuvatīḥ śobhanā upadiśati*) [18]).

Mention has also been made [19]) of Viṣṇu's co-operation with Agni and Soma [20]) in constituting an arrow: see e.g. ŚB. 3, 4, 4, 14. In § 15 it is stated that Agni is the day, Soma the night, and Viṣṇu what is between the two. As the day belongs to Agni, and the night to Soma (1, 6, 3, 24), the last identification probably is an addendum, formed for the sake of the parallelism. The Mbh., 8, 34, 18; 49, 56 etc., discussing the same topic observes (49) that the entire universe is nothing but Agni and Soma, but also nothing but Viṣṇu. This view is in accordance with the important position given to the god in post-Vedic times.

Let us now inquire into Viṣṇu's relations with Agni. Agni, who could be represented as a he-goat or he-ass, who was held to be a giver of rain and a promotor of fertility and prosperity [21]) and passed for "a possessor of food" (TS. 2, 2, 4, 1 f.), who was believed to beget offspring for the sacrificer which grows through Indra's influence (TS. 2, 2, 4, 4) [22]), who was a benefactor besought to grant boons and

---

16) See Macdonell, o.c., p. 67.

17) See also section VI.

18) I refer to Eggeling, SBE. 44, p. 366.

19) See section VI.

20) For Agni-and-Soma see Hillebrandt, Vedische Mythologie, I, p. 398, ff.

21) I refer to Meyer, o.c., III, p. 287.

22) Compare also Hopkins, JAOS. 36, p. 260 "as heat Agni for obvious reasons is said to set the embryo in all beings, vegetable and animal".

to deliver from poverty, demons and childlessness, this Agni is often mentioned together with Viṣṇu. They (and Indra) are even identified: ṚV. 2, 1, 3; cf. 5, 3, 3, and 10, 1, 3 [23]). AV. 18, 3, 11 Agni is implored to anoint with splendour, Viṣṇu to do the same with mental vigour (*medhā*), i.e. with creative power of mind. In the "consecration offering" (*dīkṣaṇīyeṣṭi*) [24]) both gods are invoked conjointly and a cake is presented to them on eleven potsherds. Cf. e.g. also ŚB. 3, 1, 3, 1 ff.; GB. 2, 1, 12; ŚB. 6, 6, 1, 2 ff.; 12, 1, 3, 1; and AiB. 1, 1, 1 ff. (cf. KB. 7, 1 ff.) "Agni is the lowest of the gods, Viṣṇu the highest; between them are all the other deities". Whereas Sāyaṇa referred these words to the place of the deities in the litanies of the Agniṣṭoma, Haug [25]) insisted that they originally pointed to a locality in the universe. Keith seems right in assuming that both sides of the relation were present to the author of the brāhmaṇa. Agni and Viṣṇu, the same text (1, 4, 10) holds, are the guardians of consecration of the gods; they are lords of the consecration (*dīkṣā*), conferring it on man. In these functions and connections of Viṣṇu we may see one of the germs of his later greatness.

Elsewhere Agni is, in accordance with his nature, the fire and Viṣṇu the sacrifice: cf. e.g. TS. 1, 1, 12 e. All the gods are Agni [26]) and the sacrifice is Viṣṇu: 2, 2, 9, 1 where an offering to both of them is prescribed. Cf. also 5, 5, 2, 4; 2, 3, 11, 1 f.; 3, 5, 1, 4; KauṣB. 16, 8; ŚB. 5, 2, 3, 6. By offering to these two gods one appropriates the gods and the sacrifice of one's enemy: TS. 2, 5, 4, 2. Cf. also ĀpŚS. 8, 19, 5; 9, 14, 10; 10, 4, 2; 18, 10, 5; 19, 23, 10. TS. 4, 7, 1, 1 f. in describing the piling of the fire altar, inserts an invocation of both deities: ". . . . come ye with radiance and strength" (*dyumnair vajebhiḥ*), adding the prayer that for the person speaking strength, instigation, influence, thought, inspiration, fame, light, breath, mind, voice, life, and other faculties etc. may be attained by the sacrifice. In the subsequent paragraphs prayers for pre-eminence, victorious power, prosperity, firmness, procreation, wealth, various sorts of food and an abundance of other wishes are subjoined. The same brāhmaṇa, 5, 7, 3, 2, supplies us with the information that "wealth (*vasu-*) is Agni, and this stream (of wealth) is his; wealth is Viṣṇu, this stream is his". — AV. 7, 29, being dedicated to Agni and Viṣṇu, is used by Kauś. 32, 3 in a remedial rite, in Vait. 8, 1 to accompany an offering to these gods at the beginning

[23]) I refer to Geldner, o.c., I, p. 275 f.; II, p. 5; III, p. 122. See also Bergaigne, Rel. Véd. II, p. 416.

[24]) The reader might be referred to W. Caland et V. Henry, L'agniṣṭoma, Paris 1906, p. 15 f.

[25]) Cited by Keith, Rigveda Brahmanas, Harvard 1920, p. 107, n. 2.

[26]) For Agni as all other gods see TS. 6, 2, 2, 6; TB. 3, 2, 8, 10.

of a parvan ceremony. It is also found TS. 1, 8, 22, 1 and ŚŚS. 2, 4, 3.

There may be room here for the observation that Agni is closely allied to the goddess Śrī who is to become Viṣṇu's spouse in later times [27]). ṚV. 1, 72, 10 it is stated that the gods in creating the two eyes of the sky (sun and moon) placed lovely *śrī-* (*śríyam.... cârum*) in Agni; 2, 1, 12 all *śrī-* is to be seen in his excellent outward appearance (*spārhé várṇe*); 10, 45, 5 the god of fire is called "a liberal giver of *śriyaḥ*", etc. etc. [28]). In the Śrīsūkta it is Agni Jātavedas who at the very beginning is invoked to bring near the goddess Lakṣmī; cf. also st. 13 ff.; 18 he is requested to preserve an increasing prosperity; cf. further st. 19; and 20, where Agni, Vāyu, Sūrya, Vasu [29]), Indra, Bṛhaspati, Varuṇa are said to pour or grant possessions. From these frequent connections between Agni and the range of ideas centring in the terms and names *śrī-* and *lakṣmī-* we may derive another argument in favour of the thesis that the relations between the same god and Viṣṇu were based upon community of interests and similarity of activities rather than similarity in their connection with natural phenomena (Viṣṇu being, then, a solar deity and Agni representing a form of the sun [30])). References to an association between Viṣṇu and Savitar, the sun as the stimulator of motion in the universe, are, in a curious manner, almost conspicuous by their absence: 10, 181, 3 the *gharma-*, i.e. the hot milk beverage offered as an oblation to the Aśvins, is by way of mystical speculation described as having been brought from Savitar, Viṣṇu, and the sun (*sūrya-*); see also st. 1 and 2 [31]). In such enumerations of gods as are found in Ṛgvedic sūktas addressed to a variety of deities Savitar and Sūrya appear only in a minority of cases side by side with the god who is the subject of this book: 6, 21, 9; 50, 12 f.; 8, 35, 1; 9, 96, 5 (and, besides, *svar*: 7, 44, 1; 10, 65, 1). These facts contrast in a remarkable manner with the frequent references to Viṣṇu's associations with Indra. The difference of the functions of these gods was, in all probability, not foreign to this. Although the sphere of their activities sometimes coincides with that of Indra and Viṣṇu, the domain and the range of interests common to the two deities mentioned last were, to all appearance, more extended [32]).

---

[27]) See also I. Scheftelowitz, ZDMG. 75 (1921), p. 43, n. 1.

[28]) See ch. II, p. 180.

[29]) Cf. Macdonell, o.c., p. 148.

[30]) See Macdonell, o.c., p. 93.

[31]) See Oldenberg, Religion des Veda³, p. 446 ff.

[32]) Some additional references to passages bearing upon these points may find a place here: TS. 5, 6, 18 (offering to Agni and V., cf. 14 etc.); in the *Viṣṇu-atikrama-* formulas Agni, Indra and the All-gods are mentioned (TS. 3, 5, 3 a-c; cf. also ĀpÇS. 4, 14, 10 a; Baudh.ÇS. 14, 20, and see Keith, Veda Black Yajus

We now come to Viṣṇu's relations with Aditi. In a few passages she is called his consort: VS. 29,60 and TS. 7,5,14, (in formulas accompanying a set of oblations to various deities). They occur in the same context in the mantras accompanying the girding of the sacrificer's wife (VS. 1, 30 etc. [33])): by this act the priest initiates her as her husband's associate in the rite. Aditi here is the earth, represented by this woman. They further appear together in the formulas used in the VS., 2, 2, and explained in the ŚB., 1, 3, 3, 4 f., which are to accompany the pouring of water on the sacrificial grass and the subsequent taking of a bunch of grass: Aditi is stated to be the earth, Viṣṇu the sacrifice. These texts are of some importance because they corroborate the other evidence of the god's relations, and even matrimonial relations with the earth.

Aditi is, indeed, often declared to be the same as the earth: ṚV. 1,72,9; AV. 12,1,61; 13,1,38 and especially ŚB. 5,3,1,4; 7,4,2, 7 [34]). As is well known modern explanations of the 'original character' of the goddess differ widely [35]). There seems, however, to be no occasion for supposing this side of her nature to be a younger development as was suggested by Keith, although the opinion expressed by Pischel [36]) and Hardy [37]) to wit that she essentially was the earth, is too farfetched. The navel [38]) of the earth, Aditi's lap [39]) is the place where an oblation is put down (VS. 1, 11; cf. 4, 30); "on Aditi's head (= the surface of the earth) I sprinkle thee, on the earth's place of sacrifice": 4, 22. In a passage discussed elsewhere the sacrifice in the form of Viṣṇu is related to have entered the earth (TS. 6,2,4,2): because it usually resorted to the lap or bosom of this deity? Aditi is also the great mother; motherhood is her main characteristic. See e.g. JUpBr. 1, 41, 4 ff. In the epic and purāṇic mythology she is the mother of the gods in general, and particularly of Vivasvat, the Sun, and of Viṣṇu

School, p. 280); Agni, Indra, Soma, Sarasvatī, Viṣṇu and the gods: TS. 7, 3, 11, 2 f. — Soma, Agni, Āditya, Viṣṇu, Sūrya, Bṛhaspati ṚV. 10, 141, 3 etc.; cf. e.g. also AVPar. 14, 1, 7; 17, 1, 8; MānGS. 1, 21, 10 etc.

33) *adityai rasnāsi* etc., see Vedic Conc., p. 51. See also s. VII.

34) See also Meyer, o.c., III, p. 233 f. She is also worshipped in housebuilding (Diksitar, Purāṇa Index (1951), p. 44).

35) For a résumé of the main views see Macdonell, o.c., p. 123; Keith, Religion and philosophy, p. 216 f.; F. B. J. Kuiper, De goddelijke moeder in de Voor-Indische religie, Groningen 1939.

36) R. Pischel, in Pischel-Geldner, Vedische Studien II, p. 86.

37) E. Hardy, Die vedisch-brahmanische Periode der Religion des alten Indiens, Münster 1893, p. 94.

38) For the navel concept see section XI.

39) "The bosom of infinite Earth"; R.T.H. Griffith, The texts of the White Yajurveda, Benares 1927, p. 4. — ṚV. 3, 62, 13 speaks of "the lap of *ṛta-*" (*ṛtasya yoni-*).

the Dwarf (Mbh. 3, 272, 62; 13, 83, 26). Aditi can also be another name for Vāk, with whom Sarasvatī[40]) is identified in the brāhmaṇas[41]).

As we have, in the course of our discussions, repeatedly to touch upon the divine earth and her relations with Viṣṇu it may be of some use to enter here into a brief review of some of her main characteristics as far as they may have a bearing upon our subject. In the Veda the Earth[42]) is stated to produce vegetation: ṚV. 5, 84, 1; 3[43]); AV. 3, 23, 6. Hence she is called a mother: 1, 89, 4; VS. 2, 10[44]). She is a place of abode for all the gods: ŚB. 14, 3, 2, 4, and occasionally said to be connected with the Aśvins: 12, 8, 2, 8; with Agni and the creator-god Prajāpati: 6, 2, 3, 1 f. (where plants, cattle, fire are stated to be not separated from the earth); with the sun[45]). She forms a pair with the sky: AV. 3, 23, 6; or with Parjanya: 1, 2, 1; 12, 1, 42; receives the embryo of existence: 5, 25, 2. The earth is Agni's womb: ŚB. 7, 4, 1, 8. The same goddess is Aditi to the gods, Sītā (Viṣṇu-Rāma's wife) to the ploughmen, Earth to the living beings in general (*bhūta-*): Hariv. 58, 18. In the great epic she is also called Gaurī: Mbh. 13, 146, 10. She is the goddess of apsaras and gandharvas: AV. 12, 1, 50; of demons and spirits[46]). The earth constitutes the feet of Viṣṇu as All-god: Mbh. 3, 189, 7. The later epic regards her as belonging to Viṣṇu: Mbh. 3, 200, 127; 13, 91, 25[47]). In another section[48]) it is related how the earth complained to the gods of the nuisance and affliction caused by the asuras, how they applied to Viṣṇu for help and how the god combats the evil powers on her behalf.

In the Hinduistic mythology, for instance in the Varāha myth, in Viṣṇu's marriage with the goddess Bhūmi and in that of his avatāra Rāma with the Furrow (Sītā) the god's relations with various aspects of the earth are crystallized.

Reverting for a moment to Aditi attention may be drawn to another point. Both Viṣṇu and the goddess were, so to say, divinities of width and broadness[49]): for Aditi reference may be made to ṚV. 5, 46, 6; 8, 67, 12. The very character of this representative of motherhood and

---

40) Whose relations with Viṣṇu are discussed in chapter II, II.
41) For other particulars see Macdonell, o.c., p. 121.
42) See also Macdonell, o.c., p. 34. I have reduced references to a minimum.
43) Cf. also Meyer, o.c., I, p. 207 ff. etc.
44) See also Hopkins, Epic Mythology, p. 78.
45) See Meyer, o.c., III, p. 295, l. 1.
46) Hopkins, o.c., p. 79.
47) For the earth and Viṣṇu-brahman: ViPur. 1, 4, 13.
48) See s. XIX.
49) See s. VII; Macdonell, o.c., § 41, al. 3 (see also my 'Ojas', p. 46); cf. ṚV. 5, 2, 7; AV. 12, 5, 15.

freedom [50]) predisposed her to forms of activity corresponding to those in which we find Viṣṇu engaged: generation, extension, 'protection'. I am, however, not able to adduce textual evidence to prove their actual co-operation in these fields.

In the Ṛgveda the number of Aditi's sons, the Ādityas, is once stated to be 7, and once 8 (9, 114, 3; 10, 72, 8). In some brāhmaṇa passages they are 12 (ŚB. 6, 1, 2, 8; 11, 6, 3, 8), Pūṣan, Savitar, Tvaṣṭar and Viṣṇu joining the original group [51]). In the text mentioned last they are said to be the twelve months of the year. Though the youngest Viṣṇu is the most important of them, the Mbh. says: 1, 65, 14 "the best in merit"; 6, 34 (= BhG. 10), 21; and especially, 12, 207, 26 f. *teṣāṃ viṣṇur vāmano 'bhūd govindaś cābhavat prabhuḥ* "amongst them was V. the Dwarf, otherwise called Govinda; he became their principal"; *tasya vikramaṇāc cāpi devānāṃ śrīr vyavardhata.* 3, 80, 2 Viṣṇu is called the refuge of the Ādityas, and 5, 97, 3 he alone is eternal among them. 1, 66, 36 Indra is called the first of the Ādityas (*śakramukhyāḥ*), but the worlds depend upon (*pratiṣṭhitāḥ*) the youngest, Viṣṇu [52]). These passages may reflect the late admission of the then already mighty god to an ancient group [53]). It can, on the other hand, be shown that he maintained relations with this group at an early date: AV. 11, 6, 2 he occurs together with Varuṇa, Mitra, Bhaga, Aṃśa, Vivasvant, — Savitar, Dhātar, Pūṣan, Tvaṣṭar appearing in st. 3, Indra in 1, Aryaman in 4; various other deities are, it is true, also enumerated in 1, 4 and in the following stanzas. As the group of the Ādityas is rather indefinite both as to the number of its members and as to their names, we cannot know for certain if Viṣṇu is 'still' an outsider here. There is room for the hypothesis that particular circles already included him

---

[50]) If, as seems probable, the name Aditi comes from *dā- dyáti* "to bind" this meaning "being loose, freedom", proposed by Oldenberg, o.c., p. 202 f., must in all probability be preferred to such interpretations as "limitless, unlimited, undividedness, Unermeszlichkeit etc.", the root expressing the idea of "binding, fettering" (for the negative form of the word compare the remarks made by J. Wackernagel, Vorlesungen über Syntax, II², Basel 1928, p. 284 ff. and such Skt. words as *abhaya-*, *amṛta-* etc.). We should not consider the term an abstract concept in the traditional sense of the word; see my observations in 'A. Ind. ojas etc.', p. 46 f.

[51]) A convenient résumé of the main data may be found in Macdonell, o.c., p. 43 f.

[52]) Mbh. 5, 98, 13 Varuṇa is called the *jyeṣṭhaḥ śreṣṭhaḥ* of the Ādityas. Cf. e.g. also Nīlamata 350.

[53]) I also refer to the rather speculative explanations in Ruben's Eisenschmiede, p. 283 (Aditi: mutterrechtliche Schicht, Viṣṇu mit den drei Schritten: nördliche schamanistische Komponente, die vor den Ārya aus Innerasien bis in den Dekkhan gelangt ist... vielleicht im Zusammenhang mit Megalithkultur...).

among the members of the group before their number was made to agree with the number of the months.

In the oldest texts Aditi had no husband, later she is the wife of Kaśyapa, the "tortoise", who is mentioned as a creator in the AV., 8, 5, 14 — in the ŚB., 7, 5, 1, 5 Prajāpati is related to have created living beings after having assumed the form of a tortoise (*kūrma-*) —, and to whom the earth was promised by Viśvakarman (AiB. 8, 21, 10) [54]). In post-Vedic literature this figure was, then, considered the father of the twelve Ādityas, and by his other wives, of all kinds of living beings. This form of the creator-god also survives in Viṣṇu's tortoise-avatāra.

Casual references to Viṣṇu and other gods, e.g. Bṛhaspati (ĀpŚS. 16, 29, 2 a, cf. KS. 39, 2) may be passed over in silence.

When other deities came to fuse with Viṣṇu, their names and epithets could pass to him. Thus he is called Yama (Mbh.), occupying this god's post (Mbh. 3, 142, 35 ff.[55])). His names Vāyu, Anila, Pavana, Samīraṇa (Mbh.) were borrowed from the Wind-god, who in the epos was also identified with several other deities (Indra, Kṛṣṇa, Śiva). It is not surprising to come across associations between Viṣṇu and this god who was believed to give rain and to maintain connections with the sunlight [56]).

It would be worth studying the god's relations, in comparatively recent times, with minor deities of local importance. In Benares he is, for instance, associated with Dālbhyeśvara, a divinity supposed to exercise great power on the clouds in procuring rain; who is revered in a cistern, also associated with the goddess of small-pox, Sītalā, and known as "the poor man's friend", causing his poverty to disappear [57]).

XVI. THE GOD'S EXPLOITS.

It is now time to consider the terms in which the ancient Indians viewed the exploits and performances attributed to Viṣṇu in the oldest documents. Although he is no warrior-god and great warlike achievements seem to be foreign to his character mention is often made of his *vīryāṇi* "deeds of manly power or heroism". It is small wonder that this term should be used with reference to his famous three steps:

---

54) See also Macdonell, JAOS. 27, p. 166 f.

55) Cf. J. Hertel, Himmelstore, Leipsic 1924, p. 26 ff. Here the motive of Yama being a partial incarnation of Viṣṇu combines with the boar motive.

56) See Hillebrandt, Ved. Myth.[2] II, p. 297.

57) See M. A. Sherring, The sacred city of the Hindus, London 1868, p. 68.

ṚV. 1, 154, 1 ∾ AV. 7, 26, 1 "I now would speak of the heroic deeds of Viṣṇu who traversed (or: measured) the spaces of the earth, who established the upper abode striding out triply, he the wide-going one"; st. 2 "So Viṣṇu is praised on the strength of his heroic deeds (ṚV.) like a fearful wild beast, wandering, mountain-staying, upon whose three wide out-stridings dwell all beings". The AV. here inserts: "From a far distance may he come hither (cf. ṚV. 10, 180, 2). Id. 6 (= ṚV. 1, 22, 19) "Behold the deeds of Viṣṇu, from where (the deeds evidently being the strides [1]); cf. also AV. 7, 26, 8) he beholds (your, man's) practices (*vratāni*; i.e. whether they follow his ordinances)". ṚV. 1, 155, 4 the god's *pauṃsya-* "manly strength or deed" is extolled: "We praise just this manly deed of his, ...the powerful protector who has widely traversed the terrestrial (spaces) .... unto wide scope for movement, unto life". ṚV. 7, 100, 1 the widely striding Viṣṇu is called *narya-* "manly, strong, heroic". It may, further, suffice to recall here also that he is held to have made his strides for man in distress (ṚV. 6, 49, 13), or to bestow the earth on mankind for a dwelling (7, 100, 4). Compare also ṚV. 6, 69, 5; 8, 77, 10, and especially 1, 154, 2. ṚV. 3, 54, 14 the god is compared to a successful favourite of fortune, if this may be considered the sense of the words *bhágasyeva kāríṇaḥ* [2]): yet the far-stepping giant is described as followed by women, not by warriors. Nor is Agni-and-Viṣṇu's greatness praised on the ground of warlike exploits (AV. 7, 29, 1 f.). When Viṣṇu and Varuṇa are adressed conjointly, the two "who by heroisms are most heroic, most mighty" (*víryair vīrátamā śáviṣṭhā*), mention is made of their establishing or supporting the spaces (7, 25, 1), the next stanza adding that whatever shines and breathes is "in their direction". Viṣṇu, indeed, fixed the earth (ṚV. 7, 99, 3; VS. 5, 16). He is, moreover, in some way or other associated with *tapas* "fervour, fiery energy" in the sacrifice, as Bhaga is with blessings, Tvaṣṭar with the forms, Indra with heroic deeds (AV. 5, 26, 7). AV. 18, 3, 11 he is requested "to anoint wisdom (*medhā*) into the mouth" of the person speaking.

The protecting character of Viṣṇu's activities is emphasized by Sāyaṇa who in commenting upon ṚV. 1, 22, 19 furnishes us with the explanation: *karmāṇi pālanādīni*. His protecting function is, indeed often recorded: ṚV. 3, 55, 10 "Viṣṇu the protector (*gopāḥ*) watches the highest place assuming his dear 'immortal' appearances". Cf. also 1, 22, 18 f. Without negating the qualities of benevolence and guardian-

---

1) In the preceding and following stanzas the three steps are explicitly mentioned.

2) Geldner, o.c., I, p. 398: "eines siegreichen Glückshelden".

ship in the other divinities, we cannot help attaching some importance to the cumulative evidence of such texts as ṚV. 1, 186, 10 "Viṣṇu who is not malevolent" (*adveṣa-*), i.e. "benevolent"; 7, 100, 2 "Do thou, ...Viṣṇu, favour us with thine universal benevolence (*sumati-*) and thine attentive concern, in order bountifully to grant us abundant prosperity (*suvita-*) and wealth consisting of horses and much brilliant (metal)"; 1, 156, 5 his kind disposition is said to surpass Indra's benevolence. Cf. also 8, 25, 12. VS. 1, 4 he is invoked to be the protector of the oblation [3]). ṚV. 8, 31, 10 the protection is implored of the mountains, the rivers and Viṣṇu, the "associate" or "companion" ("Beisteher" Geldner: *sacābhū-*). Other relevant passages are 6, 49, 13; 7, 100, 4; 1, 154, 2; 4; ŚB. 4, 2, 2, 10 "May Viṣṇu guard thee with his power (*indrya-*)". In the AiB., 3, 38, 3, the god, inter alia, protects the sacrifice preventing its defects from producing any consequences. He is also the protector of embryos: ṚV. 7, 36, 9.

The same observation may be made with regard to various episods of the epics, however much his character had developed in the early post-Vedic times. It was Nārāyaṇa who caused the ocean to be churned in order to obtain the amṛta (Mbh. 1, a. 18, Viṣṇu-Nārāyaṇa who, disguised as a woman, recovered the divine draught from the asuras (a. 19). "In former times he pervaded the three worlds in three strides, procuring the amṛta and destroying the asuras; he suppressed the great asura Bali and raised Indra to the throne of heaven, he is the lord of the gods, and this entire universe is pervaded by him", these words (5, 10, 6 ff.) may justly be considered as summarizing the main acts of kindness and benevolence performed by the god in the interest of both mankind and the universe. It was Viṣṇu who (3, 101, 10 ff.) bestowed his energy (*tejas*) on Indra, enhanced his prowess and protected him (*viṣṇunā gopitaṃ śakram*); Viṣṇu who (3, 204, 13) fillled Kuvalāśva with his energy (*aviśat.... tejasā*) with the object of doing good to the three worlds (*lokānāṃ hītakāmyayā*); Viṣṇu who by his willingness to assume human form (e.g. Rām. 1, s. 15 f.) time after time extends his sympathy and kindness to the good and virtuous. It is a matter of common knowledge that Hinduism often laid special emphasis upon this protecting and conserving aspects of the god's nature. The epos (Mbh. 6, 67, 17) calls him the protector (*bhartṛ-*) of the gods and the gods and the universe (3, 102, 20), the father and the mother of all living creatures, the purāṇas the guardian of the world, and the great poets never tire of describing his readiness to protect humanity and his condescension in being born for the salvation of the world (see e.g.

[3]) See also section III.

Kāl. Ragh. 10, 25; 31)[4]. Viṣṇu upholds the universe, he is the Lokādhiṣṭhāna (Mbh. 13, a. 149). Viṣṇu, that is to say: "le conservateur de toutes choses"[5]. In the above Vedic texts these Hinduistic functions are already anticipated. They can also contribute to our understanding of the fact that it should have been this god who became the centre of the sentiments and movements usually indicated by the term *bhakti-*.

Thus Viṣṇu, having risen to the position of the Highest Being and being revered as the creator, protector, and destroyer of the gods and the universe is, apart from his avatāras and heroic exploits in destroying the enemies of gods and men, in the epic and purāṇic mythology constantly praised on account of the yeoman service he always renders to the world: he restores peace by destroying all evil, he preserves the dharma and the bounds of morality and propriety. He is the source of happiness for all men (Mbh. 3, 189, 34). Permeating everything in the universe he fills it with his energy called *vikrama-* (12, 47, 88). Being ever occupied in achieving the salvation of the world (7, 29, 26), he assumes a variety of forms and bodies. He becomes food, drink, and fuel, and keeps up the existence of the beings by multiplying their vital powers (12, 47, 71). All that is manifestation of might and abundance, spiritual essence and energy, prosperity and illustriousness, strength and importance has arisen from, or owes its existence to its being, an integral part of Viṣṇu's fiery energy (*yad yad vibhūtimat sattvaṃ śrīmad ūrjitam eva vā | tad tad evāvagacchadvaṃ viṣṇos tejo'ṃśasambhavam* BḍPur. 2, 3, 121 f.; VāPur. 66, 140; practically identical with BhG. 10, 41)[6].

In Śivaitic texts which acknowledge Śiva as their Supreme God Viṣṇu is also represented as a very mighty divinity. Thus, Viṣṇu-Nārāyaṇa is held to be the best among the gods (*surāḥ*), and to be the creator of the universe (though he himself owes his existence to Śiva). All the gods are pervaded by him. His world is even said to be

---

[4]) In describing the manifold nature of the Supreme God Kālidāsa obviously follows the purāṇas or similar storehouses of tradition. See Bh. S. Upadhyaya, India in Kālidāsa, Allahabad 1947, p. 305 ff. — Mention must also be made of such stories as are found in the Mbh. 3, a. 102 f.; 12, a. 65; a. 122 where Viṣṇu helps, gives advice, creates beneficent institutions etc.

[5]) J. A. Dubois, Moeurs, institutions et cérémonies des peuples de l'Inde, nouvelle édition, Pondichéry 1921, II, p. 254; 368. — See also Bh. Kumarappa, The Hindu conception of the deity, London 1934, p. 86 ff. who calls Viṣṇu "the god of helpfulness".

[6]) Purāṇas often ascribe to Viṣṇu the possession of all vibhūtis (e.g. ViPur. 3, 1, 46). *Çrīmat-* is already in the Mbh. one of his favourite epithets (e.g. 5, 111, 7).

the best goal. In accounts of the creation of the universe Viṣṇu is often identified with Brahmā, who in his turn is called Nārāyaṇa.

A god who for many centuries gains in importance and assembles ever-growing numbers of devotees is apt to absorb cults and forms of adoration, myths and characteristics of other gods. He will easily assume qualities belonging to any great god. After his identification with the One and Supreme (cf. e.g. Mbh. 12, 48, 17) any quality of a Highest Idea or Being could be attributed to Viṣṇu [7]): he is the creator of the world, the founder of all-important institutions, the guide and goal of humanity, the regulator of the cosmic processes.

Yet, it cannot be regarded as a matter of mere chance that it was Viṣṇu who rose to such a high position. It was not only his ancient friendship with Indra which paved his way for gaining a paramount status. There must have been essential features in his character which enabled, and so to say predisposed, him to do so. One of these was his unremitting concern with man's weal and woe, another his interest in the furtherance of, and his association with, the useful energy given out by the sun and in the atmosphere in general, and his co-operation in annihilating the destructive influences.

In studying the god's character one will, indeed, witness a development of fighting spirit on his part. Demons and similar evil beings which in earlier times were regarded as special enemies of Indra are eventually combated and destroyed by Viṣṇu. Thus the asura Namuci [8]), who is always described as being slain by Indra in the Veda and the Mahābhārata, is according to the compilators of the purāṇas, e.g. Bḍ. 2, 73, 81 f.; Vā. 98, 81, killed by his former assistant. In the same texts Viṣṇu destroys Śambara who in the Veda was struck down from a great mountain by Indra, although he is once (ṚV. 7, 99, 4 f.) said to have been defeated by both gods conjointly. In the Mahābhārata he is vanquished by Indra, Kṛṣṇa, or Pradyumna, the son of Kṛṣṇa and Rukmiṇī. Prahrāda, who was defeated by Indra in the great epic, was slain by Viṣṇu in the above purāṇas; cf. e.g. also Saurapur. 28, 17 ff. Similar remarks might be made with regard to the demon Tāraka (e.g. Brahmapur. a. 71). In other narratives gods or men are related to have applied to Viṣṇu for help against the demons: Mbh. 3, 101 ff. Indra, it is true, defeats Vṛtra, but he is so afraid of the demon and his supporters, the Kāleyas, that he immediately asks Viṣṇu for protection. Favoured by Viṣṇu he becomes more powerful; Vṛtra is slain, but Viṣṇu's intervention is needed before the Kāleyas can be conquered [9]).

---

[7]) See also W. Ruben, Krishna, Istanbul 1943, p. 36 ff.

[8]) I refer to Macdonell, o.c., p. 161 f.

[9]) Demons slain by Viṣṇu are, e.g.: Jambha (Mbh. 3, 102, 24; elsewhere he is

These and similar deeds give evidence of, and contributed to, his increasing popularity. Even Vṛtra becomes a devotee of Viṣṇu and ascended, when killed, to his highest region (Mbh. 12, 283, 60 f.).

In the ŚB., 7, 5, 1, 25, the term Viṣṇu's deeds (*karmāṇi*) occurring VS., 13, 33 is explained as "power, valour, heroism" (*vīryam*); cf. 3, 5, 3, 21. Also in ṚV. 1, 154, 1; 2 and AV. 7, 26, 1; 2 the same word which refers to the faculty, or deeds, of manly vigour and heroism, is used. The epos in which *tejas* "fiery energy, ardour, energy, spirit, efficacy; spiritual, moral, or magical power or influence, etc." naturally was an oft mentioned quality of kings, warriors and ascetics[10]), ascribes this power not only to gods like Agni and Sūrya, but also to Viṣṇu and Kṛṣṇa. Cf. Mbh. 3, 202, 29 f.: he who will kill the wicked asura Dhundhu (who at the end of every year wakes up and by breathing causes the earth to tremble and the sun to be covered by clouds of sand) will be pervaded by the *tejas* of Viṣṇu himself, which is hardly to be borne by any other on earth. 3, 101, 10 Viṣṇu enhances Indra's prowess by imparting to him his own *tejas*. Viṣṇu is *amitatejas-:* 12, 283, 60. Mbh. 3, 99, 64 Rāma Bhārgava (Paraśurāma) bows to his namesake Rāma Dāśarathi who is in possession of Viṣṇu's *tejas*. Cf. also Bh.G. 10, 41 and 15, 12.

This is a convenient place to mention the frequent references to Viṣṇu's 'invincibility'. The term *aparājita-* "unconquered" which in the Ṛgveda is given to Indra-and-Agni and to the victorious Indra (1, 11, 2) to indicate their invincibility — 5, 25, 6 it is an epithet of the term "conqueror" — and which in the Atharvaveda applies to the world of the gods (5, 30, 17), to a stronghold (10, 2, 33), an amulet (8, 5, 22), and a physician who slays the snakes (10, 4, 15) is in the brāhmaṇas an epithet of Indra's world (śāB. 20, 1), of that part of the universe where Āditya, the Sun, dwells (JB. 1, 334), of the north-eastern quarter, where the gods were not conquered by the asuras (AiB. 1, 14, 5); ChUp. 8, 5, 3 brahman's stronghold is called *aparājita-*[11]). In the Mbh. the epithet applies to Viṣṇu: 3, 102, 19; 13, 149, 89; 105, likewise in later texts. Another epithet of his, occurring e.g. in the VP. and the Rām. is *Ajita-* "invicible"; in the Hariv. he is called *Ajaya-*. He is *Jiṣṇu-* on the strength of his victoriousness (*jayād jiṣṇuḥ* Mbh. 5, 70, 13). In the minor upaniṣads, purāṇas, and other texts this quality

slain by Kṛṣṇa, Nara-Arjuna, Indra), and the famous Madhu and Kaiṭabha. In general, see e.g. 8, 51, 54; 73, 57 ff. where his demon-slaying activities appear to be a matter of common knowledge.

[10]) J. Ph. Vogel, Het sanskrit woord *tejas*..., Amsterdam 1930.

[11]) Other instances of the use of the verb *jayati* are e.g. found TS. 5, 2, 1, 1 *yad viṣṇukramān kramate viṣṇur eva bhūtvā yajamānaś chandobhir imāṃ lokān anapajayyam abhi jayati*; 1, 7, 5, 4; 2, 1, 2, 3 etc.

of the god is also alluded to [12]). "The god of gods Janārdana is invincible (*ajeya-*) in the three worlds", the SauraP. 31, 60 holds. Now, "invincibility" means permanent victoriousness. We cannot help remembering the idea expressed by the phrase *Sol invictus*. Viṣṇu was always connected with the sun, as e.g. may appear from the dhyānaśloka: *dhyeyaḥ sadā savitṛmaṇḍalamadhyavartī* etc., from the worship of Sūrya Nārāyaṇa [13]), from the occurrence of an image of the sun where we might expect an avatāra of Viṣṇu etc. [14]). It is the sun which in its daily course suggests immortality in the primitive sense of an endless continuation of phenomenal life. That is not to say that that luminary was always present to the mind of those who addressed the god with one of the above epithets. The god who could be called *avyaya-* "imperishable" etc. could easily be addressed with similar names without any such association. — We should not omit mentioning that according to Rāmānuja (on BhG. 18, 43) the very *tejas* attributed to God implies the idea of his invincibility: *parair anabhibhavanīyatā* [15])

XVII. THE AVATĀRAS.

The next point to which I would now draw attention concerns Viṣṇu's avatāras. The phenomenon of the god's multiformity, metamorphosis and reincarnation in itself is no matter of great surprise, as similar adventures were also attributed to other gods. Indra, from whom Viṣṇu borrowed some of his features, was especially the god who wandered about in many forms (cf. ṚV. 6, 47, 18): a well-known characteristic of gods concerned with the processes of fertilization, and one shared by Agni and Rudra. Indra could assume the form of a ram, of a bull (e.g. ṚV. 1, 55, 4; cf. 1. 9, 4); Varuṇa coming out of the point of an arrow, presented the appearance of a bull (Mbh. 8, 34, 101) In a comparable way, Viṣṇu transformed his own self into Daṇḍa. Punishment (Mbh. 12, 122, 24).

Among the god's 'primary' avatāras the forms of boar, man-lion, dwarf, and tortoise were the foremost. The former three in the classic series are in a striking way theriomorphous, and the five after the man-

---

12) See e.g. Hohenberger, o.c., p. 106 and 178.

13) See also J. N. Banerjee, IA. 54 (1925), p. 161 ff.; D. P. Pandey, Sūrya, Leyden 1939, Introd.

14) See Nihar-ranjan Ray, Brahmanical gods in Burma, Univ. of Calcutta 1932, p. 43. See e.g. also Crooke, Pop. rel. and folkl. I, p. 5.

15) Compare also the use of the epithet *anihata-* "unconquered" in the Ghosundi inscription (1st cent. B.C.) in connection with Vāsudeva and Saṃkarṣaṇa.

lion are anthropomorphous [1]). In the animal manifestations the well-known motive of the animal aiding or assisting man was given a more universal and elevated application. In general the Viṣṇuite avatāras have essentially diverged from the primitive motive of a god descending to the earth [2]). The god is born each time for a specific purpose. When the dharma is not followed Viṣṇu appears on earth in one of his avatāras for the rescue of the good, for the preservation of the world and its culture, for the destruction of the evil-doers and the establishment of dharma (see BhG. 4, 7 ff.) [3]).

Although particulars may be a matter of opinion, we can be sure that various stories and motives regarding transformations and adventures have co-operated in composing the Viṣṇuite cycle of avatāras. Part of these did not originally belong to Viṣṇu. Thus his theriomorphous appearance as a swan or flamingo (*haṃsa-*) [4]) seems to have been borrowed from ancient speculations in connection with this bird, which was identified with the sun, with Agni, with the soul etc.[5]). It is usually assumed that the elements of the fish avatāra were suggested by the story of Manu who was saved from a flood by a great horned fish (ŚB. 1, 8, 1, 1 ff). But how far did the characteristics of this animal — it symbolizes growth because of its rapid reproduction — and such speculations as gave it a place in the religious conceptions of other peoples contribute to its becoming a manifestation of the High God Viṣṇu? And what is — to give another instance — the element of 'historical truth' in the tradition preserved in the Viṣṇupurāṇa (5, a. 38) that the gopīs, the wives of Kṛṣṇa were the apsarases who had been cursed by the ascetic Aṣṭāvakra? Terrestrial divinities of female sex are again and again the partners of the god's avatāras: Sītā, Satyabhāmā, Kṛṣṇa's wife who was considered a partial embodiment (*aṃśa-*) of the goddess Earth. Viṣṇu's relations with the earth are, indeed, a very important element in the avatāra conception which in its classical form may be regarded as a more exalted development of the

---

1) I also refer to E. Abegg, Der Messiasglaube in Indien und Iran, Berlin-Leipsic 1928, p. 40 ff. and 141. See also Hohenberger, o.c., p. 118 ff. — In the epic period the theory of avatāras was still developing. The Mbh. has no systematic account of them. In its appendix, the Harivaṃśa, the list is not yet that of the well-known series. See e.g. Hohenberger, o.c., p. 122 ff. Even in purāṇas we come across lists of avatāras other than the classic ten. Apart from these *tanūs* "bodies, embodiments" of the god are mentioned.

2) See also the observations made by W. Ruben, Krishna, Istanbul 1943, p. 48 f.

3) In a more popular form this doctrine is already foreshadowed in such texts as Mbh. 3, 272, 51 "assuming what form shall I rescue the earth from water?"

4) See Abegg, o.c., p. 41; 70.

5) See e.g. Macdonell, Ved. Myth., p. 185; Hopkins, Ep. Myth., p. 244; Meyer, o.c., III, p. 5 f.; Hohenberger, o.c., p. 115.

god's helpful and loving interest in our planet and its occupants. The avatāras not seldom proved to be, in the history of the Indian people, living myths: because for instance the re-establishment of a definite country resembled the renowned deed of Viṣṇu's boar-incarnation it was henceforth called *Kroḍadeśa-* "Hog-country" [6]). The power inherent in the myth manifested itself once again [7]).

XVIII. THE TORTOISE; THE CHURNING OF THE OCEAN.

After the collections of data concerning the character of the tortoise published by Meyer [1]) and Ruben [2]) Viṣṇu's second avatāra hardly needs comment. The animal played, and still plays, an important rôle in the cosmogonic, cosmographic, and genealogical conceptions of Indian peoples. It is, to begin with, often believed to serve as a fun-

---

[6]) M. N. Srinivas, Religion and society among the Coorgs of S. India, Oxford 1952, p. 245.

[7]) Some of the avatāras gave occasion for speculations on ethnic substrata, geographical names etc. (see e.g. A. P. Karmarkar, The Matsyāvatāra of Viṣṇu, Festschrift Kane, p. 253 ff.) which we cannot consider here.

In accordance with the conception of Viṣṇu's pervasiveness — which no doubt largely contributed to his ascendancy in the high position of God and personal aspect of brahman which is expressly defined as all-pervasive — is the comparatively late theory of his āveśas. The Pāñcarātra philosophers hold that Viṣṇu's manifestations are of various character. The so-called *āveśāvatāra-* is either a *svarūpāveśa-* (as in the case of the avatāras like Rāma) or a *śaktyāveśa-* (when there is an influx of special powers or functions of God). These āveśas are by God's will produced in the form of human beings, animals, trees. Other manifestations, *sākṣādavatārāḥ*, are of a transcendent nature, being derived directly from the Supreme Being just as a lamp is lighted from another. As the term *āveśa-* expresses such ideas as "entering, taking possession (often of states of mind taking possession of a person), devotedness to an object, obsession (by evil spirits)" the underlying idea is clear. (For particulars see: F. O. Schrader, Introd. to the Pāñcarātra, Madras 1916; S. Dasgupta, Hist. of Ind. Phil. III, p. 38 f.; M. Das Gupta, IHQ. 8, p. 64 ff.).

A few words may be said on the well-known passage BhG. 10, 19 ff., where Kṛṣṇa, the Bhagavat enumerates his prominent *vibhūtis* or 'manifestations'. Although the tenor is to show that the Lord, though omnipresent and manifesting himself everywhere, is especially identical with the most eminent individuals of their respective classes, it may strike us that many figures and entities occurring in the list may have been living realities to the mind of the Indians of that period (see also Radhakrishnan, Bhag., p. 263). They play also an important rôle in early Viṣṇuism: the Bhagavat is, inter alia, identified with Viṣṇu, the sun, Indra, Kubera, Agni, the aśvattha, Nārada, the king, the vajra, Kāma, Vāsuki, Ananta, Varuṇa, Garuḍa, Rāma, Vāsudeva etc. One might be tempted to conclude that the author in drawing up this list made ample use of existing 'identifications' of a god who in Viṣṇuite circles had already much advanced in his career towards the position of a Highest Being.

[1]) Meyer, o.c., III, p. 221 ff.

[2]) Ruben, Eisenschmiede, p. 241 ff.

dament on which the earth rests. It warrants the stability of the world [3]). The purāṇic account of Viṣṇu supporting India in the form of a tortoise (MārkPur. 58) may, like the god's appearance in the shape of this animal to be the base or pivot of the mountain Mandara when the gods and asuras churned the ocean (Kūrma-avatāra), be considered a Viṣṇuite adaptation of an old mythical function attributed to the animal in popular belief: in Rām. S. 1, 45 and ViPur. 1, 9, 87 the tortoise is Viṣṇu, in Mbh. 1, 18, 11 f.; Rām. N. rec. (G. 1, 46) and elsewhere it is not (not yet) identified with the god. This aiding and supporting function of the tortoise coincided with the conceptions entertained by Viṣṇu's devotees of the purpose and significance of the god's incarnations to such a degree that they could identify the animal of folklore with their god in the phenomenal form of a helpful living being. Other beliefs regarding the tortoise may have contributed to this identification. Its shells are sky and earth, what is between the shells, the air; it thus is these worlds (ŚB. 7, 5, 1, 2). Viṣṇu on the other hand, was rather early associated with the three divisions of the universe (cf. e.g. also Mbh. 5, 10, 6 ff). In ancient mythology the tortoise belonged to Varuṇa, the lord of the waters; it was the lord of the waters (ŚB. 7, 5, 1, 9) [4]). It did duty for Varuṇa himself lying as a husband beside a representative of the earth (ŚB. 7, 5, 1, 6; cf. 6, 5, 3, 1). Viṣṇu is also the earth's husband. The tortoise is also able to exert fertilizing influences [5]). In accordance with the nature of the animal Kaśyapa "the Tortoise" enters the earth (Mbh. 13, a. 154). The tortoise was, moreover, considered the father of all creatures, and Prajāpati, in creating, assumed the form of this reptile (ŚB. 7, 5, 1, 5). It is able to draw in all its limbs and serves, in later times (e.g. MārkPur. 39, 33 f.) as a model for the man who wishes to repress all emotions and to restrain the activities of his senses, "always delighted in soul, self-collected, and seeing soul in soul". Has this curious habit of the reptile, in addition to other factors, led man to consider it 'breath' or 'life' of the world (cf. ŚB. 7, 5, 1, 7; 1), and a representative of the self-sufficient High God and Universal Soul? Whatever causes have contributed to this result, it is not surprising that this queer animal, which always played so important a part in folklore, should have become a representative of the aiding and supporting Viṣṇu at the moment he enabled the gods to acquire the draught of life.

---

[3]) Ruben, o.c., and Liter. vorar. Stämme Indiens, p. 52; Kramrisch, Hindu temple, p. 111; 113.

[4]) Meyer's opinion (p. 222), that Varuṇa originally was nothing but a tortoise cannot be substantiated.

[5]) For particulars see Meyer, o.c., p. 222.

A brief comment on the famous event, the churning of the ocean, will not be out of place here. The churning staff is, according to the various versions of the story, the 'immeasurable' Meru [6]) or a similar mountain, the Mandara, or also Śiva's liṅga, all of them representing the axis of the world [7]). The basis of this axis is in Further India sometimes placed in a *kumbha-* [8]). It is made to rest on the tortoise or Viṣṇu, who thus occupies the centre of the world. The snake Ananta, a manifestation of Nārāyaṇa (Mbh. 1, 18, 15) serves as a rope. The beings and objects arisen from the ocean are also highly significant. There is some variety in the order and number of articles [9]), but among them are the moon, i.e. the lord of plants, which is closely connected with fertility, vegetative life, and the souls of the deceased [10]); ghee which is of an erotic and magic character, identified with *retas* and used in fertility ceremonies [11]); Śrī-Lakṣmī sitting on a lotus and holding a water-lily in her hand; Surā or Vāruṇī, the goddess representing spirituous liquor — which is usually drunk on the occasion of religious festivities [12]) —; the great horse and the *kaustubha*-jewel which are discussed in other sections of this book; the *pārijāta-* or coral tree (erythrina indica), the delight of the nymphs of heaven which perfumes the world with its blossoms and which served as an aphrodisiac (Varāh. BS. 77, 37) on the strength of its presumed 'erotic' i.e. fecundating character; the apsarases, fertility spirits who are not seldom mentioned as a kind of Indian houris of paradise [13]); Surabhi the renowned cow of plenty, a very fountain of milk and curds; Dhanvantari the instructor in medical science and divine physician; the amṛta itself, to gain which the churning was undertaken; the elephant Airāvata which came to be Indra's vehicle; sometimes also the tulasi; the bow and conch of Viṣṇu; the famous ear-rings of Aditi [14]); the white horse of the sun; and the umbrella taken by Varuṇa, which are likewise objects of an auspicious character.

Another observation was made by Miss Auboyer [15]) with regard to

---

[6]) I refer to W. Kirfel, Die Kosmographie der Inder, Bonn-Leipsic 1920, p. 375; 379.

[7]) See section X.

[8]) I refer to Auboyer, Trône, p. 97.

[9]) See e.g. ViPur. 1, a. 9; Wilson-Hall, o.c., I, p. 146 ff.; Baldaeus, o.c., p. 47 ff.

[10]) See Meyer, o.c. III, p. 311.

[11]) Ibidem, p. 319.

[12]) Compare also the use of spirits in the vājapeya and in wedding ceremonies (see Meyer, o.c., III, p. 184).

[13]) For particulars see Meyer, o.c., III, p. 288, and Sexual life in ancient India, London 1930, p. 568.

[14]) See section XV.

[15]) Auboyer, o.c., p. 96 ff., to which I refer for particulars.

this event which impresses us as a creation myth. When the churning staff is turned round, the Khmer iconography of Further India makes Viṣṇu ascend to the top of it on which is Brahmā's seat. This must be, the French scholar holds, a representation of the god traversing the universe.

XIX. THE BOAR.

The next point to be discussed concerns the very important *varāha*-avatāra. Viṣṇu, as a boar, delivered the world from the power of a demon called Hiraṇyākṣa, who had seized the earth and carried it down into the lowest depths of the sea. The god, after having dived into the abyss slew the monster and raised the earth. Before entering into a discussion of this myth in connection with the character of the god it may be useful here to expatiate upon the rôle played by boars and pigs in popular belief, the more so as some particulars bearing upon this point do not — as far as ancient India is concerned — seem to have been explained in a satisfactory way.

Much has been written on the pig — which may, generally speaking, be called the animal of the farmer and the planter — and on the boar which can justly claim to be one of the bravest wild animals and one of the best-armed [1]). In the folklore of the peoples of central and northern Europe the grunting hogs and boars which root and grub in the earth were very often believed to represent storm- or thunder clouds, cyclones etc. Their tusks were identified with lightning [2]). They were also supposed to be on friendly terms with evil powers such as witches. With the Celts and the Germans they were apt to be regarded in a sinister light and might well be the embodiment of demoniac beings, haunting and walking about [3]). They are supposed to know about the weather and to have foreknowledge of it. Sometimes they are "Seelentier". Often parts of their bodies are used in popular

[1]) Compare e.g. J. G. Frazer, Spirits of the corn etc., = The Golden Bough V, 1, London 1912, p. 298 ff., and passim; L. Herold, s.v. Schwein, in Handwörterbuch d. deutschen Aberglaubens VII, Leipsic 1935 f., 1470 ff.; O. Schrader, in Hastings' Encycl. of Rel. and Ethics II, 38; and other books and papers to be mentioned in the following notes.

[2]) See also W. Mannhardt, Die Korndämonen, Berlin 1868. In Indian texts the grunting or roaring of the boar is often mentioned and sometimes compared to the sound of thunder-clouds: cf. Mbh. 3, 272, 54 Viṣṇu assumes the form of a boar roaring like big clouds and being as black as these.

[3]) See e.g. J. A. Macculloch, Celtic myths, in L. H. Gray, The myths of all races, III, Boston 1918, p. 126; E. Hull, Folklore of the British isles, London 1928, p. 144 ff.

medicine, love spells, or in magic intended to promote fertility. These animals are, indeed, almost generally held to concern themselves with fertility and agriculture. This inter alia appears from the wide-spread belief that a boar or a sow is the animal embodiment of the spirit of the corn. In Germany and other countries bounded by the Baltic the last of the harvest is called the Rye-boar; it gives occasion for songs praying for plenty of food and other good things. The corn-spirit in the form of a pig — which is believed to have a fertilizing power — plays his part also in sowing-rites: as a pig he is put in the ground at sowing-time [4]). In the customs connected with the Scandinavian Yule boar the corn-spirit, immanent in the last sheaf, is held to appear at mid-winter in the form of a boar made from the corn of that sheaf; part of it is given to the ploughman and his cattle to eat, in the conviction that it will exert a quickening influence on the crops. — These animals often were symbolical of 'Wachstumskraft' to such a degree that solemn vows intended to promote luck and fortune were made over their heads, that the god of agriculture Freyr and his sister Freyja had their special boars [5]), and that they were thought to be closely connected with the goddess of the clouds whose task it was to fecundate the earth. "Mit (der mütterlichen Göttin Erde) steht das Schwein einmal als 'Symbol' [6]) der Fruchtbarkeit und dann um seiner erdaufwühlenden Natur willen in nächster Beziehung" [7]). — In the Celtic world they were also connected with the spirits of the earth [8]).

Although in ancient Greece the boar was sacrificed on various occasions it was especially sacred to Demeter and Dionysus whose concern again was agriculture. In the mysteries of these deities pigs were regularly sacrificed [9]). It may be observed that the flesh of the animals offered to chthonian gods was not eaten; their blood had to fall on the earth to be absorbed by it. The Greeks were also acquainted

---

[4]) I also refer to the data mentioned by Frazer, o.c., p. 300 f.

[5]) For particulars see Herold, Handwtb. d. deutschen Aberglaubens II, 1929 f., 517 ff. For Freyja now see E. Tonnelat, La religion des Germains, in Mana, Introduction à l'histoire des religions, II Les religions de l'Europe ancienne, III, Paris 1948, p. 373; De Vries, o.c., II, Register, p. 446, s.v. (p. 98; 268 ff.).

[6]) For obvious reasons I have put this term in inverted commas.

[7]) U. Jahn, Die deutschen Opfergebräuche bei Ackerbau und Viehzucht, Breslau 1884, p. 106.

[8]) See Hull, l.c.; see also J. Rhys, Celtic folklore, Oxford 1901, II, p. 500 f. — Compare also Chantepie de la Saussaye, Bertholet-Lehmann, Lehrbuch der Religionsgeschichte[4], II, p. 536; 589; 606; 616; J. Vendryes, in Mana (see n. 5) II, III, p. 281 f.

[9]) Orth in Paulys Real-Encyclopädie der classischen Altertumswissenschaft, ed. by G. Wissowa and W. Kroll, s.v. Schwein (II, 2, Stuttgart 1923); M. P. Nilsson, Geschichte der griechischen Religion, I, München 1941, p. 628; O. Kern, Die Religion der Griechen, I, Berlin 1926, p. 159.

with the custom to swear by a pig. An interesting ceremony is the 'Eidopfer' described by Homer, Il. 19, 250 ff.: a wild boar is slaughtered as an offering to Zeus, the Earth (*Γῆ*), the Sun, and the Erinys (the avengers of perjury). Of greater relevance to our argument is the much discussed rite in connection with the *μέγαρα*, or pits sacred to Demeter and Persephone: At the moment when Pluto carried off Persephone a swineherd chanced to be herding his swine on the spot, and his herd was engulfed in the chasm down which the god had vanished with the young goddess. In commemoration of this fact young pigs were annually, at the Thesmophoria — a women's festival in honour of Demeter —, let down into caverns. Afterwards the decayed remains of these animals, and of cakes and other objects, were fetched by women called *ἀντλήτριαι* ("they who draw up") who descended into the caverns and brought up these remains. Whoever got a piece of the decayed flesh and cakes and mixed it with the seed-corn which he was to sow in his field, believed himself to be sure of a good crop [10]). The objects thrown into the pits together with the pigs were imitations of the male sexual organ made of dough, snakes, and twigs with pine-cones, all of them being well-known ingredients in fertility rites [11]). — A hog was, further, remarkably enough, one of the animals which nursed the young Zeus, the god who, in a way typical of deities concerned with vegetation, according to the Cretan belief, was periodically reborn [12]).

The Roman author Varro (De re rustica 2, 4), in discussing harvest and marriage customs, mentions also the sacrificial boar. At harvest time the Roman peasant offered a female pig to Tellus, the goddess of the earth, and to Ceres, who presided over the growth of the crops. The slaughtering of the so-called *porca praecidanea,* offered to these goddesses conjointly had a double purpose: it served as an introductory rite to the harvest and as an expiatory ceremony intended for the deceased who, as is well known, maintain close relations with the powers controlling fertility [13]). In celebrating the ludi saeculares a pregnant swine was immolated [14]).

In ancient Egypt pigs and their relatives were from the ritual point of view impure. Yet, a more original attitude towards these animals

---

[10]) See e.g. Nilsson, o.c., I, p. 109; J. E. Harrison, Prolegomena to the study of Greek religion, Cambridge 1903, p. 123 ff.

[11]) I refer to Nilsson, o.c., I, p. 109.

[12]) For Zeus, see Eliade, Traité d'histoire des religions, p. 78 f.; Nilsson I, p. 198; 297 f. See also Nilsson in Chantepie de la Saussaye, o.c., II, p. 319 f.; O. Kern, Die Religion der Griechen, I, Berlin 1925, p. 16.

[13]) For particulars see also G. Wissowa, Religion und Kultus der Römer², München 1912, p. 193.

[14]) See also L. Deubner, in Chantepie de la Saussaye, o.c., II, p. 470.

is still recognizable: once they were regarded as representatives of 'fortune' and associated with the great goddess Isis, or what may have been the preceding stage, with Nut, the sky-goddess who was at the same time a mother-deity [15]).

Although we cannot always know for certain that the pig, which is very often the cheapest and most common animal, is offered up because it is, or was, associated with fertility, agriculture etc., attention may, further, be drawn to the wide area of occurrence of pig and boar ceremonies, offerings, rites — during pregnancy, on behalf of the deceased, in connection with sowing and reaping, in taking an oath, etc. — and of various beliefs with reference to these animals in many other parts of the world. In the island of Borneo the bridal couple is for the sake of offspring smeared with the blood of pigs or with a mixture of eggs, water, earth, and pig's blood, materializing prosperity, wealth, and fertility [16]). In the, likewise Indonesian, island of Savu black pigs are sacrificed in order to obtain rain, red ones when the rice is being planted [17]). The inhabitants of the Sandwich-islands sacrifice a pig to allay the evil consequences of a volcanic eruption [18]). On various occasions religious swine festivals are celebrated by the Papuas of New Guinea, who consider these ceremonies as an indicium of prosperity [19]).

We saw above that, apart from its prolificacy, the boar's well-known habit of rooting up the soil must have induced man to associate this animal with the fertility of the earth. Although there seems to be ample room for other considerations — the wild pig and the boar usually do great damage to the crops so that they have to be conciliated for the sake of a successful harvest — the popular belief concerning the rooting snout seems to be, in connection with our argument, a matter of special interest. In Lithuania the earth is held to bring forth like a

---

15) I refer to H. Kees, Der Götterglaube im alten Aegypten, Mitteilungen Vorderasiat. - Aeg. Gesellschaft 45, Leipsic 1941, p. 70 ff., and to W. R. Dawson, in JRAS. 1928, p. 597.

16) G. A. Wilkens, Verspreide geschriften, Semarang 1912, I, p. 544, n. 48. The theories underlying the author's expositions have gone much out of date.

17) Ibidem, III, p. 179 f. See further also I, p. 104; II, p. 149; 497; III, p. 28 f.

18) Ibidem, III, p. 495. In the northern part of Celebes (Minahasa) a boar is considered to cause earthquakes. As this animal is represented as carrying the earth (ibidem III, p. 277), Hindu influence may have led to this particular boar-conception. In India a common explanation of earthquakes is that *varāha-*, the boar who supports our planet, is changing its burden from one tusk to the other (cf. e.g. W. Crooke, The popular belief and folklore of Northern-India, I, Westminster 1896, p. 35). — For pig ceremonies in Sarawak see A. C. Haddon, Head hunters, London 1901, p. 305.

19) I refer to C. C. F. M. le Roux, De Bergpapoea's van Nieuw-Guinea..., Leyden 1950, passim, and esp. ch. 17, p. 586 ff.

mother; after a period of rest she can be fecundated again, but at sowing-time a festive dinner-party is given in which the head and the legs of a hog are made obligatory, in order to signify that "die Pflüger leicht den Acker mit einem Eisen umwerfen mögen, wie ein Schwein wenn es in der Erde wühlet" [20]). Perhaps the curious method of sowing and reaping described by Herodot (2, 14), but actually very rarely met with [21]), may also be mentioned here: after having sowed his land the Egyptian farmer turned hogs into it which were expected to tread in the seed; afterwards, at harvest-time he had the corn trodden out by the same animals. Of greater relevance is a tradition recorded by Grimm [22]): the boar by rooting up the soil taught the art of ploughing to man. This detail of German folklore has its counterparts elsewhere. The furrows were considered the earth's belly or female organs [23]), and such acts as e.g. the ancient Indian soma-pressing — already ṚV. 1, 28, 2 the pounding and the receiving parts of the pressing-apparatus are compared to the male and female organs [24]) —, or as the production of fire by rotating one stick in another stick prepared to receive it, acts which are analogous to the sexual act, were therefore identified with it or being regarded as a sort of coition: it is therefore not surprising to find many instances of ploughing and cohabiting being regarded as 'identical'. It is the less surprising as the parallelism between human procreation and the cultivation of land is often expressed in language: Skt. *kṣetra-* "land, soil" and "fertile womb, wife"; Gr. *ἀροτήρ* "plougher" and "father"; *ἄροτος* also "procreation of children"; *ἄροτρον* also "organs of generation", etc. In Sanskrit, the word *lāṅgala-* designates the plough as well as the penis. The original meaning seems to have been that of "a club or cudgel" [25]), which is

---

20) E. Wolter, in the Archiv für Religionswissenschaft, II (1899), p. 358 ff. According to the same author hogs were, in ancient times, often immolated to the earth by the Lithuanians and other peoples in their neighbourhood.

21) I follow Dawson, o.c., p. 597.

22) J. Grimm, Deutsche Mythologie⁴, II, Berlin 1876, p. 555.

23) See e.g., L. Jungblut S.V.D., Magic songs of the Bhils of Jhabua State C.I., in the Intern. Archiv für Ethnographie, 43 (1943), p. 18, and p. 23, n. 106: "to tear the earth's belly" means "to tear furrows in the soil"; for "pulling the sowing-plough" the expression "filling the earth's belly" is used. This locution is also explained by the Bhils themselves when invoking Mother Earth the moment they start the monsoon's first ploughing: "O Mother Earth, fill thou my belly, as I will fill thy belly". — See, further, V. Pisani, La donna e la terra, Anthropos 37-40 (1942-5), p. 241 ff.; Eliade, Traité d'histoire des religions, p. 226 ff.; 230 f.

24) Cf. also Meyer, o.c., I, p. 229; III, p. 187 f.

25) For this word see J. Przyluski, in Mémoires de la Société de linguistique, 22, p. 205 ff. (= Lévi, Przyluski, Bloch, Pre-Aryan and Pre-Dravidian in India, transl. by P. Ch. Bagchi, Calcutta 1929, p. 8 ff.); T. Burrow, Loanwords in Sanskrit, in the Transactions of the Philological Society 1946, p. 25 f.; F. B. J. Kuiper, Proto-Munda words in Sanskrit, Amsterdam 1948, p. 112; 127 f.

already probably on a priori considerations, because the primitive plough was, and sometimes still is, a pointed branch or stick (cf. Skt. *gokīla-* lit. "a sharp piece of wood for driving cows": "plough", and "pestle"[26])). Words for the penis have, on the other hand, often sprung from words meaning "rod, stalk, club, pointed object etc."[27]), and the sexual act itself is often denoted by verbs originally or properly meaning "thrusting, pricking, beating, scratching etc."[28]).

So the conclusion does not seem too bold that the boar's rooting, viewed as similar to ploughing[29]) or even as the example imitated by man, was considered a form of tilling, fertilizing, or generative activity. In Sanskrit, the word *potra-* "the snout of a hog" was also used for "ploughshare". A third meaning, given by a lexicographer: *vajra-* "thunderbolt" is likewise interesting: we have already pointed out that lightning and thunder were regarded as processes co-operating in the fertilization of the soil[30]). Even to-day, the Indian Muria call the thunderbolt "the seed", thunder meaning that the heavenly semen is falling to earth[31]). One is almost tempted to attach, in this connection, some importance to the boar-form assumed by Hinduistic gods in the act of creation: e.g. VāPur. 6, 10 ff. *Brahmā varāharūpa-*; Viṣṇusmṛti, a. 1 and Hariv. a. 219 Viṣṇu creates all beings after having rescued the earth in his *varāha*-form.

Turning now to the boar and the hog in Indian folklore we can only give a selection from the material available. The Gonds immolate pigs to their god Busa Deo and the Hindus of the central parts of India sacrifice them to their deity Bhainsāsur, or the buffalo demon, for the protection of the crops: when crops are beaten down at night by the wind it is supposed that Bhainsāsur has passed over them and trampled them down. In Germany the boar itself, being the corn-spirit, was

---

[26]) I refer to my paper 'Indogerm. *ser-* "(spitziger) Ast usw."', Mnemosyne III, 6 (Leyden 1938), p. 153 ff. The semantic change "pointed piece of wood" > "plough" was also discussed by R. Meringer, Indogerm. Forsch. 17, p. 116 f.; O. Schrader-A. Nehring, Reallexikon der indogermanischen Altertumskunde II, Berlin-Leipsic 1929, p. 184 ff.; C. D. Buck, A dictionary of selected synonyms in the principal Indo-European languages, Chicago 1949, p. 495 f. For the plough see also A. Nehring, in W. Koppers, Die Indogermanen- und Germanenfrage, Vienna 1936, p. 118 ff.; J. Bloch, La charrue védique, BSOS. 8 (1936), p. 411 ff.

[27]) Cf. e.g. J. Scheftelowitz, Indogerm. Forsch. 33, p. 141 ff.; Buck, o.c., p. 258 f.

[28]) Buck, o.c., p. 278 ff., and my above paper, p. 168 f.

[29]) See also Meyer, o.c., II, p. 38.

[30]) See section VI.

[31]) V. Elwin, The Muria and their ghotul, Oxford 1947, p. 261. We also refer to the views expounded by H. H. Diephuis, Naturkräfte und ihre Verehrung in der altrömischen Religion, Thesis Utrecht 1941, p. 138 ff.

believed to trample the corn down[32]). In order to ensure a rich harvest the Raj Gonds present an offering to the Earth Mother: she is one of the few deities who accept pigs: the most usual time for this ceremony is when the crop is half grown[33]). The Sema Nagas and other peoples still perform the very important ceremony of eating pork in order to promote the growth of the crops: if pork is not eaten at the proper moment the grain will not form[34]). The Santals believe the hog to be engaged in ploughing[35]). The Kharias leave the last ear of the crop to their god Ghorea who is a boar[36]).

Although the ancient Indians have not left us much information on these animals the facts found in the texts seem to admit of the conclusion that they entertained similar beliefs. In works dealing with omens and prognostication hogs and boars are more than once mentioned together with animals and objects which are closely related to water, moisture, and fertility, or which generally forebode rain: AVPar. 61, 1, 7 boars, makaras (i.e. monsters living in water, often confounded with dolphins, crocodiles etc.), herons etc.; 65, 1, 4 aquatic plants, makaras, serpents, crocodiles, alligators or similar rapacious animals living in water, porpoises, conchs, trees, tortoises, fresh lotus-flowers, reed, etc. etc. together with buffalos and boars are signs of immediate rain when clouds assuming their outward appearance become visible; 65, 2, 2; Varāh. BS. 28, 14 "clouds resembling in shape waves, hills, crocodiles, tortoises, boars, fishes.... give water within short time". A boar or hog can, however, also be a bad omen: Jagaddeva 2, 16; 41 etc., where the point at issue is not rain or fertility, but wounds, attacks, and hostilities[37]). There are other indications of the boar's supposed connections with the powers residing in the fertile soil: pearls made of conch-shells, 'dolphins', bamboo, elephants[38]), boars, snakes, and

---

[32]) R. V. Russell, The tribes and castes of the Central Provinces of India, London 1916, IV, p. 8 ff.; p. 11: "It may be suggested that pigs are offered... because the pigs were the corn-deities who damage the crops". — For boar-hunting, sacramental eating of hogs, and the boar as the enemy of Gaurī see also J. Tod, Annals and antiquities of Rajasthan, ed. by W. Crooke, Oxford 1920, p. 660 f.

[33]) C. von Fürer-Haimendorf, The Raj Gonds of Adilabad, I, London 1948, p. 353.

[34]) J. H. Hutton, The Sema Nagas, London 1921, p. 223.

[35]) W. Ruben, Literatur der vorarischen Stämme Indiens, Berlin 1952, p. 102. For non-Aryan influences in connection with the point at issue ibidem, p. 52.

[36]) S. C. Roy and R. Ch. Roy, The Kharias, Ranchi 1937, p. 428. See also the same, The Oraons of Chotanagpur, Ranchi 1915, p. 441 f.

[37]) J. von Negelein, Der Traumschlüssel des Jagaddeva, RGVV. 11, 4, p. 237.

[38]) The elephant is Indra's animal. It is especially worshipped on the very auspicious *dasahrā-* day which immediately follows the *navarātra-* festivals, and like these is sacred to Devī. On this day, it is said, Rāma marched against Rāvaṇa,

clouds, Varāh. BS. 81, 29 states, may not be perforated: they are of immense value. Men with countenances like a monkey [39]), buffaloes, boars or bucks are, according to the same authority, 68, 104, owners of sons, riches, and happiness. Its appearance in dream was in ancient India of so much importance as to deserve comment: AiĀr. 3, 2, 4.

It is stated in the Atharvaveda, 8, 7, 23 that the boar knows the plant (*varāhó veda vīrúdham*) [40]). AV. 2, 27, 2 (= 5, 14, 1) and KauśS. 38, 18 ff. inform us of a ceremony to be performed with a plant in order to be victorious in a disputation; the plant the root of which is to be chewed is addressed as follows: "the eagle discovered thee; the hog (*sūkara-*) dug thee with his snout". In the boar-myth, to which we shall turn in an instant, the *varāha-* is said to be in possession of *odana-* "grain mashed and cooked with milk", food par excellence (cf. AV. 12, 3, 4) [41]). JB. 2, 267 the *varāha-* is described as having arisen from the testicles of the sacrificial horse.

The casual references to Rudra as the boar of the sky [42]) may lead us to the assumption that there existed an Indian counterpart of the German Wodan with the boar. Yet, this animal is, in some way or other, also associated with several other gods. According to PV. 1, 8, 14 the boar, rice and barley are due to Prajāpati. ṚV. 10, 99, 6 "the slaying of the boar" is attributed to Trita [43]). ṚV. 9, 97, 7 the animal is connected with soma [44]), 10, 67, 7 Brahmaṇaspati is said to have, together with the bulls, the boars, and with "those perspiring with heat", come into possession of goods [45]). VS. 24, 40 the boar is for Indra.

---

on which account it is also called *vijayadaśamī*. For details see B. A. Gupte, Hindu holidays and ceremonials, Calcutta-Simla 1919, p. 185 ff. According to R. E. Enthoven, The folklore of Bombay, Oxford 1924, p. 214, there is a tradition that in ancient times the coronation waters were poured over the king by a she-elephant. — See also Filchner und Marāthe, Hindustan im Festgewand, p. 138 ff.

[39]) For monkeys see section XXI of this chapter.

[40]) This text is addressed to the plants in order to achieve somebody's restoration to health. With the Lhota Nagas the pig plays a rôle not only in marriage ceremonies or in the rites connected with the first fruits and the deceased, or with the founding of a village, but also in medicine: J. P. Mills, The Lhota Nagas, London 1922, p. 79 (see also p. 149; 53; 171; 6).

[41]) F. B. J. Kuiper, An Austro-Asiatic myth in the Rigveda, Amsterdam Academy 1950, p. 12 f. is under the impression that "the *odana-*... must be a symbol for goods of a universal religious importance, in Vedic terminology: Agni-Soma, or one of these". According to Von Schroeder, SitzBer. Akad. Wiss. Berlin 166, 2, p. 16 ff., it was the sun. Cf. also Nirukta, 6, 34: *odanam udakadānaṃ megham.*

[42]) ṚV. 1, 114, 5. For Rudra compare Oldenberg, Religion des Veda[4], p. 221 ff.; E. Arbman, Rudra, Uppsala Univ. Arsskrift 1922, 2 (see p. 9 f.).

[43]) See K. Rönnow, Trita Āptya, Uppsala Univ. Arsskr. 1927.

[44]) See Geldner, Der Rig-veda, III, p. 95.

[45]) Sāyaṇa's paraphrase is worth quoting: *vṛṣabhiḥ: varṣitṛbhiḥ varāhaiḥ: varāhārair varasya varaṇīyasyodakasyāhartṛbhiḥ gharmasvedebhiḥ: dīptāgamanaiḥ,*

An early, but unfortunately too short reference to an association between a *varāha-* and the earth is found AV. 12, 1, 48. It forms part of the important so-called hymn to the earth [46]), which is here, as often in later times, represented as being over-burdened by the follies of mankind [47]). The stanza runs as follows: "Bearing the fool, bearer of what is heavy (or: important, wise, venerable?), patiently enduring the settling down (?, or: destruction) of the excellent and of the evil (or, rather, of the prosperous and the unfortunate), the earth, in concord with the boar, opens itself to (or: becomes expanded for) the wild pig (*sūkarāya*)". What are we to understand by the *varāha-*, what by the *sūkara-*? Are they the same animal? [48]) What does the verb *ví jihīte* mean precisely? Anyhow, this stanza cannot be made an early piece of evidence for proving the existence of something like the varāha-avatāra in 'Atharvanic' times.

Before turning to that famous achievement of the god Viṣṇu it would be convenient to say some words on the much discussed boar-myth [49]). In the Ṛgveda, 1, 61, 7; 8, 77, 10, mention is made of a myth in which Viṣṇu carried away a hundred buffalo and cooked rice-milk which were guarded by, or had at least something to do with, a boar, called *Emuṣá-* [50]) who had apparently taken up his station on the other side of a mountain. This boar has been regarded as a 'figurative designation' of Vṛtra [51]). Now, the TS., 6, 2, 4, 2 f., relates that once the sacrifice went away from the gods in the form of Viṣṇu and entered the earth. As Indra declares himself to be "a slayer in an inaccessible place", Viṣṇu replies: "I am a carrier off from an inaccessible place", adding that a boar, "stealer of precious objects", keeps the goods of the asuras concealed on the other side of the seven hills, and asking Indra to slay that boar. Indra does so [52]), and asks Viṣṇu to carry the

---

yad vā kṣaradudakaiḥ ... taṃ prati gantṛbhiḥ marudbhiḥ ...; ṚV. 10, 99, 6 the same commentator explains *varāha-* by *udakavantaṃ megham;* 1, 61, 7 by *megham*; 8, 77, 10 by *jalapūrṇaṃ megham.*

46) For particulars see Whitney-Lanman, o.c., p. 660 ff.; M. Lindenau, Ein vedischer Lobgesang auf die Mutter Erde als die grosse Allgottheit, Festschrift Jacobi, Bonn 1926, p. 248 ff.; H. Beckh, Der Hymnus an die Erde, Stuttgart 1934.

47) The earth is also supposed to shake for that reason.

48) Cf. also Beckh, o.c., p. 51 f. The reading of the Paipp. text *sūkareṇa* does not keep us in the dark as to the identity of the two members of the subfamily suinae, but forces us into translating: "... expanded for the deer".

49) Bibliographical references may be found in Kuiper, Austro-Asiatic myth.

50) The name is evidently non-Aryan and probably Austro-Asiatic, irrespective of the correctness of Kuiper's etymologic combinations. See also Ruben, Lit. vorar. St., p. 52.

51) See Macdonell, o.c., p. 151; L. Renou (et E. Benveniste), Vṛtra et Vṛϑragna, Paris 1934, p. 163; Kuiper, o.c., p. 12.

52) On this occasion Indra in a remarkable way figures as an archer-god: cf. Kuiper, o.c., p. 13 and 17.

boar away. (Viṣṇu), the sacrifice, then carried him off "as a sacrifice for them". Thus they won the wealth of the asuras. In the succeeding paragraphs it is related that the gods won the earth, which first belonged to the asuras [53]). In the Maitrāyaṇīya version (3, 8, 3: p. 95, 3 ff.; cf. also KāṭhS. 25, 2: p. 104, 1 ff.) Viṣṇu's name is not mentioned: the sacrifice "was apart from the gods" and, after being found by Indra, asked that god to slay the boar. The main purport of this myth is clear: The demon-killer slays the representative of the enemy, now called asuras and the sacrifice, Viṣṇu, the divine power concerned with winning what is most vital and essential for gods and men, manages to secure his treasure. The *odana-* or "valuable goods of the asuras" (*ásurāṇāṃ vásu vāmám* MS.) no doubt embodies the idea of life-sustaining food, nourishment of longevity, primary substance essential to life: AV. 12, 3, 4 an *odana-* is called *amṛta-* [54]). These two divinities again act in close co-operation. It is significant that Indra alone is able to find the sacrifice, and no less worthy of note that the boar should be the keeper of the much desired substance.

In the Śatapathabrāhmaṇa this animal is called Emūṣa and said to have raised up the earth (14, 1, 2, 11): "and he", the author adds, "was her lord (husband) Prajāpati: with that mate (*mithuna-* [55])), he (i.e. the officiating priest by performing the requisite ritual act) thus furnishes him (makes him prosper) and makes him (that is Prajāpati and hence also his counterpart, the sacrificer) complete". The ritual act referred to consists in taking earth torn up by a boar [56]). TĀ. 1, 10, 8 the earth is stated to have been lifted up by a black boar with a thousand arms; TĀ. 10, 1, 8 by a similar animal with a hundred arms. TB. 1, 1, 3, 5 ff. it is Prajāpati who, having assumed the form of a boar, plunged into the water; finding the earth down below he raised it to the surface. In a more concise form TS. 7, 1, 5, 1 says that this (universe) was in the beginning water; on it Prajāpati, becoming wind, moved; he saw this (earth); becoming a boar he took it up;

---

53) For this story and some variants see also Macdonell, Mythological studies in the Rigveda, JAOS. 1895, p. 180 f.: Kuiper, o.c., p. 1 ff.

54) The sense of this word was recently discussed by P. Thieme, Studien sur indogermanischen Wortkunde und Religionsgeschichte, Leipsic Academy 98, 5, Berlin 1952, p. 15 ff.

55) For the ideas of *mithuna-* and "completing" see my Reflections on the numerals "one" and "two" in ancient Indo-European languages, Utrecht 1953, p. 31, and passim.

56) The stanza accompanying the act (VS. 37, 5) forms part of a series of mantras related to the Makha-myth, to which we shall have to revert in another section of this volume (ch. II, s. XXIV).

becoming Viśvakarman, he wiped (the water from) it (or: he rubbed it); it extended and became the extended one (*pṛthivī*).

The boar, whose name [57]) points to its being identical with the boar of the former myth, apparently is the husband of the earth, that is to say: the one who fecundates her: this conclusion does not seem to be too far-fetched. That the brahmanical circles should have tended to replace the animal by their favourite creator-god cannot be a matter of surprise. After having come into contact with the boar-deity who raised her, the earth expanded: that means, in my opinion, that she became the abode for mankind and the producer of their food. Thus the 'idea' of "broadness" was once again realized.

In contradistinction to Kuiper [58]) I am not convinced that the Emūṣa of the cosmogonical myth originally had nothing to do with the Emūṣa etc. of the boar-myth. Both mythological animals [59]) might, as far as I am able to see, be considered to represent the same powerful being: the guardian [60]) of the substance containing the potentialities of life, who on the one hand is believed to be also instrumental in generating and in producing food (or at least in enabling the earth to fulfil its purpose), but on the other hand does not voluntarily give up his treasure [61]). Be this as it may both myths evidently testify to the important part played by the boar in the most ancient period of Indian religious thought as far as this is known from written documents [62]).

In the course of time the boar which takes pity on the earth became identified with Viṣṇu [63]). In the Mbh., 3, 142, 28 ff. it is told that once

---

[57]) If the word *emuṣa-* etc. originally, or actually, was a name and not a common noun.

[58]) Kuiper, o.c., p. 18, esp. n. 3.

[59]) Described by Kuiper as "a conqueror of the nether world and of Death" (a concise statement which I would not like to adopt) and "the very one who withholds Life from the upper world and the human race" respectively.

[60]) Cf. also Eliade, o.c., p. 253.

[61]) The opinion expressed by Charpentier, Kleine Beiträge zur Indo-Iran. Mythologie, Upsala Univ. Arsskr. 1911, p. 34 may lead to misunderstandings. It is not necessary to suppose any direct connection between the Viṣṇu of the boar-myth and the much later varāha-avatāra of the same god.

[62]) In ancient Mesopotamia the shepherd-god Dumuzi or Tammuz was in charge of the tame animals (cf. ṚV. 8, 77, 10); incarnating the creative powers of spring he is also the husband of the goddess Inanna who represents the fertility of nature. See also Frazer, Golden Bough, I, p. 281; 288; IV, 1, p. 8; 164. — The sun-god (or a god related to the sun) not seldom marries the earth: Frazer, o.c. II, p. 98 ff.; V, p. 47; D. P. Pandey, Surya, Leiden 1919, p. 11; Meyer, Trilogie, III, p. 154, n. 1; Ruben, Eisenschmiede, p. 234; see also N. E. Parry, The Lakhers, London 1932, p. 486.

[63]) For particulars see Macdonell, JAOS. 1895, p. 178 ff.; Keith, Rel. and Phil., p. 111; Hopkins, Epic Myth. p. 79; 114; W. Ruben, Eisenschmiede und Dämonen in Indien, Intern. Archiv für Ethnographie, 37 Suppl., Leyden 1939,

the population of the earth, the support of all beings and the producer of all sorts of grain, increased to such an extent that this planet sank down under the weight; then Viṣṇu assuming the form of a boar lifted her up from the nether regions into which she had sunk. Mbh. 3, 83, 18; 310, 28 (*aparājita-*) and elsewhere the same occurrence is alluded to. 12, 43, 8 Kṛṣṇa is called the great boar, fire, and the sun. 1, 21, 12 his name Govinda is explained by the fact that he, as a boar, got hold of the earth (*gāṃ vindatā....*)[64]). In the same epic 12, a. 209 we find the detailed account of how Kṛṣṇa-Viṣṇu assumed the form of a roaring boar, penetrated into the nether regions and destroyed the daityas, dānavas, and asuras who had become jealous of the prosperity of the gods and oppressed the earth with a heavy load, so that "she seemed as if going down into the nether region". This version of the story approaches the 'classical' form of the varāha-avatāra — Hiraṇyākṣa turns up e.g. 13, 126, 12. Besides, the Mahābhārata in all probability informs us of a religious veneration accorded to any boar rising out of water with some of the earth he tore up on its head: persons seeing such animals, Viṣṇu himself is held to declare (13, 206, 4) shall never meet any evil and become freed from sin. Although the context would make us believe that the respect paid to these animals is due to Viṣṇu staying in them the passage may reflect an ancient 'boar-worship'.

In the Rāmāyaṇa it is Brahmā who becomes a boar, raises up the earth and creates the whole world; before, all was water only (2, 110, 3). Yet, in the NW. recension Viṣṇu's name has crept in. In the Viṣṇuite purāṇas (ViPur. 1, 4, 1 ff.; BhāgPur. 1, 3, 7; cf. also LiPur. 1, 4, 59 ff.) it is of course only Viṣṇu who, again, acquits himself of this protective and creative task with regard to the earth[65]).

Two significant facts remain to be recorded. First, it is the varāha-avatāra which enjoys special popularity, being regarded, in some purāṇas, as the most important of all 'incarnations' and immortalized by many Indian sculptors[66]). In the second place: it can scarcely be a

p. 243. — Mbh. 3, 142, 52 f. the gods do not recognize that that boar is the eternal Viṣṇu.

64) For other details the reader may be referred to Hopkins, o.c., p. 210.

65) Johansson, Solfågeln i Indien, p. 34, n. 3 is inclined to consider Viṣṇu's penetrating into the earth an instance of the periodic self-immolation of the fertility-god. As far as the correlate concept is concerned, to wit the god's return to the earth from which he has arisen, and the revival of nature resultant on it, this may have combined with the 'boar-concept' proper.

66) See e.g. H. Krishna Sastri, S. Indian images of gods and goddesses, Madras 1910, p. 22 f.; T. A. Gopinatha Rao, Elements of Hindu Iconography, I, 1, Madras 1914, p. 131 ff. — The third day of the bright half of the month Caitra (March-April) on which day Viṣṇu-Varāha saved the earth is an occasion for earth-

matter of mere chance that in the description of the festivities in connection with Indra's banner — a fertility ceremony par excellence [67]) —, as related by Varāh. BS. 43, 54, Viṣṇu's 'varāha-avatāra' should have been referred to: when the standard, that "source of vigour", is being 'decorated', raised, brought into town etc., the king himself should, without breaking his fast, recite some auspicious stanzas. One of them runs as follows: "Thou art the unborn.... One; thou art Viṣṇu, the boar, the primeval puruṣa; thou art Death, the all-destroying fire....".

If the boar really is a fertilizing divinity [68]) the idea that he cohabited with the goddess earth cannot be a matter of great surprise [69]). The relevant myth as narrated in the Kālikāpurāṇa [70]) may be young and perhaps of a more or less local character, the story of Bhūmi's son Naraka or Bhauma [71]) and the way in which he was procreated is well-known and, in various forms, of wide distribution: cf. e.g. Mbh. 3, a. 142 [72]); Hariv. a. 55; 120 etc.; ViPur. 5, 29, 23; BhāgPur. 10, 59, 30. His adventures did not fail deeply to impress both poets and devotees [73]).

The divine power or being going by the name of Naraka is mainly a representative of dung [74]), "der Genius des Misthaufens", "the demon of filth or manure", "the god of the filth of the farm-yard". As such he is also a "Genius der Trieb- und Zeugungskraft der Erde" [75]). Filth and manure, the favourite home of hogs and their relatives, actually are a product of the earth and the rooting and messing activities of these animals; no wonder that Naraka should have been a son of the goddess Earth and a god in the form of a boar. Nor is it surprising either that Naraka appears, in the purāṇical accounts, as a very rich and powerful ruler (e.g. Hariv. ch. 120) [76]). It seems possible reason-

---

worship (see R. E. Enthoven, The folklore of Bombay, Oxford 1924, p. 83).

67) See ch. III, s. II.

68) See also Meyer, o.c., II, p. 54.

69) The spirit of the forest worshipped by the Kharias (see Roy, o.c., II, p. 324 ff.) has come to be regarded as one of the principal village gods and the husband of the Earth-goddess.

70) See further on.

71) I also refer to Ruben, Eisenschmiede, p. 245; the same, Krishna, p. 182 f.

72) See Hopkins, Epic Myth., p. 51.

73) Many particulars were collected by A. Teeuw, Het Bhomakāwya, een Oud-Javaansch gedicht, Thesis Utrecht 1946, ch. II.

74) For details see Meyer, o.c., III, p. 312; Gupte, Hindu holidays..., p. 37 f.

75) Meyer, o.c., II, p. 47.

76) See also Teeuw, o.c., p. 113.

ably to explain this mythological figure without resorting to a hypothesis based on totemism [77]).

Now, it is worth while to observe that Naraka's father, who in most passages dealing with Bhūmi's son is passed over in silence, according to the Southern recension of the Mahābhārata [78]), was Nārāyaṇa, a fact unknown to other parts of the epic in which he is an asura, son of Bhūmi. Mbh. 12, 209, 7 he is called "the first of the asuras" who are to be destroyed by Viṣṇu in the form of a boar [79]). After the god has slain him in his boar form, the demon's bones are to be seen at Ganges' Gate (*Gaṅgādvāra-* [80])). Whereas in the great epic, 7, 29, 29 the goddess Pṛthivī is said to have asked Viṣṇu to give her the *vaiṣṇava*-weapon for her son without alluding to his paternity, the Viṣṇupurāṇa 5, 29, 23 is quite explicit on this point: after describing the combat between Viṣṇu and Naraka and the latter's defeat and death it relates how the goddess Bhūmi appearing and addressing the god gives him the ear-rings of Aditi [81]). In doing so the goddess says: "When you, assuming the form of a boar (*śūkara-*) lifted me up, this son, begotten through the contact with you, was born from me" [82]). The Kālikā Purāṇa, a comparatively late text describing rites and traditions of a partly local character, furnishes us with a detailed account [83]): Naraka's father was Viṣṇu who procreated him when he had assumed the shape of a boar and bore the goddess Earth in his arms after he had rescued her from sinking away in the waters (KālPur. a. 30 ff.). He was brought into the world (38, 34) on the same spot where Sītā, Janaka's daughter, had made her appearance from the furrow.

The question arises whether the boar was known to be his father also by the authors of those many texts who do not mention a father at all. Was the boar-god his father in the oldest versions of this mythical narrative? Has the stanza AV. 12, 1, 48, reference to which has already been made [84]), anything to do with it? Would it be altogether impossible to consider the passage TS. 6, 2, 4, 2: "the

---

[77]) "Diese göttliche Zeugung erinnert an das Schwein als Totemtier", Ruben, Eisenschmiede, p. 245.

[78]) Hopkins, o.c., p. 51.

[79]) The boar-form is not mentioned in the references to Kṛṣṇa's slaying the demon: 3, 12, 17; 5, 68, 4; 12, 340, 80 etc.

[80]) Hopkins, l.c.

[81]) These famous and precious ear-drops, being a source of amṛta and removers of grief, had been stolen by Naraka and kept at Prāgjyotiṣa (Mbh. 5, 48, 80); they were subsequently recovered from him by Kṛṣṇa (3, 12, 17), and then given to Sūrya (3, 307, 21).

[82]) Cf. BhāgPur. 10, 59, 31.

[83]) See also Meyer, o.c. II, p. 51 ff., where a summary of this episode is given.

[84]) See p. 137.

sacrifice went away from the gods in the form of Viṣṇu, and entered the earth" as reflecting an ancient story of Viṣṇu penetrating into the earth? [85]) Although Meyer [86]) is probably right in remarking: "Viṣṇu ist auch da jedenfalls später eingedrungen" the question remains: from what time and from what source does the conception of a god of manure, son of the earth and the boar-god, originate?

We shall conclude these observations on the boar by noticing some of the salient features of the Indonesian version of the story of Naraka's origin. In the Old-Javanese Bhomakāwya [87]), 2, 1-9, the narrative of Viṣṇu's passion for the beautiful goddess Earth, whom he made sit on his knees and violated in spite of his boar-form [88]), her millennial gestation, and the birth of the young demon who is called Naraka and made a universal and victorious king by Brahmā-Prajāpati, is linked with another well-known episode: the *liṅgodbhava-* motive, which in itself is a glorification of the paramountcy of Śiva [89]). Before Viṣṇu and Brahmā who are discussing their high position a liṅga consisting of jewels makes its appearance. When they try to lay hold of it the liṅga grows considerably in length and withdraws from them. Finally, Viṣṇu assumes the form of a boar and tries to grub up the lower end of the object, and Brahmā in the shape of a bird tries to find the top. Neither of them is successful. Their activities occasion an inundation, and the earth is on the point of sinking down. Viṣṇu, by request of the gods, prevents her from being lost in the waves. — In the Malay version (Hikayat Sang Bhoma, p. 7 f.) Viṣṇu likewise assumes the shape of an enormous boar; grubbing up earth and penetrating into the terrestrial body he sees a palace, transforms himself into a rākṣasa, meets the goddess Earth and violates her.

It may be remembered that the representation of Viṣṇu, in the form of a boar, trying to find the lower end of the liṅga is not foreign to the Indian sources: cf. e.g. ŚivaPur. 1, 6-9 and 2, 5. The story must have been extremely popular as it was often related, or alluded to, by European authors. Let it suffice to cite some lines from the Relation

---

85) Cf. Dandekar, Festschrift-Kane, p. 109. (See also TB. 1, 1, 3, 6).

86) Meyer, o.c. II, p. 55.

87) Translated into Dutch by A. Teeuw, o.c., p. 40 ff. (with an introduction and notes).

88) The order in which the events succeeded each other is, according to the Javanese author, this: Viṣṇu and Brahmā discussing universal dominion saw the liṅga. Viṣṇu transformed himself into a boar. The earth sank away. The god's passion, etc.

89) I refer to Ruben, Eisenschmiede, p. 245. See also Bosch, BEFEO. 31, p. 491 f.

des erreurs (1644) [90]): "La troisieme incarnation de Vichnou fut en cochon [91])…. Ils disent donc que les Dieux, etant en dispute entre eux pour sçavoir lequel (d'eux) etoit le plus grand, Rutren dit a Bruma et a Vichnou qu'il s'alloit cacher, et que celuy qui trouveroit ses pieds et sa teste, seroit le plus grand des Dieux. Bruma se transforma en cigne…. Vichnou se transforma en porc pour luy trouver les pieds et fut creuzer et fouillir la terre jusqu'aux abimes, et n'ayant pu les trouver, il s'en retourna plus vilain et plus sale qu'il n'etoit auparavant, mais ces pauvres Gentils sont sy brutes, que par rapport à cette fable ils ont beaucoup de veneration pour le cochon" [92]) [93]).

We can make an attempt to solve the problem of the association of the boar with Viṣṇu by referring to the god's penetrating abilities and to his relations with pits: when the sacrificial horse falls into a pit an oblation is due to Viṣṇu (ĀpŚS. 20, 7, 19; a similar injunction:

[90]) Edited by W. Caland, Twee oude Franse verhandelingen over het Hindoeïsme, Amsterdam 1923, p. 9 f.; see also Caland, Drie oude Portugeesche verhandelingen over het Hindoeïsme, Amsterdam 1915, p. 155 ff.

[91]) Mark the departure from the 'classic' tradition with regard to the motive of the boar-avatāra.

[92]) Baldaeus (Ph. Baldaeus, Afgoderye der Oost-Indische heydenen, re-edited by A. J. de Jong, Thesis Utrecht 1917) telling a similar story gives a curious detail: Viṣṇu rooting in the earth met a terrible serpent and, having returned to the surface for fear of this monster, declared Ixora (Īśvara, Çiva) to be his superior.

[93]) Some additional remarks in connection with the boar may find their place here. For a general survey of the above and other appearances of the god in the body of a boar the reader may be referred to Ruben, Eisenschmiede, p. 243 ff. He may find there also a compilation from modern ethnographical works. In my opinion matters are often more complicated than this author seems to suggest. There is, to my mind, already in the documents of the oldest period such a wealth of superstructural elaboration and implications that it is in many cases not possible to give more than a general delineation of tendencies, influences, and 'primitive origins'. As I have endeavoured to show in the above expositions, such complex conceptions as "Viṣṇu is the sacrifice" and "Viṣṇu assumes the form of a boar" cannot be regarded as being completely explained by pointing out that today so-called primitive inhabitants of India immolate hogs and by recalling the sacramental character of eating.

A conspicuous trait of Viṣṇu's appearance as a boar sometimes is his having, or using, a single tusk. (See also such inscriptional evidence as may be found in the IA. 9, p. 251. — For the 'unicorn' see R. Ettinghausen, Studies in Muslim iconography, I, Washington 1950, p. 94 ff. For various types of varāha: B. C. Bhattacharya, Indian images, I, Calcutta 1921, p. 14). Hence his name *Ekaśṛṅga*. (Mbh. 13, 149, 70 he is also called *Mahāśṛṅga-*). See also Mbh. 3, 142, 45; Rao, o.c. p. 137 (In other cases the boar is sculptured with two tusks; he is often represented en profile). One cannot help being reminded of the 'symbolical' value of a single horn or tusk — the word *śṛṅga-* can have both meanings and also stand for a variety of other horn-like projections —: the penis erectus (cf. Meyer, o.c., II, p. 301). This significance of the single tusk would be in perfect harmony with the generative function of the boar. — In this connection it may be recalled that the word *sīra-* "plough" (cf. above, p. 99 ff.) is given the sense of "the sun"

22, 21, 10; the context leads us to the conclusion that this relation was similar to that existing between drowning and the Lord of the waters, blindness and the Sun etc. [94]), and, especially, due to his associations with the earth.

XX. THE DWARF.

The Dwarf avatāra — the historical development of which was at the time studied by Macdonell [1]) — is, as it would seem to my mind, also very illustrative of the god's character. In this manifestation Viṣṇu gives unmistakable evidence of protecting and preserving capabilities. The essential element of the Vāmana myth, the three steps taken by the god for the good of the world, was already known to the authors of the Ṛgveda. In the Vedic Vṛtra combat it was Viṣṇu who, being associated with Indra, helps, by striding, the latter to vanquish the demon. In this avatāra it is Viṣṇu who takes his strides to overcome the demons himself and to regain possession of the earth for the gods after conquering Bali. In both cases Viṣṇu exerts himself to rescue gods and men from a disaster, but in the avatāra he is the central figure and, unlike the other gods, personally active.

In ŚB. 1, 2, 5, 4 ff. we find the germ of the dwarf myth: Viṣṇu was a dwarf (cf. also 6, 5, 2, 8; 6, 2, 12 etc.[2])). References to it are, for instance, made Mbh. 5, 10, 6; 8, 73, 58; 9, 33, 25. In this manifestation the god was very popular [3]). Leaving the relations between the dwarf and the soul, the allusions to a thumb-like puruṣa etc.[4]) undiscussed, it seems warranted to suppose the Vāmana to be the most famous Indian instance of the widespread belief in the miraculous abilities of beings who are considerably below the usual size [5]). In ancient Germany they were held to assist man in ploughing, harrowing, and reaping.

(*āditya-*) in the Nirukta, 9, 40: might this note perhaps reflect an 'identification' of Viṣṇu = the sun and the plough?? — See also Onians, Origins, p. 245 f.

[94]) It may however be asked whether these passages presuppose the identification of the god and the boar. — Is there any use in mentioning here that ṚV. 1, 22, 17 bearing upon V.'s strides is, side by side with stanzas referring to Varuṇa, recited in a ceremony conducted to consecrate ponds, wells, and tanks (ÇāṅkhGS. 5, 2, 6)? (ibid. 5, 3, 3 with Indra, Agni, Viśvakarman: consecration of a garden). — GobhGS. 2, 9, 13 the razor used in the *cūḍākaraṇa-* ceremony (the 'tonsure', performed on a child) is addressed: *viṣṇor daṃṣṭro 'si* "you are V.'s tusk" (= MB. 1, 6, 4).

[1]) Macdonell, JRAS. 1895, p. 165 ff.

[2]) I refer to JRAS. 1895, p. 168 f. Cf. also KaṭhUp. 5, 3.

[3]) Hillebrandt, Vedische Mythologie² II, p. 321. — Cf. also Rao, Elements of Hindu iconography, I, 1, p. 161 ff.

[4]) See section XII.

[5]) See e.g. O. Schrader-A. Nehring, Reallexikon der indogerm. Altertumskunde, II, Berlin-Leipsic 1929, p. 707 ff.; Gonda, Drama, p. 412 ff.

This aid might also mean good luck for the cattle [6]). The very idea of the divine, but dwarfish or misshapen, helper is from of old familiar to Indians: the yakṣas who are described as helpful beings in possession of supranormal powers are often thought of as dwarfs [7]). Johansson [8]) seems therefore to be right in considering Viṣṇu's appearance as dwarf in the Veda to be more than an occasional stratagem — as was supposed by Macdonell [9]) —; it probably has something to do with a feature in his character. An animal below the usual size of its species has Viṣṇu for its deity, and it serves for prosperity, the TS., 2, 1, 8, 3, states, and also that by offering such an animal to this god, who is the sacrifice, one has recourse to him with his own share. A dwarf animal affords support to cattle when born (2, 1, 5, 2). The *lūnāṅga-* "crippled" is *maṅgalāvaha-* "auspicious": Rājataraṅginī 7, 289. TS. 2, 1, 3, 1 relates that Viṣṇu seeing a dwarf offered it to its own deity; thereupon he conquered these worlds. By offering such an animal to this god a man who is engaged in a struggle becomes this god and conquers these worlds [10]). It may be remembered that the deities of vegetation are not seldom said "to be sacrificed to themselves". — I would not be able to provide evidence in favour of the supposition, which in itself would not be unreasonable, that the dwarf represents the light or energy of the sun which after small beginnings soon grows considerably [11]).

One observation remains to be made: Viṣṇu, the dwarf, is able to enlarge himself, in a miraculous way (cf. ŚB. 1, 2, 5, 1 f.; TB. 3, 2, 9, 7, and the puranic stories), to such an extent as to encompass the whole universe. He is, or can make himself, or show himself to be, co-extensive with all existence [12]).

---

[6]) W. Müller-Bergström, in the Handwtb. d. de. Abergl. 9, 1086 f.; De Vries, Altgerm. Religionsgesch. I, p. 284 ff.

[7]) See e.g. A. Foucher, in A. Getty, Gaṇeśa, Oxford 1936, p. XV; cf. also Ruben, Eisenschmiede, p. 60; 250. — For the associations of the yakṣas with fertility see e.g. Meyer, Trilogie, I, p. 98 ff.

[8]) Johansson, o.c., p. 7.

[9]) Macdonell, Ved. Myth., p. 41.

[10]) See also 2, 1, 5, 2; ÇB. 13, 2, 2, 9.

[11]) In the ceremonies observed at the Jayā and Vijayā festivals Viṣṇu the dwarf is revered: Saurapur. a. 15; see esp. st. 36 f. — S. K. Saraswati, A rare type of Viṣṇu image, Proc. Ind. Hist. Congr. 9 (1946), p. 72 makes mention of an image representing the god riding on the shoulders of a fat dwarf which may be recognized as Garuḍa. — For the offering of a dwarf-bull to Viṣṇu: ĀpÇS. 21, 23, 4. — See also Filchner-Marāthe, o.c., p. 112 ff.

[12]) I am not convinced that the epithet *bṛhaccharīra-* (ṚV. 1, 155, 6) refers to this power of the god (according to Sāyaṇa it means: *virāḍ ātmanā sarvadevamanuṣyādiśarīrāṇāṃ svaśarīratvāt*). — In this connection such passages as Matsyapur. 245, 80 may be of some interest: *prabhavasva prabhāvana | prabhavāyāsya viśvasya viśvātman* ...

XXI. ANIMALS.

Having already discussed the great bird, Garuḍa, the god's vehicle or *vāhana-* and his intimate relations with the boar, we must now review a number of other animals with which he, in various ways, associated, because they, too, may be expected to shed light on important traits of his character. Animals, widely believed to have superior power, to sustain, for instance, the potency of vegetation, to have mysterious relations, to be a sort of reservoir of power for the socio-religious community, could even be representatives of the god whom they accompanied. Some animals are especially 'divine' or apt to be worshipped and deemed to be bearers of special potentialities; others are of secondary importance [1]).

There are striking relations between Viṣṇu and the horse, an animal of great interest from the point of view of the comparative study of religions [2]). The horse is on the one hand connected with vegetation and the nether world, on the other hand related to, or identified with the sun [3]). Sunlight and fecundity are, for all we know now, also two of those 'concepts' which are especially associated with the name of Viṣṇu. In the cults and beliefs of Indians and other peoples the sun-god often assumes the form of a horse. In other cases the animal is conceived as sky-going [4]). It may be of some interest to dwell for a moment on the most famous of Ṛgvedic horses, Dadhikrā or Dadhikravan because he gives evidence of qualities often mentioned in the preceding sections. He is extolled as a hero, as swift, victorious, booty-winning, bird-like; he is a *vājin-* expected to be able to give longevity, strength, refreshing food; he "extends himself" over the nations of mankind, and in this he resembles Sūrya pervading the water with his light. He is praised at dawn, when the ritual fire is kindled. He is invoked together with the Dawns, Agni, the Sun (ṚV. 4, 38-40). Like the other horses of similar character in the Ṛgveda Dadhikrā 'symbolizes' the celestial

---

1) For the rôle of animals in religion see Van der Leeuw, Religion, ch. 8.

2) See e.g. H. Hindringer, Weiheroß und Roßweihe, München 1932, p. 36 ff.; A. Nehring, in Koppers, Indogermanen- und Germanenfrage; Koppers, ibidem, p. 279 f.; L. Malten, Jahrb. d. kais. deutschen Archaeol. Inst. 29 (1914), p. 181 f.; E. Abegg, Der Messiasglaube in Indien u. Iran, Berlin 1928, p. 39 ff.; Meyer, o.c., III, p. 314 (cf. esp. II, p. 250, n.). Compare also P. E. Dumont, L'Aśvamedha, Paris 1927, p. I ff.; W. Kirfel, in Beiträge zur indischen Philologie und Altertumskunde, Hamburg 1951, p. 39 ff. — In the cults and beliefs of various Indian tribes and communities the horse plays an important part. See e.g. also Ruben, Literatur der vorarischen Stämme Indiens, Berlin 1952, p. 75.

3) In the latter case the animal is often white in colour, cf. e.g. ÇB. 7, 3, 2, 16. For the horse = the sun, see Abegg, o.c., p. 54, n. 10.

4) See, in general, Keith, Rel. and Phil., p. 189 ff.; Macdonell, o.c., p. 148 ff.

light (cf. 7, 77, 3; 1, 163, 2) [5]). Particulars may be a matter of opinion and the search for a well-defined 'original' 'substratum' — if something like this has existed at all — an impossible task. Anyhow, we can easily conceive that the power and energy, the force active in the universe, called Viṣṇu was apt to attach to a divine horse or to a mythical figure of an equine hero.

Relations with the horse are, to begin with, expressed by some of the epitheta given to Viṣṇu. Mbh. 1, 23, 16 we find *Hayamukha-* "having a horse's face" (applying to Garuḍa); 3, 315, 14 *Aśvaśiras-* "horse-headed": in 12, 127, 3 this form of Viṣṇu is said to read the eternal Vedas, in a. 347 it is related how the god, in horse-headed form, rescued the Vedas from Madhu and Kaiṭabha who had stolen them from Brahmā at the very moment of their being created [6]). The same story is narrated in the Harivaṃśa a. 53 and 293. The ṛṣi *Vaḍavāmukha-* is, Mbh. 12, 342, 60, an incarnation of Nārāyaṇa. Viṣṇu often appears as *Hayaśiras-*: cf. e.g. Mbh. 5, 99, 5. In the passage last-mentioned and 3, 315, 14 the god is called the son of Aditi; as this goddess is often regarded as Mother Earth [7]) this relation may point to the chthonian character often inherent in the horse [8]). This fact, however, also shows the width of the range of ideas and conceptions which at the epic period could be represented by the name of Viṣṇu.

It is, moreover, worthy of note that the horse is already mentioned as an avatāra of the god in the ViPur. 5, 17, 11, where it occupies the place which in the usual series of avatāras is taken by the dwarf incarnation (*matsyakūrmavarāhāśvasiṃharūpādibhiḥ....*). The commentary observes that "the horse" here stands for Hayagrīva, the horse-headed shape of the god. In a much later period the horse occupies the 18th place in a longer series of incarnations. In the belief of the masses it is considered one of the minor avatāras, and as such looked upon as a god of learning, with functions similar to those which are usually attributed to Sarasvatī [9]). In literature and iconography this theme was often treated of, as appears also from a passage in one of the works of Hemādri: "The horse-headed god should be made (by

[5]) In later times the Sun is more than once described as assuming the form of a horse: Mbh. 12, 262, 41 *sūryo 'śvaḥ*: ViPur. 3, 2, 7.

[6]) For the horse-headed god see also R. H. van Gulik, Hayagrīva, Thesis Utrecht 1935.

[7]) For Aditi see section XV.

[8]) Cf. e.g. J. v. Negelein, Das Pferd im Seelenglauben und Seelenkult, Zs. des Vereins für Volkskunde, 2, p. 406 ff.; L. von Schroeder, Mysterium und Mimus im Rigveda, Leipsic 1908, p. 429 ff.; F. Altheim, Terra Mater, Giessen 1931, p. 117 f.

[9]) I refer to Rao, Elements, I, p. 260. For other details see also Van Gulik, o.c., p. 17 ff.

the sculptors) with his spread feet placed in the hands of the goddess Earth" [10]). Van Gulik [11]) is in all probability right in concluding that the identification of Hayagrīva and Viṣṇu must be ascribed to the fecundating character of the deified horse [12]). Sexual and chthonian considerations as well as the ancient relations between the horse and the all-pervading powers early associated with the name Viṣṇu (celestial light, vegetation, services rendered) may have contributed to this process of uniting. The very fact that in early times the steed was a *vājin-* par excellence, and that the performances of the race-horse were looked upon as pre-eminently helpful in winning and generating divine power, may also have been an important factor in preparing the minds for this identification [13]).

Viṣṇu's future avatāra as Kalkin is for the first time mentioned in the Mahābhārata, where he appears as a brahman, called Kalkin *Viṣṇuyaśas-* (3, 190, 94). In view of the compounds *yajñayaśas-* "the glory or dignity of the sacrifice" (to be conferred on the sacrificer etc.: TS. 5, 1, 1, 3; 6, 5, 1, 4 f.) and *brahmayaśas-* ("the glory of B." which enters the person who succeeds in approaching unto the throne of Brahmā: Kauś. 1, 5) this name must probably be taken to mean "being, representing Viṣṇu's glory or dignity, i.e. an essential element in the total divine personality known as Viṣṇu". This brahman Kalkin Visṇuyaśas, being a hero of great manly power, intelligence and prowess, will, the above text says, in the renewed beginning of the kṛta age, exterminate the mlecchas and institute a great horse-sacrifice. In studying this figure Abegg [14]) rightly distinguishes between two lines of tradition. The first is of a popular character, holding Viṣṇu himself to be a white horse [15]). The other is followed in the literary

---

10) Discussed by Krishna Sastri, South-Indian images of gods and goddesses, Madras 1916, p. 55.

11) Van Gulik, o.c., p. 95 f.

12) Passing mention may be made here of such texts as ÇB. 5, 1, 4, 5; 13, 2, 2, 19 (the horse is produced from the womb of the waters).

13) The horse is explicitly identified with the sun and, as such, called a thunderbolt: ÇB. 6, 3, 1, 29; 3, 10; the horse is a thunderbolt: 6, 3, 3, 12; cf. also 7, 3, 2, 10. The horse is sacred to Prajāpati: 6, 5, 3, 9 (cf. 13, 1, 2, 4), who in a very interesting passage (7, 3, 2, 14) is narrated to have become a white horse in order to go in search of Agni: from this time on anybody seeking Agni in that form will find him. The sacrificial horse is believed to have been generated by sky and earth: 13, 1, 6, 1. Lying down near it is a means of securing fertility (see Eggeling, 44, p. 322). It is the noblest, most vigorous, powerful, swiftest, and most famous of animals: 13, 1, 2, 5 ff.; 3, 3, 1. In view of the importance attached to the sacred footprint in Viṣṇuism, the offering in the horse's footprint (6, 3, 3, 22) may be mentioned too.

14) Abegg, o.c., p. 47 ff. and 138 ff.

15) Reference may be made to Ph. Baldaeus, o.c., p. 174 f.

texts which describe the tenth avatāra as a warrior on horseback. In the former way of looking on the identity of the horse and Viṣṇu the animal and the god are simply regarded as one in bodily appearance, in the latter the god is represented in the form of a human being and the animal pervaded by his essence is given to him as his inseparable and most characteristic attribute. It would appear to be too bold a supposition to conclude from this that in this case an originally theriomorphous divinity was split up into an anthropomorphous figure and an animal accompanying him [16]). There are first, no ancient indications of a horse-god Viṣṇu. And if, in the second place, the Supreme Being of Hinduism were to be regarded as having originated in a horse (and in nothing but a horse-shaped divinity), why should he not have arisen from a boar, a fish, a tortoise, a dwarf, a warrior? It does, on the other hand, appear to be a more prudent conclusion to say that the theriomorphous divinity formed part of old popular conceptions connected with power embodied in the horse. This power was similar to that ascribed to the god called Viṣṇu. That Viṣṇuism in becoming influential and in tending to absorb other cults and beliefs could identify this divinity with its central figure can, to my mind, only be explained by pointing to the strong affinity between the conceptions represented by that horse and certain striking features in the character of Viṣṇu himself [17]).

In addition to what has already been said with regard to the serpent and the dragon in the section dealing with the Vṛtra-combat some remarks must be made here on the rôle of the snake in Hinduistic Viṣṇuism. Generally speaking this animal is often an antagonist of the powers of sky and light, but its potency is not always experienced as menacing and calamitous. It is very often associated with the water. According to the ancient Egyptians the primaeval waters were inhabited by four frogs and four snakes which brought forth the sun-god and creator Atum. The Pueblo Indians conceive their great water-serpent in a way which is very similar to the god or goddess of germination, i.e. earth. He is the father of all life, just as the earth is its mother [18]). In a similar way TS. 7, 3, 1, 3 etc.: the earth is the queen of serpents. When seen in the fertility of the earth or the earthly waters the generative force in nature has also in other countries often become a snake.

---

[16]) Abegg, o.c., p. 48 f.

[17]) Ruben, Krishna, p. 118 ff.; Eisenschmiede, p. 270.

[18]) J. W. Fewkes, A study of summer ceremonials at Zuñi and Moqui Pueblos, Bulletin of the Essex Institute, 22, p. 110; Haeberlin, Memoirs American Anthrop. Assoc. 3, p. 23; 51 etc. See also Onians, o.c., p. 248 ff.

Its emerging from the ground easily led man to connect this reptile with the secrets of death, whereas its resemblance to the penis relates it to the origins of animal life. When their skins become old, snakes slough them off and are, so to say, reborn in youthful vigour. Hence their reputed association with life and immortality [19]). The well-known Indian nāgas or serpent-genii [20]) often occur in association with a variety of other divine representatives of fertility and prosperity. Inhabiting subaquatic or subterranean countries, they are keepers of the life-force or life-energy which is preserved in the waters. Serpents are called Varuṇa's children: PārGS. 2, 14, 4, and have their abodes in the west (ŚB. 3, 1, 1, 7), the region of hope (*āśā*) and *śrī-* (ŚB. 11, 1, 6, 23) protected by Varuṇa.

Coming now to the enormous serpent which carries the earth, Śeṣa, we can dismiss the information (Mbh. 5, 103, 2) that he is able to do so in consequence of his ascetic austerities as being an interpretation and justification given by the brahman redactors. Of greater moment is the fact of his being an incarnation or transformation of Nārāyaṇa (3, 189, 10) who is, however, also said to sleep upon this reptile (3, 272, 38). There would be no use in quoting texts or archaeological evidence for Viṣṇu being represented as resting on the coils of this animal. Suffice it to recall that the Supreme Being is, in the interval between two periods of creation, the only existence, the only without a second: so the cosmic ocean as well as the serpent are manifestations of this One who is Reality, of Viṣṇu himself. "The anthropomorphic figure, the serpent coils that form his bed, and the water on which this serpent floats, are triune manifestations of the single divine, imperishable, cosmic substance, the energy underlying and inhabiting all the forms of life" [21]). The very names of the animal are significant: *Ananta-* "the Endless or Infinite One" [22]), because he is the 'emblem' or 'personification' of eternity — compare TUp. 2, 1 *satyaṃ jñānam anantam brahma* "Brahman is the real, 'knowledge', the infinite"; Śaṅkara,

---

19) See e.g. J. Morgenstern, The role of the serpent in Semitic mythology, Zs. für Assyriologie 1914/5, p. 284 ff.; Frazer, The Golden Bough IX, London 1933, p. 302 ff.; Bergema, o.c., p. 318 f. n.; Meyer, o.c., III, p. 231, and in general III, p. 318; C. H. Tawney-N. M. Penzer, The Ocean of story, London 1924 ff. IX, p. 48 n.; Zimmer, Myths and symbols, passim and esp. p. 72 ff.; J. A. MacCulloch and W. Crooke, in the Encycl. of Rel. and Eth. 11 (1920), p. 399 ff.

20) J. Ph. Vogel, Indian Serpent-lore, London 1926. See also Macdonell, Ved. Myth., p. 152 f.; Hopkins, Epic Myth., where particulars may be found. It may only be recalled here that they form part of Indra's weapons: Mbh. 3, 42, 6.

21) Zimmer, o.c., p. 61.

22) Ananta is also the name of one of the minor avatāras of Viṣṇu (cf. e.g. Rao, o.c. I, p. 257 f.) and a name of the god (e.g. ViPur. 2, 13, 9).

Brahmasūtrabhāṣya 1, 1, 22 *tac cānantyaṃ brahmaliṅgam* "and this infinity is a characteristic of brahman" — and *Śeṣa-* "the residue or remainder": the figure "representing the residue that remained after the earth, the upper and infernal regions, and all their beings, had been shaped out of the cosmic waters of the abyss" [23]). In order to render more clear the ideas attached to the term *śeṣa-* it may be recalled that, to cite so important a thinker as Rāmānuja (Gītābhāṣya 7, 8 ff.), *śeṣa-* is, so to say, the spilling of the plenitude of God's being; all the entities in the universe, where they exist as bodies, senses, material objects and their causes, with their individuality and characteristics have originated in God and are his *śeṣa-*. The individual ātman also is essentially a "rest" of God. All this constitutes God's body which to him serves no purpose at all [24]).

Thus, Viṣṇu sleeps on Śeṣa and Viṣṇu is Śeṣa, Śeṣa is a form of the Supreme Being (cf. also Mbh. 6, 65, 52) [25]). Besides, this serpent bears the entire world upon its numerous heads. For the benefit of the world, he deprives all the asuras of their power. In his hands he holds a plough (*lāṅgala-*) and a *muṣala-* "a mace or pestle", objects already known to us. These and other interesting characteristics of the great serpent are, for instance, given in the Viṣṇupurāṇa, 2, 5, 13 ff. "The unborn who in the form of Brahmā creates the universe, in his own shape as the soul and source of the universe provides for its duration ... upholds it with the body of Ananta" (ViPur. 4, 1, 29). That the purāṇas made Śeṣa one with Balarāma or Baladeva, Kṛṣṇa's elder brother, was another method of expressing the idea of a close relation between the cosmic serpent and the High God.

The 'holiness' of the snakes [26]), evidence of which is given by various religious customs and literary documents, is now perfectly clear. It is on one hand a representative of the terrestrial waters and all the powers for good related to them, and on the other hand closely associated with Viṣṇu himself. Kāliya, the huge serpent which was defeated by Kṛṣṇa, the herdsman born to fight all evil, was even marked with the god-

---

[23]) Zimmer, o.c., p. 62; Vogel, o.c., p. 313.

[24]) See also Mīmāṃsāsūtra 3, 1 f. — Another explication MtPur. 248, 34 *yugāntāgnyavalīḍheṣu sarvabhūteṣu kiṃcana | yāteṣu śeṣo bhavasi tasmāc cheṣo 'si kīrtitaḥ.*

[25]) See e.g. MtPur. 249, 27; Hohenberger, o.c., p. 102. — Cf. Frankfort, Kingship and the gods, p. 145 f. "... the secret nature of the sun-creator is one with the universal symbol of chthonic life" (Egypt).

[26]) See also Ruben, Krishna, p. 90 f.; Dubois, o.c., I, p. 179; Vogel, o.c., passim; J. S. F. Mackenzie, Tree and serpent worship, in the Indian Antiquary 4 (1875), p. 1 ff.; W. Kirfel, Der Hinduismus, in H. Haas, Bilderatlas zur Religionsgeschichte, Leipsic 1934, p. XXVI f.

man's sacred footprint. The conqueror of this reptile himself might, inversely, be represented with attributes typical of serpent genii. Images of serpents, carved on stone, are frequently adored, inter alia and for obvious reasons, by women desirous of offspring. A *śālagrāma-* marked by a *cakra-* which resembles a *nāga-* (cobra) is very auspicious[27]).

A reference to the identity of Viṣṇu and the cow is conspicious by its rarity: AV. 10, 10, 30 "The cow is the sky, the cow the earth, the cow Viṣṇu, Prajāpati" [28]).

Occasional information regarding a connection between the god and the monkeys, however, deserves more than passing notice. Like the boar, the wild elephant, the hare, and other animals which destroy the crops, the wild ape was, and is, revered in order to get on the right side of him. In various parts of India it is a divine being presiding over the maize-crops or performing similar functions [29]). Ruben is therefore doubtless right in writing that the powerful monkey Dvivida, known from Kṛṣṇa's biography, who was destroyed by Balarāma, the hero with the plough (see e.g. ViPur. 5, a. 36 [30])), and the faithful Hanumat, Rāma-Viṣṇu's mighty supporter, are only two sides of the same character. What is remarkable, in the case of the snakes as well as that of the monkeys, is that their ageless 'sanctity' should, in the course of time, have become an element in Viṣṇuism. Such narratives as that describing the birth of the king of apes from a tear of Viṣṇu (Rām. 7, 37, pr. 1, 7 ff.) and the identity of names borne by the god and these animals (*Kapi-, Kapīndra-, Vṛṣākapi-*) are only to place this fact in relief. However, the comparatively frequent identification of Vṛṣākapi, the lascivious and naughty ape of ṚV. 10, 86 [31]), with Viṣṇu, and the explanation of his name when applied to the god as given in the Mbh., 12, 342, 89: "*kapi-* denotes the foremost of the boars and Dharma is otherwise known by the name of *vṛṣa-*" are not without signification [32]).

---

[27]) See Rao, o.c., I, p. 10.

[28]) For Aditi see section XV. — V. as a bull: Hohenberger, o.c., p. 108.

[29]) Ruben, Eisenschmiede, p. 258 f.; Krishna, p. 208 f.; Lit. vorar. Stämme, Index s.v. See also J. F. G. Careri, Voyage III, ed. by S. Sen, Indian travels of Thevenot and Careri, N. Delhi 1949, Index, s.v.

[30]) Compare also Wilson-Hall, o.c., V, p. 139.

[31]) For particulars see Macdonell, o.c., p. 64; Keith, o.c., p. 133; Geldner, o.c., III, p. 273 ff.; F. E. Pargiter, Suggestions regarding Rigveda 10, 86, JRAS. 1911, p. 803 f. (V. represents some ancient Dravidian monkey-god).

[32]) On account of the incompleteness of our information we cannot be so positive with regard to the Vṛṣākapi figure as is Güntert, o.c., p. 310, according to whom "der freche, lüsterne Affe" is a "faun- und silenartiger Vegetationsdaemon ... der in engster Beziehung zu Viṣṇu steht". From the main text, ṚV. 10, 86, no connection whatever between this ape and Viṣṇu appears to exist. For

Apes indeed remind us of boars in the above respect. They also have the name of being lascivious [33]). In the epics all the great apes are of divine origin: the Sun, the Aśvins, Dharma, Agni etc. are their fathers. Hanumat was the son of Māruta or Vāyu [34]). He was able to expand in size till he was larger than a mountain, and also to become as small as a thumb. In the Rāmāyaṇa he is described as having a tail like Indra's banner and as making a noise like this god's vajra. He is as glorious as the sun. Like Garuḍa, to whom he is (Rām. 4, 66, 4) likened, he sits — and even roars — on a standard (Mbh. 3, 151, 17). He resembles this bird in swiftness, the wind in strength (Rām. 4, 67, 28). The monkeys are even able to move in the space traversed by Viṣṇu 4, 37, 17 *padaṃ viṣṇuvikrāntam,* i.e. *ākāśam* comm.), travelling on the roads of the birds and the luminaries. Caland, recalling the rôle played by the Maruts in assisting Indra against Vṛtra (AiB. 3, 20, 1; ŚB. 4, 3, 3, 6 ff.; ṚV. 3, 32, 4 etc.) ventured the supposition that the apes which helped Rāma in conquering Rāvaṇa originally were (the same) wind- of storm divinities. His thesis is worth considering [35]).

XXII. KṚṢṆA.

It is not my intention to enlarge here upon the vexing and much-discussed [1]) problem of the origin of the Kṛṣṇa-Vāsudeva worship, and upon the relations between this great figure and Nārāyaṇa. Yet a few remarks must be devoted to Viṣṇu's Kṛṣṇa avatāra in general. The arguments of those scholars who hold that Kṛṣṇa Devakīputra was originally a deity will not, in my opinion, bear scrutiny; one receives

---

all we can see in the documents we cannot go farther than supposing this animal to have been identified, by later generations, with the god under discussion, probably on account of a point of resemblance in their characters.

[33]) Folklore: E. Oder, in Pauly-Wissowa, I (1894), 707; Stemplinger, in the Hdwtb. de. Abergl. I, 206 f.; N. W. Thomas, in Hastings' Encycl. I, p. 522 f. In India they are invoked to avert sterility or damage arising from whirlwinds; see also W. Crooke, Pop. rel. and folklore, I, p. 87 ff.; Dubois, o.c., I, p. 179.

[34]) I refer to Hopkins, Epic Mythology, p. 13 ff.

[35]) Caland, De incarnaties van den god Wishṇu, Provinciaal Utrechtsch Genootschap v. K. en W. 1927; cf. Pargiter, Vṛṣākapi and Hanumant, JRAS. 1913, p. 396 ff.; S. K. Chatterji, Buddhist survivals in Bengal. B. C. Law commemor. volume I, Calcutta 1945, p. 78 ("... a primitive Dravidian word, as in O Tam. *aṇ-manti,* meaning "the male monkey" was in all likelihood both translated into the Indo-Aryan Vedic as *Vṛṣākapi-,* meaning the same thing, and then aryanised into the Skt. *Hanumant-* or *Hanūmant-* as the Great Monkey God ..."). See also H. Jacobi, Das Rāmāyaṇa, Bonn 1893, p. 131 ff.

[1]) See e.g. J. E. Carpenter, Theism in medieval India, London 1926, p. 235 ff.; 265 ff.; 371 ff.; D. C. Sircar, in R. C. Majumdar, The history and culture of the Indian people II, Bombay 1953, p. 431 ff.; R. G. Bhandarkar, Vaiṣṇavism, Çaivism and minor religious systems, Strassburg 1913, esp. p. 30 ff.; Konow, in Chantepie's

on the other hand, in reading the long 'biography' of the great hero, the impression that the Indians already at an early period took delight in ascribing all possible forms of heroic and superhuman action, all characteristics of divine championship to this figure. It is already in the most ancient sources on Kṛṣṇaism difficult to distinguish between the originally Viṣṇuite and the originally Kṛṣṇaite elements [2]). Ruben [3]) is no doubt right in emphasizing that Kṛṣna —who beside Rāma is the most celebrated hero of Indian 'mythology' — is a so-called 'Wanderheld'. There seems to be no limit to his strength and power, no end to the number of his victories. Sprung from the pastoral race of the Yādavas the hero in youthful energy sets out on many dangerous adventures, slays terrible enemies, giants, demons, and monsters sent against him to kill him. He enters the ocean filled with terrible marine beings and overcomes Varuṇa; he obtains from Agni the fiery weapon, the discus and the club Kaumodaki and drives away Indra; he mounts on Garuḍa and alarms the city of the same god who is defeated.

That the (for all we know) younger Kṛṣṇa cult was antagonistic to the ancient worship of Indra, the latter being the losing party, is also apparent from other narratives in the epic and the early purāṇas. In enumerating Kṛṣṇa's feats Arjuna (Mbh. 3, 12, 18 f.) also relates that he slew all the daityas and dānavas and bestowed on Indra the sovereignty of the universe. When Naraka Bhauma had stolen the earrings of Aditi, the gods with Śakra at their head were unable to conquer him and therefore employed Kṛṣṇa whose strength, prowess and irresistible weapons were known to them, for slaying that wicked being (5, 48, 80 ff). "In this war I preferred the help of Vāsudeva (Kṛṣṇa) to Indra with the vajra in his hand" (ibid. 68). "That man whose conquest is merely desired by Kṛṣṇa is sure to gain the victory over all enemies though they be the gods themselves with Indra" (ibid. 70). Once, the Viṣṇupurāṇa (5, 30) narrates, Viṣṇu visited the gardens of Indra "who saluted him respectfully" (st. 28). When his wife Satyabhāmā who accompanied him saw the famous pārijāta tree, the

---

Lehrbuch, II, p. 142 f.; 150 ff. etc. (see p. 681); the papers by Keith to be mentioned farther on; J. Kennedy, JRAS. 1907, p. 961 ff. and 1908, p. 505 ff. ("solar type"); G. Bühler, in the Indian Antiquary 1894, p. 248; G. A. Grierson, ibidem 1908, p. 603 ff.; A. Barth, Religions de l'Inde[5], Paris 1914, p. 100 ff.; Hopkins, Religions of India, p. 465 f.; R. Garbe, Die Bhagavadgītā[2], Leipsic 1921, p. 26 ff.; Ruben, Krishna; Bhagavan Das, Kṛshṇa, Madras-Adyar 1929; H. Raychaudhuri, Materials for the study of the early history of the Vaishnava sect, Calcutta 1936; Radhakrishnan, The Bhagavadgītā, London 1948, p. 28 ff.; Bh. Kumarappa, The Hindu conception of the deity, London 1934, p. 86 ff.

[2]) I also refer to Keith, JRAS. 1908, p. 172.

[3]) Ruben, o.c. I agree with his views on this point with reservations as to detail.

favourite of Indra's consort Śacī, which was produced when the ocean was churned for the amṛta, she asked him to carry it off and to plant it in her own garden. "What right has Śacī, what has Śakra to the tree? It is the common property of all the world, just like the moon and the goddess Śrī herself. Let Indra prevent my husband from carrying off this tree. I know Śakra, the sovereign of the divinities, and I, who am a mortal, take this tree from her" (st. 43 ff). In the following conflict between Indra, vajra in hand, attended by the army of the celestials, and Kṛṣṇa, the former was defeated and derided by Satyabhāmā. But the god acquiesces in the course of events: "What disgrace is it, to be discomfited by him who is the cause of creation, continuance, and dissolution (of the universe)?" (st. 77). In the same purāṇa, 5, a. 10 f. [4]) the interesting story is related of Kṛṣṇa's persuading the cowherds to abandon the worship of Indra and his recommending them to venerate cattle and the mountains. They accordingly worshipped the mountain Govardhana [5]), presenting to it various offerings of curds, milk, and flesh. Kṛṣṇa then, having become the mountain, partook of the food [6]). These stories no doubt intimate that Kṛṣṇa directly overrode the older Vedic gods, especially Indra, his own cult becoming superior not only to that of local and contemporaneous divinities, but also to the Vedic worship of Indra cum suis. In the latter case, too, Indra plays a losing game: offended by the deprivation of his offerings, he causes heavy rain to deluge the country; but Kṛṣṇa by holding up the Govardhana shelters men and cattle, forcing Indra to desist from raining. The god then came to Gokula where Kṛṣṇa, assuming the person of a cow-boy, was tending cattle, and installed him as Upendra.

It is clear that Kṛṣṇa is one of those heroic figures who devote their lives to fighting all kind of evil represented in the shapes of wicked men, terrible animals and powerful demons, and who champion the cause of the good and the righteous. In doing so he even acquired part of Indra's inheritance: when the latter's star was waning it became possible to credit Kṛṣṇa with the victory over hundreds of asuras, inter alia, to mention only this feat of prowess, with the destruction of the great demon Śambara, a sort of replica of Vṛtra, who in the Ṛgveda is vanquished by Indra [7]) — cf. also Mbh. 3, 168, 81; 5, 16,

---

[4]) Cf. also Harivaṃśa, a. 71 ff.; Ruben, o.c., p. 101 ff. — A brief résumé of this and other feats of the man-god Kṛṣṇa may be found in J. Dowson, A classical dictionary of Hindu mythology etc., London, p. 160 ff.

[5]) For its 'holiness' see Ruben, Eisenschmiede, p. 271, and F. S. Growse, IA. 1 (1872), p. 230 ff.

[6]) I also refer to Wilson-Hall, The Vishṇu Purāṇa, IV, London 1868, p. 313.

[7]) See Macdonell, o.c., p. 161. ṚV. 7, 99, 5 he is defeated by Indra and Viṣṇu.

14 etc. —; Mbh. 5, 68, 4 [8]). Like Indra young Kṛṣṇa combated a terrible serpent, dwelling in the water, Kāliya (ViPur. 5, a. 7) [9]).

Kṛṣṇa considered as an avatāra of Viṣṇu, the saviour, is conspicuous by his helpful character. Residing in Dvārakā he is to conquer and to protect the whole earth (Mbh. 13, 147, 36). That man who seeks the protection of Keśava, who is an instructor in dharma, will be victorious and attain heaven (st. 41 f.). When the Earth was oppressed by the demons, a new saviour-incarnation was to be born. The goddess Earth applying to the gods argues that the supreme Nārāyaṇa is her guru and protector, who is Brahmā, one with time, and who assumes the form of all components of the universe (ViPur. 5, a. 1). — Before the great battle between the Pāṇḍavas and Kauravas both parties seek his aid (Mbh. 5, a. 7). In the human form of their ally and companion Kṛṣṇa, Viṣṇu served the Pāṇḍavas, the epic recipients of his favour, as adviser and charioteer. Eternal friendship exists between Kṛṣṇa and Arjuna who is Indra's son and was often compared to this god contesting with Vṛtra: a replica of the Vedic relation between the warrior Indra and his helpful companion Viṣṇu. Viṣṇu always performs what is agreeable to Jiṣṇu (Arjuna; Mbh. 7, 79, 9). He rescues him from danger, acts as his charioteer, promises him victory. In the Bhagavadgītā section this helpful friendship culminates in moral and spiritual assistance and guidance towards salvation. In enumerating Kṛṣṇa's exploits (Mbh. 3, 12, 19; 25 f.) Arjuna does not forget to mention that after having vanquished the daityas he bestowed on Indra the sovereignty of the universe, that he becoming Viṣṇu even while a child pervaded in three steps heaven, firmament and earth, that he, standing in the abode of the Sun, outshone him by his splendour.

Radhakrishnan [10]) finds trace of the conflict between Indra and Viṣṇu in the episode ṚV. 8, 96, 13—15, where a certain Kṛṣṇa, black like a cloud, was destroyed by Indra for the benefit of his favourite Drapsa [11]). If this Kṛṣṇa actually was the same as the later hero and god — which is far from certain, "the Black" being a common name [12]) — he may have been then already an adversary of the mighty god. It is here preferable to neglect this episode.

A few words may also suffice with regard to the untenable doctrine

---

[8]) In the ViPur., 5, a. 27, Çambara is slain by Kṛṣṇa's son Pradyumna.

[9]) See also Zimmer, Myths and symbols, p. 81 ff.; Rao, o.c., 212 f.

[10]) S. Radhakrishnan, Indian philosophy, London 1927 (1948), I, p. 87.

[11]) I refer to Geldner, o.c., III, p. 422 f.

[12]) See J. A. van Velze, Names of persons in early Sanskrit literature, Thesis Utrecht 1938, p. 108; ṚV. 8, 85, 3 f.; Sørensen, Index, p. 425 f.

professed by Keith [13]), according to whom Kṛṣṇa originally was a vegetation demon and the contest between him and Kaṃsa a reflection of the battle between summer and winter and of the periodic slaying of the vegetation spirit. His far-fetched conclusions with regard to a supposed original significance of this struggle for superiority and the connection of the early literary drama with the story of these two figures may be said to rest on misunderstandings and preconceived opinions to such a degree [14]) that it seems advisable not to make them an element in a discussion regarding the early history of the god Viṣṇu.

As may appear from the above Güntert [15]) was no doubt right in drawing the Kṛṣṇa avatāra into the discussion of Viṣṇu's nature and character. Yet I cannot agree with him that it was merely libido raised to the higher state of amor dei [16]) which makes it understandable how an originally phallic god (Viṣṇu), whose cult must have been orgiastic, eventually came to be revered, as Kṛṣṇa, by later generations in an attitude of bhakti. There is no denying that bhakti as a rule implies a considerable element of sublimated erotic, and even sexual, feelings, but this is not to conclude that its only source was sexual appetite [17]). Besides, in the earliest versions of the Kṛṣṇa biography no great stress is laid upon his erotic adventures, his sporting with the gopīs, his thousands of wives and 180000 sons [18]).

The figures of Kṛṣṇa and Viṣṇu must have been long in fusing. In the Mahābhārata Kṛṣṇa's cult is still growing: he is a human chief and warrior, a superhuman hero, a teacher of a path and doctrine

---

[13]) Keith, The child Kṛṣṇa, JRAS. 1908, p. 169 ff.; The origin of the Indian drama, ZDMG. 64, p. 534 ff.; The Vedic ākhyāna and the Indian drama, JRAS. 1911, p. 979 ff.; The origin of tragedy and the ākhyāna, JRAS. 1912, p. 411 ff.; The beginnings of the Indian drama, JRAS. 1916, p. 146 ff.; The Sanskrit drama in its origin, development, theory and practice, Oxford 1924, p. 36 ff. A German résumé of his views was given by Lüders, Die Çaubhikas, Berliner Sitzungsberichte, 1916, p. 278 ff., re-edited in 'Philologica Indica', Göttingen 1940, p. 391 ff., esp. p. 409.

[14]) See especially, Lüders, o.c., p. 406 ff.; Gonda, Ursprung und Wesen des Indischen Dramas, Leyden 1943 (Acta Orientalia 19), p. 330.

[15]) Güntert, Weltkönig, p. 308.

[16]) In support of his supposition Güntert quotes Max Weber, Ges. Aufsätze zur Religionssoziologie II (1921), p. 338.

[17]) As to the essence of bhakti see my paper 'Het begrip bhakti' in the Tijdschrift voor philosophie, 10 (Louvain 1948), p. 607 ff., and A. M. Esnoul, La bhakti, in Renou et Filliozat, L'Inde classique, Paris 1947, p. 661 ff.

[18]) Here again, the applicability of an argumentum e silentio and the character of the texts in which the data under discussion do, or do not, occur should be balanced. An occasional reference to the gopīs in the Mahābhārata (2, 68, 41 the epithet *Gopījanapriya-* "dear to the girls tending cows" turns up) may induce one to suppose them to have been of greater importance to contemporaneous circles which took no part in redacting the epic. See also Ruben, Krishna, p. 109 ff.

leading to final emancipation, an 'incarnation' of the god he proclaims, the All-god, and sometimes an avatāra of Viṣṇu. But the belief in Kṛṣṇa as All-god is comparatively recent (cf. e.g. BhG. 7, 19; 9, 11). Features in his character may have been adapted to the great example given by Viṣṇu. Some stories from ancient 'Viṣṇu legends' may have been early transferred to the cowherd-hero. The question, however, arises, why Kṛṣṇa was identified with Viṣṇu and not with any other Vedic deity. Raychaudhuri [19]), in endeavouring to solve this problem is in my opinion right in pointing out that the benevolent Viṣṇu always was a deliverer of mankind in distress and a great helper of the other gods against the asuras. This feature, indeed, not only fitted him to be the centre of other famous avatāras (cf. BhG. 4, 8), they made also acceptable the conception underlying the Rāma, Kṛṣṇa, and Buddha avatāras: noble and heroic men who are great benefactors of mankind represent Viṣṇu. In the above reference has already been made to other possible factors in this process. Special attention must be drawn to Kṛṣṇa's association with Arjuna and to the significance of their way of acting as a pair (cf. also BhG. 18, 78).

We grope in the dark as to the origin of the close connection between these two figures, Kṛṣṇa and Arjuna. It is difficult not to remember the stanza ṚV. 6, 9, 1 *áhaś ca kṛṣṇám áhar árjunaṃ ca* "the dark day and the bright (white) day...." [20]): these two here constitute a complementary pair, the 'dualité-unité' of the natural day (cf. 1, 49, 3 where *arjuna-* is used in connection with *uṣas-* "dawn", and 1, 113, 2 where *kṛṣṇa-* applies to the night) [21]). Moreover, VS. 31, 22 the creative power Prajāpati in the form of the sun is addressed as follows: "Śrī and Lakṣmī are thy wives; each side of thee are day and night". There is, however, as far as I am able to see, no possibility of identifying, or of tracing any connection between, these black and white ones with the epic Kṛṣṇa and Arjuna. It may, for all that, be worth noticing that in the Ṛgveda the adjective *kṛṣṇa-* is, in a natural way, also applied to demons (4, 16, 13); *arjuna-*, on the other hand, 3, 44, 5 is used to qualify Indra's *vajra-*. 1, 122, 5 *Arjuna-* is the name of an otherwise unknown man [22]).

According to a tradition preserved in the Jātaka collection (vol. V,

---

[19]) Raychaudhuri, Materials for the study of the early history of the Vaishnava sect, p. 108.

[20]) See Geldner, o.c., II, p. 601 and A. Bergaigne, La religion védique, II, p. 423.

[21]) This stanza is quoted AB. 5, 15, 5; ÇāB. 23, 8: these passages throw no light on the point at issue.

[22]) See Geldner, o.c., I, p. 168.

p. 424 ff.) Ajjuna, "the eldest of the five sons of king Pāṇḍu" was married to Kaṇhā, who was also the wife of his brothers. This Kaṇhā "the dark or black one" is the epic Draupadī who, in Sanskrit, is often called Kṛṣṇā (cf. e.g. Mbh. 1, 167, 45 ff.). Of no greater relevance is probably another Jātaka story, found in the Ghata (no. 454, vol. IV, p. 79 ff.) which describes the adventures of the ten sons of Devagabbhā by Upasagara who were brought up as the children of Nandagopā and Andhakaveṇhu [23]).

The Śatapathabrāhmaṇa 2, 1, 2, 11 and 5, 4, 3, 7 informs us that Arjuna is a secret or mystical (*guhya-*) name of Indra [24]). The king, the latter passage states, is Indra for a twofold reason, because he is a kṣatriya and because he is a sacrificer; therefore he pronounces the formula VS. 10, 21 [25]). Pāṇini, who gives evidence of knowing names connected with the epic, informs us (4, 3, 98) that the words meaning "an adorer (or: lover, admirer) of Vāsudeva", "an adorer of Arjuna" (cf. 95 *bhaktiḥ*) are formed in the same way, to wit by the suffix *-ka-* [26]). Does this grammatical rule imply, as Hopkins would have us believe, that Pāṇini "recognizes the Arjuna-Krishna cult"? There is, as far as I am able to see, nothing in the context to warrant the conclusion that the great grammarian refers to a strictly religious cult only. It is, moreover, in my opinion, not certain whether this sūtra proves that Arjuna and Vāsudeva formed, in Pāṇini's times, a pair or companions. These words were the only instances for the rule under discussion and it may be that this is the only reason why the grammarian mentioned them together. The common suffix *-ka-* may point to actual companionship of the bearers of the names underlying the derivatives,

---

[23]) See E. B. Cowell, The Jātaka, translated ..., IV, Cambridge 1901, p. 51 n.; Hopkins, Epic Mythology, p. 214 f.; E. Hardy, Eine buddhistische Bearbeitung der Kṛṣṇa-Sage, ZDMG. 53, p. 25 ff.; Lüders, ZDMG. 58, p. 687 ff. (= Philologica Indica, p. 80 ff.); H. Jacobi, Die Jaina-Legende von ... dem Tode Kṛishṇas, ZDMG. 42, p. 496 f.; Ruben, Krishna, p. 248 ff. This text is a turbid and secondary source of information. It may however be noticed that Ajjuna here appears as a younger brother of Vāsudeva before Pajjuna who, according to Hardy, o.c., p. 33, n., and Lüders, Phil. Ind., p. 91, represents Pradyumna. "Wohl hauptsächlich durch den Anklang an Pajjuna veranlaßt, scheint auch der Name des Ajjuna hierher geraten zu sein" (Lüders). Or has a reminiscense of the ancient god of rain, Pajjunna, who is not foreign to the Jātakas (see G. P. Malalasekera, Dict. of Pāli proper names, II, London 1938, p. 98) caused the name of Ajjuna = Sakka, Indra, to have crept in here, after the Moon, the Sun, Agni, and Varuṇa??

[24]) See also A. Weber, Ind. Studien I, p. 189 f.

[25]) Cf. also TB. 2, 7, 16, 1; KÇS. 15, 6, 17.

[26]) For this sūtra see, inter alia, Hopkins, The Great Epic of India, New York 1902, p. 390; Raychaudhuri, o.c., p. 24 and 101; see also M. Winternitz, Geschichte der indischen Literatur I², Leipsic, p. 400, n. 2.

but this is not necessarily so. Besides, how are we to know for certain that Pāṇini's Vāsudeva was already identified with Kṛṣṇa?[27])

Now, the Mahābhārata repeatedly states that Arjuna Pāṇḍava is Nara, and Kṛṣṇa-Vāsudeva is Nārāyaṇa[28]). Referring for the factors determining the latter's fusion with Viṣṇu to Bhandarkar's description, I only recall here that according to Indian traditions (see e.g. Manu 1, 10) as well as deductions of modern scholarship he was a divine being of rather early occurrence and associated, in some way or other, with the water. Such texts as ŚB. 12, 3, 4, 1 ff.; 13, 6, 1; TĀ. 10, 11 enable us to trace some stages in his career towards the dignity of the Supreme Soul and origin of the world and towards his merging in Viṣṇu, the pervader and All-god. Nara, the original man, with whom Arjuna is identified, is, on the other hand, the son of Indra (Mbh. 1, 67, 110 f.). Apart from other aspects of their eternal friendship — for which I refer to the observations of my predecessors[29]) — we may consider it, in a way, a counterpart of the mythical alliance between Indra and Viṣṇu. In the great epic war Kṛṣṇa though assisting the Pāṇḍavas and rendering valuable services to Arjuna, refused to take any active part in military operations. In this background rôle he resembles the Vedic Viṣṇu.

There are other such pairs of divine or heroic friends, one of whom is more active than the other who acts as his helper or adviser. That they were at least sometimes considered reproductions or representatives of a mythical 'Urbild' may appear from the standing epithets given to them by the epic poets and from the recurrent similes illustrating their character and activities. Rāma and Lakṣmaṇa are compared to Indra and Viṣṇu (Rām. 3, 68, 38). Describing the combat between Lakṣmaṇa and Indrajit (Rāvaṇa's son) the author says that they fought like Indra and Vṛtra (6,88, 35; cf. 90, 74). Caland[30]) tried to show that Valmīki in depicting the character and adventures of these brothers followed the Vedic exemple of Indra and Viṣṇu, giving, however, precedence to Rāma-Viṣṇu, because in his times this god was the greater. A passage like 6, 91, 4 where Lakṣmaṇa is compared to Viṣṇu might, then, be

---

27) In his comment on this sūtra Patañjali says that Vāsudeva is the name of the "worshipful" (*tatrabhavat-*). See also R. G. Bhandarkar, JRAS. 1910, p. 168 ff.

28) See, for the sake of brevity, Miss Das Gupta, IHQ. 8, p. 64 ff.; Bhandarkar, Vaiṣṇavism, etc., p. 30 ff.; Sorensen, Index, p. 504 and 508 ff.; for Nārāyaṇa see also the facts collected by Ruben, Eisenschmiede, p. 237 ff., of some of whose inferences I am, for the time being, sceptical. For the philosophical conceptions underlying the Nārāyaṇa mythology see Radhakrishnan, Ind. philosophy I, p. 492.

29) See e.g. Radhakrishnan, o.c., I, p. 489 ff. — Compare also Bh. S. Upadhyaya, India in Kālidāsa, Allahabad 1947, p. 308.

30) Caland, Verslag Prov. Utrechtsch Genootschap v. K. en Wet. 1927.

regarded as a relic of the original relation. The identity of Rāma and 'Indra-Parjanya' was, as early as 1893, a thesis defended by Jacobi [31]). Points of resemblance between Rāma and Arjuna Pāṇḍava, Indra's son, are not wanting [32]). I, for one, would, more cautiously, suggest the poets of the Rāmāyaṇa to have conceived the Rāma-Lakṣmaṇa theme under the influence of a general mythical scheme concerning the co-operation of an active figure, a warrior and destroyer of enemies, and a helper, an idea which inter alia found expression in the Vedic Indra-Viṣṇu myth [33]).

The conclusion might be that the idea represented by the ancient myth concerning the contest between the champion of the good and righteous, the promoter of life and fertility, and the power or being withdrawing these goods from gods and men, which forms the theme of the central mythical complex of the ancient Vedic period, was repeatedly expressed in variations. The mythical essence of the ever-renewed battle between the god Indra, assisted by the Maruts, by Viṣṇu or other divinities, and the dragon or demon Vṛtra always survived. It was recast and remoulded and made its influence felt in later times. Rāma's contest with Rāvaṇa, Buddha's continuous endeavour for victory over Māra, Kṛṣṇa's innumerable exploits, the very idea underlying all avatāras is the selfsame antagonism between the great upholder of the cause of the good, and the evil power of destruction, starvation, and death. The Indians were always ready to associate new ideas with, or to create new 'personalizations' of ideas to, those forms or concepts with which they were, at a given moment, already familiar. Taking into account their belief in the continuation of life and in ever-recurring earthly existence it was only natural that all those defenders of mankind and conquerors of the wicked and evil powers were considered to be essentially identical. And also that their consorts and female complements were reincarnations of the same divine power. Sītā, the Furrow, is like Nārāyaṇa's wife, and like Rukmiṇī who was married to Kṛṣṇa,

---

31) Jacobi, Rāmāyaṇa, p. 131; 134.

32) I refer to M. Winternitz, Geschichte der indischen Litteratur², Leipsic, I, p. 428. — It may be observed that in folk tales the younger brother is often the braver, see e.g. Ruben, Krishna, p. 58; 108.

33) Dual deities or gods acting in pairs: Macdonell, Ved. myth., p. 126 ff.; Keith, Rel. and philos., p. 220 f.; Haeberlin, Memoirs American Anthrop. Ass. 3 (1916), p. 35; Abegg, Messiasglaube in Indien und Iran, p. 84, n. 2 (with lit.). Bertholet-Lehmann, Lehrbuch, II, p. 664, s.v. Götterpaare; G. Dumézil, Mitra-Varuṇa, Paris 1948. — It would not be improper here to recall the co-operation of the active prakṛti and the pervading ātman. Nara-Nārāyaṇa are also a pair forming unity (Mbh. 5, 49, 20).

Śrī-Lakṣmī reborn [34]). It is a curious detail that in the beginning the champion was a great god with an assistant, that during the ensuing centuries the might and influence of the assistant gained in importance, that, finally, in the classical form of the Viṣṇu avatāras, under the influence of the belief in a High God, that ancient assistant had risen to the paramount position of mankind's Saviour.

This development did not preclude part of the Indian population from revering Viṣṇu and the deities associated with him in a manner different from those forms of Rāmaism, Kṛṣṇaism, Bhāgavatism as are best known to us from literary sources. Nor is it a matter of astonishment either that Viṣṇu-Kṛṣṇa becoming popular and increasing in importance intruded himself upon cults and festivals of other gods [35]).

It would, finally, appear to me that the very identifications of Kṛṣṇa and Rāma with Viṣṇu, this very merging of Bhāgavatism etc. in Viṣṇuism, must, on the other hand, have much contributed to ennobling and humanizing the god's character, to broadening the circle of his interests, to deepening his divinity, to pushing into the background the ancient naturalistic traits, his connections with natural phenomena, his interest in such special fields as generation, fertility, and atmospheric activity. The selfsame identifications were no doubt largely instrumental in winning for him the lasting devotion of many millions. Certain aspects of his character obtained enhanced significance by fusing with other figures. His traversing and pervading action could be viewed in a new light when he was identified with Puruṣa-Nārāyaṇa "who is everything here" (ŚB. 13, 6, 1, 1), "in whom are light, might, and glory" (cf. 12, 3, 4, 6), that is: earth, atmosphere, and heavens (ibid. 7), Agni, Vāyu, and Āditya (the Sun, ibid. 8) [36]).

---

[34]) Aditi is reborn as Devakī, Kṛṣṇa's mother (Hariv. 55, 37 f.) — As to Rādhā, her name is doubtless related to the Vedic *rādhas* "success, prosperity, wealth, bounty, favour, liberality", *rādhā* itself being not entirely unusual instead of *samṛddhi*- etc. At a later period Kṛṣṇa's beloved was deified and occasionally regarded as an avatāra of Çrī-Lakṣmī (compare the decided opinions defended by Bh. Krishna Sastri, The bhakti cult in ancient India, Calcutta 1922, p. 105 f.). — Like Viṣṇu, Rāma is supposed to have the disposal of *śrī*- and to be able to protect (cf. e.g. Rāmarah.Up. 2, 81; Rāmapū.Up. 4, 15). — For Sīta now compare also C. Bulcke S.J., La naissance de Sītā, BEFEO. 46 (1952), p. 107 ff., with whom I cannot agree in all particulars. — In particulars opinions may vary: Lakṣmaṇa e.g. represented one eighth part of Viṣṇu's divinity, but Tulsī Dās also follows the Adhyātmā Rāmāyaṇa (see H. von Glasenapp, Abh. Akad. Wiss. u. Lit. Mainz 1951, 6, p. 76) in considering him an incarnation of the snake Çeṣa.

[35]) I refer to Meyer, o.c., III, p. 306; Raychaudhuri, o.c., p. 166 ff.

[36]) The reader might also be referred to the papers by Miss M. Das Gupta, in the IHQ. 7 (1931), p. 93 ff.; 343 ff.; 655 ff.

XXIII. VIṢṆU AND KINGSHIP.

There is a striking parallelism between the special emphasis laid already in Vedic texts upon Viṣṇu's protecting activities and his intimate relations with kingship, the first function of which is to protect the world and its inhabitants and to defend the dharma, to punish the wicked [1]). Viṣṇu indeed is a protector: AV. 6, 3, 1 is not very significant, Indra-and-Pūṣan, Aditi, the Maruts, the child of the waters, the seven rivers, heaven being invoked for protection at the same time, but other ancient texts are: TS. 3, 1, 10, 3 "O Viṣṇu, as our nearest, O mighty one, grant us protection"; ibid. 1, 1, 11 s; 2, 2 g; 4, 10 b; 11 b; VS. 1, 4 "Be thou protector of the oblation, Viṣṇu"; 2, 6; AiB. 3, 38, 3; 7, 5, 4 "Viṣṇu guards that of the sacrifice which is ill-offered, Varuṇa that which is well-offered" [2]); ŚB. 1, 3, 4, 16 "Protect these, O Viṣṇu, protect the sacrifice, protect the lord of sacrifice"; 7, 1, 21; 4, 2, 2, 10; 3, 5, 8; and, in addition to these Vedic passages, Mbh. 2, 24, 34; 3, 249, 26 where he is stated to look after the celestials; 8, 45, 34 where he protects all creatures; 12, 48, 70 etc..

King Pṛthu Vainya was his favourite. It was Viṣṇu himself who crowned him and confirmed his power. He even entered his body, for which reason the entire universe bows to the king as to a god (Mbh. 12, 59, 127 ff.). The king is really, the text adds, endowed with Viṣṇu's greatness on earth (*mahattvena ca saṃyukto vaiṣṇavena naro bhuvi*). And at that very moment the golden lotus sprang from Viṣṇu's forehead, from which the goddess Śrī was born who became the wife of Dharma and the mother of Artha. These three were firmly established (*pratiṣṭhita-*) in the king, i.e. in the king in general. Pṛthu Vainya first milked the earth in the form of a cow which yielded the milk in the outward appearance of food-grains. In other texts the self-born creator is described as milking the earth himself and starting agriculture [3]).

Thus the god entered all kings. Already in the TB. 1, 7, 4, 4, it is observed that by identifying himself with Viṣṇu the king is able to

---

[1]) For kingship in ancient India see e.g. P.V. Kane, History of Dharmaśāstra, II, Poona 1941, Index, p. 1313 f. s.v.; J. J. Meyer, Das altindische Buch vom Welt- und Staatsleben, Leipsic 1926, p. 913; the same, Trilogie III, p. 306; the same, Sexual life in ancient India, London 1930, p. 578; J. Gonda, Ursprung und Wesen des indischen Dramas, Acta Or. 19, p. 417 ff.; Patil, Cult. hist. from the Vāyu Pur., p. 161 ff.; Upadhyaya, India in Kālidāsa, p. 83 ff.; compare also Mānavadharmaśāstra, esp. a. 7.

[2]) These passages were recently discussed by D. J. Hoens, Çānti I, Thesis Utrecht 1951, p. 41. — For Viṣṇu as a protector see also Miss Das Gupta, o.c., 7, p. 105.

[3]) Patil, o.c., p. 90. See e.g. also Saurapur. 27, 7 ff.

conquer the worlds: *viṣṇur eva bhūtvemāṃl lokān abhijayati.* Hence also such comparisons between a great sovereign and the god as Mbh. 3, 126, 2 (both of them ruling the three worlds), such mythical tales as that regarding Puraṃjaya, the illustrious prince, into whom the god descends with a portion (*aṃśa-*) of his own being, in order to destroy, on earth, all the enemies of the gods (ViPur. 4, 2, 6 ff.), and such blessings as: "May this king.... long protect the earth — he who is Viṣṇu himself in the form of a king, to whose tusk when he had assumed the form of the boar fitted to grant protection, the earth, in days of yore, clung...." (Mudrārākṣasa 7, 19). All cakravartins or paramount sovereigns bear a portion of Viṣṇu's personality which is sometimes more precisely stated to consist of *tejas* "fiery energy". Cf. e.g. VāPur. 57, 72 *viṣṇor aṃśena jāyante pṛthivyāṃ cakravartinaḥ manvantareṣu sarveṣu atītānāgateṣu vai.* This is the ancient conception of the divinity of kingship in the setting and foundation given to it by Viṣṇuite Hinduism.

Viṣṇu, the supreme ruler and protector of the universe[4]), is also often represented on a royal throne. In India proper and in Greater India cases are not rare in which kings by erecting statues of themselves in the garb of the god established and confirmed their identity with him[5]). These customs and the conceptions underlying them are in harmony with the ideas regarding divine kingship current among other peoples. Ancient civilizatons of the Near East likewise admitted that the king and the 'high god', or the fertility deity, or the high god in his fertility aspect, were identical[6]). In the king the high god's power was embodied in a living figure.

Apart from other considerations, attention to which shall be given presently, this conception regarding the king representing Viṣṇu is also understandable from the point of view of the ruler's function with respect to the furtherance of vegetation. It was an essential part of the

---

4) The god is also a *cakravartin-*.

5) S. Stevenson, The rites of the Twice-born, London 1920, p. 89, n. 1; J. Auboyer, Le trône et son symbolisme dans l'Inde ancienne, Paris 1949, p. 163 f.; G. Coedès, L'apothéose au Cambodge, Bulletin de la comm. archéol. de l'Indochine 1911, p. 28; the same, Les états hindouisés d'Indochine et d'Indonésie, Paris 1948, p. 207. — The Bhāratīya Nāṭyaśāstra, 1, 59, describing the presentations made by the chief gods to the initiators of dramatic art, provides us with the interesting detail that Viṣṇu gave a throne (lion-seat, *siṃhāsana-*). As the other gods gave objects typical of their functions and characters (Indra his banner, Varuṇa a golden pitcher, the Sun an umbrella etc.), the throne may be considered as 'belonging to' Viṣṇu.

6) I refer to I. Engnell, Studies in divine kingship in the ancient Near East, Thesis Uppsala 1943, p. 6 f.; 22 ff.; 53 (Egypt, Mesopotamia, Hittites); see also Van der Leeuw, Religion, ch. 13; Birket-Smith, Geschichte der Kultur, p. 316 ff.; Frankfort, Before philosophy, passim.

king's duty to make rain and to cause the crops to be good. It was he who by his conduct made the sun to shine, or drought to vex mankind. In short, he was responsible for the welfare of his subjects and the course of nature determining it [7]). The same functions are attributed to Viṣṇu who is always concerned with generation and fertility, whether he is believed to be active in the atmosphere or in other provinces of the universe. Neither the generative power rightly ascribed to the sunlight [8]) nor the intimate connections between the sun and the earth [9]), or on the other hand the similarity or 'identity' supposed to exist between the king and the Supreme god who represents inter alia the fertilizing rays of the celestial light [10]) seem to require further comment.

Now it is important to remember that there are, in the older literature, many allusions to a similar association between Indra and kingship. In those texts of the Atharvaveda which pertain to kings and their functions Indra, the king of gods, is the heavenly prototype of the earthly ruler: cf. e.g. 3, 4, 6 (used in establishing a king) where the ruler is addressed as being like a human Indra [11]); 6, 87, 2 (which is a document of similar purport): "O Indra, stand thou fixed just here; here do thou maintain royalty". The king and Indra, if not tending to merge their identity in each other's, are companions: 4, 22, 5 f. It is Indra who puts great splendours in the ruler: 22, 3, who makes him victorious: 22, 5 f., who is invoked to establish him: 3, 3, 6. In the brāhmaṇas Indra, the chief of gods (cf. e.g. ŚB. 3, 4, 2, 2) and the strongest of them (ŚB. 4, 6, 6, 3), the valiant hero, is, in a very appropriate manner, the representative of the ruling class. Indra is the *kṣatra-* "ruling power" (5, 3, 1, 3; 10, 4, 1, 5; cf. 8, 4, 3, 10). The vital power or energy called *ojas,* which 'belongs to' Indra as "brilliance, illuminating power" (*varcas*) is associated with fire, and "the power of shining radiantly" (*bhrājas*) with the sun, is often mentioned in connection with kings and kingship [12]). In the epics [13]) the warriors are supported by the hope of reaching Indra's heaven, and although the gods seldom interfere in human conflicts , Indra still maintains some

---

7) See Gonda, o.c. (n. 1), p. 417 ff.; J. J. Meyer, Sexual life, p. 286 f.; Coomaraswamy, Yakṣas II, p. 37 f. and the texts and papers adduced by these authors. See e.g. also Mānavadhś. 7, 1 ff.

8) I refer to Eliade, Traité, p. 118; 123 ff.; 132 ff.

9) See Eliade, o.c., p. 124.

10) See Eliade, p. 126; 128.

11) I refer to Whitney-Lanman, o.c., p. 90.

12) See my treatise on *ojas,* p. 17 ff.

13) The reader might be referred to E. W. Hopkins, The social and military position of the ruling caste in ancient India..., JAOS. 13 (New Haven 1889), p. 315.

bonds with the rulers who are called *narendra-* "Indras, i.e. lords of men", though it is not exclusively his essence that pervades a king: Rām. 7, 76, 31 f. the king is said to be Indra, Varuṇa, Kubera, and Yama incorporated. In a similar way, Manu, 5, 96 and 7, 4, describes the king as being formed of particles of the eight guardians of the world, Indra, the Wind, Yama, the Sun, Fire, Varuṇa, the Moon, and Kubera [14]). Mbh. 12, 59, 118 Śakra-Indra is said to bestow wealth on Pṛthu Vainya who in st. 98 was described as *rūpeṇendra ivāparaḥ*.

These facts may suffice to demonstrate that in this point too, Viṣṇu in the course of time inherited part of the functions of his "elder brother", or to express ourselves more precisely: that in younger texts it is Viṣṇu who is credited with power, influence, functions, activities which in the older literature were mainly the concern of Indra, and that by having these transferred to him he (to all appearance) brought his personality to a state of greater completion [15]).

XXIV. THE MYTH OF VIṢṆU, THE SUN, AND INDRA.

There is an ancient and highly interesting myth, the latter part of which has, in contradistinction to the former half, not found the attention which it deserves [1]). It is told at length in the ŚB. 14, 1, 1, 1 ff.; compare also TĀ. 5, 1, 1 ff.; MS. 4, 5, 9 [2]). The gods Agni, Indra, Soma, Makha, Viṣṇu and the Viśve Devāḥ, excepting the two Aśvins, performed a sacrificial session. Entering upon it they thought: "May we attain excellence (*śrī-*); may we become glorious (*yaśas*); may we become eaters of food". They said: "Whoever of us, through austerity...., shall first reach the end of the sacrifice shall be the most excellent (*śreṣṭha-*) of us". Viṣṇu first attained it and he became the most excellent of the gods. Hence people declare him to be so. Now Viṣṇu is the sacrifice, and the sacrifice is the sun. But Viṣṇu became unduly puffed up with the glory (*yaśas*) which he had won. He took his bow and kept standing and resting on the end of it. Not

---

14) Cf., e.g., also Kauṭilya, Arthaś. 13 (9, 10): see Meyer, Das altind. Buch v. Welt- u. Staatsleben, p. 26, n. 2.

15) It may be useful to touch here upon another point. VS. 14, 24 and in other texts the mantras are mentioned which are to accompany the laying down of the so-called freeing bricks in building the fire-altar. These bricks are symbolical of Prajāpati's deliverance, with the assistance of the gods, of all beings from evil, from death. Each divine being which aided this work received a portion and an *ādhipatya-* or "lordship". Among them are Viṣṇu, Varuṇa, the Rudras, Pūṣan etc.

1) Keith, Rel. and phil. p. 112 is in my opinion mistaken in denying any symbolic sense to it.

2) See also n. 5.

daring to attack him, the gods sat themselves down all around him. The ants [3]), on the promise of the reward of being able constantly to enjoy food and to find water even in the desert, gnawed the string of his bow. When it was cut, the ends, springing asunder, cut off Viṣṇu's head. It fell and became the sun. — So far the myth may be regarded as referring to a rather close connection between Viṣṇu and that luminary.

It must, however, be emphasized that only the upper part of the god, his head, is identified with the sun. The story continues: The gods rushed forward to him, even as those eager to secure gain will do. Indra, reaching him first, applied himself to him limb after limb and enclosed him in his own self, so that he became possessed of that glory of his. Because Makha "Sacrifice" is the same as Viṣṇu Indra became *makhavat-* (possessed of *makha-*) which is mystically identical with *maghavat-*, a well-known epithet of Indra [4]).

In this myth the figure of Viṣṇu, who is the sacrifice, becomes two, the sun and a substance which is absorbed by Indra. Indra contains, embraces, represents, the very body and 'glory' of Viṣṇu, minus the head. Or to express ourselves otherwise: Indra has borrowed the very essence of the other god; the sun and Indra together essentially coincide with, derive their existence or important qualities, from Viṣṇu. We have already had occasion to point out the manifold connections of the latter god with Indra as well as with the sun and the solar energy.

In the above version of the myth Makha is one of the gods present. ŚB. 6, 5, 2, 1 he is said to be the sacrifice, and in the very text under discussion, 14, 1, 1, 13, he is, as we have seen, identified with Viṣṇu. Elsewhere it is this divinity who is the central figure of a similar myth: PB. 7, 5, 6 ff. the gods Agni, Indra, Vāyu and Makha, desirous of *yaśas,* performed a sacrificial session, saying that the yaśas which would come to (one of) them should be in common to (all of) them. Makha (who is identified with the sacrifice), to whom it came, took it and went off. When the other gods tried to take it from him, the end of his bow springing upwards cut off his head — the ants are not mentioned [5]).

---

[3]) See R. T. H. Griffith, The texts of the White Yajurveda translated, Benares 1927, p. 349 f.; J. Muir, Original Sanskrit texts IV, London 1873, p. 123 ff.

[4]) For Makha "Sacrifice" see Keith p. 226 and 381; Hillebrandt, Ved. Myth.[2] II, p. 415, n. 4. See also ṚV. 9, 101, 13; 10, 171, 2.

[5]) According to the Kāṭhakas (Kāṭh. Āraṇyaka, ed. L. von Schroeder, Berl. Sitz. Ber. 137, p. 114) it was Indra who in the shape of an ant gnawed through, with the same effect, the bowstring of Rudra who was excluded by the gods from the sacrifice. ṚV. 10, 171, 2 alludes to a story in which Indra severed the head of the recalcitrant Makha from his body. The same motive occurs in the Skanda-purāṇa; see Caland, Incarnaties, p. 13.

in the latter's victory: the daitya Hiraṇyakaśipu had wrested the sovereignty of the heavenly realm from Indra; his son Prahlāda drove him to frenzy by becoming an ardent devotee of Viṣṇu, who, as man-lion, killed the father in order to avenge Prahlāda and to vindicate his own insulted majesty. Mythologically, his high position came to be expressed by a variety of identifications — he was not only impersonated as Indra and Rudra, but Agni and other gods were considered forms of, or identical with, him: e.g. Mbh. 12, 343, 15 and 3, 88, 24 f. where Dharma is identified with Viṣṇu-Kṛṣṇa — and by genealogical relations: Gaṇeśa, the son of Pārvatī (and Śiva), is sometimes regarded as having sprung from Viṣṇu [12]) — and so is Manmatha — but Mbh. 13, 149, 79 Ganeśvara is a title of this god himself. Although Śivaites tended to trace his origin back to their great god Śiva (e.g. SauraP. 55, 27), they usually acknowledged him as superior to the other divine beings: considering him the best of the gods (*surāḥ*), the lord of the ādityas and other divinities, they often held those to contain his essence [13]). The superior position and the fervent adoration of millions who consider him or his main avatāras to be God, have, on the other hand, not prevented some groups from continuing to worship him as a being of lower rank. There are many, even now, who do not adore him as the omnipotent deity [14]), but emphasize special aspects of his manifold character. As a matter of course in mythological and miraculous stories, cults and ceremonies much has been preserved which could also belong to divine beings of a lower position [15]).

However, it cannot be part of my task to summarize here the later development of Viṣṇuism in which the fusion of the old god with Kṛṣṇa and Nārāyaṇa and the bhakti movement were, beside other historical processes, essential factors.

XXV. EPILOGUE.

An attempt may now be made to recapitulate the most salient points in our argument and briefly to sketch the main features in the character of the early Viṣṇu.

We are, to begin with, fortified in our opinion that any effort to give

---

[12]) See e.g. Sonnerat, o.c., p. 276 f.; Caland, Portug. Verh., p. 88 ff. — In temples G. is also worshipped together with V.'s animal avatāras: Getty, Gaṇeśa, Oxford 1936, p. 1; 7 ff. There appears to have been no sharp division between Viṣṇuism and Çivaism in various parts of India in early days.

[13]) For other particulars see Patil, o.c., p. 84.

[14]) See e.g. also Dinesh Chandra Sen, The Bengali Ramayanas, Calcutta 1920, p. 114.

[15]) See e.g. H. von Glasenapp, Heilige Stätten Indiens, München 1928, p. 96 ff.

a historical account of the rôle played by the god in the spiritual and religious life of ancient India can for reasons peculiar both to the character of our sources and to the nature of the subject itself only end in an unsatisfactory substitute of what a historical study should be. We have therefore preferred to focus attention mainly on the various aspects in which the god manifested himself to those who left their writings to us, without attempting to combine them in a chronological scheme and without assuming that one of them had, at a more remote period, represented the 'original character' of the god. In doing so it has been our endeavour to understand, as far as possible, what must have been the complete sense conveyed by the term Viṣṇu, what may be regarded as the significance of the figure Viṣṇu as it presented itself to the minds of the ancient Indians themselves.

It would appear to the present author that there is much truth in the time-honoured Indian interpretation of the god's character as representing pervasiveness. The quality expressed by that term, the actual penetration of the provinces of the universe must indeed be considered a central feature in the vast complex of ideas and representations denoted by the name Viṣṇu[1]). The frequency of the terms conveying the ideas of permeating and penetrating, of distribution and spatial extensiveness, the identification with *virāj-*, i.e. the idea of ruling far and wide, which is at the same time regarded as the totality or sum of all existence and often identified with *śrī-* or "prosperity" point in the same direction as Viṣṇu's famous striding activity which enabled him to traverse the worlds and cover the universe. The general idea originally underlying this central mythical act seems to have been the eternal phenomenon of the pervading and omnipresent, mighty and blessing stream of celestial light, warmth, and energy. But Viṣṇu was more than this. The universe being tripartite the act intimates, in a way, the god's universal character[2]). All beings abide in these three steps. By his striding movement and other activities Viṣṇu, moreover, essentially contributes to Indra's greatness and to his success in combating the evil and obstruction, known as Vṛtra and other demoniac beings. The close association between the Vedic Viṣṇu and Indra who was mainly a representative of power in nature (and especially in the atmosphere), of victorious display of power for the well-being of man-

[1]) To reassure those scholars who seem to distrust any result of investigations in the field of Indian cultural history if it happens to agree, to a certain extent, with the traditional opinions of the Indians themselves, it may be noticed here that this point was far from clear to me when I commenced my researches.

[2]) The universal character of the god is for instance also expressed AiB. 1, 14 *agnir vai sarvā devatā, viṣṇuḥ sarvā devatā.*

kind and the maintenance of those processes on the earth and in the atmosphere on which man's life and subsistence depend, has often and rightly been emphasized in books on ancient Indian religion. The unfortunately rather scarce references to Viṣṇu's entering Indra's bolt may probably be considered another indication of his pervasive character as well as his intimate relations with the descent of the celestial blessings to the earth and the processes resulting from it. By striding Viṣṇu obtains, for the gods: their all-pervading power, for man: ample room and 'living space'. In doing so he is instrumental in protecting 'Aditi's lap', i.e. the place of universal creation, from narrowness and obstruction. He, moreover, acquires the power of pervasion and penetration for the sacrificer who by imitating the god's activity reaches his goal, the highest light, the heavenly world, the safe refuge [3]).

Like the creator-god Prajāpati, who is to fuse with Viṣṇu in later times, the latter is also identical with the powerful device for ensuring the operation of all powers for good and means of gaining entrance into the celestial worlds, the sacrifice. The sacrifice is supposed to be localized in the omphalos; and in epic and other texts Viṣṇu's omphalos is the place from which Brahmā arises. It is the centre of the universe, the source of existence. The sacrificial post (*yūpa-*), like the tree, belongs to him. Being a path to heaven, a representative of the idea of the axis which connects the 'centre' of the earth with the summit of the sky, it is erected in the immediate neighbourhood of the altar and constitutes an essential feature of the ritual.

Being concerned with the axis, the navel, the descent of celestial light and the transmission of the heavenly blessings to the world of mankind, assisting Indra in destroying and warding off the powers of evil, Viṣṇu was in a natural manner considered a protector who rendered services of the utmost importance to gods and men, developing (often, but not always, as Indra's successor) a fighting spirit, and being regarded as invincible.

These qualities of character involved a deep concern for the weal and woe of mankind and the world. Viṣṇu was, often in co-operation with other gods, intent on promoting the processes and maintaining the phenomena connected with vegetation, fecundation, and fertilization, with the means of supporting life and with the continuance of the human race in general. Hence also the intimate relations with kingship which become manifest in later times.

It would appear to us that many points discussed in the preceding

---

[3]) See e.g. also the very instructive passage ÇB. 1, 9, 3, 10. — For the rays of the sun as a means of approaching that luminary, see e.g. JUB. 1, 30, 1 f.

sections illustrate an often unmistakable continuity in the god's history. Various details shed light upon those characteristics of the Vedic deity which have persisted and reached maturity in the subsequent period or enable us to gain an insight into those factors which helped, or even predisposed, him to gain the high position which he occupies in Hinduism. Although he became the Supreme Being only after a long process of amalgamation, many particulars of which have unfortunately been lost for ever, Viṣṇu's omnipresence [4]), his ruling, protecting, and supporting activities, his interest in human welfare, his ascent to the high position of a Saviour, are not only due to his being considered, in the course of time, the personal aspect of brahman, nor to the composite character of the great God who had borrowed functions from Vedic deities and fused with the central figures of pre-existent popular cults. However much the process of amalgamation has contributed to deepening the god's character we are still in a position to understand, in the main, why it has been Viṣṇu who could rise so high among the gods of the early period. We see that his chief avatāras recall ancient traits in his character: helpfulness, rescuing activity, willingness to descend to, or even to penetrate into and to serve as support of, the earth, resistance to the evil powers of varied provenance. It is not incomprehensible that the avatāra idea as well as the bhakti cult and movement [5]) developed within the circles of Viṣṇu's adherents. Owing to the search of the ancient Indian mind for one ultimate principle which could be regarded as 'manifold', for an omnipresent and universal power on which all existence depends and which is the eternal firm foundation of the world, for an all-pervading Divine Spirit in which all phenomenal spiritual beings have a share on the one hand, and owing to the need for a personal god who proves to be a reliable friend and companion, an unremitting helper, and a safe refuge on the other hand, Viṣṇu could be looked upon in various circles and by men of different culture and education, as God, whose qualities, though beyond human understanding, are described with fervour and imagination by poets and compilers of devotional literature, with subtlety and intellectual acuteness by philosophers and theologians, each of whom emphasized those aspects in which he himself or his readers and followers felt special interest.

It was the figure of Viṣṇu ripened to maturity and keeping a firm hold over the hearts and minds of millions who led his followers to

---

[4]) He encompasses the universe, e.g. ViPur. 2, 7, 29. Viṣṇu is "the pervader with reference to his omnipresent energy", Carpenter, Theism, p. 235.

[5]) Cf. also Bhandarkar, Viṣṇuism etc., p. 28; Sircar, o.c., p. 432; M. Das Gupta, o.c., esp. IHQ. 7, p. 93 ff.

insight and inspiration, who made them understand that He is in the sun and in the daily food, that the carrying capacity of the earth comes from Him, because He enters into it, carrying and nourishing all beings [6]), and that by entering into the soma, He becomes all plants; who taught them that when the human soul, in disinterested devotion to duty, is enlightened and united with His Divine Being, the union of vision and energy will ensure well-being (*śrī-*), victory (*vijaya-*), welfare (*bhūti-*), and morality (*nīti-*) [7]).

---

[6]) See BhG. 15, 13 and Rāmānuja's commentary.

[7]) BhG. 18, 78 (last stanza). "Energy": *pārtho dhanurdharaḥ:* cf. *Indra-vajrabhṛt-* etc.

CHAPTER TWO: ŚRĪ.

I. ŚRĪ-.

It seems to be relevant to survey first a number of passages showing the word *śrī-* as a 'common noun'. Commencing our discussion with texts of the Ṛgveda it is interesting to notice that Sāyaṇa often explains the term by *saṃpad-* "benefit, advantage, riches, prosperity" and sometimes also by *samṛddhi-* "thriving, welfare, plenty, abundance", *vibhūti-* "plenty, abundance, manifestation of power", or *śreyas-* "wellfare, bliss, fortune, happiness" in verses where these equivalents and meanings would, in my opinion, certainly do duty. Modern translators have been perhaps too readily inclined to assume such a sense as "lustre, radiance, splendour, beauty, grace" as having been intended by the poets. Why should, for instance, Agni Vaiśvānara, 4, 5, 15, be a "zur Schönheit entflammter Bulle" (Geldner, and similarly Grassmann)? The more 'materialistic' rendering "for the benefit (of the sacrificers)" proposed by Sāyaṇa is, to my mind, easily conceivable in connection with a god who in the same verse is called "a dwelling of wealth" [1]). Cf. also ṚV. 4, 2, 20; 1, 20; 3, 2, 15. In a comparable way probably 4, 23, 6 [2]). ṚV. 1, 188, 8 some female divinities are invoked: Iḷā who represents the offering of milk and butter, or plenty derived from the cow, with which she is often connected, her very name being also used for "nourishment" and "refreshing draught" [3]), Bhāratī, the offering of the Bharatas as a divine being, and Sarasvatī, the river-goddess who bestows vitality and offspring, who yields riches of every kind and is often said to give plenty and nourishment [4]): *tā naś codayata śriye*. I would prefer "excite, inspire us with a view to the increase of wellbeing" to Geldner's [5]) "eifert uns zur Vortrefflichkeit an" (*saṃpade*

---

[1]) Compare also the adj. *sudṛśikarūpaḥ* "looking beautiful" (ibidem) which might, in the circles of the Vedic "Viehbarone" have also occurred without a tendency to aestheticism on the poet's part. A Dutch farmer, replying to a remark of a tourist who admired the fine poplars and chestnuts of the surroundings, pointed to the dung-hill: "that is beauty: it means money".

[2]) See also K. F. Geldner, Der Rigveda in Auswahl, II, Stuttgart 1909, p. 70.

[3]) See also A. H. Macdonell, Vedic Mythology, Strassburg 1897, p. 124.

[4]) Cf. Macdonell, o.c., p. 86 f.

[5]) Geldner, Der Rig-Veda aus dem Sanskrit ins Deutsche übersetzt, I[1], p. 243; [2]p. 269.

Sāyaṇa). 10, 45, 5 Agni is stated to excite, or to give liberally, "various kinds of prosperity" and to be a holder or keeper of riches: *śrīṇām udāro dharuṇo rayīṇām* (*vibhūtīnām* S.). 6, 48, 19 Pūṣan is equal to the other gods in *śrī-*: as this divinity is often called a possessor and bringer of wealth, a bestower of blessings, a friend of abundance etc., and scarcely ever as "splendid" or "glorious"[6]), I should like to interpret *śrī-* in this passage as *sampad-*. 1, 139, 3 the Aśvins are said to be in the possession of all *śriyaḥ pṛkṣaś ca*; as the latter term means "refreshment, nourishment" and the Aśvins are succouring deities par excellence — they heal diseases, restore sight, give riches and children, they ward off death — I would propose to render the first word by "benefits, prosperity etc." (*sevanīyāḥ sarvā lakṣmīr dhanakanakādirūpāḥ* S.; "Herrlichkeiten" Geldner). Compare also 1, 64, 12; 3, 44, 2 and 8, 92, 20 *indra yasmin viśvā adhi śriyo raṇanti,* cf. e.g. 10, 42, 2; 7, 37, 3 etc.[7]).

Side by side with the phrase *sahase jātaḥ,* 4, 20, 6, "zum Siegen geboren" (Geldner), we find, 9, 94, 4, *śriye jātaḥ* "born in order to enhance well-being" (*sampadartham* S.): the phrase is used in connection with Soma who, in the same stanza, is said to bestow *śrī-* and *vayas* "vigour, vigorous age" upon the invokers, who thereupon are regarded as *śriyaṃ vasānāḥ*. This locution does not necessarily mean, in a literal sense, "in Glanz gekleidet" (Grassmann[8])) or "mit Herrlichkeit sich umkleidend" (Geldner[9])), for 9, 80, 3 it reads *ūrjaṃ vasānaḥ* (Soma) "dressed in strength"; 10, 16, 5 *āyur vasānaḥ* (Agni) "....in longevity", etc. The same phrase *śriye vasānaḥ* is applied to Agni (2, 10, 1), where, like 3, 38, 4, the outward appearance or qualities of a prosperous being are rather referred to. 9, 102, 4 Soma is stated to have been directed or instructed, *śriye,* by seven mothers: this god, the king of plants, the drink of immortality itself, is constantly described as a bestower of wealth[10]), for which, in the same stanza, he is said to be responsible; so the sense seems to be "for the benefit, well-being viz. of the sacrificers": *yajamānānām aiśvaryārtham* (S.). 9, 16, 6 and 62, 19 the soma juice is stated to afford all *śriyaḥ* "valued objects, benefits"[11]). Cf. also 6, 29, 3; 44, 8; 63, 5; 8, 102, 9. 1, 81, 4 although the sense of "ostentation of well-being" could also be thought

---

6) I refer to Macdonell, o.c., p. 36 f.

7) Macdonell, o.c., p. 62 f.

8) H. Grassmann, Rig-Veda übersetzt, Leipsic 1876, II, p. 260.

9) Geldner, Der Rig-Veda... übersetzt, III (Harvard Oriental Series vol. 35, 1951), p. 90.

10) I refer to Macdonell, o.c., p. 110.

11) 9, 16, 6 Sāyaṇa explains the word under discussion by *śobhāḥ,* 62, 19 by *sampadaḥ.*

of. 1, 92, 6 where Uṣas shines and *śriye smayati,* Geldner felicitously translated by "glückverheißend" (*saṃpadartham* S.). Cf. 1, 64, 12. 10, 45, 8 *āyuḥ śriye rucānaḥ* (Agni) "zum Heile.... Leben strahlend" (Grassmann) seems to be more to the point than "in.... Lebenskraft zur Pracht erglänzend" (*vibhūtyai* S.). 2, 23, 18 we might be tempted to translate *tava śriye* by "to your advantage, for your benefit". Cf. also 4, 41, 8; 8, 26, 4. 10, 95, 3 *iṣur na śriye* seems to mean: "of no use (to me) was my arrow" [12]).

In other passages the correct rendering seems to be "exhibition or display of welfare, well-being or capability". It is not probable that the axles of the chariots of the Maruts were nothing but ornaments [13]); so I would disagree with Geldner who 1, 88, 3 translates *śriye* by "zur Zierde". Sāyaṇa, however, explained it by *aiśvaryāya* "for (supranormal) power". Does 8, 20, 7 where the Maruts *śriyam.... vahante* refer to their bringing prosperity?: one of their main functions is to shed rain [14]). Cf. also 5, 60, 4; 9, 104, 1 [15]); 10, 77, 2. Sometimes the meaning of the plural may be something like "the qualities, or perhaps also the phenomena by which mighty beings show that they are prosperous or well-off, or by which they display their welfare", or the "various aspects of their potency to do so". Modifying Oldenberg's interpretation [16]), in which *śrī-* is rendered by "Schönheit", we might also say: "es ist die Gesamtheit der *śrī*-potenzen gemeint, die dem *śrī*-begabten Wesen anhaften". Cf. 1, 85, 2 *arcanto arkaṃ janayanta indriyam adhi śriyo dadhire pṛśnimātaraḥ,* where Geldner's translation "haben.... (sie) ihre Prunkstücke angelegt" can hardly be adopted, unless we take it 'figuratively' [17]); 1, 166, 10; 5, 57, 6 "....victorious power (*sahas*), vital energy (*ojas*) [18]), strength has been put in your arms, courage in your heads, weapons on your cars, the totality of *śrī-* or the display of every aspect of *śrī-* (*viśvā.... śriyaḥ*) has been

---

[12]) See also H. J. de Zwart, Ṛgveda 10, 95, in Orientalia Neerlandica, Leyden 1948, p. 363 ff.

[13]) Cf. Macdonell, o.c., p. 79.

[14]) Geldner, Der Rig-Veda... übersetzt, II, p. 323, translating "...führen... die Schönheit mit sich" tries to make sense of it by observing: "Die Schönheit könnte die Rodasī sein, wie in den Aśvin-liedern die Sūryā *śrī-* heißt (s. 1, 116, 17)".

[15]) See my treatise 'The meaning of Vedic *bhūṣati*', Wageningen 1939, p. 14.

[16]) H. Oldenberg, Die vedischen Worte für "schön" und "Schönheit" und das vedische Schönheitsgefühl, in Nachr. königl. Ges. d. Wiss. Göttingen, ph.-h. Kl. 1918, p. 35 ff., esp. p. 39.

[17]) Oldenberg, l.c., drawing attention to the frequent use of *adhi* in this connection observes: "es scheint danach, daß die *śriyaḥ* als auf dem Körper ruhend vorgestellt wurden". Compare also the above *śriyaṃ vasāna-*.

[18]) For ojas see my treatise 'Anc.-Ind. *ojas,* Latin **augos* and the Indo-European nouns in *-es-/-os*', Utrecht 1952.

laid on your bodies". 7, 72, 1 where the Aśvins are described as "looking handsome by" or "preparing themselves with" (*śubhānāḥ*) *spārha-* i.e. "desirable, enviable" *śrī-* — this adjective which 7, 15, 5 is also connected with *śrī-* elsewhere accompanies such words as *reknas* "(inherited) property'; *rādhas* "gift, munificence"; *vasu* "property, wealth"; *iṣ-* "refreshing draught"; *mayas* "refreshment"; *ranti-* "pleasure" etc. — the term *śrī-* is put in the singular: "display of welfare etc.". Cf. also 5, 61, 12.

The outward splendour of well-being seems to be emphasized: 8, 20, 12 (cf. 5, 57, 6, see above) addressed to the Maruts: *anīkeṣv adhi śriyaḥ*; 1, 46, 14; 122, 2; 4, 44, 2; 5, 28, 4; 6, 66, 4 etc. Hence also such meanings as "splendour, beauty, glory, etc.". Whereas 7, 67, 2, where the banner of Uṣas *aceti.... śriye.... jāyamānaḥ,* the sense of "for the good (of mankind), in order to bring prosperity" may, to my mind, be preferred, the goddess being often implored to bring wealth and children, to confer glory, and to bestow protection [19]), other passages (cf. 4, 10, 5; 8, 7, 25; 10, 110, 16) may rightly be considered as showing the sense of "beauty". Yet, it is important to remember that, even if 8, 7, 25 and in texts of the same tenor Geldner's translation "bemalen sich die Schmucken zur Schönheit" (*śubhrā vy añjata śriye* for *śubh-* cf. Rām. 2, 118, 20;) happens to express the poet's intentions, the adornment of the body, the laying on of ointments, the use of ornaments etc. often were at the same time magic practices. So-called ornaments served, or also served, as amulets against illness, sorcery, or other misfortunes or as talismans to bring good luck or to enhance the wearer's power, success of invincibility [20]). But, not only is Oldenberg right in comparing such phrases as *viśvāni pauṃsyā, amṛtāni viśvā* to the above *viśvāḥ śriyaḥ,* the verb *adhi dhā-* is also frequently used in connection with other 'concepts' or, rather, 'power-substances' part of which are not primarily of a visible order: *nāma* "name" 1, 123, 4; *śravas* "fame" 1, 117, 8; *śravāṃsi* 3, 19, 5; *pṛkṣaḥ* "satiation, Stärkungen" 6, 35, 4. In the last text the noun is qualified by the adjectives *aśvaścandrāḥ* "brilliant with horses, durch Rosse ausgezeichnet" and *vājaśravasaḥ* "famous for steeds or wealth": the 'Stärkungen' consist of a donation of horses. Elsewhere an "ornament" undergoing the process of *adhi dhā-* is a hymn of praise: 4, 36, 7 (see further on).

---

19) See Macdonell, o.c., p. 48.

20) The reader might be referred to H. Webster, Magic, Stanford Cal. 1948, p. 502; F. M. Olbrechts, Ethnologie, Zutfen 1936, p. 156 ff.; K. Birket-Smith, Geschichte der Kultur, Zürich 1946, p. 210 ff., and for the Vedic period, my papers on the terms *alaṃkāra-* and *ābharaṇa-* in the New Indian Antiquary, I, p. 97 ff., and II, p. 69 ff.

We should, however, above all things remind ourselves that the ancient Indians did not distinguish between concrete and abstract concepts, between visibility and invisibility in the modern scientific way [21]). Their relevant terms often clearly denote a 'concept', a quality, condition, mode of being as well as the phenomena by which they manifest themselves, the circumstances attending them. Thus *tejas* does not only stand for a special "fiery energy, ardour or spirit", but also for its manifestations, be they, in our eyes, of the 'moral' or 'spiritual' order ("prestige, moral or spiritual influence, energy") or visible: when, for instance the lamps are deprived of their lustre by the *tejas* of the new-born prince Raghu (Kāl. R. 3, 15) [22]).

Nor can I subscribe to Oldenberg's view [23]) that the frequency of the passages in which *śrī-* is connected with derivatives of *dṛś-* proves the former's primary sense of "erfreulicher Anblick". Such texts as 7, 15, 5; 2, 1, 12; 1, 122, 2 only show that *śrī-*, its manifestations, consequences and attendant circumstances can be, and often are, visible, that the possession of *śrī-* can be displayed. Passages like 5, 3, 4 *tava śriyā sudṛśo deva devāḥ purū dadhānā amṛtaṃ sapanta* "durch deine, des Schönen, Herrlichkeit (*samṛddhyā* S.), O Gott, mehren und wahren die Götter die Unsterblichkeit"; 4, 23, 6; 5, 44, 2 etc. do not necessarily imply that *śrī-* was employed by the poet from the aesthetic point of view. Are we right to translate 10, 91, 2 *sa darśataśrīr atithir gṛhe-gṛhe vane-vane śiśriye takvavīr iva* by "of conspicuous beauty...."?: Agni who abides in every piece of wood displays his *śrī-* when kindled (cf. 5, 28, 4); so "whose *śrī-* is, becomes, visible, or.... is worth seeing" might be a more adequate rendering. As to Agni's *śrī-*, from 10, 45, 5 (see above); 8, 102, 9 *ayaṃ viśvā abhi śriyo 'gnir deveṣu patyate | ā vājair upa no gamat*, where Sāyaṇa explains *ś.* by *saṃpadaḥ*; 2, 8, 3; 4, 5, 15 (*śriye*, to wit *yajamānānām* S.); we may infer that it was at least not always of an aesthetic or preponderantly aesthetic order. Compare also 3, 1, 5 *śocir vasānaḥ pary āyur apāṃ śriyo mimīte bṛhatīr anūnāḥ* "arraying himself in radiance, and in the vitality of the waters he (Agni) displays (or: apportions) his substantial [24]) and complete prosperity [25])", i.e. the prosperity which he, according to 1, 1, 3; 31, 10

---

[21]) For the sake of brevity I refer to H. von Glasenapp, Entwicklungsstufen des indischen Denkens, Halle (S.) 1940, p. 9 ff., and to my treatises 'Notes on *brahman*', Utrecht 1952, and 'Anc.-Ind. *ojas*...' (see above), passim.

[22]) See especially J. Ph. Vogel, Het sanskrit woord *tejas*..., Amsterdam Academy 1930.

[23]) Oldenberg, o.c., p. 37.

[24]) For *bṛhat-* in the sense of "firm, solid, substantial" see my above-mentioned book 'Notes on *brahman*', p. 31 ff.

[25]) Here and elsewhere the plural may also be regarded as a so-called "Plural

etc. abundantly commands [26]). 10, 1, 5 *śriyā tv agnim atithiṃ janānām* seems to admit of a similar interpretation ("vermöge seines Vorrangs aber der Gast der Menschen ist" (Geldner) [27]). Attention may finally be drawn to 6, 64, 1 ff.: Uṣas who is implored to grant wealth is said to have arisen: *bhadrā dadṛkṣe* and *ud u śriya uṣaso rocamānāḥ*; here the verb *dṛś-* is connected with a term which according to Oldenberg himself [28]) denotes an entity which "spendet Glück von sich selbst aus, oder etwa.... es steht.... in mystisch-zauberhafter Korrespondenz mit der glückspendenden Macht, ist in gewissem Sinn mit ihr identisch". — It may not be out of place here to discuss also 5, 55, 3: the Maruts, called *subhuvaḥ,* i.e. either "strong, powerful", or "handsome, beautiful" or, rather, only "of an excellent nature, thriving, prosperous", are said to grow or prosper *śriye.* As one of their main functions is to shed rain [29]), and as they also dispel the darkness, as their singing strengthens Indra for the slaying of Vṛtra, I feel inclined to translate *śriye* by "for (our) prosperity" and not by "zur Schönheit" (Geldner).

It must, however, be conceded that is not always possible to distinguish between well-being or prosperity and the outward appearance of the person who enjoys them — in China "growing fat" is equivalent to "producing fortune" —: 2, 1, 12 Agni is called the "highest vigour, wealth and property", in his enviable colour (or lustre) the *śriyaḥ* are stated to be present; Agni is also concerned in 10, 91, 5 "thine *śriyaḥ* are like the lightnings of the rain-clouds"; 1, 43, 7 Soma is implored to grant the *śrī-* which consists in a hundred men, great glory (*śravaḥ*). Sometimes the joy or happiness accompanying (the furthering of) well-being seems to be emphasized: 10, 105, 10 ("dir zu Ehren" Geldner). Now and then the choice of an English equivalent must be left undecided: 7, 56, 6.

In the Atharvaveda the term under discussion is connected with *bhūti-* "growth, thriving, prosperity": 12, 1, 63 "O mother earth (*bhūmi-*), do thou happily set me down well established (*supratiṣṭhi-*

---

der affektischen Verallgemeinerung" (intensivus), see e.g. W. Havers, Handbuch der erklärenden Syntax, Heidelberg 1931, p. 160 f.

[26]) Cf. also Macdonell, o.c., p. 97 f. Cf. the phrase *mimīte... ojas,* e.g. 5, 31, 7.

[27]) I must also disagree with Oldenberg (p. 39) in respect of 10, 95, 6 *śriye gāvo na dhenavo 'navanta:* I fail to see that an audible act performed for (the sake of) *śrī-* can be an argument for *śrī*'s audibility. May we take this lowing as an auspicious acclamation? (see my remarks in the Acta Orientalia, vol. 19, p. 438 ff. and 21, p. 81 ff., cf. also 8, 69, 11; 9, 26, 2; 32, 5; 80, 2).

[28]) Oldenberg, o.c., p. 49.

[29]) I refer to the abundance of texts quoted by Macdonell, o.c., p. 79 f. "They come with cows with distended udders: the cows can scarcely be anything other than the swollen rain clouds" (A. B. Keith, The religion and philosophy of the Veda and Upanishads, Harvard Univ. 1925, p. 151).

tam [30])...., do thou set one in well-being (*ś.*), in prosperity (*bhūtyām*), and with other substances or entities which are essential to man's bodily or material well-being: 10, 6, 26 "the (amulet) which Bṛhaspatī bound on for the gods, (as) a destruction of the asuras, ...together with invigorating food (*ūrj-*), with milk (*payas*), with property (*draviṇa-*), with fortune or well-being (*śrī-*)". In st. 10 the word is used as a member of an enumeration of much-desired power-substances (10, 6, 6-17): *ājya-* "sacrificial butter", *bala-* "strength", *varcas* "lustre", *bhūti-, vājina-* "vigour", *mahas* "greatness", *sūnṛtā* [31]) "youthful vitality", *amṛta-* "'immortality', longevity", *satya-* "truth", *jiti-* "gaining, victory" and "everything". 9, 6, 36 *śrī-* appears after *payas* "milk" and *rasa-* "sap", *ūrj-* and *sphāti-* "fatness, increase, prosperity", *prajā* "progeny", and *paśu-* "cattle", *kīrti-* "fame" and *yaśas* "glory", and before *saṃvid-*, which was tentatively translated by "alliance" (Whitney-Lanman), although "possessions" (Petr. Dict.) seems better; anyhow, "fortune" (*śrī-*) here likewise applies to concrete and visible welfare or prosperity. Compare also 9, 5, 31 where "he thrives (*bhavati*) himself" is opposed to "he burns out his rival's *śrī-*" and 32 ff., where *śrī-* is successively accompanied by the adjectives *kurvatī* "making", *saṃyatī* "self-contained", *pinvatī* "fattening", and *udyatī* "rising, increasing"; and, further, 11, 1, 12; 21.

As to the adjective *aśrīra- aślīla-*, AV. 4, 21, 6 "Ye, O kine, fatten whoever is lean; make the *aśrīra-* one of good aspect", I would propose to translate it by "shrunken" rather than "unlovely" (Whitney-Lanman). 14, 1, 27 ∾ ṚV. 10, 85, 30 it may be considered to form an ancient counterpart of *aśrīka- aślīka-* which in post-Vedic texts expresses such ideas as Manu 4, 206 *aślīkam etat sādhūnāṃ yatra juhvaty amī haviḥ | pratīpam etad devānām....* "it is inauspicious, unlucky (*śrīghnam* "destroying the *śrī-*") for the correctly living men and it displeases the gods", and Mbh. 3, 173, 64 "the city of the dānavas deprived of its lords and afflicted with sorrow and distress" was *aśrīka-* "unlucky". I fail to see why the bridegroom's body (AV. 14, 1, 27) should become "unlovely" [32]) if he should wrap his own body (or member) with the bride's undergarment after the defloration. This garment which is highly dangerous, "walking witchcraft" (*kṛtyā padvatī*, st. 25) and

---

30) See my paper *Pratiṣṭhā*. Cf. also GB. 1, 1, 34.

31) According to Mādhava, quoted by Devarāja p. 49, 12 *sūnara-* = *sudhana-* "very rich, fortunate". F. B. J. Kuiper (*Νώροπι χαλκῷ*, Amsterdam Academy 1951, p. 14 ff.) tries to show that *sūnṛtā* must have denoted "the state of being **sūnar-* "full of youthful strength", or "the (personified) Vitality".

32) Whitney-Lanman; cf. also Geldner, Der Ṛig-Veda... übersetzt, III, p. 71; Oldenberg, o.c. p. 38.

regarded as extremely ill-omened if not given away [33]), was no doubt supposed to injure the bridegroom's *śrī-* if he should be so incautious as to put it on himself: the next words, *ruśatī pāpayāmuyā* which I would render by "malignant (injuring) in that evil way" (cf. 7, 56, 6; the idea expressed by *pāpa-* is very often opposed to *śrī-*) [34]) seem to corroborate this interpretation. ṚV. 8, 2, 20 the *aśrīra- jāmātā* seems to be an inauspicious son-in-law, one whose *śrī-* (see above) has gone, cf. the adj. *durhaṇāvat-* in the same stanza which expresses the idea of "harmful, pernicious, inauspicious by being harmful". ṚV. 6, 28, 6 *yūyaṃ gāvo medayathā kṛśaṃ cid aśrīraṃ cit kṛṇuthā supratīkam | bhadraṃ gṛhaṃ cit kṛṇutha bhadravāco bṛhad vo vaya ucyate sabhāsu* likewise has the adj. *aśrīra-* in connection with such ideas as "gesegnet" and "Lebensstärkung" (Geldner), and in opposition to "lean, weak, emaciated"; it is "looking under-nourished or ill" rather than "unschön".

Similar remarks may be made in connection with the use of the substantive *śrī-* in Vedic prose.

The gods, who are *śrī-*, are glorious and immortal (ŚB. 2, 1, 4, 9); cf. 10, 1, 4, 14. In conferring *śrī-* on a person, neither *tejas*, nor *indriya-* (the faculty of senses), nor cattle, nor prosperity (*śrī-*) go away from him: ŚB. 13, 2, 6, 7. 11, 4, 4, 11 *śrī-* is said to be surrounded by *tejas*, *yaśas*, and *brahmavarcas* "fiery energy, renown, and pre-eminence in holiness and sacred knowledge". — Food, drink, *śrī-*, light and immortality constitute the fivefold nature of the year, of fire and man: ŚB. 10, 2, 6, 16. 1, 6, 3, 15 the *devās* "divine beings or powers", *vidyās* "special knowledge as a key to supranormal achievements", *yaśas*, food and *śrī-* are put on a par. Soma is ŚB. 4, 1, 3, 9 considered to be *śrī-*. There sometimes exists a correlation between *śrī-* and a complete lifetime (*sarvam āyuḥ*): JaiUB. 1, 4, 8. — ŚB. 3, 1, 1, 12 increase of substance (*rāyaspoṣa-*) is stated to be equivalent to abundance (*bhūman-*), and abundance to *śrī-*; and, it is added, people say of him who enjoys *śrī-* "prosperity" that he rejoices in *iṣ-*, i.e. "refreshing draught, freshness, comfort, increase". — The terms *śrī-* and *prajā* "offspring" are

---

33) See the anukramaṇī quoted by Whitney-Lanman, Atharva-veda saṃhitā, Harvard Univ. 1905, p. 739; Kauś. S. 79, 20; M. Winternitz, Das altindische Hochzeitsrituell, Denkschriften Akad. d. Wiss. Vienna 40, 1 (1892), p. 100; 113; Meyer, Sexual life in ancient India, p. 43; B. Kummer, in the Handwörterbuch des deutschen Aberglaubens, I, Berlin-Leipsic 1927, 1532; V. Elwin, in the British Journal of medical psychology, 1943, p. 439 f.; N. M. Penzer, Poison damsels, London 1952, p. 36 f. and 43; Srinivas, Religion and society among the Coorgs, Oxford 1952, p. 103; (also J. P. Mills, The Lhota Nagas, London 1922, p. 152).

34) For *ruś ruṣ hiṃsāyām* see the Dhātupāṭha 28, 126; Whitney-Lanman, o.c., p. 134; see e.g. AV. 3, 28, 1, and 14, 1, 38 where this meaning suits the context better than "glistening".

often found in the same context: ŚB. 2, 3, 1, 13; 4, 4, 2; 4; AiĀr. 5, 3, 2.

Special attention may be drawn to such passages as the following: ŚB. 1, 8, 1, 36 "May I live, may I have offspring, may I obtain prosperity (*śriyam*). Now in praying for the blessing of cattle, he prays for *śrī-*, for cattle means *śrī-*...."; cf. also 12, 4, 1, 11. Cf. 1, 2, 2, 3 where dough is expected to bring offspring, *śrī-*, and food to the sacrificer. Life, offspring, and *śrī-* go together 1, 8, 1, 36. 2, 4, 4, 1 offspring, cattle, *śrī-*, being glorious (*yaśas*) and being an eater of food, i.e. having plenty of food (*annāda-*) are the wishes formulated by Prajāpati himself in sacrificing. Cf. 1, 6, 3, 15; 4, 2, 4, 23; 6, 9, 1; 3; 13, 2, 6, 3. — AiĀ. 5, 1, 6 *śriyam aha gor aśvam ātman dhatte* "he thus wins the profit of a cow and a horse" (Keith)[35]): *śrī-* consisting of a cow. TaiU. 1, 4, 2 *śrī-* is called *lomaśa-* "hairy, woolly" — consisting of sheep or other woolly animals (as property)[36]) — and is implored to grant, in a short time, clothes, cows, food and drink[37]). See also SVB. 3, 2, 6. — Cattle is food and *śrī-* is food: ŚB. 8, 6, 2, 1. See also ŚB. 1, 5, 4, 5; 8, 1, 36; ŚāB. 21, 5; PB. 13, 2, 2 cattle is *śrī-*: because people regard a cattle-owner as *śrīmān*, the commentary adds; here Caland's translation[38]) "cattle is a beautiful manifestation" fails to emphasize the economic element; I would prefer "manifestation of prosperity". Cf. also 5, 4, 5 f. When *śrīr yaśāṃsi* left Indra's mouth they entered the cattle: ŚB. 12, 8, 3, 1; GB. 2, 5, 6. Cf. TĀ. 7, 4, 2. The "end" of food is *śrī-*, i.e. plenty of food leads to "Wohlfahrt, Ansehen" (Caland), the JaimBr. 2, 184 holds. Food is *śrī-* and *śrī-* is food: JB. 1, 117; GB. 1, 5, 4; 2, 1, 19; *śrī-* and food appear together KauṣU. 1, 5 = ŚāĀ. 3, 5. See also AiĀ. 5, 3, 2; 1, 1, 3; MahU. 2, 64, and other texts. ŚB. 12, 7, 3, 13; 22; 8, 1, 21 milk is called *śrī-*; cf. 8, 1, 20 where milk is regarded as vital air (*prāṇa-*) and food; in the same connection *śrī-* and longevity. Cf. also 2, 6, 3, 6; and 1, 4, 5, 6. The gravy of the animals (*vasā*) means *śrī-*; it is the essence (*rasa-*) of cattle, the highest food: ŚB. 12, 8, 3, 12. In other passages *śrī-* and *rasa-* "life-sap" are mentioned together: ŚB. 6, 1, 1, 4; 9, 2, 3, 51. ŚB. 5, 5, 3, 1 and 6 the collected or concentrated essence (*rasaḥ saṃbhṛtaḥ*) of the waters is called *vīrya-* "strength" and *śrī-*. ŚB. 11, 1, 6, 23 the earth is considered to be *śrī-*; there is no need to translate this text: "....is the source of prosperity", Eggeling). In a comparable way: AiB. 8, 5, 4. ŚB. 2, 6, 3, 2 the *śrī-* which came to the gods on performing definite offerings

---

[35]) A. B. Keith, The Aitareya Āraṇyaka, Oxford 1909, p. 273; see his remarks in n. 3.

[36]) Monier-Williams, A Sanskṛit-Engl. Dict., s.v.

[37]) However, the syntactic structure of this sentence is not evident.

[38]) W. Caland, Pañcaviṃśa-brāhmaṇa, Calcutta 1931, p. 311.

and gaining the victory over Vṛtra is identified with *śuna-* which is elsewhere used to express such ideas as "success, growth, welfare"; the term is connected with the name of the *śunāsīrīya-* offering which may be regarded as a consecration of the plough [39]). In the same text the *rasa-* "essence" which belonged to the year is identified with the second component of the name of that offering. Cf. also 2, 6, 3, 4. — Elsewhere, ŚB. 2, 1, 1, 7 it is stated that the man who has gained *śrī-* is *purīṣya-* "rich in manure or loose earth" [40]). A molehill is therefore conducive to the attainment of *śrī-*; ŚB. ibid.[41]). See also BJābU. 3, 8. The commentator Mahīdhara interpreted *śrī-* in ŚB. 13, 2, 6, 16 as referring to the earth. — Rain is *śrī-* ŚB. 12, 4, 1, 11 *śriyo* ("blessings" Eggeling) *vai parjanyo varṣati.* Cf. also JB. 1, 117. Water is *śrī-*: cf. TĀ. 3, 11, 6; TritāU. 3, 24. — It is not surprising that loss of *śrī-* means hunger: ŚB. 11, 4, 2, 10; cf. JaiU. 3, 12, 3. Sometimes a text testifies to an unmistakable connection between *śrī-* and property: ŚB. 3, 9, 3, 34.

It is, further, also clear that various other objects of entities can be denoted by the same term, if they essentially are *śrī-* or add to the *śrī-* of their owner. ŚB. 8, 6, 2, 1 the chandasyas (bricks pertaining to the metres) are called *śrī-*; they were given to him who wishes to obtain *śrī-*, which in the same passage is specified as "distinction, either in regard to kingship or to headmanship". ŚB. 8, 6, 2, 4 the great recitation of praise (*mahad uktham*) is said to mean *śrī-*. The ninth day of the ten-day rite is called *śrī-*, because of the great number of the sāmans etc. (cf. the commentary): PB. 15, 4, 5. It is understandable that women, too, are mentioned in this connection: ŚB. 13, 2, 6, 7 in describing the anointing of the horse which is destined to be offered (*aśvamedha-*) by the wives of the sacrificer, remarks that this is the wives' task because wives are a form (*rūpam*) of *śrī-* ("prosperity or social eminence" Eggeling). — In another passage (ŚB. 13, 1, 5, 1; also TB. 3, 9, 14, 1), the lute (*vīṇa-*), the sound of which is auspicious (cf. e.g. ĀpŚrS. 21, 1, 8, 8) [42]) is called a *rūpa-* of *śrī-*; by playing this instrument one confers *śrī-* upon a person.

Now, *śrī-* and *yaśas,* i.e. "honour, glory, dignity", constitute a frequent combination: ŚB. 2, 3, 2, 11 "if one wishes to be like Indra in

---

39) A. Hillebrandt, Vedische Mythologie², II, Breslau 1929, p. 199 ff.; H. Oldenberg, Die Religion des Veda (ed. 1923), p. 442.

40) Cf. Eggeling, in the Sacred Books of the East 12, p. 279, n. 1.

41) For the mole see e.g. J. J. Meyer, Trilogie altindischer Mächte und Feste der Vegetation, Zürich-Leipzig 1937, III, p. 77 and 219; R. Riegler, Hdwtb. de. Abergl. VI, 1934, 14.

42) For the auspicious character of the lute see also ÇB. 13, 4, 3, 3.

ś. and *y.....*"; 3, 13; 4, 6, 7, 20; 5, 3, 2, 3, where these power-substances are opposed to darkness; 11, 6, 2, 2; cf. 2, 1, 4, 9; GB. 2, 5, 6. JaiUB. 4, 24, 11 says that the *brahmayaśas* is encompassed (*parivṛḍham*) by *śrī-*; the man who knows this, being *brahman-*, is encompassed by *śrī-* and *yaśas*. — Id. 1, 17, 3 *śrī-*, reverence (*apaciti-*), the heavenly world, *yaśas* and food are mentioned together. Id. 1, 46, 2 Prajāpati, being the Veda, and desiring to be manifold, divides himself into 16 parts: *bhadraṃ ca samāptiś cābhūtiś ca saṃbhūtiś ca bhūtaṃ ca sarvaṃ ca rūpaṃ cāparimitaṃ ca śrīś ca yaśaś ca nāma cāgraṃ ca sajātāś ca payaś ca mahīyā ca raśaś ca*; 47, 6 *śrī-* appears to be his speech; thence he created the ocean. Compare also the enumeration of qualities id. 1, 43, 11 *jyotiṣmān pratiṣṭhāvāñ chāntimān ātmavāñ chrīmān vyāptimān vibhūtimāṃs tejasvī bhāvān* etc. "bright, well-established, free from evil influences, self-possessed, 'fortunate', pervading, might, energetic, luminous etc.". In addition to these texts see AiĀ. 5, 1, 5; TĀ. 2, 10, 1; 4, 41, 1-3; 10, 1, 5; Māhānar. 2, 63; SVB. 3, 1, 2, 4. *śrīś ca hrīś ca* appears TĀ. 4, 42, 5. The negative *nāsmāt tejo 'pakrāmati* is, AthVPar. 1, 20, 1, followed by the more explicit *tejasvī prajayā paśubhiḥ śriyā gṛhair dhanena bhavati.*

Specially interesting is the frequent opposition between *śrī-* and *pāpman-* "evil, misfortune, unhappiness, misery, wickedness, the state of being affected by sin". ŚB. 4, 1, 3, 9 Soma, the king of plants and drink of immortality, means *śrī-* and physical evil or 'disease' (*yakṣma-*)[43]) *pāpman-*. ŚB. 5, 1, 2, 10 ff. truth (*satya-*), *śrī-* and light (*jyotis*) are opposed to untruth (*anṛta-*), *pāpman-* and darkness (*tamas*); see also 5, 28; 2, 3, 3, 13; 5, 3, 2, 3; 14, 1, 1, 31. 10, 2, 6, 19 hunger ceases through food, evil or misery (*p.*) through *śrī-* ("well-being, goodness" Eggeling), darkness through light. Cf. also 4, 1, 3, 9; AiB. 7, 15, 1. JaiU. 1, 1, 4, 7 "he has now put *śrī-* ("fortune" Oertel) outside, he will become worse ("afflicted", *pāpīyān*). Cf. GB. 1, 1, 38. This opposition is the more remarkable as *pāpman-* accompanies the word for "death" *mṛtyu*: ŚB. 8, 4, 2, 1 ff.; 3, 1; cf. 4, 2, and *pāpimant-* is a standing epithet applied to Māra "(the) Evil, the Wicked One" in ancient Buddhism[44]). Māra, 'originally' "death" representing such ideas as destruction, suffering, misery, and all evil contrary to the final emancipation taught by the Buddha who was inspired by the insight called *amṛta-*, is of course opposed to the ideas expressed by the term *śrī-*. *Śrī-* is, therefore, closely associated with life and the maintenance of this

---

[43]) Cf. J. Filliozat, La doctrine classique de la médecine indienne, Paris 1949, p. 40 ff.

[44]) See e.g. H. Beckh, Der Buddhismus, Berlin-Leipsic 1916, II, p. 66 f.

highest good. — By a definite rite one repels distress (*śuc-*) and comes to *śrī-* (*saṃpad-* Comm.) and *haras* (*tejas* Comm., "fire"), PB. 12, 6, 10 says.

In the brāhmaṇas *śrī-* is rather frequently identified with the *virāj-*. This metre, the name of which is also used to express such ideas as "excellent, splendid, ruling far and wide, pre-eminence, high rank, majesty", is not seldom mystically regarded as food: ŚB. 8, 3, 2, 13; 9, 2, 3, 40; AiB. 4, 11, 18; 6, 36, 6; GB. 1, 5, 20 (*śrīr vai virāḍ yaśo 'nnādyam*). In the Atharvaveda the *virāj-* is extolled as the first and creative principle (8, 9 and 10) [45]). After having "ascended and descended" in various fires, in the assembly etc., gods and men invited her, calling her by such names as *ūrjā* "strength, sap, refreshment", *svadhā* "the libation of clarified butter etc. offered to the deceased ancestors", *sūnṛtā* "youthful vitality" [46]), *irāvatī* "granting refreshment or satiation". Appearing in the shape of a cow, Indra the god of power and fertility in nature being her calf, and the cloud her udder, she was milked by the gods: medicinal herbs, *vyacas* i.e. "expanse or wide space", water and the sacrifice were her milk. When invited and milked by men she produced agriculture (*kṛṣi-*) and *sasya-* "grain", "upon which men subsist" (8, 10, 24); "successful, one to be subsisted upon, becomes he who knows thus". — Thus GB. 1, 5, 4 it reads: *annaṃ vai śrīr virāḍ annādyam*. Invocations are directed to be made in the *virāj* metre when food is the especial object of prayer. For the identification of *śrī-* and *virāj-* see e.g. ŚB. 11, 4, 3, 18 (the texts continues: "he thus establishes (the sacrificer) in the virāj, in *śrī-* and food"); ŚāB. 1, 1 "*śrī-* and proper food are the virāj"; 2, 3; 14, 2; 16, 3; 10; 17, 3; 19, 5; 7 etc.; TB. 2, 6, 19, 2. ŚāB. 16, 10 "he who sacrifices with the sautrāmaṇī obtains *śrī-*, offspring, and the virāj...." The virāj is *śrī-* and food; GB. 2, 1, 19 *annaṃ vai śrīr virāṭ*.... The virāj is also identified with the earth, e.g. ŚB. 12, 6, 1, 40; Mbh. 12, 262, 41. — The bṛhatī metre to which cattle are related (ŚB. 12, 7, 2, 15; ŚāB. 4, 3), is likewise called *śrī-* (ŚāB. 28, 7; 29, 5); see also ŚB. 12, 8, 3, 24; cf. TB. 3, 11, 1, 20.

A short note on the *pṛṣtha-* (i.e. a particular arrangement of sāmans) being identified with *śrī-* (AiB. 6, 5, 2; GB. 2, 5, 11) may not be out of place here, because they are elsewhere regarded as identical with

---

45) For *virāj-* and its being *anna-* "food" see M. Mauss, Mélanges-Lévi, Paris 1911, p. 333; L. Renou, Virāj, J.As. 240 (1952), p. 141 ff. The metre virāj was highly magnified because it was a cosmic symbol. Consisting of ten syllables it may have been considered an "accomplissement numérique" or *saṃpad.* — The text AV. 8, 10 was briefly discussed in connection with ancient Indian cow-worship by M. A. Muusses, Koecultus bij de Hindoes, Thesis Utrecht 1920, p. 22 f.; 33.

46) See above, n. 31.

the seasons (ŚB. 13, 3, 2, 1). The *abhiplava-* ceremony by which the sacrificer obtains food, animals, plants, trees, etc. is also regarded as *śrī-* and cattle (ŚāB. 21, 5).

There exist also connections between *śrī-* and *kṣatra-* "ruling power, dominion, chieftaincy", whereas TB. 3, 9, 14, 2 states that *śrī-* does not associate with *brahman-*. Cf. also 3, 8, 10, 3; 9, 7, 1. By executing a definite rite in a definite manner one attaches *kṣatra-* and *śrī-* to a single person: ŚB. 8, 7, 2, 3; 9, 3, 1, 14; 4, 3, 2. Cf. also 6, 6, 1, 8; JB. 1, 272. Such texts as AiB. 1, 30, 30 "this is the divine chieftaincy, this *śrī-* ("prosperity, material well-being"), this the overlordship.... this the resort or support (*āyatana-*[47])) of Prajāpati, this the self-rule (*svārājya-*)" are illustrative of the same close connection between *śrī-* and *kṣatra-*. We also find such passages as ŚB. 2, 1, 3, 7 *kṣatraṃ śriyā yaśasā syām iti* "may I become ruling power in welfare or prosperity and renown": here the Kāṇva text reads: *kṣatrasya pratimā syām śriyā yaśaseti* "....become an image of *kṣatra-* in *ś.* and *y.*" (1, 1, 3, 6). Rule (*rāṣṭra-*) itself is also regarded as *śrī-*: ŚB. 6, 7, 3, 7; 13, 2, 9, 1. Elsewhere, JaiU. 2, 7, 5; 7; 9 *śrī-* and *īśā* "dominion, lordship" form a couple. Compare also JB. 3, 152 *aśnute śriyaṃ gacchati rājyaṃ ya evaṃ veda*: the *sāman-* under discussion is a *śrīsava-*, i.e. "a consecration leading to majesty" (*śrī-*; Caland). The house-lord's position and dignity (*gārhapatam*), too, means *śrī-*: ŚB. 5, 3, 3, 3; 4, 3, 15. TĀ. 6, 1, 3 *śrī-* is connected with the three highest classes of society. — In later times we often find *rājaśrī-*, *rājyaśrī-*, and *śrī-* in connection with a royal position. Cf. also Mbh. 14, 16, 22 *brāhmī śrī-*.

In considering this point the curious fact may not be omitted that the cushion of the royal throne is (JB. 2, 25; AiB. 8, 12, 3) identified with *śrī-*. Vedic metra and sāmans, ṛks, yajus etc. are the other parts of the throne, and such important divinities as Prajāpati, Bṛhaspati, Soma and Varuṇa (AiB. 8, 12, 3) appear as its legs; cf. also DŚS. 10, 4, 7. On this seat, it is added, Āditya, the sun, was anointed; the vasus consecrated him to kingship (*rājyāya*), the rudras to extended sovereignty (*vairājyāya*) and other gods to other forms of lordship. As the materials of which the throne is constructed are no matter of indifference and as this ceremonious seat confers power upon the king, or, at least, consolidates his power [48]), the identification of the cushion and *śrī-* is not fortuitous or meaningless. The cushion no doubt adds to the king's *śrī-* "prosperity", his kingship rests on it. It is evident

---

47) See my paper on *pratiṣṭhā* (see above, n. 30).

48) J. Auboyer, Le trône et son symbolisme dans l'Inde ancienne, Paris 1949, p. 16 ff.; 177 ff.

that the function of the cushion is similar to that of the well-known tiger's skin used in the rājasūya ceremony (inauguration of a king): ŚB. 5, 4, 1, 11 "He then makes him step upon the tiger-skin, saying: "Thou art Soma's "brilliance-and-impetuosity" (*tviṣi-*)" — for because when Soma flowed through Indra, the latter thereupon became a tiger, and therefore he is Soma's *tviṣi-* — (and) "May my *tviṣi-* be like unto thine". The tiger's *tviṣi-* he thereby bestows upon him...." [49]). The power of the throne may also be illustrated by PB. 5, 5, 2, where it is said to be made of udumbara wood, which is food: "he thereby retains food for himself". Cf. also the above-mentioned Ait. text 8, 12-14, esp. 8, 12, 3. — In an elaborate description of Brahmā's throne Vicakṣaṇā (KauśU. 1, 5 = śāĀ. 3, 5) *śrī-* is the cushion on which Brahmā sits. It may be important to add that according to AiB. 8, 7, 5; 7; 9 a king is anointed for strength (*balāya*), *śrī-*, glory (*yaśase*), and food[50]). A similar passage is found AiĀ. 1, 2, 4: the hotar mounts the swing, the udgātar the seat of udumbara wood, ...the former is food, the latter prosperity (*śrīḥ*).

As it is important to emphasize the relations between *śrī-* and kingship reference should also be made to a verse in the AiB., 8, 27, 7: "in this kingdom I make prosperity to dwell" (SMB. 2, 8, 6 f.); cf. 8 "I place *indriya-* (a special aspect of power) in this kingdom". AiB. 7, 34, 9 f. a number of great kings are said to be, like Āditya (the sun), established[51]) in *śrī-*; obtaining tribute from all quarters they give heat. — ŚB. 2, 4, 4, 6 the idea arises of a royal man's being wedded to *śrī-*, who here is represented as a female being: *rājyam iha vai prāpnoti.... eteno hāsyāsapatnānupabādhā śrīr bhavati.*

Few would dispute the contention that the possession of prosperity and well-being leads to distinction and gives a claim to social pre-eminence. Yet, some words may be added on the character of prosperity and the meaning and evaluation of being well-to-do[52]). Well-being,

---

49) See e.g. also ĀpÇS. 18, 15, 5 and other texts quoted by A. B. Keith, The Religion and Philosophy of the Veda and Upanishads, Harvard Univ. 1925, p. 340 ff.

50) There is ample evidence that the throne was in other civilizations also considered an object charged with the power of kingship; see e.g., H. Frankfort e.o., Before philosophy, Harmondsworth 1949, p. 26.

51) For the sense of this term see my paper on *pratiṣṭhā*.

52) The reader may be referred to R. Bunzel, in F. Boas, General anthropology, New York 1938, p. 361 ff.; A. Goldenweiser, Anthropology, New York 1946, p. 152 ff.; B. Malinowski, Argonauts of the western Pacific, London 1932, p. 156 ff.; K. Birket-Smith, Geschichte der Kultur, Zürich 1946, p. 135 f.; 183; 187; J. Ph. Duyvendak, Inleiding tot de ethnologie van de Indische Archipel, Groningen-Batavia 1940, p. 109; G. van der Leeuw, Religion in essence and manifestation, p. 115 ff.; the same, L'homme primitif et la religion, Paris 1940,

prosperity, wealth, and property did, in those times, certainly not mean what they mean in the modern world. In most societies, ancient and modern, welfare and prosperity lend prestige, or show their value in their social aspects only or especially if they are evident to other people, if they are displayed. In so-called primitive or undeveloped societies the natural tendency to display is of a social and ceremonial character and has nothing to do with an economic use of goods and property. As a wealthy and successful cattle-owner one is a great and admirable man, even if one's flocks have no economic value at all. Food, ornaments and other valuable objects are stored up or shown in order to enhance the owner's prestige; the very manifestation of prosperity and liberality means esteem and satisfaction. A prosperous man is a honoured man, because he gives evidence of possessing uncommon abilities. Prestige and admiration are, further, essential in making a leader or ruler, and for 'primitive' or, rather, natural man it is just luck, prosperity, and extraordinary power which produce the more or less mystical element of admiration. Kingship and chieftainship are powers superior to their bearers themselves, power, prosperity, luck, admiration constitute a status or impersonal dignity which is imposed on a human being and, fusing with his own will and personality, makes him king or chief. The Scandinavian sagas which ascribe victory in battle and invulnerability to the king's luck, the ancient Egyptian texts which speak of the superhuman character and the closely guarded secret of kingship, the Malay 'concept' of *andeka* or *daulat* (the sacrosanctity investing a ruling chief, the divine element in kingship hedging its bearer), the *maiestas* of the Roman *imperium* and our own ceremonious forms of address: *Your Majesty* etc. may be quoted in evidence. The Indian ruler was in a similar way "a great deity in human form" (Manu 7, 8), and such descriptions of bearers of majesty as are given by Kālidāsa: "he outshone all in power and transcended all in majesty" (Ragh. 1, 14 *sarvātiriktasāreṇa sarvatejobhibhāvinā*) are far from rare. The king's majesty ought to be manifest, his power ought to overflow; he should bestow gifts, his prosperity should be visible, his position illustrious. "Because a king" Manu (7, 5) says in a discussion of Indian kingship, "has been formed of particles of those lords of the gods (to wit: Indra, etc., mentioned in st. 4), he surpasses

---

p. 67 ff.; C. M. Bowra, Heroic poetry, London 1952, p. 197 ff.; Frankfort, o.c., p. 82 etc.; the same, Kingship and the gods, Chicago 1948; J. H. Hutton, The Sema Nagas, London 1921, p. 145; J. J. Meyer, Trilogie altindischer Mächte und Feste der Vegetation, Zürich 1937, II, p. 156 ff.; B. S. Upadhyaya, India in Kalidasa, Allahabad 1947, p. 74 ff.; D. R. Patil, Cultural history from the Vāyu Purāṇa, Poona 1946, p. 48.

all beings in fiery-energy-and-lustre (*tejas*)". Like the ancient German kings who were called dispensers of gold and other treasures, like the Arab king who deserved this title only if he distributed gifts, like the chief of the Indian Sema Nagas who is expected to feed his dependents and even to provide them with wives when they are not able to buy them themselves, the ancient Indian chief was, by virtue of his office, generous and charitable; he was, at least, supposed to be able to be so. Already in the Ṛgveda the ruler was marked out from his subjects by his retinue and his glittering apparel; there is also evidence of royal gifts and liberality: ṚV. 1, 126; 8, 4, 19; 21, 18. "Adorning his bodily appearance", the Mahābhārata says (15, 5, 34), (the king) should sit prepared to make offerings (gifts) in profusion (*bhūridakṣiṇa-*)"; cf. also 12, 66,10 etc.; Kubera himself was said to increase a king's treasury (Kāl. Ragh. 17, 81).

A few examples may suffice to illustrate the way in which these widespread conceptions are reflected in various languages. Words for "being prosperous" are not seldom used to convey such meanings as "wealthy, displaying wealth, etc."; terms which originally denoted "good luck, good fortune" easily assumed the sense of "prosperity, wealth, large possessions". The Engl. *wealth* derives from *weal* "prosperity, state of well-being" which is etymologically related to *well*, OE. *wel* "in a great degree, very, fully" (compare, in the 'prayer for the King's Majesty': "Grant him in health and wealth long to live"). The Lat. *fortuna* stands for "(good) luck" as well as "wealth". "Fulness, plenitude" goes together with "wealth" and "power": Lat. *plenarius* "full" > AncFr. *plenier* "strong, wealthy, powerful, full-grown" [53]). Words of this semantic category can often also express the ideas of "excellency (in general)", "beauty", "social esteem" and "political power". The Tontemboan (an Indonesian idiom spoken in the north of Celebes) *siya'* stands for both "wealthy" and "handsome, fine"; *wa'ilan* means "rich, distinguished, prominent; powerful, fortunate (in connection with the deified ancestors)". The Busang (Borneo) *jaya'* means "wealthy, prominent, splendid, grand, of high rank". "Being possessed of special power or fortune" seems to have developed into "wealthy" in the Malay *kaya*, an older meaning of which survives in "mighty" (of God's works), "Almighty" (of God), and in *oraṅ kaya* ("magnate", *oraṅ* "human being") — cf. also the etymologically identical Philippine word *kaya* "power", and the N. Celebes *kakaya* "magical

---

[53]) E. Gamillscheg, Französische Bedeutungslehre, Tübingen 1951, p. 107. In this connection reference may also be made to C. D. Buck, A dictionary of selected synonyms in the principal Indo-European languages, Chicago Ill., p. 781.

power or means" —; the modern sense is "wealthy (in association with power)"; hence also "gentleman". Possession and political power go together in the Sem. *mlk*: Arab. "possess, being in possession of, reign", Hebr. "being king". The outward dignity and the insignia of royalty are, e.g. in the Gayo language of Sumatra, denoted by *kĕröjöön* "kingship; high dignity", but also "fortune, good luck" (the word derives from the Skt. *rājā* "king"), and "insignia of royal dignity". The Lat. *magnates* (from *magnus* "great") "the men of high (political) position, the chiefs of a people" lies at the root of the Engl. *magnate* "man of high position, power, authority, wealth". The Bare'e (Celebes) *mokole* "chief, prince" must be connected with words for "great", cf. also Engl. *great* in the sense of "of high rank, birth, or station". The Engl. *rich* "wealthy, fortunate in the possession of; fine, valuable; fertile; plentiful, copious etc. etc." and the corresponding Germ. *reich* (the Fr. *riche* is an O. German loan), Dutch *rijk,* Dan. *rig,* Sw. *rik* etc. in the older period mostly meant "strong, powerful", or "mighty, noble"; it derives from the Common Germ. **rīk-* "mighty, ruler" (cf. Goth. *reiks* "ruler") and is related to Germ. *Reich* which must etymologically be connected with Skt. *rājya-* "kingship, kingdom"; in this case "royal" implied "powerful" which was interpreted, and survived, as "rich".

Special stress must, in this connection, be laid upon a number of Indian words. The adj. *revant-* (from *rayivant-* "possessing goods or 'wealth' ") means "prosperous, opulent", and "brilliant, splendid, beautiful", "Reich in der Erscheinung"[54]) (cf. ṚV. 3, 61, 6 *ā revatī rodasī citram asthāt,* subj. Uṣas; 10, 35, 4). The identical Av. *raēvant* similarly applies to a rich and prominent or powerful man, and to a splendid or beautiful star. The adj. *viśiṣṭa-* "distinguished, excellent" is sometimes used for "splendid", or "showing, manifesting". The ideas of "disposing of wealth, possessing goods" and "ruling, reigning" go, for instance, together in the verb *īś- īṣṭe,* which can, in addition to this, also express the sense of "being valid, powerful, able"; cf. the Av. *is- ište* "to be able, powerful, master of, to rule over". In this respect some derivatives of *bhū-* are especially worthy of attention. The word *vibhūti-,* deriving from *vibhū-* "to be developed or manifested, to expand and be adequate, to fill or pervade" (the caus. meaning, inter alia, "to display"), stands for "manifestation of might" as well as for "welfare, prosperity, splendour" and "wealth or riches". The subst. *vibhu-* conveys the meanings "mighty, powerful, great, strong, able, excellent" and "lord, ruler, king". In Pāli *vibhava-* means "prosperity, wealth, power", *vibhūti-* "splendour, majesty"; the same variety of

---

[54]) Petr. Dict. IV, 435.

meanings has persisted in the NIA. period: Hind. *vibhūti* "welfare, prosperity, great success, wealth, influence, dignity, magnificence, (great) power, might, supremacy, dominion". Cf. also *prabhu-* "abundant, rich, excelling, mighty, powerful; chief, lord, king" and other words related to it. In the light of these facts the etymology proposed by Lanman and Osthoff [55]) for the well-known *bhavat-* "your honour, you" seems preferable to other explanations (contraction of *bhagavat-* [56]); "the gentleman present" [57])): the original sense of the root *bhū-* is "growing, thriving, prospering" (cf. Gr. *φυτόν* "plant, creature"; *φυά, φυή* "growth, stature, race"; *φύσις* "origin, natural form as a result of growth, nature", *φύω* "to bring forth; grow, spring forth" etc.; OHG. *būan* "to cultivate, dwell"; Russ. *bytĭ* "being"); cf. ṚV. 7, 52, 1 *sanema mitrāvaruṇā sananto bhavema dyāvāpṛthivī bhavantaḥ* (*bhūtimantaḥ syāma* Sāyaṇa); the frequent phrase *tato vai devā abhavan,* followed by *parāsurāḥ* and *bhavaty ātmanā parāsya bhrātṛvyo bhavati* in the brāhmaṇas; such locutions as *bhūyāma putraiḥ paśubhiḥ* (ŚB. 1, 6). AiB. 1, 13, 11 *bhū-* and a derivative of *śrī-* run parallel: *yo vai bhavati yaḥ śreṣṭhatām aśnute* "he who is successful, he who attains pre-eminence". Attention may also be drawn to the subst. *bhūti-* "well-being, thriving, prosperity, might, power, fortune, wealth", often explained by *saṃpad-, saṃpatti-, aiśvarya-, vibhūti-, vibhava-* (see above), also used as another name for the goddess Lakṣmī, and applied to such objects as represent well-being and conduce to it: "ornamentation [58]), esp. that consisting in the paint of ashes", and "the (fecundating and evil-averting) ashes" in general [59]).

Let us now return to the term *śrī-*. The possession of well-being and prosperity meaning, or leading to, distinction or giving a claim to social pre-eminence — see e.g. AiB. 7, 20, 5 *śriyam aśnute, aśnute ha prajānām* ("men, people") *aiśvaryam ādhipatyam* — the word appears in the sense of "excellence, precedence, superiority": ŚB. 3, 4, 2, 1 the gods, being peers, were unwilling to yield to each other's *śrī-*; at last they felt themselves compelled to come to an agreement and to yield to Indra's *śrī-*; then it was said that Indra is all the deities, that they have him for their chief. In the same sense it is found 5, 3, 4, 21: the

---

55) Ch. R. Lanman, A statistical account of noun-inflection in the Veda, JAOS. 10, p. 509; H. Osthoff, Morphologische Untersuchungen, I, 1878, p. 263. Cf. however, Lanman, A Sanskrit reader, Boston 1888, p. 205.

56) W. D. Whitney, A Sanskrit grammar, § 456; L. Renou, Grammaire sanscrite, Paris 1930, p. 337; and especially J. Wackernagel, Altindische Grammatik, III, Göttingen 1930, p. 259.

57) Monier-Williams, Dict. s.v.

58) See my papers mentioned in note 20.

59) Reference may be made to Meyer, Trilogie, III, p. 288.

sun-motes do not yield to one another's 'superiority' (*śrī*-). PB. 6, 9, 12 the foremost point (*agra*-) of speech is identified with *śrī*-, because, the commentary says, *bahūnāṃ madhye yasya vāk prathamaṃ pravṛttā sa śobhate,* and ŚB. 12, 8, 2, 28 "speech" (*vāk*) is called a *śrī*- ("distinction" Eggeling), that is to say *prāṇānāṃ śrīḥ*. By acquiring the *śrī*- of the gods, who hitherto prevailed, the cause of the asuras became victorious (JaiU. 1, 16, 1 ff.; cf. however also Mbh. 12, 228, 26). Thus we find the phrase *śriyaṃ gacchati* "to become notable or distinguished": JB. n° 153 C.; AiB. 5, 22, 5 [60]). — The term *pṛthuśrī-,* which Mbh. 3, 64, 46 is applied to a king, is remarkable for containing the adjective "broad" which we discussed in chapter I: one might compare the Greek *εὐρὺ κρείων* (Iliad 1, 102) and the mediaeval German use of *breit* in connection with good luck and fortune.

It seems useful to deal with some related words because they throw some light on the ancient Indian conceptions in the economic, social and political spheres. The adj. *śrīmat*- "possessed of *śrī*-" is used in association with *yaśasvin*- and *annāda*- ŚB. 10, 4, 1, 11; cf. also AiĀ. 1, 1, 3; ChU. 3, 13, 2; KauṣU. 2, 6. Ath.V.Par. 68, 28 it is apparently opposed to *adṛḍharogin-,* expressing the idea of "enjoying well-being". In later texts it is often synonymous with *īśvara-, śrīmatī* with "lady", e.g. Mbh. 3, 42, 11 (Indra); 69, 23 (Damayantī); it may also be translated by "illustrious". Possession of *śrī-,* however, means endowment with prosperity and prospering power: hence the prescription that the king in attending a lustration ceremony for the horses should take his stand or seat on a tiger-skin [61]), being *śrīmat-,* i.e. "in full pomp", or "mit seinen Insignien" (Pet. Dict.), for insignia are power-bearers (Vār. BS. 44, 13) [62]). Cf. also Boehtlingk, Ind. Spr. 3553 *nātaḥ śrīmattaraṃ kiṃcid.... prabhaviṣṇor* (see above) *yathā.... kṣamā,* and Rām. 2, 26, 9 where the adjective is used of an auspicious and favourable constellation. It is, moreover, worth noticing that it is not only used as an epithet of Viṣṇu, whose connection with the *śrī*-concept we shall have to concern ourselves with further on, but also as a significant name of

---

60) It is not my intention to deny the existence of such shades of meaning as "splendour, lustre, beauty" for the term under discussion. Yet even in those passages where "splendour" or similar concepts are mentioned *śrī*- is not always unequivocally synonymous with them. Cf., e.g., JaiU. 1, 4, 1 where both *śri*- and the sun are regarded as *bhās*-; when it is stated, ÇB. 12, 8, 3, 24 that the sun shines established on the *bṛhatī* as his *śrī*- and *pratiṣṭhā* this does not imply that *śrī*- is splendour; such texts as TĀ. 2, 11, 1 *savitā śriyaḥ prasavitā,* and ÇB. 6, 7, 2, 2 being a comment on VS. 12, 1 = ṚS. 10, 45, 8 where Agni (as the sun) is said to shine "for welfare" (*śriyo eṣa rocate*) do not contain this meaning either.

61) See above, p. 190.

62) See also Meyer, o.c., II, p. 127.

Kubera, the god of wealth and material happiness, the lord over all treasures, who was held to be immanent in a king (Rām. 7, 76, 31) and doubtless represents a fecundating divinity, a promoter of productivity: he is united with *Ṛddhi-* "Increase, Success, Abundance" who in the Mahābhārata is considered his consort, with Lakṣmī who in the epics is not yet called his wife, and with Soma's daughter Bhadrā ("the Happy, Prosperous, or Fortunate One"); the yakṣas who are without any doubt concerned with fertility and vegetation are his attendants [63]). Kubera is also believed to be in the possession of *śrī-*, which, Hopkins[64]) is right in saying, means "material prosperity", and which, Mbh. 2, 17, 15 implies, belongs to him as *tejas* belongs to the sun, *kṣamā* ("patience, indulgence") to the earth, and anger to Yama. — We must leave the question undecided whether the adj. *śrīmat-* in the sense of "rich (i.e. "plentiful, abundant, luxuriant"), charming, splendid etc." was also preferably associated with trees, lotus- and other plants, fruits, gardens, rivers, mountains, āśramas and similar objects. It could also express the idea of 'majestic' (tiger: Mbh. 3, 64, 31).

The rare *śreman-* "distinction" forms a pair with *mahiman-* "greatness" ŚB. 12, 4, 1, 11, where the context clearly shows that this substantive expresses a quality originating in the possession of *śrī-*: by keeping for oneself the agnihotra-cow which is unable to bear one's *śremānaṃ.... mahimānam,* one shall become *śreyān* (i.c. acquire more *śrī-*) and take *śrī-* to oneself. With this passage we might compare such texts as 3, 9, 1, 1: when Prajāpati, the lord of creatures, had created the living beings, he felt himself, so to say, exhausted; the creatures turned away from him, they were no longer at his disposal for his *śrī-* and food. These creatures or subjects constituted his *śrī-*. The same phrase returns in the next paragraphs: by offering P. regained strength, the creatures were at his disposal for his *śrī-* and food; by offering he became better (*vasīyān*) [65]). A somewhat different shade of meaning occurs AiB. 7, 15, 5 *sūryasya paśya śremāṇaṃ yo na tandrayate caran* "....the pre-eminence or excellence of the sun who does not tire of wandering". The explanation given in Sāyaṇa's commentary: *śremānam*: *śreṣṭhatvaṃ jagadvandyatvam,* is worth mentioning, because it shows the social element of appreciation,

---

63) For Kubera and his attendants and associates see E. W. Hopkins, Epic Mythology, Strassburg 1915, p. 142 ff.; A. K. Coomaraswamy, Yakshas, Smithsonian Misc. public., Washington 1928-31. Meyer, o.c., I, p. 98 and III, p. 307; 329.

64) Hopkins, o.c., p. 146. The author rightly invites attention to the points of resemblance between Kubera and Indra.

65) Eggeling (SBE. 26, p. 217 f.) is not right in translating *śrī-* by „joy".

praise, respect, and veneration enjoyed by those who possessed *śrī-*.

Similar interpretations are handed down in connection with *śreṣṭha-* to which we shall turn now: *praśasya-, praśasyatama-* "praiseworthy", *sarvātiśayin-* "surpassing everything or anybody", *atyutkṛṣṭatama-* "taking a very high position, excellent".

The relation between or identity of, the possession of *śrī-* and a state of thriving and prosperity, of enjoying economic, social, and political pre-eminence is often elucidated by the use of the terms *śreṣṭha-* and *śreyas-*, which from the point of view of the formation of words are nearly related to *śrī-*, (*a*)*śrīra-* (see above), and *śrīmant-* [66]). The terms *śrī-* and *śreyas-* or *śreṣṭha-* are often used in the same context: ŚB. 11, 1, 6, 23 the earth is *śrī-*, therefore he who obtains most of it becomes *śreṣṭha-* "well-to-do, prosperous, (and hence:) distinguished". AiB. 3, 7, 11 if he desire of a man "may he be (more) prosperous (well-to-do: *śreyān*), he should....; < in doing so > he places him from *śrī-* in *śrī-*". ṚV. 2, 33, 3 *śreṣṭho jātasya rudra śriyāsi tavastamas tavasām* (*aiśvaryeṇa praśasyatamaḥ* Sāyaṇa) is a very instructive text. Cf. also 5, 60, 4 *śriye śreyāṃsas tavaso.... mahāṃsi cakrire tanūṣu* (subj. the Maruts) and 6, 26, 8. ŚB. 1, 3, 5, 12 instructs the priest to recite only for a man of established prosperity (*gataśrī-*) who would not wish to become (economically) better (*śreyān*) or worse (*pāpīyān,* see further on). An interesting passage is AiB. 5, 22, 5 "let us not speak ill of prosperity (*śrī-*), for it is wrong to speak ill of a man who is well-to-do (or: who is one's better, one's superior: *śreyas-* [67]))": *loke 'pi śreyaso vidyaiśvaryādinādhikasya puruṣasyācaraṇaṃ duravavadaṃ hi... ata eva pitrācāryādīnāṃ nindāṃ na kurvanti, dveṣibhiḥ kriyamāṇāṃ api na śṛṇvanti* [68]). Cf. also GB. 2, 3, 3; MaiU. 1, 11, 3. KāśB. 1, 2, 2, 14 ....*evaṃ haiva kīrtyā yaśasā śriyā śvaḥ śvaḥ śreyān bhavati,* whereas in 15 it reads: ....*kīrtyā* ....*pāpīyan bhavati.* See also AiB. 7, 17, 6-7; ŚB. 12, 2, 2, 23; PB. 2, 2, 3.

It is, moreover, perfectly clear that these words are very often used in connection with welfare, prosperity, advantage, food, material comforts etc. Whereas AV. 5, 20, 9 the meaning of the phrase *śreyo vanvānaḥ* seems to be "winning advantage" (of the war-drum) — cf. also 10 *śreyaḥketo vasujit* — and a similar indeterminate sense is also found elsewhere (cf. e.g. 2, 11, 1-5), the substantive accompanied by

---

[66]) See also L. Renou, Grammaire de la langue védique, Lyon-Paris 1952, p. 164. — Cf. already Oldenberg, o.c., p. 35, n. 1.

[67]) As is well-known the so-called comparative very often serves to express the idea of "rather, in a more or less considerable degree, not the opposite of the idea expressed by the root etc."

[68]) Cf. e.g. P. Sartori, Hdwtb. de. Abergl. VII, 1038 f.

either of the two adjectives is: ŚB. 13, 8, 1, 14 offspring (in the same context: "productiveness" (*prajanana-*)): *prajā hāsya śreyasī bhavati* ("more prosperous" Eggeling). Soma, the drink of immortality (life) and magically potent bestower of wealth, is the *śreṣṭha-* of the plants: AV. 11, 6, 15, where the plants themselves are invoked to deliver man from distress; cf. PVB. 1, 6, 7 (Soma) *subhūr asi śreṣṭhaḥ* [69]) "well thriving art thou, most possessed of *śrī-*": *tvaṃ suṣṭhu bhāvayitā vṛṣṭyādidvāreṇa sarvajagata utpādayitāsi, śreṣṭhaḥ sarvebhyo devebhyaḥ praśasyatamaḥ* (Sāyaṇa). Cf. also ṚV. 10, 76, 2. A *śreṣṭhatama vīrudhām* is addressed AV. 6, 138, 1. ŚB. 9, 5, 2, 13 becoming *śreyas-* day after day is opposed to becoming a withered trunk. AiB. 2, 1, 6 ff. the man who desires food (*anna-*) and "increase, or a well-nourished condition" (*puṣṭi-*) is advised to make a sacrificial post of bilva wood, which is a *rūpa-* "material form, sensuous appearance, representative" [70]) of food; it should be covered with branches from the very root, which is a rūpa of *puṣṭi-*. The man who knowing thus makes such a post prospers (*puṣyati*), he becomes the *śreṣṭha-* of his own people, and a light among them, because, they say, *bilva-* is "light" (*jyotis*). But the bilva [71]) is also connected with *śrī-* and *Śrī-*: it is also called *śrīphala-*. This word originally denoted the bilva fruit, cf. e.g. Manu 5, 120 *śrīphalair*: *bilvaphalair* Kullūka; it was also called *vṛddhināmauṣadha-* "the herb called after prosperity". The bilva tree is among the symbols sacred to Śrī-Lakṣmī, side by side with the conch, the mace, the lotus, the disk, the luck-bringing svastika, the footprints of a cow, the mango tree (which is a representative of fertility etc.) [72]). That its fruits are used as a cure for barrenness may perhaps be attributed to its relations with the same goddess [73]). By offering them one can win gold (AVP. 31, 6, 4). Already in the Śrīsūkta the bilva is called Śrī's tree, st. 6: "O Sun-coloured One (= Śrī) from *tapas* ("asceticism") your tree

[69]) Chinnaswami's edition (Kashi Sanskrit Series, Benares 1935) has *s. a. ś. raśmir devānāṃ saṃsad devānām*...

[70]) I refer to M. Falk, Nāma-rūpa and dharma-rūpa, Calcutta 1943, esp. p. 19 ff.

[71]) The bilva is the wood-apple tree (Aegle marmelos), now commonly called *bel*. In Hinduism its leaves are used in the ceremonial of the worship of Çiva, its fruit when unripe medicinally. It is also connected with the sun: the man who desires pre-eminence in holiness or sacred knowledge has also to make a sacrificial post of bilva wood (cf. also ĀpÇS. 7, 1, 15), because it has grown up on the very spot on which the sun before being lifted to the sky had been established on the earth (see TS. 2, 1, 8, 1; MS. 2, 9, 3: 116, 12). Cf. also Varāham. BS. 85, 3. — In later times bilva leaves were used in Çivaite rites. For the power of a bilva amulet see ÇāṅkhĀr. 12, 20 f.

[72]) See for instance B. A. Gupte, Hindu holidays and ceremonials, Calcutta 1919, p. 40 (and plate 5).

[73]) See e.g. R. E. Enthoven, The folklore of Bombay, Oxford 1924, p. 286.

came into being, to wit the bilva tree; its fruits must, through (the power of) *tapas,* remove the illusions (*māyā(ḥ)*, implying tricks, sorcery, cunning) and (all kinds of) evil fortune (*alakṣmīḥ,* implying distress, poverty, adversity), be they internal or external". When performing an oblation of bilva to Śrī, the fuel of the fire must, according to the prescriptions laid down in the Ṛgvidhāna (2, 19, 3 ff.) [74]), also consist of wood of the same tree; when a man who is desirous of prosperity (*śrī-*) performs this act, he will obtain endless fortune (*śrī-*). In the same text, 3, 42, 4, a bilva leaf and a lotus are among the leaves and flowers which cause Hari's satisfaction. According to the Varāhapur. 79, 1 ff. the lotus which bears Śrī grows in the neighbourhood of a vast bilva-wood.

Returning now to *śreyas-* and *śreṣtha-* we call attention to ŚB. 12, 4, 2, 10: when it rains upon a person's agnihotra-milk he should know that *śukra-* "pure juice or essence" (but the word can also mean "gold, wealth" and "semen (of men and animals)") has come to him from above, that the gods have rendered assistance to him (*upa māṃ devāḥ prābhūvan*), that he shall become *śreyān,* i.e. that his *śrī-* shall increase. Cf. also 12, 4, 1, 11 *śriyo vai parjanyo varṣati tad vidyāc chremāṇaṃ me mahimānam adhārayamāṇopāvikṣac chreyān bhaviṣyāmīti* "Parjanya (the rain-cloud) showers down blessings (prosperity); let him therefore know: "Unable to bear my well-being (distinction) and 'greatness', she (the agnihotra-cow) has lain down; I shall become possessed of greater prosperity" ". Ibid. 7 it rains, herbs and trees come into being, seed flows from man and animals, therefrom everything here comes into being.... abundant (*bhūyasī*) generation (*prajātiḥ*) has accrued unto him, he will be multiplied in offspring and cattle, he shall become *śreyān* ("more prosperous")". 12, 5, 1, 4 one becomes *śreyān* by using milk of a special cow.

ṚV. 5, 82, 1 *śréṣṭhaṃ sarvadhâtamaṃ túram* is used in connection with the food to be procured to man by the god Savitar, the sun, who here seems to be identified with the well-known distributor of wealth, Bhaga, or, what is perhaps also possible, whose food is regarded as a "promoter of welfare [75])". JaiB. 1, 108 *annādo vā ayaṃ śreṣṭho bhaviṣyati* "dieser fürwahr wird ein Esser von Speise, ein Ausgezeichneter, sein" (Caland); I would prefer "he shall have what to eat, he shall not lack sufficient food, (nay,) he shall be uncommonly (very) provided with *śrī-*". Sad to relate, the wish to be an *annāda-* often recurred in

---

[74]) I refer to my translation of this text, Utrecht 1951, p. 51.

[75]) See e.g. Macdonell, Vedic Mythology, p. 45. If the word *túra-* is a subst. (accent, see also Geldner's note, II, p. 85) it may mean "excellent food" (cf. the adj. *turá-* when accompanying words for "power" or "spirituous liquor").

a country which was frequently afflicted by drought and famine[76]). The combination *annādaḥ śreṣṭhaḥ svānām* occurs, for instance, JB. n° 157 C. (2, 305); 186 C. (3, 128); 191 C (3, 171). In my opinion *śreṣṭha-* refers to a position or situation of economic welfare leading to social distinction.

Now, the AiB. 1, 5, 23 states that *virāj-* is food (see above); therefore, the text continues, can the man who here has most food be considered "most illustrious or eminent in the world (*bhūyiṣṭhaṃ loke virājati*); he is illustrious (eminent) among his own, most prosperous (*śreṣṭha-*, or "best") of his own, who knows thus". By way of digression to this text and in addition to the remarks already made with respect to the connection between *śrī-* and *virāj-* [77]), let us discuss the sense of the root *rāj-*. Like the cognate Lat. *rēx* Ind. *rājan-*, mention of which has already been made, not only denoted a "king or prince" but also implied the sense of a "wealthy, influential, or mighty man". When applying to the pattern king *rājan-* stood for a man who was considered an essential factor in the well-being of his people, a man who was, or ought to be, handsome, virtuous, victorious, generous, and very rich, whose very constitution was held to be more healthy and robust than that of other men [78]). It is not surprising that the word, in a fairly large number of cases, came to express the idea of "the best, largest, or principal of its kind": *rājadanta-*, *rājamaṇi-* etc. In a comparable way, the verb *rājati,* the denominative character of which may be taken for granted [79]), assumed the sense of "being kingly", i.e. "to distinguish

---

[76]) The reader might be referred to C. A. F. Rhys Davids, in the Cambridge History of India I, Cambridge 1922, p. 203; W. H. Moreland and A. Ch. Chatterji, A short history of India[2], 1945, p. 4 and passim; for a discussion of Megasthenes' affirmation to the contrary see B. C. J. Timmer, Megasthenes en de Indische maatschappij, Thesis Amsterdam 1930, p. 131.

[77]) See above, p. 187.

[78]) The reader might be referred to E. W. Hopkins, The social and military position of the ruling caste in ancient India, in JAOS. 13 (1889), p. 57 ff., and esp. p. 113 ff.; Jagdish Chandra Jain, Life in Ancient India as depicted in the Jain canon, Bombay 1947, p. 49 ff.; R. Fick, Die sociale Gliederung im nordöstl. Indien zu Buddha's Zeit, Kiel 1897, p. 63 ff.; The Pāli Text Society's Pali-Engl. Dict. VII, 1924, p. 26 ff.; H. Zimmer, Altindisches Leben, Berlin 1879, p. 162 ff.; Macdonell and Keith, Vedic index of names and subjects, London 1912, II, p. 210 ff. — Remember also the compound *nīrājana-* denoting a lustration, a ceremony bringing victory etc.

[79]) W. D. Whitney, The roots ... of the Sanskrit language, Leipsic 1885, p. 138. There is no need to assume, with Grassmann and Monier-Williams, two different roots: 1° "to reign", 2° "to be illustrious or resplendent". We might compare the history of Lat. *regalis* > Engl. *regal* "pertaining to a king; fit for a k.; splendid, stately"; Fr. Eng. *royal* "pertaining etc. to a king; splendid, magnificent; of superior importance etc."; in Dutch *royaal* means "open-handed, liberal, munificent; ample; generous; sportsmanlike"; *vorstelijk* (from *vorst* "prince,

oneself, to be illustrious or resplendent, to be conspicuous for splendour, beauty, loftiness etc.". The compound *vi-rāj-*, which is very usual, is ChU. 2, 16, 2 accompanied by *prajayā paśubhir brahmavarcasena*, and connected with *śrī-*: ṚV. 1, 188, 6 *surukme hi supeśasādhi śriyā virājataḥ* "(Dawn and Night), ...beautifully adorned.... are illustrious (eminent, conspicuous) by their display of well-being"[80]); Mbh. 3,163,21 (of Viṣṇu-Nārāyaṇa) *suśriyābhivirājate*; cf. also 1, 114, 9 *rarāja.... śrīmān*. The same verb is also connected with *bhaga-* "good fortune, prosperity", *subhaga-* etc.: ṚV. 4, 1, 6; AV. 2, 36, 3 (a text by means of which the person reciting it hoped to obtain a husband for a woman): *gatvā patiṃ subhagā vi rājatu* (Whitney-Lanman do not seem to be correct in translating "let her bear rule"); cf. also 14, 1, 64 (a nuptial text) *śivā syonā patiloke vi rāja*. The verb is not seldom used in connection with happy and fortunate women: Rām. 2, 60, 13 G. *rāmalakṣmaṇayor madhye sītā rājati te snuṣā* | *viṣṇuvāsavayor madhye padmā śrīr iva rūpiṇī*; Mbh. 3, 53, 12 *tatra sma rājate bhaimī sarvābharaṇabhūṣitā* (and in 13 *śrīr ivāyatalocanā*).

Various other words for welfare, advantage, fortune, and for means of promoting, or ways of displaying, them, are likewise frequently qualified by *śreyas-* or *śreṣṭha-*; or, these adjectives are found in the same context: AV. 6, 21, 2 *śreṣṭham asi bheṣajānām*; 44, 2; ṚV. 10, 112, 3 *śreṣṭhai rūpais tanvaṃ sparśayasva*. In a natural way *svasti* "well-being, fortune" is *śreṣṭhā*: ṚV. 10, 63, 16; AiB. 1, 9, 7. ŚB. 3, 4, 4, 27 *varīyas tapo bhavati paraḥ-paraḥ śreyāṃsaṃ lokaṃ jayati vasīyān u haivāsmiṃ loke bhavati*. Possessions, wealth etc. are often called *śreṣṭha-*: ṚV. 2, 7, 1 *ś..... dyumantam.... rayim*; 10, 35, 7 *ś..... vareṇyam bhāgam*; 24, 2 *śreṣṭhaṃ no dhehi vāryam* (Indra is addressed): *praśastatamaṃ paśvādidhanam*; cf. 3, 21, 2, and also 10, 31, 2. ṚV. 2, 21, 6 *indra śreṣṭhāni draviṇāni dhehi*; 4, 54, 1; cf. also 6, 16, 26; 68, 2; cf. also AiB. 2, 12, 11 ff. ṚV. 5, 25, 3 Agni is requested to bestow wealth on those praying with most prospering benevolence (*śreṣṭhayā sumatyā*). The "favour, furtherance, assistance" (*avas*) [81]) of the Aśvins is *śreṣṭham*; cf. also ŚB. 12, 4, 4, 2 ff.; other words in *-as-* which, generally speaking, denote power-substances which within

---

sovereign") "princely" and "munificent"; like the Dutch *heerlijk* (from *heer* "lord"), which can mean "glorious, lovely, great etc.", the Engl. *lordly* also expresses the idea of "magnificent"; besides, it can stand for "lavish, generous".

[80]) "Çrī, eigentlich das Bessersein, drückt Vorrang, Ansehen und Schönheit aus" Geldner, o.c., I, p. 269.

[81]) See J. Gonda, Anc. Ind. *ojas*, Lat. **augos* and the Indo-Eur. nouns in *-es-/-os*, Utrecht 1952, p. 52. — Cf. also the commentary on TS. 7, 4, 19b which explains *aviḥ* "kindly disposed" as *śrīḥ* because "it helps (*avati*) all living creatures".

some form of experience were supposed to be present in persons, objects and phenomena, and by virtue of which they were endowed with special qualities [82]), are likewise elucidated by these adjectives: ŚB. 2, 2, 2, 19 *tasya bhūyo-bhūya eva tejo bhavati śvaḥ-svaḥ śreyān bhavati* [83]); cf. also AiB. 1, 28, 5 ff. *ojas* and *śraiṣṭhya-*, ṚV. 4, 36, 7 *peśas*. Mitra and Varuṇa are *śreṣṭhavarcasā*, e.g. 4, 19, 2.

In addition to this mention may be made of ṚV. 6, 71, 2 *devasya vayaṃ savituḥ savīmani śreṣṭhe syāma vasunaś ca dāvane | yo.... niveśane prasave cāsi bhūmanaḥ* "may we live under [84]) the most beneficial ("heilsamst" Grassmann) guidance (stimulation) [85]) of the god Savitar (the stimulator) [86]) in order to receive wealth, (Savitar) who art concerned with giving a resting-place to, and the furtherance of, all existing things....". With the verbs *sū-* and *pra-sū-* this god is often besought to bestow wealth, cf. e.g. 3, 56, 6; 5, 81, 2. Cf. VājS. 3, 58 *vasyas-* and *śreyas-*. ṚV. 10, 170, 3 *idaṃ śreṣṭhaṃ jyotiṣāṃ jyotir uttamam* is called *viśvajid dhanajid* i.e. "all-conquering and wealth-acquiring": the often recurring conception of the sun's invincible power to promote prosperity. The AiB., 7, 20, quoting part of this stanza adds: "no harm befalls him when he is instigated by the god Savitar, he attains ever increasing prosperity (*śrī-*)". — ṚV. 7, 77, 5 Uṣas is addressed to shine upon the person praying and his relations *śreṣṭhebhir bhānubhiḥ*, and (in doing so) to promote long life for them; a request for refreshment (*iṣ-* also "sap, refreshing drink"), cows, horses, cars, no doubt to be procured by Uṣas' rays of light, is added; cf. also st. 6, and ŚāB. 7, 10.

We had already occasion to touch upon the association of *śreṣṭhatā-* and the verb *bhū-* when serving to convey ideas of thriving and prospering [87]). We may add here such passages as AiB. 3, 21, 2 *yo vai bhavati yaḥ śreṣṭhatām aśnute sa mahān bhavati* (see also Sāyaṇa's commentary); 23, 3; AiĀ. 1, 1, 1. Cf. also the phrase *bhūyiṣṭhaṃ śreṣṭhaṃ vittanām* JB. 1, 24.

ŚB. 13, 8, 1, 6 sets forth that a deceased man's offspring will become

---

[82]) See the book mentioned in n. 81, p. 46 ff.

[83]) For *tejas* see the same book, p. 49 f.

[84]) I.e. "derive benefit from", see also Renou, Grammaire de la langue védique, p. 354.

[85]) For the general function of the substantives in *-man-* see my remarks in the Mnemosyne, III, 6 (1938), p. 162, and in 'Notes on *brahman*', Utrecht 1950, p. 72 f. W. Porzig, IF. 42, p. 226 was already right in stating that the words formed by this element not seldom denoted an idea "in dem Kräfte schlummern, die ohne menschliches Zutun ihre Wirkungen hervorbringen".

[86]) For Savitar see Macdonell, Vedic Mythology, p. 34 (cf. e.g. ṚV. 3, 56, 5; 5, 82, 4 f.; 2, 56, 6).

[87]) See p. 192 f.

more prosperous (*śreyas-*) when the sepulchral mound is made on ground which inclines towards the north. On the strength of 4, 5, 8, 11 "....if she (the thousandth cow) goes northward.... the yajamāna ("sacrificer") will be *śreyān* in the world...., if she goes southward he will quickly die" and taking into account the above remarks on the god who resides in the north, Kubera [88]), I would venture to connect this relation between the idea expressed by *śreyas-* and the northern region with Kubera's relations with the *śrī*-concept [89]).

The opposition between *śrī-* and *pāpman-* [90]) is also illustrated by the frequent contrast between the related adjectives [91]). See ŚB. 1, 2, 5, 24-26 where the recurrent opposition *pāpīyāṃsaḥ: śreyāṃsaḥ* does not seem to have been correctly translated by Eggeling: "more sinful: righteous". In my opinion, those who perform the sacrificial acts in the right manner are doing well or prosper, the others suffer evil or misfortune. Cf. 11, 4, 2, 7 f. where the same author is right in translating by "more prosperous, poorer"; 14, 1, 3, 33 (cf. also ĀpŚS. 15, 9, 13); 1, 3, 5, 12; 12, 1, 3, 22, and especially 2, 2, 2, 19 by speaking the truth one sprinkles, so to say, the consecrated fire with ghee, and increases one's own *tejas* and day by day one becomes more prosperous (*ś.*); whosoever speaks untruth.... becomes, in the same way, more afflicted by evil (*pāpīyān*). Cf. also the very illustrative passages AiB. 3, 7 and GB. 2, 3, 3; and, in addition to these JB. 1, 108 (n° 17 C.) *annādo vā ayaṃ śreṣṭho bhaviṣyati pāpmā vā asya paryavartīti*. See, finally, PB. 2, 1, 4.

We found that a distinction can scarcely be made between economic prosperity and social eminence: cf. ŚB. 10, 3, 5, 8 "he who knows thus becomes the most prosperous (*śreṣṭha-* "the first" Eggeling), the leader (*puraetṛ-*) of his own people (*svānām*), an 'eater of food' (see above), a ruler (*adhipati-*)". Social distinction is meant 12, 7, 1, 10: when the asura Namuci had taken away Indra's *indriyaṃ vīryaṃ somapītham annādyam* "psychical power, manly power, soma-draught, and food", the god laid down dissolved; then the gods said that he who had been the *śreṣṭha-* of them, had now been overtaken by *pāpman-* "evil". Cf. also 12, 2, 3, 10.

By a frequent pseudo-etymological explanation the head (*śiras*) is said to mean *śrī-*, for, ŚB. 2, 1, 2, 8 holds, the head indeed means *śrī-*; hence people say of a man who is the *śreṣṭha-* of a community that he

---

88) See p. 195.

89) It may be observed that the points of the compass are sometimes indicated by the mere names of their regents.

90) See p. 186.

91) See also Oldenberg, o.c., p. 35, n. 1.

is the head of that community. Similarly, 1, 4, 5, 5. When, JaiU. 4, 11, 1 ff. says, the six self-existing divinities, to wit Agni, Vāyu, the Sun, Breath, Food, and Speech, disputed regarding their *śraiṣṭhya-* ("notability, distinction, pre-eminence"), they did not recognize each other's *śreṣṭhatā*; each of them, believing himself to be the *śreṣṭha-*, wanted to be considered and revered as *śrī-* by his colleagues (*māṃ śriyam upādhvam iti*). ŚB. 14, 1, 1, 3 f. the gods wished to obtain *śrī-* and to become *yaśas* [92]) and 'eaters of food'; it was agreed that he who should first reach the end of the sacrifice should be the most excellent (*śreṣṭha-*) of them [93]). Very interesting is also the statement (4, 1, 3, 9): soma means *śrī-*, physical evil (*yakṣma-*) *pāpman-;* even as at the approach of his superior (*śreyas-*) the man who is lower in the social scale (*pāpīyān*) would descend from his seat, so does psychical evil go down before him (soma). 12, 8, 2, 28: when in a definite ritual act the sacrificer singly and solely takes possession of *śrī-* he becomes singly and solely the most distinguished (*śreṣṭha-*) among his own people. JB. 1, 271 (n° 95 C., a passage worth reading in its entirety) it is argued that a man who in a particular way knows and reveres *śrī-* shall become the *śreṣṭha-* of his region; even the 'princes' (*rājānaḥ*, see above) shall revere him. See also ŚB. 3, 4, 1, 11, etc.; JB. 15, 7, 4. The phrase *śreṣṭhaḥ svānām* "distinguished among his own people", expressing the idea of social repute and pre-eminence in one's own circle, is frequently found: ŚB. 1, 6, 3, 22; 10, 3, 5, 10 (cf. 8, see above); 12, 8, 3, 2; AiB. 2, 22, 9; Śā. 12, 3; cf. JBr. 2, 409. Special mention must be made of AiB. 1, 5, 25 *vi sveṣu rājati, ś. svānām bhavati*.... It is, in the same way, applied to Indra: PB. 7, 8, 2; 16, 4, 3 (*praśasyatamaḥ adhikaḥ* Comm.); TB. 2, 3, 1, 3; ŚB. 1, 6, 3, 22; 9, 2, 3, 3. PB. 16, 4, 2 clearly refers to social distinction among equals: *tiṣṭhante 'smai samānāḥ śraiṣṭhyāya*.... "to him.... his equals yield the supremacy" (Caland); cf. 6, 3, 9 f.; 7, 5, 2; 3; see also ŚB. 10, 3, 5, 11. Cf. also ŚB. 8, 4, 1, 3 (of Brahmā); JBr. 2, 369; ŚB. 8, 3, 1, 3. In this connection the phrases *jyeṣṭha- śreṣṭha-* and *jyaiṣṭhya- śraiṣṭhya-* may be recalled: ŚB. 10, 3, 5, 10; PB. 21, 2, 4; AiB. 4, 25, 7 (cf. 6); JB. 2, 67. We also find *śreṣṭha- baliṣṭha-* (ŚB. 11, 5, 4, 2 Indra and Agni), *śreṣṭha-varṣiṣṭha-* ("eminent and important": ibid. 3 Prajāpati and Savitar); *ś.* and *vasiṣṭha-* ŚB. 8, 1, 1, 6; TB. 2, 3, 1, 3. ŚB. 13, 7, 1, 1 we come across *śraiṣṭhyaṃ svārājyam ādhipatyam* (of Brahmā), etc. Cf. also AiB. 8, 14, 4; 15, 1; 19, 2. In a comparable way, a horse is pre-eminent

92) For this 'personal' use of the neuter *yaśāḥ* see my book on *ojas*, p. 46 ff.; 53; 55.

93) The text adds that men now formulate the same wishes when entering upon a sacrificial session.

among the animals (ŚB. 13, 1, 6, 1: it goes beyond or surpasses them). The sun is the *ś.* ray of light (VS. 2, 26 a), the sacrifice the *ś.* work ŚB. 1, 7, 1, 5). For *śreṣṭha-* in the sense of "distinguished" and for *śraiṣṭhya-* "pre-eminence, notability" see e.g. JB. n° 141 C. Other applications could be quoted in which the semantic transition to the sense of "best" (in general) might be clearly seen: e.g. ŚB. 2, 2, 4, 9 where reproducing oneself and saving oneself from death is called *śreyas-*.

As is well known, the term *śreyas* often expresses the idea of "bliss, happiness, esp. the bliss of final emancipation" (cf. e.g. KaṭhUp. 2, 1; Manu 4, 258; Mbh.): cf., in a way, the use of *śrī-* AiB. 1, 30, 30. Viṣṇu himself is called *Śreyas-* and *Śreṣṭha-* (Mbh. 13, a. 149). Before turning to an enumeration of some passages in the later literature where the above words or compounds containing them occur in an interesting manner, let us enter into a short discussion of the cognate terms in Avestan and examine the statements made by previous scholars with regard to their meanings. According to Bartholomae and his disciples the Av. *srī- srāy-* means "Schönheit; beauty", the adj. *srīra-* "schön anzusehen, schön; beautiful", *sraēšta-* "der schönste; most splendid or beautiful" ("1. fürs Gesicht; 2. fürs Gehör; 3. im Allgemeinen") [94]; Lommel [95]) likewise translated these words by "schön etc.". There is no denying that this vague meaning can do duty in most cases, but the question arises whether at least part of the relevant passages will not gain in depth and importance if we replace the above translations, which, though adopted by Oldenberg [96]), are only seldom a necessity, by renderings resulting from the assumption that the primary sense of the IIr. *śrī-* was something like "prosperity, well-being", and not "beauty" [97]).

The adj. *srīra-* is comparatively frequent in connection with plants. Now, Av. *urvarā* especially refers to useful and edible plants which were often considered divine beings [98]). Does Vend. 18, 63 *urvaranąm uzuxšyentinąm srīranąm zairi-gaonanąm vaxšå* refer exclusively to the growth of greenish plants which are agreeable to the eye from the aesthetical point of view, or does *srīra-* mean, or imply, the idea of "thriving"? Cf. also Yt. 18, 6 where three highly important powers,

---

94) C. Bartholomae, Altiranisches Wörterbuch, Strassburg 1904, 1645 f., 1632; H. Reichelt, Avesta Reader, Strassburg 1911, p. 270 f.

95) H. Lommel, Die Yäst's des Awesta, Göttingen-Leipsic 1927, passim.

96) Oldenberg, Die vedischen Worte fur "schön" etc. (see above), Nachr. Gött. 1918, p. 36.

97) The Pahlavi translations *nēwak, nēwakīh, nēwaktar* etc. are no great help.

98) See, e.g., H. Lommel, Die Religion Zarathustras, Tübingen 1930, p. 258; 264; J. Hertel, Die arische Feuerlehre, Leipsic 1925, p. 144.

the divine star Tištrya (which brings rain [99])), the 'wind' (who blows clouds and rain [100])) and the "glory of kingly power" (*χvarənah-*) are said to bring prosperity; in the next part of the same passage the same phrase "prosperous growth of the *srīra-* etc. plants" recurs. Y. 57, 19 the haoma, which is elsewhere called *frādaṯ.gaēϑa-* "making the living beings to flourish" [101]), *dūraoša-* "he before whom death flees", *sāiri.baoγa* "rescuing from ruin" — compare also such passages as Y. 9, 19-32 and 10, 7 ff. — is, like its Vedic counterpart, the soma, brought into connection with *srī-* by being styled *srīra-*. A name for a shoot or similar part of a plant, *uruϑmi* — the word derives from *rud-* "to grow" — is likewise given the same epithet: Yt. 13, 55. The earth is, Yt. 13, 9, not only called the bearer of all that has corporeal existence, but also the mother of much that is *srīra-*. When recalling such texts as Vend. 3, 4 "Where on earth, is it best? Where one cultivates the greater number of cornfields, pastures, fruit- and kitchen-gardens (*yavanąmča vāstranąmča urvaranąmča χvarəϑō.bairyanąm,* the last word meaning "bearing edible food")", and 24 "for soil left untilled a long time is as unhappy ....as a beautiful woman, a long time without child", one is almost tempted to take the adjective in the sense of "prosperous, displaying prosperity". Besides, Satavaēsa, a rain-making divinity which drives the waters (clouds) forth, is Yt. 8, 9 called *srīra-* when he arrives at 'child-birth' [102]) (*vyāhva yaṯ jasati srīro*); "he stands still peacefully (or: bringing rest or peace) over the lands with good harvest". In consideration of the other characteristics of this divinity — Yt. 8, 43 [103]) he is said to wash off all evil or horrors, to make grow, and to heal all creatures; 32 he is called *raēvå,* which like the cognate AInd. *revant-* means "rich", and *χvarənahvå* "possessed of the *χvarənah* (see above), i.e. something like "illustrious" or "glorious" — in Neriosangh's Sanskrit translation it is rendered by *śrīmān*! — [104]), and said to rise from the sea and to produce fogs. The same divine power appears in Yt. 13, 43 f.: here it is regarded as a rain-maker who makes the grain and vegetables grow in order to save,

---

[99]) Cf. e.g. Yt. 8, 33; see e.g. also E. Herzfeld, Zoroaster and his world, Princeton 1947, p. 586.

[100]) For the 'wind' or atmosphere see S. Wikander, Vayu I, Uppsala-Leipsic, 1941; H. S. Nyberg, Die Religionen des alten Iran, Leipsic 1938, p. 300 f.; H. Lommel, Die Yäšt's des Awesta, p. 143 ff.

[101]) See Lommel, Religion, p. 103 f. and p. 83 f.

[102]) I refer to Nyberg, Religionen, p. 309 ("die 'Entlastung' der Wolke vom Wasser"); Herzfeld, o.c., p. 602.

[103]) If Herzfeld, l.c. is right in assuming that this passage must be attributed to him.

[104]) Herzfeld's translation of the two words "rich, fortunate" (p. 597) seems better than Lommel's: "prächtig glänzend" (p. 54).

or provide for, man and cattle. In 44 he is given three epithets: *srīrō bānuvå raoχšnəmå*: Satavaēsa being a star, a translation like "the beautiful, radiant, with intense light" seems correct; however, Iranian stars like the Vedic luminaries granted their gifts by shining [105]). It is, indeed, curious and possibly more than a coincidence that Ušah "Dawn" is, G. 5, 5, likewise called *srīra-* [106]). A "beautiful" wind is, on the other hand, less conceivable than a "favourable" one, especially when it is believed to bring the χvarənah, healing and strength (Yt. 14, 2). The adjective also occurs in the enumeration of the best Iranian countries in Vend. 1 [107]). Side by side with Haētumant which is called *raēvantəm χvarənaṅuhantəm*, Bactria and Arachosia are regarded as *srīrąm ərəδwō. drafšąm*: as these regions were fertile, and knew periods of considerable prosperity, I would feel tempted to take the first adjective in the sense of "prosperous": the plains of Bactria which are an excellent grazing ground, and the fields and pastures of Arachosia are mentioned by various authors.

Yima, the first man and king, ruler of the primeval golden age, when there was neither old age and death for men and cattle, nor parching for land and plants, Yima, who was closely connected with the cult of the fertilizing power par excellence, the haoma [108]), is in the Vendidad repeatedly called *srīra-*. Is it a mere coincidence that, in contradistinction to Yt. 19, 31 ff., the Vendidad contains the tradition of the surviving Yima: when the paradisiac life ended with winter and flood and with the extinction of two-thirds of all life, Yima was instructed how to save himself and the *mazišta- vahišta-* and *sraēšta-* of all men, women, and animals and the most fragrant of all plants, the best tasting viands [109]). I would venture the conjecture that *srīra-* expresses, in this text, the idea of "felicitous, fortunate, i.e. happy and bringing good luck or fortune" rather than "handsome".

To confine attention to the very frequent triplet of so-called superlatives, *mazišta- vahišta- sraēšta-* [110]), it may be noted that it is,

---

105) See J. Hertel, Die Sonne und Mithra im Awesta, Leipsic 1927, Register, p. 312 (Hertel's expositions being very one-sided and often speculative, his arguments are to be checked). Cf. e.g. such texts as Yt. 12, 29 ff.; Vend. 6, 49 ff.

106) For the Vedic Uṣas and *śrī-* see above, p. 178 ff.

107) See A. Christensen, Le premier chapitre du Vendidad..., Det Kgl. Danske Vid. Selskab, hist.-fil. Medd. 29, 4, 1943, where the translation is: "beautiful" (p. 15 and 37).

108) Cf. Nyberg, o.c., p. 84 f. ("König des Unsterblichkeitszeitalters und Unsterblichkeitsdrank").

109) The reader might be referred to J. Hertel, Die Himmelstore im Veda und im Awesta, Leipsic 1924, p. 23 ff.; Lommel, Yäšt's, p. 196 ff., and Herzfeld, o.c., p. 320 ff.

110) See Bartholomae, Altiran. Wörterbuch 1158.

generally speaking, applied to such entities as admitted of being considered bearers of a power-substance like the Vedic *śrī-*: the *daēnā māzdayasnī* (which Yt. 10, 64 is called *srīra-*) whether it refer to an inspired religious sight [111]) or to another aspect of religious experience, the so-called *airyaman* prayer which lays claim to vouchsafe succour (Yt. 3, 5 where other adjectives of the same tenor are added: powerful, firm, victorious, curative); the central religious conception of *arta* (*aša*) "Truth" [112]) (Yt. 13, 91 f.); Ahura Mazdāh; his *fravarti* [113]) — as is well known, the spirits of the deceased act for the benefit of their clans: by their fortune and glory the waters flow and the plants grow, the females conceive young ones and sons are supported in the womb (Yt. 13, 14 ff.); they endeavour to seize the water, each one for her own family and clan and they wish them prosperity and a flourishing state (st. 66 ff.) —; his name: Yt. 1, 5 ff., where he styles himself the lord of plenitude, of the herds, of truth, of all good things etc. etc.; the *ašayō* "rewards, portions in life" (Y. 52, 3) — this word is the plural of *Arti* (*Aši*), the name of the goddess of fertility [114]), who is often regarded as *srīra-*: Yt. 17, 6 where she is believed to give the beneficial *χvarənah* to those men whom she accompanies; the house which she enters becomes fragrant [115]); 60 where she is requested to stay in the *srīra- χšaϑrō.kərəta-* house of the person praying [116]); 61 and 13, 107 —; libations: Nir. 84 [117]); a place or dwelling. Compare also the triplet of substantives *masānasčā vaṅhānasčā srayanasčā* Y. 58, 4, and the corresponding so-called comparatives V. 5, 22 etc. The Vedic combination of *śreṣṭha-* and *vasiṣṭha-* has already been referred to.

---

111) Nyberg, o.c., p. 114 f.

112) I refer to H. Lüders, Varuṇa, I, Göttingen 1951, p. 27. This very important term is in the Avesta seldom qualified by adjectives or epithets; see also Nyberg, o.c., p. 129.

113) See also W. Caland, Über Totenverehrung bei einigen der indo-germanischen Völker, Amsterdam 1888, p. 48 ff.; Nyberg, o.c., p. 62 ff.; Herzfeld, o.c., p. 495 ff.

114) I refer to Nyberg, p. 66; for connections between *aši-* "lot, reward" and the goddess Armaiti who entertains relations with the earth ibid., p. 111. For the goddess *Arti* (*Aši*) see especially Yt. 17. Bartholomae (Wtb. 242) considers her a goddess of "Wohlstand"; Lommel translates her name by "Segnung".

115) For the 'heavenly fragrance', or 'odour of sanctity' of beneficial divine beings, holy men etc. and the unpleasing smell of demoniac figures see E. Lohmeyer, Vom göttlichen Wohlgeruch, Sitzungsber. Heidelberg, phil.-hist. Kl. 1919, 9 and D. J. Hoens, *Çānti,* Thesis Utrecht 1951, p. 62.

116) The exact shade of meaning of the latter adjective being not clear it can not be made out if the former is proleptically used.

117) Compare also A. Waag, Nirangistan (Iranische Forschungen herausg. v. H. H. Schaeder), Leipsic 1941, p. 89.

It is not my intention to deny that the common phrase *kainīnō* (etc.) *kəhrpa srīrayå* "in the shape (bodily appearance) of a *s.* maid" does not denote a figure producing a visual impression of beauty upon the eye; I would only doubt the correctness of a merely aesthetic interpretation of this "beauty": Yt. 5, 64; 14, 27 etc. where such adjectives as "very strong, fair of growth (form), noble" are added, this beauty may easily be conceived as implying the splendour of prosperous-looking health. The combination *spənta srīra,* applied to Ahuramazdāh's daughter (Ārmaiti?, Vend. 19, 13) may also be mentioned, *spənta-* in my opinion having the sense of "possessing a special energetic, life-promoting power, which may be enhanced by praising" [118]). A similar remark may be made with regard to the word *śrī-* itself: Yt. 17, 11; H. 2, 9.

These texts may suffice to illustrate the use of *srī-* in the Avesta. If I am not mistaken it agrees fairly well with that of *śrī-* and the group of words deriving from it in the Veda.

Let us conclude our course through those ancient passages which may be of interest for an understanding of the signification of the term *śrī-* by a very few observations on its use in Āraṇyakas, Upaniṣads, Manu, and some other texts. From our above investigations and from the notions which the Indians had formed on the character and function of lightning [119]) we may perhaps conclude that BārUp. 2, 3, 6 *sakṛdvidyutteva ha vā asya śrīr bhavati ya evaṃ veda* called up not only a mental picture of outward splendour but also of actual prosperity. — In the remarkable incantations and ceremonies for procreation added to the same Upaniṣad, 6, 4, it reads (§ 6): *śrīr ha vā eṣā strīṇāṃ yan malodvāsaḥ.* It would appear to me that such interpretations as "She is loveliness (or: Śrī) among women when she has put off the clothes of her impurity" [120]) may be disproved: as is well known the menstruation in the view of the Indians [121]) purifies a woman from magical and moral evils; during these days she is dangerous to such a degree that a man visiting her forfeits his happiness or longevity (Mbh. 13, 104, 150; 16, 8, 5 f. *gataśrī-* etc.). In the days immediately following this period, the *ṛtu-,* the married couple is under obligation to cohabit, the discharge of which is a virtue leading to heaven (Mbh.

---

118) See my paper on this word, in Oriens, 2 (1949), p. 195 ff.

119) See ch. I, section VI.

120) See e.g. R. E. Hume, The thirteen principal Upanishads, Oxford 1934, p. 169; E. Senart, Bṛhadāraṇyakopaniṣad, Paris 1934, p. 113.

121) The reader may for the sake of brevity be referred to J. J. Meyer, Sexual life in ancient India, London 1930, p. 581.

13, 144, 13 f.). The goddess Śrī keeps the company of men who enjoy their wives in the right way (cf. 13, 157, 10). I would therefore suggest explaining the upaniṣad passage under discussion as follows: a woman after the monthly cleansing is an embodiment of the great female power of fertility and prosperity, of life and generative force. TB. 3, 9, 4, 7 wives are considered a *rūpam* of *śrī-*. Compare also the 'pun' — this term is dangerous — *striyaḥ śriyo loke* etc. [122]), and especially Manu 9, 26. Varāh. BS. 68, 64 *śriyo bhājaḥ* refers to people who "participate in *śrī-*"; 65, 9 auspicious goats are called *śriyaḥ putrāḥ*. In a formula occurring TĀ. 10, 1, 5 (cf. MahānārUp. 1, 5) Agni is implored to bring or give cattle, life, etc., *śriyā mā paripātaya*, i.e. *dhanadhānyādisampadā sarvataḥ prāpaya* (comm.). — *Śrī-* (or *śriyaḥ* plur.) is sometimes said to have settled in an object or to be somewhere: AiĀ. 2, 1, 4 sight, hearing, mind etc. are called *śriyaḥ* and stated to be in the head. Elsewhere an important or vital part of an entity is called *śrī-*: TB. 3, 9, 7, 4 *śrīr vai vṛkṣasyāgram* (because the top of a tree is, in a sense, the seat of its vegetative force?). — Such enumerations as *satyaṃ yaśaḥ śrīḥ* (ĀśvGS. 1, 24, 29); *āyuṣyam, yaśasyam, śriyam, ṛtam* (Manu 2, 52; cf. also 4, 231) continue to be in use. — As we have stated above the idea expressed by *puṣṭi-* "a well-nourished condition" is not seldom expressed in the same context. It is interesting to notice that *puṣṭa-* qualifies *śrī-*: Manu 4, 231; Varāh. BS. 62, 1. Mention may finally be made of the synonyms given by lexicographers: *vṛddhi-* "growth, increase, advancement, welfare, prosperity etc."; *siddhi-* "accomplishment, complete attainment, success, good luck, prosperity etc." [123]).

Turning now, for a moment, to some compounds, we see that *Śrīda-* "Giver of *śrī-*" is a name of Kubera and of Viṣṇu; *Śrīdā* = Viṣṇu-Kṛṣṇa's beloved Rādhā; *Śrīdhara-* "bearer or possessor of *śrī-* (*Śrī-*)" and *Śrīkara-* "causing *śrī-*" = Viṣṇu who is also called *śrīmatāṃ varaḥ*, *Śrīnidhi-*, *Śrīgarbha-* etc. But why does *Śrīkaṇṭha-* which is usually taken as "beautiful-throated" apply, in the epic and afterwards, to Śiva? This god often bears the name of *Nīlakaṇṭha-* "the Blue-necked One": according to the well-known story his throat became dark-blue or bluish black when he drank the deadly poison which was one of the products of the ocean when it was churned (Mbh. 1, 18, 42 ff.). It may, however, be recalled that vegetation demons and men representing them are often believed to have, or bound to make themselves, a black face.

---

122) References may be found in the Petr. Dict. VII, 364.

123) The above expatiation is not meant to be exhaustive. Some more relevant passages may be found in the Petr. Dict. VII, 362 ff.

Black or dark-blue is on a wide area a, or the, colour of the subterranean powers, of the genii of vegetation, of the earth, and of magic connected with these [124]). This colour representing those powers and phenomena which constitute *śrī-*, or are the foundation of *śrī-*, a 'dark-blue-throated deity' may have meant a '*śrī*-faced god'. This name would, then, be in harmony with another epithet of the same divinity, *Nandīmukha-* (Mbh. 12, 284, 83); which, in my opinion [125]), means "whose face means, expresses, bears, produces, prosperity, thriving, strengthening" rather than "Freude auf dem Gesichte habend" (Petr. Dict., s.v.). Another name of Śiva is *Śrīvardhana-* "increaser of *śrī-*" (Mbh. 13, 17, 153).

As other trees and plants connected with Śrī and Viṣṇu are dealt with elsewhere we now consider only the *śrīkhaṇḍa-* "sandal-tree, sandal" and a few other botanical names. I doubt whether the explanation of the word *śrīkhaṇḍa-* given in the Petr. Dict., s.v., to wit "Prachtstück" is correct. The latter part meaning "piece, part, fragment" (cf. also Kāl. Megh. 30 *divaḥ.... kh.* "a fragment or part of heaven"), the word appears to express the idea of a fragment (i.e. 'a manifestation') of *śrī-*". A synonym is *bhadraśrī-* (also *bhadraśriya-*). Needless to recall the well-known fact that sandal-wood was often burnt as incense: it was believed to be agreeable to the divine powers and to ward off all kinds of evil beings [126]). *Śrīkandā* is the name of another plant used in medicine: *kanda-* "a bulb, a bulbous or tuberous root". — The incense-tree is called *suśrīka-*. The name *śrīparṇa-* was given to various plants and trees; among these is the *śālmali-* or silk-cotton tree (seemul; salmalia malabarica), the erotic and magical character of which is well-known [127]): its stem is also used in vegetation ceremonies.

One of the compounds which are illustrative of the sense of the word under discussion is *saṃbhṛtaśrī-*: AV. 19, 49, 1 night, "the vigorous or 'refreshing' woman (*iṣirā yoṣā*), the household maiden of

---

[124]) See e.g., A. Dieterich, Sommertag, Leipsic 1905, p. 24 f.; Mannhardt, Wald- und Feldkulte, passim; Meyer, Trilogie I, p. 63; 83 ff.; III, p. 319; C. Mengis, in Hdwtb. de. Abergl. VII, 1432.

[125]) Acta Orientalia, 21, p. 88. Çiva's bull is called *Nandin-*. One cannot help remembering the use of the term *nāndīmukha-* in connection with the śrāddha and the particular group of deceased ancestors indicated by that name (ViPur. 3, 10, 6; MārkPur. 30, 5 etc.): for the close relations between the deceased and vegetation etc. see Meyer, o.c., III, p. 323 f.

[126]) For the use of sandalwood see Hilgenberg-Kirfel, o.c., p. 827. It was, and still is, extensively used in funeral rites and other religious ceremonies. See also M. Monier-Williams, Religious thought and life in India, London 1883, p. 366.

[127]) See Meyer, o.c., p. 338 f.

Savitar and Bhaga", is called expanding over all existence (embracing all things) and *saṃbhṛtaśrī-*: I would prefer "in whom all prosperity etc. is concentrated" to Whitney-Lanman's "of assembled fortune". The night is (st. 2) compared to a friend presenting excellent *svadhāḥ* "refreshing food or drinks, libations"; it (she) is asked to save for man the objects produced and what "by prosperity" concerns the cows (3), to be propitious (*śiva-* 5); it (she) is "excellent" or "blessed, fortunate" (*bhadra-* 8), and implored to protect against thieves. The meaning of the compound must be that all objects representing welfare are in charge of the night, constituting a source of prosperity for man in daytime. — Cf. also Kālidāsa, Megh. 111.

Let us finally devote a few lines to the etymology of the word *śrī-*. It would appear to me that Oldenberg [128]) did not err when be considered *śrī- śrīṇāti* (disconnecting it from *śrā- srapayati* "to cook") to be related to *śrī-*, translating this verb — "unter Vorbehalt der genaueren Nuance" — by "kräftigen". Compare especially the use of *śrī-* in PB. 9, 6, 7 *tenātmānaṃ samaśrīṇāt prajayā paśubhir indriyeṇa* "by means of it (a particular sāman) he braced himself fully (Caland) by progeny, cattle and psychical power" (cf. 9, 5, 8 where *sat karoti* "to put all right" is used). The verb *śrīṇāti* is the counterpart or semantical opposite of *vibhraṃśate* "to fail, to be unfortunate or unsuccessful, to suffer a loss etc." [129]): cf. 14, 12, 4 ....*vyabhraṃśata* (*vibhraṣṭavīryo 'bhūt* comm.) ....*tair ātmānaṃ samaśrīṇāt* "by means of these (sāmans) he invigorated himself (*vīryeṇa samayojayat* comm.) Cf. also TB. 1, 2, 6, 7 and other texts quoted by Oldenberg, where the idea of regeneration seems to be implied, and such compounds as *kṣatraśrī-* (ṚV. 1, 25, 5 explained by *kṣatrāṇi śrayati* Sāyaṇa) [130]). I must, however, disagree with Oldenberg with respect to the basal meaning of the root *śrī-*: the hypothesis "daß in ṛgvedischer Zeit.... ein Mitteilen von Schönheit — d.h. Ansehnlichkeit, Pracht, Geschmücktheit — gemeint gewesen sein wird" [131]) is, to my mind, not felicitous. The idea of "invigorating, strengthening, (re)creating.... for good causing to prosper" — the connotations differentiating this root from similar families of words being not distinguishable — must have constituted the primary meaning. So the etymology: *śrī-* ∾ Gr. κρείων,

---

[128]) Oldenberg, Nachr. Göttingen 1918, p. 40 ff.

[129]) See also Caland, Pañcaviṃśa-brāhmaṇa, Calcutta 1931, p. 166.

[130]) Geldner, o.c. I, p. 26, observing hat these compounds are essentially synonymous with those beginning with *su-*, translates: "der die Herrschaft zu Ehren bringt"; rather "causes... to be vigorous". Cf. also ṚV. 6, 26, 8.

[131]) Oldenberg, o.c., p. 44.

κρέων "wielding, having power, ruler, lord" [132]) is, to all appearance, correct, although a supposed 'original sense' of this participle "hervorleuchtend", and a basal meaning "hervorleuchten" [133]) are erroneous.

II. ŚRĪ-, THE GODDESS.

Although the authors of older books on Hinduism or Indian religions often defined the character of the goddess Śrī tolerably well by calling her the deity of fortune and prosperity [1]), some misunderstandings were, and still are, always apt to occur. Too great emphasis was often laid on special features of her personality and on particular parts of her field of action. Sometimes attention was too exclusively focussed on her being the type of female beauty, or on the various legends connected with her springing, like Aphrodite, from the foam of the ocean [2]); in enumerations of the 'ideas' or phenomena as embodiment of which she is held to stand, 'beauty' frequently ranks above 'fortune' [3]). In other books she chiefly appears on the scene as the consort of Viṣṇu, or as his śakti [4]). Generally speaking, authors often appear to have emphasized those aspects of the goddess and of her activities which come to the fore in the Rāmāyaṇa and the kāvya literature.

However, Indian tradition as handed down in purāṇas and various other sources contains many traits which may help us in forming a more complete picture. The meritorious investigations by Scheftelowitz [5]), Miss Hartmann [6]), and Meyer [7]) have already brought to light

---

132) See e.g. E. Boisacq, Dictionnaire étymologique de la langue grecque, Paris 1923, p. 513; J. B. Hofmann, Etymologisches Wörterbuch des Griechischen, München 1950, p. 159; A. Walde-J. Pokorny, Vergl. Wörterbuch der indogerm. Spr., Berlin-Leipsic 1930, I, p. 478, etc.

133) Hofmann, l.c.; Walde-Pokorny, l.c.; Pokorny, Indogerm. etymol. Wtb., Bern 1953, p. 618. — A. Juret's supposition (*śrī-* ∾ Gr. καλός "beautiful": Mélanges 1945, Publ. de la Faculté des Lettres, Univ. Strasbourg, fasc. 108, p. 13) is fallacious.

1) Or of wealth and prosperity, cf. A. K. Coomaraswamy, Pour comprendre l'art hindou, Paris 1926, p. 88.

2) E.g. J. Dowson, A class. dict. of Hindu Mythology etc.[6], London 1928, p. 176.

3) E.g. Macdonell, Vedic Mythology, p. 120; H. D. Bhattacharya, in Majumdar's Hist. and Cult., II, p. 470 f.; Hohenberger, o.c., p. 158; S. Konow, Hinduismen, Stockholm 1927, I, p. 53; H. von Glasenapp, Brahma et Bouddha, Paris 1937, p. 115; Die Religionen Indiens, Stuttgart 1943, p. 147 f.; S. Sørensen, Index Mahābhārata, 1904, p. 215 and 445.

4) M. Monier-Williams, Hinduism, London 1890, p. 124; Konow, in Bertholet-Lehmann, Lehrbuch der Religionsgeschichte, Tübingen 1925, II, p. 61; 156.

5) I. Scheftelowitz, Çrīsūkta, in ZDMG. 75 (1921), p. 37 ff.

6) Gerda Hartmann, Beiträge zur Geschichte der Göttin Lakṣmī, Thesis Kiel 1933.

7) J. J. Meyer, Trilogie, see the 'Register'. I also refer to H. Zimmer, Myths and symbols, N. York 1947, p. 90 ff.

many interesting particulars apt to correct and complete our views of this subject. We shall here summarize the contents of the German works by these authors as far as they have a bearing upon our theme, adding some remarks of our own. According to Miss Hartmann [8]) Śrī, who as a distinct female divinity does not appear before the Vājasaneyi Saṃhitā, is a pre-Aryan goddess of fertility and other phenomena relative to it (Fruchtbarkeit, Fülle, Glück), whose symbol is the lotus, the plant growing in mud and slime, and whose cult, mythology and iconography show a variety of traits characteristic of deities concerned with fertility and prosperity in general. In the Śrīsūkta [9]), the central part of which reaches back to the Vedic period, and which supplies us with extremely valuable information, Śrī is called "moist" (*ārdra-*, also implying "fresh, green as a plant, living"), "perceptible through her odour" (*gandhadvāra-*), continually thriving or always well-supplied (*nityapuṣṭa-*), abounding in dung (*karīṣin-*). She is (Śrīs. 17*) said to have arisen from the lotus and to delight in the sound of elephants, which seems to refer to thunder-clouds [10]). She is requested to give cows and food, corn and prosperity (*bhūti-*), gold and female slaves, offspring and happiness, *yaśas* "splendour, honour, renown" and the fulfilment of all wishes. She is asked to dwell with Kardama "mud, mire, slime" and Ciklīta "mire, ooze" in the house of the man praying. Driving away hunger, thirst and "impurity" (*mala-*), fear, indigence and misfortune, *abhūti-* "disastrous circumstances", *asamṛddhi-* "ill-success, failure", and the *jyeṣṭhā alakṣmī* [11]), she is invoked to make approach *kīrti-* "esteem, renown" and *vṛddhi-* "success, welfare" and to make man vigorous giving him health and a life-time of a hundred years. Because she is the goddess of prosperity, her outward appearance is compared to that of gold or of the sun; she is *jvalantī* "shining brightly", *candrā* "having the hue of light", *prabhāsā* "splendid". Although she is beautiful, she is "nicht eigentlich Göttin der Schönheit" [12]). In Śrīs. 28*, where she is stated to be "the divinity of deities", i.e. the chief divinity, Ānanda "State of being invigorated, Happiness" Kardama, Śrīta, Ciklīta and Viśrita [13]) are called her sons and ṛṣis.

---

[8]) Hartmann, o.c., p. 6 ff.

[9]) Edited by Scheftelowitz, Die Apokryphen des Ṛgveda, Breslau 1906, p. 72 ff.; for further bibliographical reference see my Ṛgvidhāna, Utrecht 1951, p. 50.

[10]) Hartmann, o.c., p. 8 etc.; A. K. Coomaraswamy, Geschichte der indischen und indonesischen Kunst, Leipsic 1927, p. 27. For the lotus see e.g. also the data collected by D. R. Patil, Cultural history from the Vāyu Purāṇa, Poona 1946, p. 234 f.: and chapter I, section XIII. For the elephant: Hartmann, p. 32 f.

[11]) Hartmann, o.c., p. 15 and 18.

[12]) Hartmann, o.c., p. 7; compare also Oldenberg, Nachr. Göttingen, 1918, p. 47.

[13]) Representing a divine power "to which to have recourse"?

In this sūkta, part of which was already quoted in ancient texts [14]), Śrī is pictured as a guardian deity of the farmer. The commentary on TĀ. 10, 1, 43 — where the line *gandhadvārām* etc. is quoted as one of the mantras used in sanctifying lumps of earth at the line of ritual bathing — calls her the *mṛttikābhimāninī devatā.* Besides, the Ṛgvidhāna, 2, 17, 6 ff. quotes some stanzas in describing a series of rites requiring bilva fruits and lotus flowers and intended to invite the goddess to come into a lotus or into gold; it is added that she should by no means be invited for the sake of a miser (2, 21, 1). — When, in the purāṇical narrative of Śrī's birth from the ocean, the goddess, splendidly beautiful and bearing a lotus, has appeared, the apsarās dance before her, the rivers and the elephants of the quarters of the sky supply her with bathing-water in golden jars, the Ocean gives her an unfading lotus-garland and Viśvakarman beautiful ornaments, the great ṛṣis praise her with the same Śrīsūkta (cf. ViPur. 1, 9, 100 [15])) : in spite of the magnificent setting of the mythologizing narrative the authors are aware of Śrī's original and essential character. The small text has indeed enjoyed popularity up to the present day.

Śrī and Lakṣmī, who at the beginning were different divinities, tended to merge into each other in the upaniṣads [16]). In full Hinduism Viṣṇu's consort is denoted by both names. I doubt whether Miss Hartmann is perfectly right in contending [17]) that the originally dual personality of the goddess survives in the well-known representation of Viṣṇu with two wives: "Lakṣmī und die (wegen des Uebergangs dieses Namens auf Lakṣmī) zwar nicht Śrī genannte, aber deutlich mit ihr als Vegetationsgöttin identische Bhūmī oder Puṣṭi". Apart from the fact that such epithets and formulas as *viṣṇu- śrī-mahīyukta-* are not seldom used (cf. in the AtriSaṃh. 2, 37; *devyau śrībhūmyau* 4, 22; *devasya dakṣiṇe pārśve śriyaṃ vāme mahīṃ tathā; śrībhūmidevyoḥ* 16, 18 etc.), it would appear to me that Bhūmi is another divine character. We shall

---

[14]) I refer to Scheftelowitz, ZDMG. 75, p. 41 f. Passing mention may be made of an observation found in the VidhPur. 2, 128, 2 ff.; the hymn to Çrī is different for each veda, the text under discussion being the one for the Ṛgveda; the text TB. 2, 7, 7, 2 is the śrīsūkta for the Yajurveda (*rathe akṣeṣu vṛṣabhasya vāje | vāte parjanye varuṇasya śuṣme | indraṃ yā devī subhagā jajāna | sā na āgan varcasā saṃvidānā*), the stanza SV. 1, 267a; ṚV. 8, 99, 3 for the Sāmaveda; *śriyaṃ dhātar mayi dehi* (cf. ĀpÇS. 6, 20, 2) is the one for the Atharvaveda. Besides, there exist other śrīsūktas, see Kane, Hist. of Dharmaś. III, p. 77, n. 110. As to ṚV. 1, 165 see my Ṛgvidhāna, p. 32. According to the VidhPur., l.c., a *śrīsūkta-* is *puṣṭivardhana-*.

[15]) For other particulars see Hartmann, o.c., p. 17 f.

[16]) I refer to Hartmann, o.c., p. 16 f.

[17]) O.c., p. 17.

have to revert to her[18]). Yet, the fusion of Śrī and Lakṣmī is sometimes incomplete[19]).

In those stanzas of the Śrīsūkta which are addressed to Lakṣmī it appears that this deity was conceived as the goddess of gold and wealth. Her name is doubtless identical with the appellative *lakṣmī-* "mark, sign, token" which, like *lakṣman-* "(good or lucky, or also bad) mark, sign, characteristic" derives from *lakṣ-* "observe, recognize, know by means of indicating characteristics". It may therefore be expected to express an idea relating to the process of deriving knowledge from the observation of outward appearances (cf. ṚV. 10, 71, 2). I would hesitate to subscribe to the distinction drawn between *lakṣmī* and *lakṣman-* by Oldenberg[20]): "*lakṣman-* ist das äuszere Merkmal glücklicher oder unglücklicher Disposition; *lakṣmī-* ist diese Disposition selbst, die durch ein *lakṣman-* angezeigt wird oder angezeigt werden kann". Making allowance for the scarcity of the Vedic occurrences of these words I feel inclined to modify this statement in the following way: a *lakṣmī* is an object or a being the very existence or presence of which means something (auspicious: *puṇyā l.*, or evil: *pāpī l.*[21])); a *lakṣman-* is, more vaguely, a token or mark, a fact connected with the external form of beings or objects as perceived by the senses, which may induce man to infer that there is something auspicious, favourable etc. It seems worthy of notice that the feminine polysyllabic *-ī-* stems in Vedic denote, as a rule, beings or objects[22]); part of them refer to power-substances believed to lead an independent existence[23]): *tandrī-* "weariness' (cf. AV. 8, 8, 9; 11, 8, 19 *svapno vai tandrīr nirṛtiḥ.. śarīram anu prāviśan*); *nāndī-* "refreshment, bliss which causes joy or favourable conditions, and inter alia appearing in the form of an auspicious benedictory stanza"[24]). Of the neutra in *-man-*[25]) *marman-*

---

18) See further on.

19) I refer to Hartmann, o.c., p. 25 and Hohenberger, o.c., p. 106. She quotes, inter alia Indische Sprüche 6281 the śrī of kings and the lakṣmī of merchants. However, Lakṣmī is very often the name of the goddess who resides with the king. As to *siriñ ca lakkhiñ ca* in Jāt. III, p. 443 cf. TĀ. (Andhr.) 10, 64 and VS. 31, 22 (cf. also Wackernagel-Debrunner, Altindische Grammatik, III, Göttingen 1930, p. 172). — See e.g. Mbh. 3, 37, 33; Rām. 3, 46, 17, where Çrī is, according to Rāma's commentary: *aiśvaryapradhānā* (*ai.*: any success and attainment in this world), and Lakṣmī: *saubhāgyapradhānā* (*s.*: welfare, happiness).

20) Oldenberg, o.c., p. 46.

21) See Hartmann, o.c., p. 3.

22) A. A. Macdonell, Vedic Grammar, Strassburg 1910, p. 269 f.

23) The reader might be referred to H. von Glasenapp, Entwicklungsstufen des indischen Denkens, Halle S. 1940, p. 1 ff.

24) I refer to Acta Or. 21, p. 81 ff.

25) See my Notes on *brahman*, Utrecht 1950, p. 73.

"mortal spot" (√ *mer-* "to die"); *sadman-* "seat, abode, dwelling, place"; *varman-* "envelope, defensive armour, shelter, protection"; *hanman-* "stroke, an object enabling man to strike"; *sāman-* "conciliating words" etc. perhaps deserve some attention with reference to the force of the suffix in *lakṣman-* (an object or place which may in a sense be powerful by itself, in or by which the process expressed by the root is or can be actualized). Thus, ŚB. 8, 4, 4, 8 the metres are identified with cattle, cattle are said to be *puṇyās.. lakṣmyaḥ* "(objects of) good fortune" (Eggeling), and these *p. l.* are the sun. 8, 4, 4, 11 bricks are called a *puṇyā lakṣmīḥ* ("sign of good fortune" E.); they are laid down on the south side, whence the man who has a *lakṣma* (*lakṣaṇaṃ kāyasya vā varṇe vā* comm.), i.e. a mark, on his right side is said to have good luck (*puṇyalakṣmīkaḥ*); see also the same paragraph, in fine and 8, 5, 4, 3. In the Atharvaveda the difference is fairly well discernible: 7, 115, 1 (used in rites against *nirṛti-* „perdition", part of which consists in driving away a 'scape-goat') "fly forth from here, O evil sign" (*pāpi lakṣmi*), 2 "the flying *l.* has mounted me", 4 "let the good *l.* stay; those that are evil have I made disappear": the *l.* may be a crow to the legs of which certain objects have been fastened. As appears from st. 1 the ill-luck represented by it may be attached to an enemy. AV. 1, 18 is intended to drive away a *l.* which is at the same time an *arāti-*: a kind of evil spirit frustrating good intentions and disturbing happiness; it is likewise conceived as a demoniac being: 4 "antelope-footed, bull-toothed..". AV. 11, 7, 17 *lakṣmī-* is put on a par with *ṛta-, satya-, tapas, rāṣṭra-, vīrya-, bala-* and similar entities; 12, 5, 6 the kṣatriya who appropriates the brahman-cow loses his *sūnṛtā* [26]), *vīryam*, and *puṇyā lakṣmīḥ*: here it is not far from "luck". AV. 6, 141, on the other hand, has the word *lakṣma* (st. 2; 3) in connection with marks made in the ears of cows: the text, which is included among the *puṣṭika*-mantras [27]), is to accompany the ceremony of earmarking cattle for the sake of prosperity. In st. 3 the Aśvins are requested to make the *lakṣma* in order to thousand-fold thriving (*poṣa-*). See also 12, 4, 6. AV. 1, 23, 4 the white spot(s) of the leper are called a *lakṣma*. See also TS. 7, 4, 19, 2 *ya āsāṃ kṛṣṇe lakṣmaṇi sardigṛdiṃ parāvadhīt* (used in connection with the female organs) and also ṚV. 10, 10, 2 [28]); 12, 6. Note should however be taken of the fact that Varāhamihira, Bṛh. at a considerably later time uses *lakṣman-* not only in the sense of "prognostics" (e.g. from limbs being touched, 51, 44), a significant collection of hairs at an unusual place of the body likewise being a *lakṣma* (52, 10), but also

---

[26]) See ch. II, s. I, n. 31.

[27]) See Whitney-Lanman, AthVSaṃh., p. 386 and 694 f.

[28]) Cf. also Geldner, Der Rig-Veda übersetzt, III, p. 134.

in a sense which we might expect to be expressed by *lakṣmī-:* 43, 58; 67 Indra's ensign or standard is called a *lakṣma;* but for Varāhamihira and the other post-Vedic authors in general *lakṣmī-* denoted "luck, fortune" (cf. e.g. BS. 71, 5; 84, 2; 93, 13 where significant occurrences bring, reveal or increase a person's *lakṣmī-*). This sense is 'developing' in the Vedic texts: TS. 2, 1, 5, 2 "the humpbacked *is* a thousandfold *lakṣmī*"; in AiB. 2, 40, 8 "the offering verse is acquisition, is *puṇyā lakṣmī-;* verily thus he creates (or furthers) *p. lakṣmī-* ("a prospering destiny, a condition of prosperity).." both 'shades of meaning' occur. TĀ. 3, 13, 2 Hrī and Lakṣmī are the two wives (*hrīś ca te lakṣmīś ca patnyau*) of the Puruṣa, who is identified with the creation; the commentary adds that Lakṣmī is the deity who lays claim to prosperity in the world, power or eminence (*aiśvarya-*). Mantrabrāhmaṇa 1, 4, 5 a brahman invokes the help of Agni, Vāyu, Moon, and Sun in order to beat off from a woman the *pāpī lakṣmīḥ,* which is specified as *patighnī, aputratā, apasavyā,* these 'varieties' being conceived as *tanū-*, i.e. 'manifestations'.

With the distinction made here between *lakṣmī-* and *lakṣman-* the fact is in harmony that the first term is also applied to a variety of plants which are thought to bring, or to represent, luck or fortune: the white tulasi [29]), the turmeric [30]); other names for the same are, inter alia, *siddhi-* "success", *ṛddhi-, vṛddhi-* "growth, increase, prosperity"; also to a pearl (*muktā*) [31]); such connotations are on the other hand foreign to *lakṣman-*. *lakṣmaṇa-,* which is interpreted by *lakṣmīvant-, śrīmant-*, however, can be used instead of *oṣadhi-* "(medicinal) herb" and of particular botanical names. It is not surprising that *vibhūti-* "manifestation of abundance or power" should, beside "Padmā (Śrī)", have been given as the meaning of the word *lakṣmī* [32]). So, Lakṣmī may 'originally' have been the divinity representing the signs, evidence, or prognostications (of luck and prosperity) [33]).

---

29) See ch. I, section II.

30) See Meyer, o.c., I, p. 22 f.; 49. Cf. also Caland, Vaikhānasasm. transl., p. 79, n. 7.

31) For pearls and other precious stones see e.g. AthVPar. 1, 43, 3; 18, 3, 1 etc.; H. Webster, Magic, Stanford Cal. 1948, p. 123 f.: Eliade, Images et symboles, p. 190 ff.

32) Ujjvaladatta, US. 2, 57; 3, 160; see Harmann, o.c., p. 3.

33) I am not convinced that Miss Hartmann, o.c., p. 13 ff. is right in arguing that *lakṣmī-* originally expressed the sense of *alakṣmī-* alone, and that Lakṣmī first was the goddess of poverty. Nor can I subscribe to the view expounded by F. D. K. Bosch either (in a paper 'Gouden vingerringen uit het Hindoe-Javaansche tijdperk', Djåwå 7 (Solo, Java 1927), p. 310 ff.): *lakṣmī-* and *śrī-* "1⁰ token > 2⁰ bodily mark or token, lucky mark, the collectivity of these marks, esp. in connection with the god or the king > the goddess of luck and fortune, the king's śakti > majesty, splendour, power, abundance, wealth etc."

Meyer collected a sufficiency of data to show that Lakṣmī was closely connected with the yellow ripe corn [34]). To this day a corn-basket filled with unhusked rice is at her festival believed to represent fortune, i.e. the goddess herself. She admits of being identified with Gaurī, "the Indian Ceres" (Tod), "the Reddish-yellow One", the goddess of the ripe corn. She is sometimes considered to exist or to manifest herself in the shape of seedlings grown in the winnowing basket (*śūrpa-*, e.g. Bhav.Pur. 28, 58). She "is evidently the beneficent Annapūrṇā ("the goddess who is possessed of plenty of food") in another garb" (Tod). Piṣṭapurī, a goddess mentioned in an inscription of the king Saṃkṣoba (529 A.D.) seems to be a form of hers (cf. *piṣṭapūra-* "a sort of cake"). She lives in maidens, in 'ornaments', in sacrifices, in rain-clouds, in byres, in lakes filled with lotus-flowers, in rivers, elephants, in kings on the throne.. (Mbh. 13, 11, 14 ff.).

According to the Śrīsūkta which, being called a 'benediction' (Bṛhad-devatā 5, 91), is intended to achieve growth or increase (st. 17: *saṃbhūti-*) Kardama "mud, slime, the mud of the rice-field" and *Ciklīta* "liquid slime" [35]) are Śrī's sons (st. 11 f.). The poet is fully conscious of the great importance of mud and mire: Śrīs. 17 "we, the creatures have come into existence through Kardama". In st. 9 he calls the goddess *karīṣiṇī* "abounding in dung".

It is convenient here to notice that the Śrīsūkta was ritually used in the remarkable ceremony called Saṣṭhīkalpa and described in the MānavaGS. 2, 13. The goddess Ṣaṣṭhī (see KāṭhGS. 19, 7; BaudhPar. 4, 2) is connected with new-born children [36]). The Mānavas had the rite performed on the 6th day of a lunar fortnight, invoking Ṣaṣṭhī "who gives treasures, possesses goods, grants the fulfilment of wishes, who is propitious and full of splendour", asking her to give "sons and cattle, treasures and corn, etc. etc." (2, 13, 6, I ff.), and identifying her with other powerful 'conceptions', among which is a female being Padmacāriṇī "the Lotus-footed One" (ibidem V). In the subsequent stanzas the author imperceptibly proceeds to commingle Ṣaṣṭhī's individuality with that of Śrī, quoting the Śrīsūkta, concluding his recitation by a number of invocations: "To Śrī, to Hrī ("Modesty or Conscientiousness", who is often mentioned bracketed together with

---

[34]) Meyer, o.c., II, p. 85 ff. See also J Tod, Annals and antiquities of Rajasthan², Oxford 1920, p. 695 f., cf. also p. 665 f., and such customs as are described by B. A. Gupte, Harvest festivals..., IA. 35 (1906), p. 61 and by R. S. Dinesh Chandra, The folk-literature of Bengal, Calcutta 1920, p. 85. — The yellow colour is *pauṣṭika-* (Atris. 44, 10). — Cf. also such injunctions as are given Manu 2, 29.

[35]) See also Scheftelowitz, Apokryphen, p. 80.

[36]) Cf. M. J. Dresden, Mānavagṛhyasūtra, Thesis Utrecht 1941, p. 154 ff.;

Śrī — cf. e.g. Mbh. 3, 37, 33; Rām. 3, 46, 17 — Kīrti, Dyuti, Lakṣmī, Puṣṭi, Sarasvatī etc. keeping them company), Lakṣmī, Upalakṣmī, Nandā [37]), Haridrā (as an appellative noun the "curcuma longa" [38])), Ṣaṣṭhī, Samṛddhi ("Intensive prosperity, Abundance"), Jayā ("Victory" [39]), who was to be a mother-goddess or a companion of Pārvatī in the purāṇic mythology), and Kāmā ("Desire"). These 'beings' may be regarded as representing special aspects of 'Prosperity'; their names may elsewhere be given to Śrī-Lakṣmī herself. AiB. 8, 5, 4 Śrī and the earth are identified in a similar way. According to Mahīdhara (on VS. 23, 12) *śrī-* in ŚB. 13, 2, 6, 16 likewise refers to the earth. Rām. 5, 22, 32 she is mentioned together with the apsarases.

In the rites relative to the furrow (Sītāyajña; PārGS. 2, 17, 9) Śrī is invoked together with Sampatti ("Success, Plenty"), Bhūti ("Thriving, Welfare", as a goddess e.g. Rām. 3, 46, 17 [40]); Mbh. 13, 149, 80 the name is given to Viṣṇu himself), Bhūmi ("the Earth"), Vṛṣṭi ("Rain"), Jyaiṣṭhyam ("Excellence") and Śraiṣṭhyam ("Preeminence"); after these names it reads: *śrīḥ prajām ihāvatu svāhā.* It may be noticed that this sacrifice is performed in a field of rice or of barley, on a clean spot which has been ploughed, so that the crop be not damaged. Indra is invoked, and his wife Sītā in whose substance (*bhāve*) dwells the welfare (*bhūti-*) of all Vedic and wordly works [41]).

Festivals in honour of Śrī-Lakṣmī are often recorded. In addition to the descriptions and references supplied by Meyer and other authors mention may be made of Baldaeus' [42]) account: in September a festival is celebrated for "Laetsenu, Vistnum's consort": during nine days married woman of the Coromandel coast revere the goddess in order to obtain wealth and a long life for their husbands. — To do justice to the facts it should be observed that the goddess, fusing with the figures of Aditi, the apsarases and other female divinities, and being considered 'identical' with the earth and the lotus represented "all the

---

Meyer, o.c. III, p. 320; M. M. Underhill, The Hindu religious year², Calcutta 1921, p. 104. — For other ritual use see e.g. VidhPur. 2, a. 128.

37) See Acta Orientalia, 21, p. 81 ff., and U. P. Shah, in the Journal of the Or. Inst., Univ. of Baroda 3 (1953), p. 66 f.

38) See Meyer, o.c. I, p. 22 f.; 49, and N. M. Penzer, Poison-Damsels, London 1952, Index, p. 318.

39) See also Meyer, o.c., II, p. 92. Cf. also V. R. Ramachandra Dikshitar, The Purana Index I, Madras 1951, p. 637.

40) Cf. also Macdonell-Keith, Vedic Index, II, p. 108; D. R. Patil, Cultural history from the Vāyu Purāṇa, p. 58.

41) The text was translated by Oldenberg, in SBE. 29, p. 333 ff.

42) Ph. Baldaeus, Afgoderye der Oost-Indische heydenen, edited by A. J. de Jong, Thesis Utrecht 1917, p. 196.

possibilities of existence substantially and maternally personified" [42a]).

According to the rules of iconography Śrī, when two-handed, often carries a lotus in each hand, or a lotus and a bilva-fruit. The trifoliate leaves of the latter, which is regarded as being related to longevity, is sometimes said to be identical with Brahmā, Viṣṇu and Śiva. When four-handed, the goddess also carries a jar (*kumbha-*) containing the *amṛta-* and a conch (*śaṅkha-*), a well-known 'Glücksding' which is often considered the auspicious emblem (*maṅgala-*) par excellence. As Gaja-Lakṣmī she was in olden days represented as sitting in the middle of a pool; on each side an elephant held a vessel, pouring out water on her person. This scene was, no doubt, interpreted as the fertilizing of a female being representing, or connected with, the earth or the fields by rain-clouds; clouds were often represented by elephants, the word *nāga-* having both meanings. In epic and post-epic works Śrī-Lakṣmī is often described as wearing Viṣṇu's attributes or mounting the Garuḍa. Mbh. 12, 228, 14 she looks like a large solar disk.

Like Viṣṇu himself, Śrī-Lakṣmī maintains relations with kingship. Śrī, Dharma, and Artha are said to enter a ruler who is really a portion of Viṣṇu on earth, obtaining superiority over others (Mbh. 12, 59, 133 ff.). She is the chief of a group of female deities representing victory and other positive qualities. The king on his part protects her. Part of the procedure of the coronation as contained in the BaudhGparS. 1, 23 is a propitiation of this goddess with "the hymn to Śrī", an act preceding the washing of the crown with cow's urine and dung, milk, curds, etc. Poets (e.g. Bhāsa, in his Bālacarita) represent her as appearing to the king in dreams etc.; in Uddyotana's romance Kuvalayamālā she presents him with a document containing the fundamental tenets of Jainism. The ancient Indonesian king was believed to maintain conjugal and other relations with manifestations of the goddess.

In the Indian Archipelago Śrī was to have a great future as a female deity concerned with the cultivation of rice, the food-plant par excellence, and with female accomplishments. Like the inhabitants of other islands the Balinese believe her to have died when she had been forced to submit to Viṣṇu's love; after she was buried several plants sprang up from her body, the rice from her navel [43]). In her Sundanese form

---

[42a]) A. K. Coomaraswamy, Elements of Buddhist Iconography, Harvard 1935, p. 22. Cf. also Gupte, IA. 32, p. 237.

[43]) I refer to K. A. H. Hidding, Nji Pohatji Sangjang Sri, Leyden 1929, p. 28 f.; J. Gonda, Sanskrit in Indonesia, Nagpur 1952, p. 132; S. Lévi, Sanskrit texts from Bali, Baroda 1933, p. XXVIII, who makes mention of a text called Çrīstava. In Bali the name of *Çrīdevī* is also given to the rice cut, but not yet thrashed, while *Umādevī* is the 'holy name' of the rice-seed, ***Girinātha*** **the name**

as *Nji Pohatji Sangjang Sri* or *Nji* (*Dèwi*) *Sri* the goddess of rice is considered to be able to descend from heaven: although she was born from a tear of Dewa Anta or Antaboga (< *Anantabhoga-*, the serpent of the nether world [44])), she is described as a divine princess, closely related to the widadaris (< Skt. *vidyādharī* [45])), a sort of kindly fairies who in part of the Archipelago are considered to preside over love, and in Java are held to be able to revive the deceased: they maintain relations with the waters and exercise a salutary influence on agriculture and on the wealth and prosperous condition of the house in which they take up their residence. These Indonesian widadaris have on the one hand taken over the rôle played by the apsaras in India and must, on the other hand, be regarded as representing a body of indigenous deities. Another figure connected with the origin of rice is Nārada — often in his Indonesian form of Kanekaputra (< Skt. *Kanyakāputra-*) "the son of the maiden or daughter", cf. Hariv. 1, 3, 13 *tato 'bhisaṃdhiṃ cakre vai dakṣaḥ tu parameṣṭhinā | kanyāyāṃ nārado mahyaṃ tava putro bhaved iti* (cf. also BrPur. 3, 13 f.; Bḍ. 2, 2, 17 f. etc.). In the Indian epic and puranic narratives Nārada, whose name can be explained as "the Water-giver", — he is described as bearing a water-pot (Mbh. 9, 54, 17) and appears (Rām. 7, 21, 3) on a cloud — is often mentioned together with gandharvas who are concerned with fecundation [46]) and presumably belonged to their class. It may be recalled in passing that the epic Nārada maintains various relations with Kṛṣṇa-Viṣṇu, whom he worships (Mbh. 5, 83, 27), identifies with Nārāyaṇa (7, 83, 19), and declares to be the supreme god (6, 34, 12 f.; 12, 207, 47); sayings of his about Kṛṣṇa are repeatedly quoted; Nārāyaṇa shows himself to him (12, a. 340), etc. etc. Besides, a fish, a pig, a crocodile, yakṣas [47]), and a princess of the sea-bottom appear in the mythical traditions about Dèwi Sri [48]), all of them maintaining intimate relations with water or the nether world, from which vegetative life

---

of the young plant, *Gaṅgādevī* of the rice after transplantation. — See also Scheftelowitz, ZDMG. 75, p. 39.

[44]) See my Sanskrit in Indonesia, p. 47; 71.

[45]) Ibidem, p. 134.

[46]) For the character of the gandharvas see for instance J. J. Meyer, o.c., III, p. 297; Macdonell, Vedic mythology, p. 137 and 179; E. W. Hopkins, Epic mythology, Strassburg 1915, p. 243; G. P. Malalasekera, Dictionary of Pāli proper names, I, London 1937, p. 746; G. Borsani, Apsaras, Milano 1938, passim; Keith, Religion and philosophy, p. 179 ff.; Coomaraswamy, Yaksas, passim. — For Nārada see also Hopkins, o.c. p. 188 f.; Sørensen, Index, p. 504 ff. According to the BhāgPur. 13, 1 ff. he is an incarnation of Viṣṇu. His companion is, in a significant way, Parvata "the Mountain" (ch. I, s. VIII).

[47]) Coomaraswamy, o.c.; Meyer, o.c., III, p. 329.

[48]) Cf. Çrīsūkta, 3 *śriyaṃ devīm*; 28 *śrīr devī*; Boehtlingk, Ind. Sprüche, no. 3768. — Sometimes the goddess herself has the form of a snake.

arises. She is destined to be married to Viṣṇu who by association with her becomes a promoter of wealth and prosperity. The rice is protected by the king who is an incarnation of Viṣṇu, his assistants in this occupation are chthonic beings. It seems incomprehensible that this 'agrarian' character of the goddess in Indonesia should have been regarded as merely indigenous and representing a later stage of development [49]).

The name of the goddess Śrī is very often found on ancient Javanese finger-rings and other golden ornaments. This shows that her cult was maintained "if not by the educated, then amongst the lower strata of society" [50]). By engraving the word *śrī* on these precious and protective objects people no doubt intended to 'establish' the goddess in them [51]), or at least to consecrate them to her, in order to gain control over the capricious (*cañcalā*) deity. For obvious reasons the akṣara expressing the name often tends to resemble the outlines of a *kumbha-*, "a water-jar" or a *śankha-* "a conch-shell" [52]).

We already touched upon Śrī's connections with other deities [53]). In the Śrīsūkta Lakṣmī is especially associated with Agni Jātavedas who is repeatedly requested to lead her towards the person praying (st. 1 f.; 13 ff.). It is certainly no mere coincidence that this task was undertaken by the god who on the one hand was an intermediary between heaven and earth, transmitting the oblations to the gods and bringing them to the sacrifices of men and who was, on the other hand, a great benefactor of his worshippers, protecting them and giving them riches [54]). As we have seen in the preceding section Agni was often considered as possessing and displaying *śrī-* (which was bestowed upon him by the gods: ŚB. 8, 6, 2, 4; cf. also such texts as ŚB. 5, 4, 3, 15); he moreover was, according to epic conceptions, the father of gold, which is truly this illustrious god (cf. e.g. Mbh. 13, a. 85). When the Śrīsūkta asks him to deliver man from *enas* and *aṃhas* [55]) and to found the thriving condition of wealth and prosperity (st. 18 *rāyaspoṣaṃ ca dhāraya*) this function is in perfect harmony with his well-known activity in repelling

---

49) W. H. Rassers, De Pandjiroman, Thesis Leyden 1922, whose mythological views were combated by Hidding, o.c., ch. IV.

50) Bosch, o.c., p. 312.

51) I once saw a ring bearing the inscription *pratiṣṭhā* "establishment of power, consecration", see my paper '*Pratiṣṭhā*'. As *Sěri-sědana* she is revered in the shape of an image made of coins, *Sědana* (< Skt. *sādhana-* "commodities") being considered a brother of hers.

52) See also Bosch, o.c., p. 313, who modified his opinions on this point in his book 'De gouden kiem', Amsterdam-Brussels 1948, p. 131 ff.

53) I refer to Hartmann, o.c., p. 20 ff.

54) See above, p. 180. Cf. also E. W. Hopkins, The mediatorial office of the Vedic fire-god, Harvard Theol. Review I (1908), p. 507 ff.

55) I refer to S. Rodhe, Deliver us from evil, Lund-Copenhagen 1946, p. 205.

evil (see e.g. ŚB. 7, 3, 2, 16 *agnir u sarveṣāṃ pāpmanām apahantā* "Agni is the repeller of all evil"; 4, 1, 34 Agni is *rakṣas*-killing light [56])). It seems worth noticing that the conceptions of Agni possessing *śrī-* and bringing Lakṣmī are in keeping with the 'original sense' of the words and the primary functions of the divinities as maintained in the preceding part of this chapter. Besides, one of Agni's forms is the sun, which is also said to belong to him (MaitrS. 1, 6, 3, 24); Agni is inter alia concerned with rain, fecundation, and procreation [57]). Śrī and Lakṣmī are, however, in the Vedic period also considered the consorts of Puruṣa (VājS. 31, 22), who is Prajāpati and Brahmā and appears in the visible phenomenon of the sun. According to the ŚB. 11, 4, 3, 1 she was created by Prajāpati. Her high rank is apparent from the mythical narrative (ibid. 3 ff.) in which ten gods took away her food (*annādya-*), royal power, universal sovereignty, kingship, power, 'pre-eminence in holiness' (*brahmavarcasa-*), dominion, welfare or fortune (*bhaga-*), prosperity (*puṣṭi-*) and forms or manifestations (*rūpāṇi*). Afterwards, the gods restored these characteristics or accomplishments: Agni, the lord of food, gave her back her food, Indra her *bala-* "power", Pūṣan the *bhagapati-* "lord of wealth or fortune" her *bhaga-*, Sarasvatī her *puṣṭi-* etc. This passage must no doubt be understood to mean that food, power, kingship, prosperity etc. are Śrī's spheres, the phenomena in which, and through which, her presence and activity manifest themselves, and to make it clear that she is only able to perform her functions through the mighty influence and the cooperation of Prajāpati and the ten gods: Agni, Soma, Varuṇa, Mitra, Indra, Bṛhaspati, Savitar, Pūṣan, Sarasvatī and Tvaṣṭar.

Before being constantly described as specially connected with Viṣṇu — this stage is not reached before the younger parts of the Mahābhārata — Śrī was associated with various gods, all of them assorting well with her. One of them was Kubera, in whose palace she stayed (Mbh. 2, 10, 19) [58]), and whose consort she was to be in the Nārada Purāṇa 84, 12. Another was Dharma, whose wife she is in the Mahābhārata and even in Viṣṇuitic purāṇas like ViP. 1, 7, 21; cf. also Mbh. 1, 66, 13 etc. where Lakṣmī belongs to the thirteen daughters of Dakṣa who were given in marriage to Dharma, Tuṣṭi "Satisfaction", Puṣṭi "Thriving", Ṛddhi "Growth, Success", Kīrti "Renown" etc. being her sisters and co-wives.

Especially fascinating are her relations with Indra [59]). In the Mahā-

[56]) See also Hopkins, Epic Mythology, p. 40; 43; 100; 107.

[57]) The reader may for the sake of brevity be referred to the indices of the books mentioned in the preceding notes.

[58]) For Kubera see p. 195 and 202.

[59]) See also Hartmann, o.c., p. 20.

bhārata she is not only related to have said to this god that she has come to him of her own accord, after having left the asuras — and in doing so she was followed by her inseparable companions: Jayā, Āśā "Hope", Śraddhā "Faith", Dhṛti "Firmness, Content", Kṣānti "Forbearance", Vijiti "Triumph", Saṃnati "Humility", Kṣamā "Patience" (12, 228, 82) [60]) — but also that she sat down beside him: then the god began to pour rain upon the crops which sprouted up at their proper season, men and gods became prosperous and cheerful, and the cows gave plenty of milk (12, 228, 90). In the same book of the great epic (12, 225, 1 ff.) she is said to have left Bali for Indra who at her own request divides her into four parts and gives her habitations in the earth, water, fire, and correctly living men. Mention may also be made of some particulars in the former of these passages: Śrī approaches Indra when he is sitting with Nārada; she rides Viṣṇu's splendid vehicle, attended by many apsaras, and looking like a solar disk; she calls herself Lakṣmī, Bhūti, and Śrī, Śraddhā, Medhā "Intelligence", Saṃnati, Vijiti, Sthiti "(High) position", Dhṛti, Siddhi etc. It may be added that Śrī is often described as accompanied by these or similar goddesses, e.g. in Bharata's Nāṭyaśāstra, ch. 3 passim, cf. especially st. 86 f. where Sarasvatī, Dhṛti, Medhā, Hrī, Śrī, Lakṣmī and Smṛti are called Mothers, being invoked for success.

There is, on the other hand, a curious purāṇic story of Indra's losing her. It is already referred to in the Rāmāyaṇa (6, 50, 25). When Indra had lost her because through his fault a garland, which was the goddess' residence [61]), had been thrown to the earth, the gods recovered her by churning the milk-ocean — it may be observed in passing that after the churning the asuras fought with the gods not only to obtain the goddess but also to take possession of the draught of immortality: *amṛtārthe ca lakṣmyarthe*: Mbh. 1, 18, 44; they are likewise bracketed together 5, 102, 12 —, but she then gave herself to Viṣṇu [62]). Would it be too rash to consider this narrative a reminiscence of a former association between Śrī-Lakṣmī and Indra [63]), which was broken off in favour of Viṣṇu when he came to be, in many respects, Indra's successor? Broken off; but not absolutely. For Indra continued maintaining some relations with the goddess: In honour of his consort Śrī-Lakṣmī Viṣṇu gave the Kaumudī festival to the Vaiśyas, expecting them to worship her who

---

60) Cf. e.g. also VaikhSmS. 3, 19 in fine.

61) For the religious value and function of garlands see K. Meschke, in the Hdwtb. d. de. Abergl. V, 381 ff.; Pauly-Wissowa, Real-Encycl. IV (1901), 1636 ff.

62) See also H. Jacobi, Das Rāmāyaṇa, Bonn 1893, p. 61 ff.; 138.

63) For her name Indirā see Hartmann, p. 4 f.

presides over wealth and prosperity [64]). This feast which is connected with the cult of ancestor worship, the rice-crop, manuring, powers presiding over agriculture and harvest is celebrated on the full-moon of Āśvina [65]). Lakṣmī's image is washed with milk, manure-heaps are worshipped [66]), etc. etc., and, according to part of our sources [67]) Indra, riding his elephant Airāvata shall have a share in the worship due to the goddess; incidentally, he may even be the principal character. He must be presented with an offering of rice boiled in milk. As Indra is one of the divinities concerned with the Āśvina ceremonies as described in the PārGS. 2, 16, 1 ff. (Indra, Indrāṇī, the Aśvins, the full moon of Āśvayuja etc.), there is, to my mind, no need to regard his share in the Kojāgara or Kaumudī as incidental, or more or less fortuitous. A similar partnership of Śrī and Indra is described by the KālikāPur. a. 91, 21 ff. (the Lakṣmī festival Śrīpañcamī).

There are more data helping to establish the strong probability of Śrī's former association with Indra: in the Mahābhārata, 1, 197, 1 ff., she is appointed to become the wife of the five Indras (who will be incarnate as the Pāṇḍavas), and therefore to be re-born as Draupadī. The MārkPur., 5, 24 ff., however, altered this story by declaring that it was Indra's own wife who became incarnate as Draupadī, without mentioning her name [68]). As, in the epics and purāṇas (cf. also MārkPur. 1, 29; 15, 70 etc.) Indra's wife is called Śacī, or sometimes Indrāṇi, it is highly improbable that Śrī is meant here. Mention may, finally, be made of an interesting stanza in the Rāmāyaṇa, 2, 60, 13 G. *rāma-lakṣmaṇayor madhye sītā rājati te snuṣā | viṣṇuvāsavayor madhye padmā śrīr iva rūpiṇī.*

---

[64]) B. A. Gupte, Hindu holidays and ceremonials, Calcutta-Simla 1919, p. 36 ff.; Meyer, o.c., II, p. 89 ff.; Underhill, o.c.

[65]) For the rites on that day see above.

[66]) It is interesting to notice that also those Hindus who emigrated to Suriname (Dutch Guyana) when celebrating their dīwalī festival kept up many old traditions; the housewife, whilst beating the sūp or winnowing basket recites the words "Lakṣmī may enter, indigence go away"; finally she rushes to the dung-hill, throws the sūp and the stick with which she has beaten it or the dung and exclaims: "stay here!". By doing so she drives off poverty. See C. J. M. de Klerk, Cultus en ritueel van het orthodoxe Hindoeïsme in Suriname, Amsterdam 1951, p. 214.

[67]) For particulars see Meyer, l.c.

[68]) See also F. Eden Pargiter, The Mārkaṇḍeya Purāṇa, Calcutta 1904, p. XVI ff.

III. VIṢṆU'S FEMALE PARTNERS.

On the other hand Viṣṇu before, and besides, being constantly associated with Śrī-Lakṣmī, maintained connections of a more or less temporary nature with other divine women. If the ancient texts had paid more attention to the female half of the human and divine societies — I for one am convinced that the female divinities occupied a very subordinate position not so much in the belief and worship of Vedic man in general as in the texts which we possess — these connections would doubtless be much clearer to us.

In AthV. 7, 46, the main ancient text dealing with this female divinity, Sinīvālī is (st. 3) explicitly called Viṣṇu's consort. The little text, which is ritually used in a remedial ceremony for various diseases and in addressing Prajāpati for obtaining benefits, describes her as the sister of the gods (= ṚV. 2, 32, 6), as "mistress of the people" [1]) — since the Vedic *viś- viśaḥ* is often used where later texts would have preferred *vaiśya-* "the third class of peasants, etc.", *viśpatnī,* which, moreover, occurs in connection with the *araṇi-* "the lower of the pieces of wood used for kindling fire" (ṚV. 3, 29, 1), may be put on a par with Agni's frequent epithet *viśpati-* "lord of the settlers" —, and as "giving birth to many" (*bahusūvarī*). She is, indeed, concerned with childbirth: AV. 14, 2, 15 and 21 "O S., let her (the bride) have progeny"; ṚV. 10, 184, 2 = AV. 5, 25, 3, MB. 1, 4, 7 etc. (the stanza being used in a ceremony for successful conception) "place the embryo, O S." (*garbhaṃ dhehi sinīvāli*) [2]). The same request is, in this stanza, addressed to Sarasvatī who keeps her company also AV. 19, 31, 10 where both goddesses are besought to bring riches, fatness of milk, and grain. AV. 2, 26, 10, used in a ceremony for the prosperity of cattle, asks her to "lead hither the van (of the cows)", addressing similar requests to Anumati — "Favour (of the gods), believed or besought to be propitious, to protect man and to grant him a long life" [3]) — and Bṛhaspati [4]). Elsewhere Prajāpati, Anumati, and S. constitute a trio engaged in "shaping" a son (AV. 6, 11, 3 used in a rite for conception of a male child), and this field of action may, all things considered, be

1) Geldner translated by "Stammesfürstin".

2) The stanza is also used in gṛhyasūtras to accompany rites in connection with conception (e.g. HirGS. 1, 25, 1 II). See also AtriSaṃh. 56, 16; Kāśyapa Saṃh. a. 58. For other particulars concerning her fecundating activities see Meyer, o.c., III, p. 161; cf. also Johansson, Solfågeln, p. 12 f.; Hillebrandt, Ved. Myth.[2] II, p. 325.

3) See e.g. Macdonell, o.c., p. 119; Keith, o.c., p. 211.

4) See e.g. Macdonell, o.c., p. 101 ff.; A. Hillebrandt, Vedische Mythologie[2], I, Breslau 1927, p. 160 ff.

especially proper to Sinīvālī [5]). In the stanzas inserted in the elaborate description of the ceremonies for procreation in the BārUp. 6, 4, 21 the husband whilst uniting with his wife asks Viṣṇu to make her womb prepared, Tvaṣṭar [6]) to shape the forms, Prajāpati to pour in, Dhātar (whose very name means "the establisher") to place the germ, and Sinīvālī to give the germ its proper place etc. In later Vedic texts Sinīvāli, Anumati and similar goddesses are identified with the phases of the moon [7]) (see e.g. AiB. 7, 11; GB. 2, 1, 10; ŚB. 4, 6, 4 ff.). In AiB. 3, 48, 1 ff. Anumati is declared to be the sky and the gāyatrī metre, Rākā to be Uṣas and the triṣṭubh, Sinīvālī to be the cow and the jagatī, Kuhū (who belongs to the same class of minor deities) the earth and the anuṣṭubh, Sūrya being identified with Dhātar. ĀpŚS. 14, 17, 3 Sinīvālī to all appearance is a name of the Earth.

The post-Vedic associations of Sinīvālī and the goddesses who bear her company in ancient texts (cf. also ṚV. 2, 32, 8 where apart from Indrāṇī and Varuṇānī, Guṅgū, Sinīvālī, Rākā, and Sarasvatī are invoked) are likewise instructive. Mbh. 3, 229, 50 identifies her with Devasenā "the army of the gods", i.e. the wife of Skanda, the general of that army, who is also identified with Lakṣmī herself, who elsewhere accompanies this god (9, 46, 64); in the former context she is also called Ṣaṣṭhī, Kuhū, Āśā, Sukhapradā, etc. In the purāṇical genealogies Ṡ., Kuhū, Rākā, and Anumati are daughters of Aṅgiras and Smṛti, and S. the consort of Vāyu [7]), the god of the wind who gives rain [8]). She is, in the epic, identified with Indra, Kṛṣṇa, and other gods (Mbh. 1, 25, 9; 12, 47, 65). Elsewhere she is married to Dhātar (see above; BhāgPur. 6, 18, 3) or identified with Durgā [9]). Especially interesting is her marriage with the prajāpati Kardama, the divine mud who is already known to us [10]): according to a purāṇical account [11]) she had two daughters, Samrāṭ "Sovereign" and Kukṣi "Womb" [12]). S. is said to have left K. for Soma: cf. e.g. MatsyaPur. 23, 23 ff., where nine

---

[5]) For other texts and particulars see Johansson, Über die altindische Göttin Dhiṣaṇā und verwandtes, Uppsala-Leipsic 1917, p. 71 f., and Meyer, o.c., III, p. 158. — Cf. also TB. 1, 7, 2, 1.

[6]) For Tvaṣṭar see above.

[7]) I refer to Johansson, l.c., and Keith, o.c., p. 199 and 201, and for the moon in connection with female deities, procreation, vegetation etc. Meyer, o.c., III, p. 311; Hillebrandt, o.c. I, p. 362 ff. See also the references given by Eggeling in SBE. 43, p. 264, n. 3.

[8]) See Kirfel, Purāṇa Pañcalakṣaṇa, p. 41 and 129; p. 196.

[9]) See the Petr. Dict. VII, 1006.

[10]) See above.

[11]) Cf. Ramachandra Dikshitar, The Purana Index I, p. 327 f. In other traditions K. had married another woman.

[12]) Cf. however Kirfel, o.c., p. 142 etc.

goddesses are related to have left their husband in order to love Soma: Lakṣmī left Nārāyaṇa, S. K., ... Puṣṭi Dhātar etc.

This much is certain that Sinīvālī on the strength of her functions and changeable affections was no stranger in the divine company under discussion. If there has really been a period or a circle of worshippers in which she was considered Viṣṇu's wife [13]), it is a curious fact that the very stanza AV. 7, 46, 3 declares her to be *indram.... pratīcī* which may be translated by "turning towards Indra" [14]).

Sarasvatī, who in Vedic times associates with Indra and the Aśvins (cf. also ŚB. 12, 8, 3, 18 where these deities are called the universe; KātyŚS. 19, 4, 14 ff.), with Indra alone, or with the Maruts, but in later ages is, as the goddess of learning and eloquence, Brahmā's wife, may also be primarily a divinity concerned with fecundation etc. [15]), with rain and food (cf. e.g. ĀpŚS. 8, 19, 5 and HirGS. 1, 20, 1 where she is worshipped for the sake of offspring; and ŚB. 12, 8, 2, 16, where healing power belongs to the Aśvins, energy and manly power to Indra, and food to S.). She sometimes enters into relations with Viṣṇu. In the ceremony of the seven steps which forms part of the wedding-rites and is executed "for sap, juice, offspring, welfare, prosperity etc.", Sarasvatī is requested to be gracious, and Viṣṇu to lead the bride up (MānGS. 1, 11, 18), in the Mbh. 6, 65, 61 she is Kṛṣṇa-Viṣṇu's tongue. In the śrauta ritual food for Agni and Viṣṇu, and an oblation for Sarasvatī are mentioned in the same passage: ĀpŚS. 5, 23, 5; cf. 19, 19, 6, and also 14, 7, 19. She is worshipped for the sake of learning (see e.g. KāśS. ch. 8), and is one of the deities worshipped in temples together with Śrī (cf. e.g. AtriS. 36, 58), with whom she is also identified [15a]). She is sometimes said to be Viṣṇu's wife (Pañcar. 2, 3, 64). Śrī and Sarasvatī are often mentioned together, in a complementary or antithetical sense (cf. also Praśnopan. 2, 13). It is understandable that this goddess, after having been identified with Vāc, that is with Eternal Speech in its transcendent reality (ŚB. 5, 2, 2, 13 f.) tended to belong to the Highest God. The universal and creative character of speech was, on the other hand, explained in the JUpBr. 1, 28 by stating that

---

[13]) See also Whitney-Lanman, ad AV. 7, 46, 3.

[14]) It may be remembered that S. is worshipped by the Vaikhānasas; cf. e.g. KaśS. ch. 58 and AS. 56, 16.

[15]) I also refer to Meyer, o.c., III, p. 317. — For Sarasvatī see also Hopkins, Religions of India, p. 451; Rao, o.c., passim; M.P.L. Sastry in the Poona Orientalist 6 (1941-2), p. 190 ff.

[15a]) See e.g. also Asiatic Researches 3 (1799), p. 272 f. — Cf. e.g. AS. 32, 69 Rudra, Pavitra, Vāg devī, Ravi, Çakra, Çrī. Or Sarasvatī is considered a 'śakti' of Çrī. On the mutual relations and essential identity of Çrī and Sarasvatī see N. N. Choudhuri, Lakṣmī in the purāṇa and tantra, Poona Orientalist 13 (1948), p. 4.

a ray consisting of speech and proceeding from Indra, i.e. from him who burns here, who is space (and who is the earth, the sky, and all existence, 1, 43, 10), becoming speech, is located in all creatures, who speak by Indra's 'ray'.

Viṣṇu's marriage with Śrī is always considered very important [16]). This may for instance appear from the fact that also philosophers did not omit it. In the introduction to his commentary on the Bhagavadgītā Rāmānuja commences his expositions by calling God, Viṣṇu, "the lord or husband of Śrī" (*śriyaḥ patiḥ*). In the Mbh. (13, a. 149) the god is already called *Śrīpati-*; cf. also his other epithets: *śrīmatāṃ vara-*; *Śrīnidhi-* "receptacle of *śrī-*"; *Śrīdhara-* "bearer of *śrī-*"; *Śrīda-* "giver of *śrī-*"; *Śrīnivāsa-* "abode of *śrī-*", etc. In the ViPur. we find a detailed and very instructive account of the various features in their character predisposing them to oneness, harmony and co-operation (1, 8, 15 ff.); their mutual relations and complementary nature are set forth in the following way: "Śrī, the spouse of Viṣṇu, the mother of the world, is eternal and imperishable. In like manner as he is all-pervading or omnipresent (*sarvagata-*), so also is she. Viṣṇu is meaning, she is speech; he is policy (*naya-*), she prudence (*nīti-*), he understanding, she intellect; he dharma, she good action. He is the creator, she creation. Śrī is the earth, Hari (Viṣṇu) the support of it.... Lakṣmī is the altar, Hari the sacrificial stake.... Keśava (Viṣṇu) is the sun, the lotos-seated goddess its radiance. Śrī is the heavens; Viṣṇu, who is one with all existence, is wide-extended space.... Śrī is prosperity, Śrīdhara (Viṣṇu) the lord of riches (Kubera) ....Lakṣmī is the light, Hari the lamp.... She is the night, he the day.... He is the standard, she the banner. He is one with all that is male, she with all that is female. Etc. etc.". Although the term *śakti-* is used in this passage (st. 27), the goddess is not yet regarded as the Lord's Śakti in the philosophical way of authors belonging to a later period [17]). Then Śrī symbolizes the Lord's creative energy, his potency, the power with which he is eternally associated and which enables him to become the efficient and the material causes of the universe. To the religious mind she at the same time becomes the divine mother of all existence, who sometimes intercedes with God on behalf of man. The story of the love Śrī, when arising from the ocean, at first sight conceived for Viṣṇu — see ViPur.

[16]) I also refer to P. N. Srinivasachari, The philosophy of Viśiṣṭādvaita, Adyar 1946, p. 166 ff.; 190 ff.; 386 ff. Hartmann, o.c., p. 22 ff., and Macnicol, Indian Theism, p. 109. See e.g. also Prapañcasāra Tantra 36, 35 ff.

[17]) For the *śakti-* concept the reader may, for reasons of space, be referred to the handbooks of Indian philosophy and religion. See e.g. also O. Lacombe, L'absolu selon le Védânta, Paris 1937, p. 322; S. Dasgupta, A history of Indian philosophy, III, Cambridge 1940, p. 41 f

1, 9, 104 — was likewise to show, now in mythological wording, the strong bonds between both divinities. In popular traditions the excellence of their marriage is elucidated by such observations as are found in ancient European accounts of Hinduism: Lakṣmī is all that can be desired or imagined [18]). Pairs of popular deities were, and are, identified with Viṣṇu and Śrī [19]).

There is, as far as I know, no certainty as to the exact period in which they came to be a couple. As Śrī-Lakṣmī had only a minor place in early Viṣṇuism (VājS. 31, 22 = MahānārUp. 1, 12 Ś. and L. are the wives of the puruṣa in the sun, who in later times is identified with Viṣṇu), their close connections do probably not reach back to very ancient times. In the Mahābhārata the goddess is called Kṛṣṇa's wife (1, 61, 44), a part of her became incarnate as Rukmiṇī, Kṛṣṇa's wife (1, 67, 56), but as we already saw she belongs also to Dharma and the five Indras. From numismatic and other evidence it however appears that under the Guptas Lakṣmī was enthroned beside Nārāyaṇa [20]).

Nor does it appear that they married annually or periodically as is the case with the god of the sun and the goddess of the earth who — e.g. with the Oraons [21]) — are believed to marry every year.

An important feature in Viṣṇuism is, on the other hand, the appearance of another goddess, usually called Bhūdevī, the Earth, as the god's second consort, beside Lakṣmī [22]). In addition to the remarks already made on Viṣṇu's association with the earth reference may be made here to a number of texts showing various sides of this connection: AV. 12, 1, 10 (the famous hymn to the earth) our planet is called "her on whom Viṣṇu strode and whom Indra made free from enemies"; 15, 14, 5 the god is said to have moved toward the fixed quarter, i.e. the nadir; 12, 3, 59 and 3, 27, 5 he is again brought into relation with that region, these texts also showing a certain 'correlation' with plants. The same idea is expressed MGS. 2, 15, 1 "May Viṣṇu and the earth and the serpents protect me from below" [23]). Mbh. 11, 8, 21 ff. it is Viṣṇu who in the midst of the celestials who had assembled in Indra's court answered the goddess Earth when she came there to argue her case, making her a promise of help [24]).

18) Caland, Port. Verh., p. 165; Fr. Verh., p. 8.

19) See e.g. M. N. Srinivas, Religion and society amongst the Coorgs of S. India, Oxford 1952, p. 233.

20) See Raychaudhuri, p. 177.

21) See Ruben, Eisenschmiede, p. 234. — For many other particulars see Hartmann, o.c., p. 22 ff.

22) See e.g. also Rao, o.c., passim (Index, p. 4); Coomaraswamy, Ind. u. Indones. Kunst, p. 161; G. Jouveau-Dubreuil, Iconography of S. India, Paris 1937, p. 62.

23) See Dresden, o.c., p. 164; cf. KS. 37, 10.

24) I also refer to Abegg, Messiasglaube, p. 79.

The divine person Earth is in the Mbh. (5, 117, 14) said to be married to Bhūmipati, the "lord of the Earth". Although this term usually refers to the human lord of the earth, the king — who was also believed to be mystically united with the goddess Earth —, we may, I think, safely suppose a divine being to have been meant here. Bhūmipati may have been the god who impregnated the earth. Anyhow, Viṣṇu afterwards took his place: Mbh. 13, 149, 119 he is called *kṣitīśa-*; see also Śrīsūkta 25 *viṣṇupatnīṃ kṣamāṃ devīm* "the goddess Earth, Viṣṇu's wife". Thus he became another example of a bigamous divinity concerned with processes pertaining to the continuance of earthly life [25]). — His close connections with the goddess Earth are also apparent from the eulogies pronounced by the latter upon her lord and protector: Viṣṇusmṛti 1, 49 ff., where Viṣṇu the boar after having, in the beginning of this cosmic period, drawn the earth from the bottom of the sea and commencing creation is addressed by her; MtPur. 248, 12 ff. [26]).

We shall pass over in silence the many popular descriptions of the god's married life with Śrī and Bhūmi [27]), as well as the speculations of a more philosophical nature concerning the mutual relations of these figures [28]). Nor can we dwell on the puranic theory of the eight śaktis or energies, faculties of Viṣṇu, the protector: Śrī, Bhū, Sarasvatī, Prīti (Love), Kīrti (Fame), Śānti (Peace), Tuṣṭi (Satisfaction, Pleasure), and Puṣṭi (Well-nourished condition), considered as the eight channels through which the protective energies of the god can display their beneficent activity [29]).

---

[25]) See also Ruben, Eisenschmiede, p. 232 f. The Roman goddesses Ceres and Tellus may, to a certain extent, also be adduced as a parallel; see e.g. F. Altheim, Terra Mater, p. 108 ff.

[26]) See Hohenberger, o.c., p. 173 ff.

[27]) See e.g. Baldaeus, o.c., p. 42; B. Ziegenbalg, Malabarisches Heidenthum, ed. Caland, Amsterdam 1926, p. 47.

[28]) Beside Çrī and Bhūmi (see e.g. Lacombe, o.c., p. 320 ff.) we also find Līlā "Sport", i.e. Çrī as far as she is concerned with God's creative 'playful activity'. See e.g. M. M. Bose, The post-Caitanya Sahajiā cult of Bengal, Univ. of Calcutta 1930, p. 158.

[29]) See also H. K. Sastri, South-Indian images of gods and goddesses, Madras 1916, p. 189.

CHAPTER THREE: SOME ASPECTS OF VIṢṆU'S CULT.

I. INTRODUCTORY.

Although it would be beyond the scope of this work to describe the Hinduistic Viṣṇu cult [1]) a few words may be said on some particulars of the ritual connected with it. The mantras used in Viṣṇu's worship (*pūjā*) contain much that originally referred to other deities [2]). Part of them has no bearing upon the god himself, but it is interesting to notice that according to the Viṣṇudharmottarapurāṇa a. 65 an offering of food (*naivedya-*) is presented to the image whilst pronouncing ṚV. 10, 121, 1-8, i.e. the greater part of the famous text which discusses the character of the Unknown God who in the beginning became Hiraṇyagarbha, and who, being born, became the only lord of creation, who gives life and strength. Another text to be pronounced is the Puruṣasūkta, ṚV. 10, 90, which declares the universe to have developed from the primaeval Puruṣa or Man, who is this all, and who in the course of time was identified with Nārāyaṇa and Viṣṇu, the Supreme Being. The god is invited with ṚV. 5, 81 which was addressed to Savitar. In the ritual as described in the Baudhāyanagṛhyapariśiṣṭa sūtra such Viṣṇu mantras occur as ṚV. 1, 22, 18; 17; 20 referring to the strides, as TS. 1, 2, 13, 2, and TS. 4, 2, 8, 2 dealing with the brahman which was first born of old, ... the womb of the existent and of the non-existent. The twelve names of the gods are repeated and stanzas taken from TB. 2, 4, 6 associated with them. Thus light is thrown upon the various sides of the god's character, the composite nature of which is clearly shown [3]).

---

[1]) Apart from the well-known books by Von Glasenapp, Farquhar, Ch. Eliot (Hinduism and Buddhism, London 1921), J. E. Carpenter (Theism in medieval India, London 1921), and others, see Upadhyaya, India in Kālidāsa, p. 305 ff.; 320 ff.; Patil, o.c., p. 188 ff.; J. N. Banerjea, in Majumdar's Hist. and Cult. II, p. 452 f.

[2]) The reader may be referred to Kane, History of Dharmaśāstra, II, 2, Poona 1941, p. 726 ff. — It may be remembered that many local cults survived by incorporation into the worship of Viṣṇu or Çiva.

[3]) For a more detailed account of Viṣṇuite ritual and mantras see section II.

In expatiating on the various aspects of Indian religions early European authors also mentioned instances of fertility rites, which are of special interest to us when they form part of the cult of Viṣṇu. Rogerius [4]) describing the festival called 'Gokoulástemi' (i.e. the *gokulāṣṭamī* or *kṛṣṇāṣṭamī*) says that people throw milk, cream, coconuts, and other fruits, and also "other objects as are found among herdsmen" at each other. Ziegenbalg [5]) informs us that on the occasion of Kṛṣṇa's birthday his votaries used to put four trees in the earth and to hang them with coconuts; a herdsman was sprinkled with water. An image of Ananta Padmanābha made of straw is mentioned by the former author [6]) : it is censed, strewn with flowers, and addressed with formulas. Round the right arm of the institutor of the festival a red cord is bound. The straw figure no doubt represents a vegetation deity [7]), probably Viṣṇu himself in a particular manifestation. Another Viṣṇuite custom, hunting a he-goat or a fox which were allowed to run away, is likewise recorded by Rogerius [8]); a hare hunt is mentioned by Dubois [9]). Similar hunts took place in ancient Rome, England, and other countries, forming part of festivals originally intended to promote fertility. The purpose of sham fights was similar [10]). According to Baldaeus [11]) the inhabitants of the Malabar coast celebrating, in August, a festival in honour of Viṣṇu had excellent meals — this, too, is a widespread means of producing health, wealth, and fertility [12]) — and performed sham fights. Processions attracted the attention of several authors [13]); some of them made mention of the devadāsīs, the Lakṣmī feast, the diwālī [14]) etc.

Many celebrations in honour of Viṣṇu, indeed, show how much the common people liked to associate him with welfare and fertility, with wealth and productivity. Some of the ceremonies performed on the occasion of the Dolāyātrā, which is now given to the Kṛṣṇa cult, consist in sprinkling an image of the god with red powder, in burning

---

4) A. Rogerius, Open-deure tot het verborgen heydendom, ed. Caland, The Hague 1915, p. 132.

5) Ziegenbalg's Malabarisches Heidenthum, ed. Caland, Amsterdam 1926, p. 88.

6) Rogerius, o.c., p. 130.

7) See Meyer, o.c., III, p. 322.

8) Rogerius, o.c., p. 128.

9) Dubois-Beauchamps, Hindu manners ...³, p. 574.

10) A. Piganiol, Recherches sur les jeux romains, Publ. fac. lettres Strassbourg 13 (1923), p. 137 ff.

11) Ph. Baldaeus, Afgoderye..., ed. De Jong, Thesis Utrecht 1917, p. 70 f.

12) I refer to my 'Drama', p. 395 ff.

13) See e.g. Rogerius, o.c., p. 124; F. S. Growse, Mathurā², 1880, p. 68 ff.

14) See e.g. W. Geleynssen de Jongh, Remonstrantie, ed. Caland, The Hague 1929, p. 91.

an effigy upon a bonfire, in placing the image in a swing [15]) and swinging it in a ceremonial manner. Being dressed in new clothes, boys who tend cows leap, dance, and sing, and people sprinkle each other with red powder or liquid [16]).

The many descriptions of the establishment of images are often instructive. Such iconographical details as the black complexion of many images or the yellow colour of his robe remind us of the dark colour of the vegetation divinities of other peoples and of the colour of springtime and ripening corn respectively. His consorts Śrī (yellow) and Bhūmi (black) are sculptured or established on his right and left. Among the divine beings attending him are yakṣas, kinnaras, vidyādharas and similar "doers of good, devoted to joy" (Rām. 4, 43, 50), who use to sport with their female partners, devoted to love and wealth [17]). The vidyādharas are essentially spirits of the air, the yakṣas connected with fertility and vegetation. The god himself as well as his consort Lakṣmī are still often worshipped together with the sun [18]).

II. VAIKHĀNASA VIṢṆU RITES.

We now proceed to discuss some aspects of the Viṣṇu worship of the Vaikhānasas, which seem to be of special relevance. Referring for a general introduction to the two expositions given by Caland [1]) we recall that this youngest school of the Taittirīya branch of the Black YajurVeda, thoug constituting a Vedic school, already in the smārta portions of its ritual books gave evidence of having introduced a considerable number of rites and other details not, or only incidentally, referred to in the books of the other schools. Apart from the sūtras which in all probability were not definitively drawn up before the IVth century A.D., they produced many other works. In the traditions of their community which in the course of time developed into a Hinduistic group of Viṣṇu adorers much information can be found which tends to confirm the occasional references to the Vaikhānasas

15) See my 'Drama', p. 348 f. For theatrical performances see also S. Konow, IA. 49, p. 232 f.

16) See also Hopkins, Religions of India, p. 453 f. and the short description of a number of festivals and ceremonies in honour of Viṣṇu, as described by the MtPur. in Hohenberger, o.c., p. 140 ff.

17) For other details see e.g. Hopkins, Epic mythology, p. 175 f.

18) Some particulars may be found in M. A. Sherring, The sacred city of the Hindus, London 1868, p. 113; 126 ff.; 185; Growse, o.c., p. 126.

1) W. Caland, Over het Vaikhānasasūtra, Amsterdam Academy 1926, and On the sacred books of the Vaikhānasas, ibid. 1928.

in Sanskrit literature. The community which, in the South of India, has survived to this day, has in the last decenniads, published some of their highly valuable texts, a thorough examination of which will no doubt enable us to deepen our insight into the early transitional stages in the history of Hinduism.

There is strong internal evidence for the antiquity and continuity of the Vaikhānasa cult: the oblations in the fire are executed according to Vedic injunctions and accompanied by old mantras; many well-known Vedic technical terms, ritual particulars etc. are still found in every treatise dealing with the conduct of worship: the institutor of a sacrifice is almost always called a *yajamāna-*, the priests are often designated by the Vedic term *ṛtvijaḥ*, the titles *hotar-*, *adhvaryu-* etc. are likewise frequently used; such objects as the *juhū* "a curved wooden ladle for pouring sacrificial butter into the fire" and the *sruc-* "a large wooden ladle for similar purposes" are often mentioned.

In places, the traditional portions of the Smārtasūtra already contain invocations of, or oblations to, Viṣṇu which are not altogether unworthy of interest. A muttering addressed to the god and consisting of ṚV. 1, 22, 16-21 in which his famous three steps are the main object of glorification — "from there the gods shall favour man from where Viṣṇu moved on, Viṣṇu, the undeceivable, Indra's intimate friend, who in striding observes the laws, the highest step of whom, always seen by the liberal institutors of sacrifices, may be considered the eye of heaven" — is repeatedly quoted (see e.g. 1, 5; 3, 17; 21; 4, 10). Only part of these six stanzas are prescribed in other smārtasūtras. A passage in the description of the funeral rites (5, 3) has the direction to throw a ball made of clay and destined for Viṣṇu into the water, whereas another ball destined for Brahmā should be buried and a third, destined for Rudra, should be put on the spot where the corpse is to be cremated [2]). — In the description of the normal paradigma for a sacrifice mantras containing Viṣṇu's name are prescribed: TS. 1, 2, 13 g-h "....From the sky, o Viṣṇu, or from the earth.... fill thy hands etc.". In gathering the grass to be used for strewing around the vedi one has to pronounce the mantras "At the west (etc.) thou art Viṣṇu's seat".

In describing the distribution of the sacrificial utensils on the corpse of the man who had employed them during his life-time the sūtrakāra has the vessel for mixing meal with water placed on his belly with the mantra "(thou art) Viṣṇu's front", which, being TS. 1, 2, 13 k is, e.g.,

---

[2]) For these three balls see 5, 2, and Caland, Die altindischen Todten- und Bestattungsgebräuche, Amsterdam Academy 1896, p. 26.

prescribed ĀpśS. 11, 8, 1 under different circumstances [3]). Especially in the chapters 6 and 7 which contain the many prāyaścittas and in the dharmasūtra Viṣṇu's name can often be found: when, for instance, the proper time for the garbhādhāna has passed, one should perform it as usual after having put an embryo of gold on the belly of one's wife and pronounce the Viṣṇusūkta (ṚV. 1, 154). If this is the case with the ceremony of name-giving one should offer an oblation to the same god (6, 3 and 4 resp.). In case of other omissions and shortcomings similar atonements are prescribed.

In the elaborate discussion of the mantras which are common to any ritual act the direction is given (1, 21) to gather all the grass used for strewing around the vedi with the mantras "at the west (south, north, east) thou art Viṣṇu's seat (*sadanam*)" and to throw it into the fire whilst pronouncing the mantras TS. 1, 1, 13 f-h (which elsewhere accompany the act of casting a piece of grass from the prastara towards the east [4])) "Swell, ye waters and plants; ye are the spotted steeds of the Maruts; fare to the sky, thence bring us rain". Similar references to Viṣṇu are made in the chapters dealing with the introductory rites: 1, 10; 12, and especially 1, 15: "for the sake of prosperity (*samṛddhyai*) he offers melted butter with the mantras ṚV. 1, 22, 16 and 17 (see above), the second of which is TS. 1, 2, 13 e, which in the rites as described by various schools often serves to accompany an offering of butter [5]).

As is very often the case in agricultural environments the worship as practised by these Vaikhānasas is intimately connected with the welfare of the community, the village, the successful growth of the crops etc.; this ritual aims at welfare, prosperity, good fortune, increase of the population, multiplication of cattle and property, deliverance from every kind of evil. Special ceremonies intended to stimulate the fall of rain are not wanting. As a special rite not described in other gṛhyasūtras their smārtasūtras (4, 8) already includes a sacrifice to be dedicated to Śrī and Viṣṇu on the day of full moon in the month of Caitra (March-April). To these deities oblations of clarified butter and a rice-mess are offered. In addition to this a number of divinities is invoked whose concern is one of the various manifestations of power in nature, most of them directly influencing the growth of the crops

---

[3]) See Caland, Todten- u. Best., p. 50.

[4]) For the prastara see e.g. Caland, Das Çrautasūtra des Āpastamba, I, Göttingen-Leipzig 1921, p. 60 f.

[5]) See e.g. ĀpÇS. 2, 6, 1; 9, 1, 11; 10, 16; 11, 6, 13; 13, 25, 8; 14, 30, 5; 31, 1; A. B. Keith, The Veda of the Black Yajus School, Harvard 1914, I, p. 32; W. Caland et V. Henry, L'Agniṣṭoma, Paris 1906, p. 81.

and the fertility of the soil, to wit the twelve months — addressed by their ancient names Madhu, Mādhava etc. [6]) —, the seasons and their deities, the herbs and the lord of the herbs (*auṣadhīśāya*), Śrī, the husband of Śrī (*Śrīpataye*) and Viṣṇu (sic!). The person performing the rites has to worship, to the west of the fire, the goddess Śrī and the god who is her husband and to present to them the sacrificial substance (i.e. the remains of the rice-mess from which he has already sacrificed). The accompanying mantras are very instructive: TS. 5, 7, 2 f "Summer, winter, and spring for us, autumn, the rains be favourable for us; may we enjoy the favour and protection of these seasons through a hunderd years" [7]); "What is deficient must be made full for me, what is full must not become wanting" [8]); "Born for *śrī-* he (Soma, in the ṚV.) came forth for *śrī-*, *śrī-* and a youthful age does he bestow on the invokers; wrapping themselves in *śrī-* they entered 'immortality'...." [9]); and the verses addressed to Viṣṇu corresponding to ṚV. 1, 22, 16-21. After the above ritual acts one had to feed some brahmins with rice which had ripened in the month of Caitra, whilst pronouncing the so-called annasūkta, or 'hymn to the food'. This text corresponds to the greater part of TB. 2, 8, 8, 1-4; its last stanza is TS. 3, 4, 11 d: *aham asmi prathamajā ṛtasya, pūrvaṃ devebhyo amṛtasya nābhiḥ.... aham annam annam adantam admi.... annam āhuḥ prajananaṃ prajānām. ahaṃ sad amṛto bhavāmi. brahmā devānām padavīḥ kavīnām.... somaḥ pavitram aty eti rebhan* [10]).

In Caitra, the second spring-month in which the crops ripen (see e.g. Mbh. 12, 100, 10), fertility festivals are numerous. Part of these festivals are, or have been, widespread and some districts have almost "nine holidays out of seven days". The Caitra-Gaurī festival in honour of Gaurī, i.e. the goddess of the colour of ripe corn — one of Lakṣmī's manifestations — is celebrated at that time by married women whose

---

[6]) See TS. 1, 1, 14 and W. Kirfel, Die Kosmographie der Inder (Bonn-Leipzig 1920), p. 131; G. Thibaut, Astronomie, Astrologie usw. (Grundriss), p. 11.

[7]) For other applications of these apposite words see Keith, o.c., p. 469 n. 4; cf. also W. D. Whitney, Atharva-veda saṃhitā, Harvard 1905, p. 322.

[8]) This mantra is used ĀśvGS. 2, 2, 3 and PGS. 2, 16, 3 (in a somewhat different form) in the Āśvayujī ceremony (see A. Hillebrandt, Ritualliteratur, Strassburg 1897, p. 77 f., and A. B. Keith, The religion and philosophy of the Veda and Upanishads, Harvard 1925, p. 362) which anyhow is intended for economic welfare in the agricultural sphere. Cf. also VaikhSmS. 4, 9 (see further on).

[9]) This mantra, RV. 9, 94, 4 which is to return VaikhSmS. 4, 11, was no doubt included in this ritual on account of the fourfold *śrī-*.

[10]) It is given in the VaikhSaṃh. 2, 12 (75-77). Cf. also TĀ. 9, 10, 6; TUp. 3, 10, 6. Part of it also occurs at the end of TUp. (3, 10, 6) in a passage giving vent to the mystical rapture of the knower of the universal unity.

husband is alive [11]). In Mewār the ceremonies of the beneficent Gaurī who then is regarded as Annapūrṇā "Satiation with food" are ushered in by the festival of flowers, celebrated on the 15th Caitra, the opening of the luni-solar year of Vikramāditya. The rites in honour of Gaurī or Īśānī, the goddess of abundance, begin by bringing earth for her image. Then "a small trench is excavated, in which barley is sown; the ground is irrigated and artificial heat supplied till the grain germinates, when the females — the festival only or mainly concerns women — join hands and dance, invoking the blessings of Gaurī on their husbands". The image of the goddess which is adored is that of a matron painted the colour of ripe corn, and holding a lotus, and often also a conch, discus, and club [12]).

After this interruption, let us return to the Smārtasūtra of the Vaikhānasas. After the Caitrī the redactor has inserted the Āśvayujī [13]), which as described by him may doubtless be considered a ceremony intended for the welfare of the cows: the fire for domestic worship is established in the cow-house, where the rites are performed, which are concluded by circumambulating and paying homage to these animals [14]).

The subsequent khaṇḍas, 4, 10-12, contain the worship of Viṣṇu (*viṣṇvarcanā*), describing, as ceremonies of the Hinduistic type, the consecration or establishment (*pratiṣṭhā*) [15]) of the god and the ordinary and obligatory worship. The introductory remarks give evidence of the Visnuite character of this religion: the worship of Viṣṇu, which is said to be equivalent to the worship of all other gods, should take place at the end of any obligatory sacrifice, for "Viṣṇu is the highest of the gods" (AiB. 1, 1, 1). Devoting to these ceremonies just as much consideration as is required for our purpose, I draw attention to kh. 11: a jar which should not be of dark colour is filled with purified water and placed at the right side of the god; a bunch of kuśa-grass, unhusked rice, a piece of gold and jewels are thrown into it. Having meditated on the spotless god as being in one's own heart and also in the clear

---

[11]) J. Tod, Annals and antiquities of Rajasthan, ed. by W. Crooke, II, Oxford 1920, p. 665.

[12]) Tod, ibidem, p. 664 ff.; B. A. Gupte, IA. 35 (1906), p. 61 ff.; Gupte, Hindu holidays and ceremonials, Calcutta 1919, p. 18 f.; J. J. Meyer, Trilogie altindischer Mächte und Feste der Vegetation, passim (see III, p. 297). — See also ch. II.

[13]) See above, n. 8.

[14]) For the sense of a circumambulation see Caland, Een indogermaansch lustratie-gebruik, Amsterdam 1898, p. 275 ff.

[15]) See my paper on *pratiṣṭhā* (see ch. I, s. 3, n. 12).

water [16]), as gold-coloured, as having a red mouth, red eyes, red hands and feet, as wearing the śrīvatsa-mark.... and a yellow garb, as having in his hands the conch and the disk, and as of benign countenance.... one should bow before him. After having sprinkled water around the fire...., one invites the god by name into the southern praṇidhi-vessel by means of the formulas: "*Oṃ, bhūḥ* (I invoke) Puruṣa etc.". The god's names are: Puruṣa (the primaeval man as the soul and original source of the universe with whom Viṣṇu is often identified, the Puruṣasūkta, ṚV. 10, 90, being part of the texts to be recited during these ceremonies), Nārāyaṇa (a name of frequent occurrence in this sūtra [17])), Satya "the True One, or Truth" (applied to Kṛṣṇa Mbh. 5, 70, 13 and elsewhere and also one of Viṣṇu's thousand names Mbh. 13, 149, 25 etc.), Acyuta "the Immovable One" (thus the epic Kṛṣṇa- and Viṣṇu-Kṛṣṇa are often called), Aniruddha "the Unobstructed or Self-willed One" (Mbh. 12, 340, 38 or 339, 41 and later works [18])). Besides, a formula is addressed to Śrī, showing that she is also invoked, in all probability after an image of her had been made. Another formula is addressed to Mahī "the Earth".

In the Ṛgveda a goddess Mahī sometimes (1, 13, 9; 5, 5, 8) appears in association with Iḷā "Refreshment, Nourishment", who represents plenty derived from the cow, and Sarasvatī, a well-known bestower of wealth, plenty, and nourishment [19]). In parallel texts Iḷā and Sarasvatī are, however, accompanied by Bhāratī (1, 188, 8 etc.). Sāyaṇa, followed by Geldner [20]) and other scholars, therefore identified Mahī and Bhāratī: *atra mahīśabdo mahattvaguṇayuktāṃ bhāratīm ācaṣṭe* (1, 13, 9). This conclusion is however open to question: compare RV. 1, 142, 9

---

[16]) The term *praṇidhi-* to designate the vessel for the *praṇītāḥ* or lustral water (see e.g. ÇB. 12, 9, 3, 8; ĀpÇS. 1, 16, 5 ff.) and the fact that there are two of them, are peculiar to the Vaikhānasas (Caland, Vaikhānasasmārtasūtram. Engl. translation, Calcutta 1929, p. 23, n. 13). Whereas the *praṇītāḥ* serve, inter alia, to protect the sacrifice (see TB. 3, 2, 4, 1 ff.), the Vaikhānasas use the *praṇidhi's* to "cause to come near" or invoke deities (cf. SmS. 1, 13; 3, 13). One cannot help remembering the Buddhist meaning of the term: "request, prayer, asking, solicitation".

[17]) For the identification of Viṣṇu and Nārāyaṇa see e.g. R. G. Bhandarkar, Vaiṣṇavism, Çaivism and minor religious systems, Strassburg 1913, p. 4 ff.; J. N. Farquhar, An outline of the religious literature of India, Oxford 1920, p. 50, 90 etc.; Hemchandra Raychaudhuri, Materials for the study of the early history of the Vaishnava sect, Calcutta 1936, p. 111.

[18]) Cf. Bhandarkar, o.c., p. 6 and 12 f.; Raychaudhuri, o.c., p. 97 ff.

[19]) For particulars see A. A. Macdonell, Vedic Mythology, p. 86 ff.; Meyer, Trilogie, II, p. 247 and III, p. 158 ("ursprünglich eine Wasser- und Fruchtbarkeitsgenie"); and ch. II of this volume.

[20]) Geldner, Der Rig-Veda übersetzt, I, p. 14.

and 9, 5, 8, which were discussed by Pischel and Johansson [21]). The suggestion made by the former scholar, that Mahī in these Āprī-hymns refers to Dhiṣaṇā is likewise liable to be questioned, for *mahī* is in the Ṛgveda a frequent epithet of divine beings and powers. It must, on the other hand, be conceded that most of the nouns qualified by this adjective, which while expressing the general meaning of "great and large" obviously implies the ideas of power, wealth, eminence and importance [22]), belong to the semantic category of power-substances and divine personalities to which man's reaction, generally speaking, is awe and amazement. Apart from Dhiṣaṇā which may have represented the earth and perhaps also abundance proceeding from the earth (or, rather, the earth as a producer of abundance, cf. ṚV. 10, 35, 7) [23]), the earth, when denoted by the word *pṛthivī* (cf. also ṚV. 1, 164, 33 *mātā pṛthivī mahīyam*), heaven (the sky), Uṣas, Aditi, Aramati [24]), Pṛśni (the mother of the Maruts), Sūnṛtā [25]), praise, a stream, the cow, a woman are styled *mahī*. The masculine forms of the adjective *mah-* likewise prefer to qualify divinities, mighty beings and such powerful entities and 'concepts' as "assistance, gift, good-will, fame, wealth, force, dominion etc." [26]). Our conclusion may therefore be that the possibility of an old epithet given to Śrī as a powerful divinity must not be left entirely out of account. As on the other hand "the earth" is the only surviving application of the Vedic *mahī* (letting alone technical meanings and proper names), this interpretation of the invocation Mahī occurring in the text under discussion is no doubt preferable, the more so as the sacrifices prescribed by the sūtrakāra are to be accompanied not only by the Viṣṇu- and Puruṣasūktas, ṚV. 1, 22, 16 ff., and 9, 94, 4 *śriye jātaḥ*, but also by the mantra beginning with "the goddess Earth": *medinī devī vasundharī syād yasudhā* (sic) *devī vāsavī | brahmavarcaḥ pitṝṇāṃ śrotraṃ cakṣur viṣṇur manaḥ* [27]). This view is rendered certain by other data found in the Vaikh. books, and by the well-known relations between Viṣṇu and both goddesses, Śrī and the Earth. —

---

[21]) R. Pischel, in R. Pischel und K. F. Geldner, Vedische Studien, II, Stuttgart 1897, p. 84 f.; K. F. Johansson, Über die altindische Göttin Dhiṣáṇā und verwandtes, Uppsala-Leipzig, 1917, p. 24 f.

[22]) Remember the Avestan *masišta-*, discussed in ch. II, § 2.

[23]) For Dhiṣaṇā see also A. Hillebrandt, Vedische Mythologie², I, Breslau 1927, p. 425 ff.; Caland, Museum 26, 204; Arch. f. Relig. 25, p. 287.

[24]) See Oriens, 2, p. 201.

[25]) See above, ch. II, § 1, p. 182.

[26]) I refer to Grassmann's Wörterbuch, 1013.

[27]) This mantra also accompanies an offering to "the sacrifice to Earth" (*bhūmiyajñāya*), forming part of the ritual performed on the occasion of founding a house: 3, 16.

The next day the votary, whilst muttering the Śakunasūkta [28]) carries the image and the jar into his house (or into a temple) and duly instals the god.

The no doubt younger kalpas, the texts prescribing the ritual and giving rules for ceremonial and sacrificial acts, constantly refer to the sūtras or prove to be in keeping with their contents. Many Vedic mantras, compiled at an early date in a special Vaikhānasīyasaṃhitā or Mantrapraśna are cited and their recitation prescribed. The first part of this text [29]) contains the mantras relating to the welfare of the individual, running parallel to the gṛhya portions of the sūtra-text. The second part is designated as *daivikacatuṣṭayam*, i.e. the four chapters of mantras relating to the God. They are used in performing the *pūjā* (honour, worship, and adoration in the Hinduistic manner) of the god Viṣṇu. The ritual is accordingly divided into the so-called invisible or Vedic Agni-worship and *samūrti-* ("visible in some form") Hinduistic worship.

The incorporation of the so-called Hinduistic forms of ritual and adoration beginning in the sūtras appears to have advanced greatly in the younger texts, which give evidence of a full-fledged temple and image ritual with various offerings, processions and many other Hinduistic rites, most of them, however, being performed with Vedic fires. Such subjects as the construction of temples, the consecration of various kinds of images, daily and special ceremonies, expiatory rites and other practices and observances are amply discussed. Essential traits of all Visnuite religion are not absent: the necessity of devotion and attachment to the Lord is over and over again inculcated, the avatāras are not only enumerated and described but also worshipped, and so on.

The character of the more or less prolonged festive processions, offerings and other ceremonies in honour of Viṣṇu as described in these other Vaikhānasīya collections is not essentially different from the greater part of the Hinduistic ceremonial, a specimen of which, the Caitra festival, has already come to our notice. The utsava section of Atri's treatise on *samūrtārcanā* "the worship (of God) in a certain material form" [30]) supplies us with such a sufficiency of data as to

---

28) See my remarks in 'The Ṛgvidhāna', p. 36.

29) The first half of this Saṃhitā was published at Kumbakoṇam in 1910, see L. Renou, Bibliographie védique, Paris 1931, p. 82. As it is printed in Grantha characters, it has been inaccessible to many scholars. A complete edition appeared in the Vaikhānasagranthamālā (ed. Bālakalānidhi D. Çeṣācārya).

30) Atri-saṃhitā (or) Samūrtārcanādhikaraṇam, ed. by P. Raghunāthacakravarti-Bhaṭṭācārya (ÇriVeṅkaṭeśvara Oriental Series, VI, Tirupati 1943). According to the tradition of the Vaikhānasīyas their cult has chiefly been expounded by four ṛṣis: Atri, Marīci, Bhṛgu, and Kāśyapa. The works held to have been composed

conclude that the chief desires of an agricultural community: appeasement of evil, rain, health, opulence, prosperity, fertility, increase of the power of the king — who is not only the protector of his peacable subjects, but also the mediator, in their interest, in stimulating the powers of fertility[31]) —, belong to the main objects in which the interest of the author centres. In spite of their predominantly formal and technical character this text and the Kāśyapa-Saṃhitā or Kāśyapa-Jñānakāṇḍa[32]) which, unlike Atri's work is written in prose, make, in places, passing reference to the various ends which the votaries of the god have in view apart from reaching Viṣṇu's highest abode and attaining final emancipation. "One shall establish Viṣṇu, the lord of the world in pleasant appearance everywhere in villages etc. in order to promote universal prosperity" (AS. 4, 33); "If Viṣṇu is adored in accordance with the rules of the Vaikhānasas the village, the institutor of the ceremony, the king, and the kingdom will obtain any welfare and prosperity" (79, 39 f.); "A king who causes the *abhiṣeka*-ceremony of the god to be performed shall rule the world and obtain *śrī-*, be happy on earth and gain final emancipation" (64, 54 f.); "If (the images of) the two goddesses[33]) are present with (the image of) the god there will be well-being, one's wife and children will prosper and there will also be other reasons for enjoyment" (39, 27); "If the ritual wedding of the god and his two consorts is celebrated with due solemnity the women of the village will have sons and grandsons; they will enjoy all possible happiness and any felicity" (39, 55 f.); "Performing the ritual based on the fivefold conception of Viṣṇu[34]) effects the expiation of evil, and gives rise to welfare and happiness; besides, it gives rain to all beings and great prosperity to the four classes of society" (37, 7 ff.; cf. also 38, 71 ff.); "A locality possessing a temple dedicated to Viṣṇu has secured prosperity, a well-nourished condition, and the increase of offspring, grain and money" (2, 29). "By duly executing the

by these authorities have not completely survived, but the publication of the valuable remainders is now in progress. The other five sections of the Atrisaṃhitā deal with the selection of the site for constructing a temple, its erection etc. (*karṣaṇa-*), the consecration of the images (*pratiṣṭhā*), the actual worship (*pūjā*), the ceremony of the holy bath (*snapana-*), and the expiatory rites (*prāyaścitta-*).

[31]) I refer to my remarks on this point in the Acta Orientalia, 19, p. 417 ff.

[32]) Vaikhānasīya Kāśyapajñānakāṇḍa, ed. by R. Sārthasārathi Bhaṭṭācārya, Tirupati 1948.

[33]) Çrī and Mahī.

[34]) The Vaikhānasa ritual is based on the fivefold conception of God Viṣṇu as Viṣṇu, Puruṣa, Satya, Acyuta and Aniruddha, who are considered manifestations of the divine being and the god's 'constituents'. Whereas Viṣṇu is regarded as all-pervading, Puruṣa is the principle of animation, Satya is static existence unlimited by time, Acyuta does not undergo any change by external influence, Aniruddha cannot be reduced.

instructions given by the author a brahmin achieves the immediate annihilation of all sins contracted by his body and obtains all possible success in worshipping, a kṣatriya will be famous and victorious and become rich in grain and money; a vaiśya will likewise be in possession of grain and money, fiery energy, sons and cattle; a śūdra will become the best of his community, and possess offspring and knowledge" (35, 73 ff.). Viṣṇu's avatāras are not forgotten either: "The man who wishes to obtain indifference to worldly objects and supranormal yoga-power must adore the Fish and Tortoise avatāras, the Boar in order to effect a prosperous condition of the king and the kingdom, the Man-lion if he wishes to destroy enemies and barbarians and desires to be invincible, the Dwarf and Jamadagni's son (Paraśurāma) if he wants to obtain a kingdom and wisdom; if he is desirous of happiness and increase of dharma Rāma, if he longs for sovereignty over the whole earth Balarāma [35]); Kṛṣṇa must be adored in order to enjoy pleasures, supremacy, happiness, and satisfaction, Kalkin in order to effect the obstruction of the flood of evil" (KS. ch. 37). The worship of Śrī is likewise often recommended: "By adoring Śrī on a definite day the man who is desirous of *śrī-* shall obtain it" (AS. 47, 58; cf. KS. ch. 38); "If one longs for welfare one must adore Śrī on Friday, using garlands of flowers and perfumes, tulasī, saffron etc. The man who devotedly (*bhaktyā*) honours Lakṣmī with rice boiled in milk, cakes, betel, cocoa-nuts etc. will obtain offspring, cattle, and complete welfare (*saubhāgya-*), after a happy life on earth he will attain final emancipation" (AS. 47, 16 ff.); "By paying worship to Śrī offspring, wealth, longevity, renown, prosperity (*śrī-*), wisdom will be in favourable condition, and the performance of yoga will succeed" (KS., ch. 38). In KS. ch. 7, after the *āyuṣkāma-* and the *prajākāma-* — and before (ch. 8) the man who is desirous of wisdom and knowledge (*vidyākāma-*) who is directed to worship Sarasvatī —, the *śrīkāma-* "the man who longs for welfare" comes up in the author's expositions. *Śrī-* is twofold: *rājaśrī-* and *brahmaśrī-*. The former consists in richness and (social and political) supremacy, the latter in the successful performance of the sacrificial rites and in complete attainment of the supranormal abilities, e.g. the power of becoming as small as an atom, besides, in homage on the part of the brahmans. After describing the material objects requisite for the worship of Śrī the author continues: "One must meditate upon Śrī as having the beaufitul appearance of a lotus (*padmaprabhā, padma-* especially denotes the red flower of the nelumbium speciosum which closes towards evening), as lotus-eyed,

[35]) He is called Balabhadrarāma.

as wearing a garland of lotus flowers, as holding a lotus in the hand etc. [36]), as wearing a bright garment and being adorned with all kinds of amulets-and-ornaments (the frequent compound *sarvābharaṇa-bhūṣita-*) [37]), heaving breasts like golden jars [38]), etc., make oblations to her whilst using lotus flowers and pronouncing the Śrīsūkta.... If one is desirous of royal prosperity one should offer a bilva-fruit [39]); by confining one's worship to the highest contemplation one will become wealthy; likewise, by offering at a definite moment. — In order to procure prosperity (*samṛddhi-*) the advice is given to plant nyagrodhas (Indian fig-trees), uḍumbaras (ficus glomerata), aśvatthas (holy fig-trees), plakṣas (waved-leaf fig-trees); after having come into contact with the wind they shall cause prosperity to the region (KS. ch. 17). Whereas famine, fall of the king and of the kingdom, illness and evil in general are enumerated among the disasters to be feared (e.g. AS. 40, 138; 66, 3), *śrī-*, "growth or abundance" (*ṛddhi-*); a well-nourished condition (*puṣṭi-*), health, longevity, advancement of the family, are, with children and happiness, the main favours, craved for. From the lists of calamities and adverse circumstances — among which unfavourable meteorological conditions and other factors detrimental to agriculture are not forgotten — we can see that, in spite of the ritual and technical character of these texts the god was readily credited with a great care for the material and spiritual well-being of his faithful adorers (cf. e.g. AS. 67, 60 f.; 82, 2 ff.; 38 ff.).

In the above account little attention has been paid to some special complexes of ceremonies mentioned in the Vaikhānasa texts. Yet we can perhaps best picture to ourselves what the character of the worship for the average votary was by a close examination of a complicated series of rituals, formulas and other forms of religious observance. We shall therefore proceed to discuss the ceremonies in connection with the main feast in honour of Viṣṇu as described in the Kāśyapa-Saṃhitā, ch. 88-90, adding such extracts and parallels borrowed from other writings of this community as may serve a useful purpose [40]).

"There are three varieties of processional festivals [41]): the festival

---

[36]) The reader might also be referred to Meyer, Trilogie, III, p. 221.

[37]) For *ābharaṇa-* see my paper in New Indian Antiquary, II (1939), p. 69 ff.

[38]) See Meyer, o.c., I, p. 170 f.

[39]) For the bilva see p. 198.

[40]) In the following account the original Sanskrit has often been abridged. A literal translation of a passage is indicated by quotation-marks.

[41]) Processional festival: *utsava-*; for this term see India Antiqua (presented to J. Ph. Vogel, Leyden 1947), p. 146 ff. Here *utsava-* denotes festivities and ceremonies in honour of Viṣṇu and other divinities including, as an essential

to be celebrated at a fixed point of time; the festival as an act of faith (or loyalty: *śraddhā*); the festival celebrated on account of ominous events and similar motives (*nimitta-*) [42]). That is to say: a festival which is regularly and with an intention celebrated each year in this or that particular month, on this or that particular day — this is the principal variety — [43]); a festival celebrated in any month when the desire to give evidence of faith has arisen [44]); a festival celebrated in order to appease (*śānti-*) inauspicious events (*aśubha-*) such as drought or famine [45]). When undertaking the festival one shall settle (the ceremonies so that) the ablution [46]) falls on the equinoctial day or on one of the following days: a solstitial point, the twelfth of the bright half of the month Bhādrapada (Aug.-Sept.) [47]) under the asterism under which

---

element, one or more processions. The *utsava*-image of the god is the idol used for taking out in processions. AS. (= Atri-Saṃhitā) 54, 2 adds: "They consider the processional festival as causing appeasement (*śānti-*) and prosperity (*puṣṭi-*) for all beings. It is an act of worship (*yajña-*) eminent above all acts of worship". For appeasement (*śānti-*) see D. J. Hoens, Çānti, Thesis Utrecht 1951. — AS. 54, 3 "because it is (the) best (*utkṛṣṭa-*) (sc. form of worship) it is called *utsava-*".

42) For this term see D. J. Kohlbrugge, Atharvaveda-pariśiṣṭa über Omina, Thesis Utrecht 1938, p. 17 ff.

43) AÇ. 54, 5 "If an *utsava-* the annual celebration of which has been instituted is omitted, this shall cause harm (*doṣa-*)".

44) AS. 54, 6 joins *bhakti-* with faith.

45) AS. 54, 7 "When bad ominous events which inspire fear and drought etc. occur..." AS. 54, 8 and 9 has an additional remark; "This *utsava-* sacred to Viṣṇu is an act of worship belonging to that category which is addressed to (the god in) visible shape. The king or a person belonging to the village community who is able to do so can, according to his ability and with due observance of the prescriptions, cause (such a festival) of the highest or middlemost class to be conducted making every possible effort. For other men who are not able (to perform these forms, which are specified further on) a festival of the lower class is established".

46) The ablution or purification (*avabhṛtha-*) of the institutor of the rite (*yajamāna-*) and of the sacrificial requisites, after the performance of the rites is meant.

47) The 12th day of the light half of a month (instead of *parva-* in the text I read *pūrva-*) is sacred to Viṣṇu (see e.g. Meyer, Trilogie, I, p. 169, n. 1). When the 12th day of the light half of Bhādrapada falls on the constellation Çravaṇa it is considered especially sacred; on that day religious observances of great efficacy are performed. Cf. also such passages as Varāhamihira, BS. 43, 38. To him who duly performs the rites mentioned in GarPur. 116 and other texts (quoted by Meyer o.c.) Viṣṇu gives wealth, corn, sons, victory, and political power (GarPur. 116, 2).

The eight festivals which nowadays are celebrated in this month are described by W. Filchner und D. Sh. Marāthe, Hindustan im Festgewand, Celle 1953, p. 105 ff. Among them is the Vāmanadvādaśī, the twelfth (of the month) sacred to the Dwarf. This however is in the first place a festival in honour of the demon Bali. The fourteenth of the same month is sacred to Ananta.

the institutor of the ceremonies, or under which the king is born" [49]). The festival lasts, in order of merit, 30, 25, 21, 15, 12, 9, 7, 5, 3 or 1 day [50]). On the day preceding the series of festival days one shall perform the ceremonial raising of the banner. Before that an offering of young shoots [51]) should be made. "(Next,) one takes, if the institutor is a brahman, a pole of bamboo, if he is a kṣatriya a nutmeg-tree, if he is a vaiśya a campaka, if (the person) who has (the erecting) performed is a śūdra: if (the ceremony takes place) for the king's intention, it may also be a nutmeg-tree, or (if not:) a betel-nut tree, or (if the ceremony is performed for the benefit) of all, just a betel-nut tree [52]), with the exception of trees which have been struck by lightning, have fallen by the wind, broken spontaneously, which are hollow, have worm-holes, or are crooked [53]); the pole must be of the same height as the temple, a quarter less, or half as high as the temple [54]), not too thick and not too slender". After having prepared and fastened a staff-support made of trees which are suitable for sacrifices one proceeds to the laborious manufacture of the banner itself: it should be made of a new piece of cotton cloth (with the exception of one which is torn or rent asunder), of definite dimensions etc. One meanwhile recites the *svastidā* mantra [55]). "In the middle (of the banner) one delineates, in

---

[49]) The enumeration of the moments in AS. 54, 12 ff. is somewhat different; it reads: *ayane viṣuve cāpi māsarkṣe viṣṇupañcake* ("the five days of Viṣṇu", i.e. dedicated to his worship) *tatrāpi śravaṇe yatnād dvādaśyāṃ mārgaśīrṣake,* adding the nakṣatra under which the village was founded.

[50]) AS. 54, 10 f.: a half-month, 13, 11, 9, 7, 5, 3, 2 days and 1 day.

[51]) In order to have good results a ritual act in honour of Viṣṇu must, according to the books of the Vaikhānasas, be preceded by an *aṅkurārpaṇa-*, an offering of shoots. We shall have to revert to this very remarkable ritual further on.

[52]) The hard and jointed bamboo stems (*veṇu-, vetasa-*), the rapid growth of which is well-known, are often mentioned among the trees used as Indra's pole. According to the Bhār. Nāṭyaśāstra 23, 164 one should select a piece of bamboo which is not worm-eaten ... after smearing it with honey and ghee and worshipping it with garlands and incense. Cf. also Mbh. 1, 63, 17. Being regarded as the flower of the waters the bamboo stem is also used in ceremonies for stimulating rain (see Meyer, o.c., III, p. 224; 256). Betel-nut trees are believed to have an aphrodisiac power (ibid. III, p. 291); nuts are 'identified' with testicles. — A detailed description of a *dhvajārohaṇa-* can now be found in K. K. Pillay, The Çucīndram Temple, Adyar 1953, p. 220 ff.

[53]) Struck etc.: not in AS. Such enumerations of trees unsuited for religious purposes are also often found in purāṇas and similar texts, see e.g. Meyer, o.c., III, p. 66 ff.; Varāham. BS. 43, 13 f. (in connection with Indra's banner).

[54]) Temple: *vimāna-*. The plan and construction of the vimāna are described in the so-called *karṣaṇa-* section of the Atri-Saṃhitā. For the term and its meaning see also S. Kramrisch, The Hindu temple, Univ. of Calcutta 1946, I, p. 131 ff.

[55]) This mantra seems to be TB. 3, 7, 11, 4 which in the VaikhSmS. 2, 2 and 4, 10 is quoted as *svastidā viśas patiḥ* and in other texts (e.g. Kauś. 14, 7) as *svastidāḥ*. It runs as follows: "Giver of well-being, lord of the people, Vṛtra-slayer, remover of enemies, controlling let the bull Indra go before us, giver of

five colours [56]), the Garuḍa.... sitting in the *svastikāsana-* or *vīrāsana-* [57]), bending its left foot and extending its right foot, or ascending to the sky, in the possession of wings, two-armed, making an añjali, its right shoulder being ascended by the serpent called Sumukha [58]). One shall (, further, attach [59])), at its right and left sides both discus and conch-shell, two chowries, and over it a sunshade. One shall then sprinkle the banner with water and attach it.... whilst pronouncing the *svastidā* mantra".

Next, "one should construct, in front of the house of God, a pavilion (*maṇḍapa-*) or a hall (*kūṭa-*), besmear (the floor with cowdung, make, by means of grain or rice, pedestals with three sacrificial altars, place the banner on the eastern pedestal, the disk on the western, Viṣvaksena [60]) on the northern, invite Garuḍa (to come) into the banner, worship (him) with twenty-seven distributions, offer him an oblation consisting of mudgabeans (phaseolus mungo)" [61]), present an oblation to the others, "invite, whilst pronouncing the words "Nandīśa of great arms, Rudra's friend, lord of the bhūtas, Nandīśa [62])" (to descend) into a kettle-drum which has been placed on the heap of corn on the right and revere him". The guru, after being honoured with a garment etc., shall "pour out food (rice) with other ingredients for the oblations into a saucepan, and then — first with a banner and a pennon, and next with the musical instruments such as the kettle-drum and the tabor, with the incense, lamps etc. and the requisites for the oblations (*bali-*), and then, being himself surrounded by a sunshade, wings, chowries, peacocks' feathers, etc. [63]), with the disk, the banner Śānta [64]), — execute a circumambulation from left to right of the temple, and the village" Then

well-being, producing security". This text forms part of a series of stanzas used against enemies (see Whitney-Lanman, Atharva-Veda Saṃhitā, p. 22), of a collection of texts securing safety ("fearlessness", cf. Kauś. 16, 8, note) and is also applied in the so-called *svastyayana-* ceremonies which are performed for well-being. ĀpÇS. 3, 12, 1 uses it in a long series of stanzas to accompany the *prāyaścittahomāḥ* of the rites of full and new moon.

56) AS. 54, 23 "White, red, greenish, black, yellow". According to the AS. the Garuḍa must wear bells, bracelets and other ornaments.

57) The AS., 54, 25 has only the *sv.* (particular modes of sitting practised by yogins).

58) A serpent (see e.g. Mbh. 1, 35, 14; 5, 104 passim) destined to be eaten by Garuḍa; see Sørensen, Index, p. 657 f.; Vogel, o.c., p. 314.

59) There is a lacuna in the text.

60) A particular aspect, or another name, of Viṣṇu-Kṛṣṇa. See F. O. Schrader, Introduction to the Pāñcarātra, Madras 1916, p. 57 etc.

61) Beans are believed to avert evil influences and to promote welfare; see also Meyer, o.c., III, p. 292. Cf. also AS. 54, 45 and 78.

62) N. is one of Çiva's attendants.

63) For the ritual use of peacock's feathers see Meyer, o.c., III, p. 313 f.

64) In the Mbh. Çānta is one of Viṣṇu's names (e.g. 13, 149, 75).

bali offerings are given to the protectors of the temple, the regents of the quarters and other divinities and the god, the lord of the world, is requested to be pleased and graciously to accept the festival. The other gods [65]) are likewise invited to attend Viṣṇu's sacrificial ceremony (*viṣṇuyāga-*). The invitation should be pronounced towards the eight quarters of the sky and one should have it proclaimed by means of musical instruments. After having dug a hole as deep as is suitable, and put down, with the respective formulas, in the centre, the east etc. a jewel (*maṇi-*), a diamond, a cat's-eye gem, a pearl, and a coral [66]), washed off the staff of the banner, one shall by means of a string of kuśa grass, to the accompaniment of music, erect the banner in such a manner that the top of its staff should be directed towards the temple [67]). At the foot of it one shall construct a pedestal with three sacrificial altars and worship the god in the banner [68]) offering him an oblation of mudga-beans. One must continue this worship as long as the banner stands erected [69]). In case of a festival organized for averting calamities one shall begin the festival proper immediately after erecting the banner, i.e. in the evening of the first day. When a banner has been raised the residents of the village concerned should not go to another village before performing the purification (*avabhṛtha-*). If they should go a serious disease would befall them [70]).

Hereafter, one shall bring together palanquins, chariots, various mechanical contrivances such as swings, lanterns, stages [71]), and various musical instruments, call near the players, dancers, and singers, the

---

65) Among the deities enumerated are the *devapatnyas* "the wives of the gods", the *mātṛgaṇāḥ* "the assemblages of the divine mothers", Pūtā (= Durgā), Pūtanā (the female demon who offered her poisoned breast to the infant Kṛṣṇa who sucked away her life), and Carakī, the evil spirit mentioned by Varāhamihira, BS. 53, 83.

66) A *maṇi-* is a gem to which special magic properties are attributed. For the ritual use of valuable stones and their wonderful character in tales see e.g. C. H. Tawney-N. M. Penzer, The ocean of story, vol. X, London 1928, p. 192; J. J. Meyer, Sexual life in ancient India, London 1930, p. 400 f.; 455.

67) "When the standard is erected troubles and diseases and the terrible spirits shall no doubt disappear" AS. 54, 75.

68) I.e. Garuḍa, see also AS. 54, 78.

69) A devout woman should cut a lump of that sacrificial food in order to have a son: AS. 54, 79. That son will be *śreṣṭha-*, *āyuṣmant-* and *balānvita-* (80).

70) A special power is inherent to them and consequently they are, to use the Latin term, 'sacer'. It would be dangerous to them to expose themselves to foreign influences. One might compare the sacrosanct person of the snātaka. Cf. C. v. Fürer-Haimendorf, The Raj Gonds of Adilabad, I, London 1948, p. 341: on First Sowing Day no one may leave the village-land before midday lest he takes in his train part of the precious virtue which causes the crops to prosper (rites aimed at attracting the powers of fertility being performed in the morning).

71) AS. 55, 2 has the time-honoured phrase *sambhārān saṃbharet,* which is, further on, also used by Kāśyapa.

devout worshippers and assistants (servants), collect the requisites: sunshades, chowries, peacock's tails, fans, banners, pennons and other 'ornaments' [72], cleanse the house of God and besmear it with cow-dung [73]), cause flowers such as the red and blue lotus, jars filled with water, and figures made of meal in the shape of elephants, horses, lions, cakravāka birds, flamingos (or similar aquatic birds), banners, pennons, plantain trees, betel-nut trees etc. to be prepared [74]), "cause the house (of the god) to be 'adorned' everywhere with incense, lamps, canopies, banners, tufts of kuśa grass, garlands, wrappings round the columns, garlands of flowers, and other 'ornaments', and place at the doors betel-nuts, full jars, and young shoots; one shall cleanse and besprinkle the roads of the village, adorn them with plantains, betel-nuts, full jars, young shoots, banners etc. and adorn also the people who dwell in the village with luck-bringing ornaments, perfumes, and garlands" [75]).

On the first day of the festival, in the evening, one shall worship Viṣvaksena and the discus with twenty-seven acts of reverence, adorn them and cause them to ascend a vehicle, "and, placing in front of them

---

72) The word used is *alaṃkāra-* for the sense of which see New Indian Antiquary I (Thomas Festschrift), p. 97 ff. For the use of the objects mentioned see e.g. Meyer, Trilogie, passim.

73) See Meyer, o.c., III, p. 311.

74) Instead of *paiṣṭikādi* (p. 150, l. 1) I read *paiṣṭikāni*. — Lotus flowers which are symbolic of, or rather represent, water are extremely frequent in rites and ceremonials for the benefit of fertility and the vegetation in general. Many relevant particulars were collected and discussed by F. D. K. Bosch, De gouden kiem, Inleiding in de Indische symboliek, Amsterdam-Brussels 1948 (see e.g. p. 133 ff.), who also paid attention to the jars filled with water, which are the vessels of abundance (p. 121 ff., etc.). See, inter alia, also A. K. Coomaraswamy, Yakṣas, passim; H. Zimmer, Myths and symbols in Indian art and civilization, New York[2], 1947. For figures made of meal see Meyer, o.c., III, p. 310. Meal itself is held to be a means of averting evil. Elephants are considered to be 'symbols' of fertility, being also associated with Çrī-Lakṣmī, cf. e.g. Zimmer, o.c., p. 92 f.; 109 etc.; the horse is not only connected with the sun, but also with corn and vegetation in general (see Meyer, o.c., III, p. 314); for the lion see Meyer, o.c., II, p. 136 and Bosch, o.c., p. 151 f. Aquatic birds (the cakravāka is the anas casarca): see e.g. Meyer, o.c., III, p. 5 f. The *haṃsa-* (this word is in the text) is also considered a manifestation (*prādurbhāva-*) of Viṣṇu: ViṣṇudhPur. 3, 118, 7; 120, 11; MatsPur. 247, 19 etc. ViṣṇudhPur. 3, 151, 3 f. it is identified with Kṛṣṇa, Dharma's son. The plantain tree is connected with vegetable life, "eine Art Schutzgottheit oder Schutz- und Wachstumszauber der Bäume" (Meyer, o.c., I, p. 105; cf. III, p. 289). It has already been observed that the betel is held to be an aphrodisiac.

75) For the ritual use and apotropaeic function of lamps see Meyer, o.c., III, p. 307 f. — For garlands see ch. II, p. 224 and n. 61. For flowers in general: Whitehead, Village gods, p. 168. — In the AS., 55, 15, the erection of *toraṇa's* ("arched doorways, festooned decorations over doorways") is recommended in addition.

a spade (or a similar instrument for digging) fitted with a sunshade, wings, chowries, etc., adorned with garments and garlands, a boiler, a pierced jar, an earthenware vessel, banners, pennons, etc., and to the accompaniment of instrumental music go to fetch the clay required for the rite. Going towards the east of the village or the temple leads to general prosperity (*sarvasamṛddhi-*), towards the south-east to loss of the corn, towards the south to loss of living beings, towards the south-west to a severe disease, towards the west to drought, towards the north to prosperity with regard to sons (abundance of sons), towards the north-east to universal happiness [76]). Next, one shall go towards a point to the north-east or north of the said place and, on a clear and attractive spot, besmear a space 'as large as a cow's hide' [77]), mark out clay as broad as 4 fingers, and model (the figure of) the goddess Earth, having the face above and the head directed towards the north-east, 8½ tālas in size, worship it with the mūrtimantras [78]), order the pronouncement of an auspicious day, ask the permission (of the goddess) and, facing the north or the east and speaking (the formula) "I dig you" [79]), take earth (clay) on (from) her forehead, arms, breast or breasts (and put it) into a vessel made of gold, silver, copper, brass or clay, enter the temple so that one's right side is turned towards it, and deposit (the clay on a spot) on the north or east side (of the building) [80]). (Then) on the 9th, 7th, 5th, 3rd day before the day of the descent into the water one shall, at night, at a lucky hour, in accordance with the ritual rule which has already been prescribed offer the shoots.

---

76) "Going towards the n., n.-e., e. leads to happiness, towards the other directions to sorrow", AS. 55, 26 f. For similar passages see e.g. Varāh. BS. 59, 13; BhaviṣyatPur. 1, 131, 35 ff.; cf. also ÇB. 14, 2, 2, 28 and Meyer, o.c., III, p. 91. Iśāna = Çiva who presides over the north-eastern region is often concerned with various aspects of fecundation (cf. also Meyer, o.c., III, p. 293); according to the brāhmaṇas the north-east is the direction of the gate of heaven (ÇB. 6, 6, 2, 4); the Viṣṇu-strides are made in this direction (id. 6, 7, 2, 12), by means of which Prajāpati created offspring. The east, in the brāhmaṇas, the region of the gods, is Indra's region.

77) Cf. ÇB. 1, 2, 5, 2; Mbh. 13, 62, 19. AS. 55, 28 *daśatālakrameṇa* (a *tāla-* is a span).

78) *Mūrtimantrāḥ* are special, or 'individual' formulas serving as a means of causing a divinity to appear in actual bodily presence. Cf. e.g. AS. 55, 43; KāśyapaS. p. 151, 4; 152, 11.

79) AS. 55, 31 has the mantra *medinī devī* used, i.e. the mantra mentioned above (p. 240). It prescribes taking the clay from head, arms, breasts, middle and abdomen, declaring the annihilation of all guilt (or disadvantages: *doṣa-*), gold, advancement of the family, universal prosperity to be the respective results.

80) AS. 55, 35 has a circumambulation of the village and inserts a recitation of the *svastisūkta-* (which is quoted by Caland, Vaikhānasasmārtasūtram, transl., Calcutta 1929, p. 40, n. 21).

Now [81]), the institutor of the ceremonies shall, at dusk, honour the guru and bid him perform the special worship, i.e. the festival, of the Lord of the gods. After having given a bath to the Lord of the gods and presented him with an abundant burnt oblation [82]), one shall also give offerings to the two goddesses [83]), to the muni [84]), to Brahmā and Īśāna, to Garuḍa, the discus, and Viṣvaksena, and, if one be able (to do so), to the divinities who are in attendance". An oblation of clarified butter is, in the fire-place, presented to Viṣṇu, and a boiled oblation (*caru-*) mixed with clarified butter to the gods presiding over the assembly; a bali-offering, the ingredients of which are rice, beans, two sorts of pulse [85]), sesame, symplocos racemosa, cakes, and parched grain [86]) and, besides, water, flowers, perfumes, incense, lamps, and unhusked barley-corns, is conducted in honour of the discus, Śānta and the Garuḍa. Offerings are made to the protectors of the doors, the gods belonging to the temple and, in the village, to the deities of the eight quarters of the sky, the bhūtas, nāgas, rākṣasas, and the hosts of Vairocana [87]) etc. Thereupon, one shall adorn the *utsava*-image, or in default of it the *kautuka*-image [88]), with white, yellow, and black garments made of silk etc., with a variety of rings, bracelets, and other golden ornaments, garlands of flowers etc., lift the god whilst pronouncing the formula "I know" [89]), conduct him whilst reciting the śakunasūkta[90]), make him ascend the vehicle and adorn him with a crown of rays [91]). According to some authorities one should, together with the

81) "After having, in this way, gone for clay, one shall, at night, begin the festival", AS. 55, 38.

82) "With double portions and additional food to be eaten with the chief dish", AS. 55, 40.

83) Çrī and Mahī, see above.

84) Vikhanas. Compare e.g. also Caland, Vaikh.SmS., p. 10, n. 8.

85) *niṣpāva-* (this appears to be a general name for several kinds of pulse of the dolichos variety) and *kulattha-* (dolichos uniflorus). For their ritual use see Meyer, o.c., III, p. 301 s.v. Hülsenfrüchte.

86) For sesame see Meyer, o.c., III, p. 319 f.; sympl. rac.: *tilva-* or *tilvaka-*, see e.g. ÇB. 13, 8, 1, 16; for the ritual use of grain: Meyer, o.c., III, p. 306.

87) Cf. VaikhSmS. 1, 3 and 4. Vairocana = Bali, whom Viṣṇu made to dwell in the nether world. Cf. AS. 55, 51 f. *grāmaṃ gatvā bahir vīthyāṃ tatra sandhau baliṃ dadet | dhvajārohaṇamārgeṇa kramāt sandhau baliṃ dadet || pradakṣiṇaṃ baliṃ dattvā praviśed ālayaṃ punaḥ | bhūtapīṭham anuprāpya tatra śeṣaṃ baliṃ kṣipet ||*.

88) The *utsava-* image is used for taking out (n. 41), the *kautuka-* for all worship (*arcana-*).

89) "I know this mighty Puruṣa, of the colour of the sun, beyond the reach of darkness. Only by knowing Him does one pass over death..." Also VS. 31, 18; TĀ. 3, 12, 7; 13, 1; ÇvetUp. 3, 8.

90) ṚV. 10, 165, against birds of ill omen, and beginning: *devāḥ kapotaḥ*. See my Ṛgvidhāna, p. 115.

91) *prabhāmaṇḍala-* "a halo of light or glory", cf. e.g. Kālid. Ragh. 5, 51; Varāh. BS. 58, 48.

god, make the two goddesses ascend also. Then circumambulations of the temple and the village are performed, the god being preceded by banners and pennons, mechanical stages, musical instruments, singers, dancers, incense and lamps in due order, and surrounded by chowries etc. and golden paraphernalia of manifold appearance [92]). After having entered the temple [93]) one shall place (the image of) the god in the 'audience hall' or 'assembly room' and honour him like a king with dance, songs, worship and bathe him, and present him with abundant burnt offerings. "Until and except the day of the purificatory bath (*avabhṛtha-*) one shall regularly, at dusk and in the morning, execute the procession (*utsava-*). One shall feed all those who have come with the view of attending it".

The subsequent paragraph in the KS. deals with the *mṛgayotsava-*, a ceremony characterized by adorning the god with a girdle, a knife and other objects, making him ascend a vehicle, collecting the requisites for hunting, and surrounding, on the day preceding the descent into the bathing-place, forests inhabited [94]) by goats, monkeys, tigers etc., by adorning the goddess Śrī, making her mount a litter and conciliating the god who is accompanied by Śrī and Bhūmi.

"In the night previous to the day of the descent into the bathing-place, at the end of the procession, one shall worship the Lord of the gods, offer a burnt oblation to him and have the discus execute a circumambulation of the village or the temple. Next, one shall bath the discus in water of the sacred bathing-place, enter the temple, place (the discus) at the right side of the Glorious One, have the benedictions pronounced, fasten the cord round the (god's) wrist [95]), cause the Lord of the gods to lie down on the couch as before, and pass the remainder of the night with dancing and singing. At dawn, one shall bathe, arouse

---

[92]) AS. 55, 69 has the brahmans and other people, each near his own house, delighted and devotedly go to salute the procession with lamps, shoots, pitchers with water etc.

[93]) Here AS. 55, 73 states that prosperity (*śrī-*), health (*ārogya-*), children, grain, money and any welfare shall fall to those looking at the god. For the 'assembly room' (*āsthānamaṇḍapa-* see P. K. Acharya, An encyclopaedia of Hindu architecture VII, p. 67.

[94]) This is a guess; the text is not clear to me. For religious hunting see Meyer, o.c., III, p. 123, and Pillay, o.c., p. 217: "Supposed to go out hunting wild beasts, the god is carried on vāhana (vehicle) in procession. As suggestive of the hunt, some weapons are placed by the side of the image in the vāhana; morever, the procession itself moves very briskly". A *mṛgayotsava-* is one of the seven ceremonies of a *mahotsava-*.

[95]) For the *pratisarābandhana-* (the *pratisara-* is a cord destined to be worn round the wrist) see VaikhSmS. 2, 2 and esp. 4, 10. See also Acta Orientalia 15, p. 311 ff.

the god, and worship him with the thirteen acts of attendance"[96]).

In the morning the *ācārya-* shall, after some preparatory acts "put down, in the court[97]) of the temple which is previously besmeared with cow-dung, a wooden mortar and a pestle, worship, in those objects, Brahmā and Īśāna, take a turmeric (curcuma longa)[98]), besprinkle it, invoke Lakṣmī (to come) into it, and cast the turmeric into the mortar whilst pronouncing the formula "born unto prosperity"[99]). Then he shall pulverize it whilst reciting the mantras "hence the gods etc."[100]), fill with the powder of it 12, 8, 4, 2 jars or one jar, put them (it) down in front (of himself), conciliate Sinīvālī[101]) therein and give the Lord of the gods a bath with that powder. The misfortune of the man who places the powder of that (turmeric) on his head, disappears.

Thereupon, at noon, one shall cause the Lord of the gods and the disc to execute a circumambulation of the village approaching the sea, a river, a pool at a distance not less than a yojana[102]). Or, (one shall do as follows:) the water which is in the proximity of the temple of Viṣṇu is like the water of the Ganges in consequence of (its getting mixed with) the water used for washing his (the God's) feet. Therefore one shall place the Lord of the gods and the disc in front of him there, or at the bank (of the sea, river etc.)[103]), fill first five jars with water, place them in the centre, east, south, west and north, pour out into them clay, kuśa, flowers, perfumes and unhusked barleycorns (*akṣata*) respectively[104]), worship the Lord of the gods, besprinkle him with the

---

96) For the *upacārāḥ* (or ways of service), which are usually stated to be 16, although the number is subject to fluctuation, see Kane, Hist. of Dharmaśāstra II, p. 729 f.

97) The printed text has *-aṅkaṇe*.

98) For the turmeric see Meyer, o.c., I, p. 22 ff.; 49; Crooke, Popular religions² II, p. 28 f. It is believed to have a fecundating power; hence also the ceremony of rubbing it on the bride and bridegroom (Hindī *haldī, hald-hāt*).

99) ṚV. 9, 94, 4.

100) Sc. (*avantu naḥ*) "must aid us" (ṚV. 1, 22, 16).

101) For the remarkable occurrence of this female divinity see ch. II, s. II. Cf. AS. 56, 16 *kalaśe dharām* (the earth) *sinīvālīm arcayed aṣṭavigrahaiḥ*. — For pots etc. as divine 'symbols': Whitehead, o.c., p. 103 ff.

102) Or *na* "without" seems to be superfluous (cf. the variant *krośād arvāg gacchet*). AS. 56, 21 it reads: *evaṃ pradakṣiṇaṃ kṛtvā tīrthasnānāya saṃvrajet* || *sindhum* etc. The water of a stream (*sindhu-*) is best, that of a pure or holy river (*puṇyanadī*), of a lake (*abdhi-*), river (*nada-*), large sheet of water (*saras*), waterfall, pool, pleasant pure water can successively do duty in default of water of a higher category. Sea-water is only pure on the days of the changes of the moon (AS. 56, 22 f.).

103) For the position of *vā* between the two words connected Caland, Vaikhānasasmārtasūtram, p. XIII.

104) AS. 56, 38 has: *ratnodair akṣatodaiś ca kuśodaiś ca yavodakaiḥ* | *candanodaiś ca sampūrṇān kalaśān saṃpragṛhya tān*. St. 30 the formule *iṣe tva ūrje* etc. for food thee, for strength thee".

water of the respective jars with the mantras recited in bathing and give, with the remainders of it, a bath to the discus. One then submerges the Lord of the gods and the discus in the water. Or the discus alone. Having bathed in the sacred water (*tīrthajale*) they are all freed from every sin. Next, one shall make the god ascend the vehicle as before and enter the temple [105]).

The *avabhṛtha-* must be performed by day. By night, the detrimental effect (sin, offence: *doṣa-*) would be great in consequence of the impurity of the water" [106]). "At the end of the processional festival (*utsava-*) one shall have a bath in the manner as explained in the chapter on bathing, offer, according to one's ability, a great burnt offering (*havis*) and present a perfume of the mouth consisting of cardamom, pimenta acris, etc. [107]). The institutor (*yajamāna-*) shall then give to the guru a dakṣiṇā consisting of gold, cattle, land, etc. and, according to his ability a dakṣiṇā to all the assistants etc." [108]).

After having described the procedure of invoking Viṣṇu's indulgence for mistakes and omissions, the KS. goes on to deal with the ceremonious striking of the banner: One shall worship the god in the banner, offer a havis, present bali-offerings in the temple, the village, at its 'junctions' [109]), in an empty building (temple), at a sacred tree (*caityavṛkṣe*), a pond, a court-place, an abode for cattle, in the dwellings of other deities, have a bath, enter the temple, approach the banner (and pronounce the words): "Those who have come together at this *utsava-* shall, all of them, go as they came. The festival has now concluded;

---

105) Like other parts of these ceremonials the bathing rites are described at greater length in AS. which inserts, inter alia, instructions for meditation (56, 33 ff.).

106) Here the author inserts special rules for executing the ceremonies when they last one day.

107) *elā* and *takkola-*.

108) ... *dattvā* ... *ca dadyāt,* the 'superfluous' *ca* noticed by Caland, o.c. p. 236. — AS. 56, 43 f. The officiants are specified: *yajamāno* ... | *ācāryādyarcakebhyaś ca paricartṛbhya eva ca* || *sarvebhyaḥ karmakartṛbhyo yathārhaṃ dakṣiṇāṃ dadet.* — Here AS. 56, 46 ff. inserts the following instructions: If in a village, by contravention of the rules laid down by the authorities, a processional festival is at the same time conducted in honour of another divinity, both festivals shall be resultless and inauspicious. When the festival for the god has begun a festival act due to men must, in the same village, not be undertaken; in the other case one shall perish. When in a village a festival is undertaken in honour of other deities who are fierce (inauspicious: *krūra-,* opposite to *saumya-*), then one shall cause another festival to be performed in honour of Hari of auspicious manifestation. When a festival is addressed to the god Hari universal prosperity is furthered in a felicitous way.

109) AS. 56, 59 *catuskoṇatrikoṇeṣu dvikoṇeṣu ca sandhiṣu* ... 61 *smaśāne 'pi mahāpathe.* For these terms see B. B. Dutt, Town planning in ancient India, Calcutta-Simla 1925, passim.

this banner is struck". Whilst speaking one shall bow, allow the god in the banner to go and strike the banner.

"By this processional festival", the author concludes, "the Lord of the gods will be much pleased. By it the cows, the brahmans and the other three classes of society will be prosperous, the crops of corn will thrive. It is an auspicious event which causes success in every respect and destroys all inauspicious influences. It is an appeasing ceremony (*śānti-*) for the village etc., and a means of obtaining all (kinds of) desires. And by it all the gods will be pleased. The man who out of devotion performs the festival of Viṣṇu will therefore make himself delivered from all sins, clandestine as well as open, whether they are committed in former existences or in this existence, and he will obtain all desires". He who always duly performs the god's worship will go to Viṣṇu's highest abode.

Although these elaborated ceremonies are intended for obtaining various blessings, for any prosperity, fertility and a prosperous state of fields and cattle, the possession of a sufficient supply of food is emphasized: AS. 54, 2 "the *utsava-* brings about *śānti-*, i.e. destruction of evil influences, and *puṣṭi-* i.e. a well-nourished condition"; 55, 1 it gives *śānti-*, rain, health and *puṣṭi-*. In this connection a special interest attaches to the banner erected during the festivities. This banner sacred to Viṣṇu has so much in common with Indra's banner, that is to say with the ceremonies expressive of the desire to rouse up and intensify Indra's fertilizing and conquering activities that a few words may be said here with regard to that important aspect of the Hinduistic worship of the latter divinity. The relevant (epic, purāṇic, and other) texts having preserved many important features, we can confine ourselves to a concise review of the contents of chapter 43 of Varāhamihira's Bṛhatsaṃhitā, adding some elucidative annotations borrowed from other descriptions [110]. The gods, unable to resist the children of darkness, approached Brahmā for assistance. He advised them to obtain from Viṣṇu the ensign (*ketu-*) at the very sight of which the demons would fall back. After being duly praised, Viṣṇu, now called Nārāyaṇa, gave them the standard (*dhvaja-*) produced from his lustre or energy (*tejas*), which was carried on an eight-wheeled fulgent chariot beaming as if it

---

[110]) The text was translated in full by H. Kern, in the J.R.A.S., NS. IV-VII, 1870-75, reprinted in H. Kern, Verspreide Geschriften, I and II, The Hague 1913; I, p. 169 ff. (see esp. I, p. 290 ff.). The ceremony under discussion was recently touched upon by S. Kramrisch, The banner of Indra, in Art and Thought, issued in honour of Dr. A. K. Coomaraswamy, London 1947, p. 197 ff.

were the sun [111]). By raising this *dhvaja-* which was adorned with many tinkling objects, garlands, sunshades, bells and trinkets [112]), Indra annihilated in battle the host of the enemy. He then presented the bamboo flagstaff (*yaṣṭi-*) to Vasu the sky-traveller (Uparicara), lord of Cedi, who treated the gift with due respect [113]). Satisfied by that festive demonstration (*maha-*) Indra declared that those kings who would act like Vasu should be rich and obeyed, their subjects being contented, free from danger and illness and well supplied with food. The banner, it is added, would also be able to forebode by tokens what good or evil consequences awaited mankind. In the days of yore monarchs desirous of victory and increase of power honoured that standard by Indra's command. After having described the ceremonial hewing of the stem selected to become a *dhvaja-* the authors state that it should be carried, in a festive way, to the accompaniment of horns and other instruments, into the town. The staff (*yaṣṭi-*) is covered with new cloth and enveloped in garlands, perfumes, and incense. Various precepts are given in connection with the ceremonious erection; we only draw attention to the sacrifice to be celebrated by the court priest, clad in white and pronouncing formulas addressed to Indra and Viṣṇu (Varāh. BS. 43, 30) [114]). The magically powerful ornaments (*bhūṣaṇāni* or *ābharaṇāni*), with which the gods once decorated the divine banner (*suraketu-*) or prototype are enumerated. They are consecrated to the respective divinities by whom they were produced (ibid. 49). Any 'historical', i.e. reproduced Indra banner must be equipped with them (cf. st. 41; 51). While a specialist acquainted with the authoritative texts is engaged with this act the king addresses the flagstaff with auspicious formulas containing, inter alia, the epithets "source of vigour" (*ūrjaskara-*), "unborn, imperishable, eternal, unchangeable one"; it is also called *viṣṇur varāhaḥ* [115]) *puruṣaḥ purāṇaḥ* (54) "Viṣṇu, the wild boar, the primeval soul". Thereupon the king invokes Agni and Indra, the killer of Vṛtra, and prays that his warriors may be victorious. — Other instructions are subjoined. Indra's ensign

---

111) "The general import of the myth appears to be that the sun, the source of light (Viṣṇu), bestows on... Indra his own *ketu-* (i.e. ensign and first gleam of day), before which the spirits of darkness must needs vanish" (Kern's note on the passage). Kramrisch, p. 198, likewise remarks: "The standard is part of Viṣṇu's luminosity and power".

112) As is well known such objects essentially add to the standard's efficacy. Cf. also Kramrisch, p. 198 f.

113) See Mahābhārata, 1, ch. 63.

114) In a similar way ViṣṇudhPur. 2, 155, 21.

115) Mark the curious occurrence of the varāha (avatāra). Kern, V.G., p. 294 translated: "thou (art) the all-fertilizing Viṣṇu".

(*lakṣma*) [116]) should be adorned with a parasol, flags (or: a, the flag: *dhvaja-*), mirrors, fruits, crescents, garlands etc. The raising of the standard must be accompanied by the shouts of the crowd, festive cries, benedictions, salutations, and music. Its point should be directed towards the residence of the enemy as if threatening death to him. Damages happening to the arrangement presage evil. After four days the king must, "for the weal of his army", with all reverence cause the standard to be removed.

There can be no doubt that this "banner" (*dhvaja-*) or "ensign" (*lakṣma*) and its accessories constituted an object of the highest religious importance. All details of the descriptions, to which Meyer devoted an elaborate treatise [117]), point to that. The standard is a divine being, originating in Viṣṇu's tejas; it is Indra himself. "Indra is worshipped in the shape of the standard (*yaṣṭi-*) which Vasu received" (Mbh. 1, 63, 21 ff.). The periodical erection and worship of the Indradhvaja, with which once, in the beginning, the gods had conquered the enemies, leads to welfare, happiness and victory. It is therefore no matter of great surprise that it should also play a very important part in the history of the Indian drama and in theatrical performances. The first drama was, according to Bhār. NS. 1, 53, staged on the occasion of the banner festival (*dhvajamahaḥ śrīmān*) of Indra. Pleased with the performance Indra gave his auspicious banner which, in historical times, is always erected when a stage-play is produced. With this very banner Indra, in honour of whose victory over the demons the first festival was celebrated, destroyed the asuras and malevolent spirits (*vighna-*) who tried to prevent the success of the play which, relating to their being killed, was to perpetuate, by way of imitation, his victory. Hence the banner was called *jarjara-*: "decayed", but folk-etymologically interpreted as an active adjective. The *jarjara-* since secures the play's success which consists in welfare for the people and victoriousness for the king. The Nāṭyaśāstra elsewhere enjoins *pūjā* ("worship, adoration") to be offered to the *jarjara-* for attaining good success at the performance, for bringing victory and prosperity (*abhyudaya-*) to the king, and welfare to cows and brahmans (3, 11 ff.; 81) [118]).

---

116) This also conveys such ideas as "sign, token, characteristic".

117) Meyer, Trilogie, III. See also the Samarāṅgaṇasūtradhāra a. 17. Some of the relevant facts are also mentioned by Miss Kramrisch, o.c.

118) See e.g. S. Konow, Das indische Drama, Berlin-Leipsic 1920, p. 37; J. Gonda, Zur Frage nach dem Ursprung und Wesen des indischen Dramas, Leyden 1943 (= Acta Orientalia, 19, p. 331 ff.), p. 442 ff.; cf. also S. N. Dasgupta, A history of Sanskrit Literature, I, Calcutta 1947, p. 49 f. The chapters 1-27 of Bharata's Nāṭyaśāstra were recently translated by Manomohan Ghosh: The Nāṭyaśāstra, Calcutta 1950; see p. 9 ff.

Now, as might be expected, this banner, though being Indra's, is also the concern of other gods: Brahmā, Hara, Viṣṇu-Janārdana, Kumāra and the Pannagas are held to protect its parts (Bhār. NS. 3, 78 f.); when Indra gave his banner, other divinities rewarded the first performers of the play with other presents [119]). Among them Viṣṇu is often mentioned: ViDhPur. 2, 157, 6: the powerful far-stepping Viṣṇu must, beside Brahmā and Śiva enhance Indra's, i.e. the banner's fiery energy; KālikāPur. 90, 22 insists on adoring Viṣṇu side by side with Indra (st. 22, cf. 57); BhavPur. 2, 2, 8, 92 has an expiation in connection with Indra's banner performed with the Viṣṇu mantras ṚV. 1, 22, 20 etc. *tad viṣṇoḥ paramaṁ padam* and with a hundred lotus-flowers; in addition to this ten thousand pippalas (fuel-sticks (?) of the sacred fig-tree) should be sacrificed into the fire in honour of Viṣṇu. According to the tradition followed by Varāhamihira [120]) and other descriptions the banner constitutes a presentation of Viṣṇu. Now, there can be no doubt that the worship of an erected tree for the sake of strengthening powers for good was older than its being connected with Indra. The cult of trees and standards, the worship of banners the staff of which is made of trees [121]), is very widespread. The tree, which is a power-bearer, was often considered to be, or to house, a divinity, to represent vegetation, vitality, life itself [122]). It is believed to sustain the power of life of the community. Reviving periodically it is considered to be a regenerative principle and revered for the sake of much desired restoration of life. Hence we find all over the world May-poles, Eastern branches, adorned with fruits, ribbons and other potent ornaments, or trunks, stems, poles of similar purport and sacredness[123]). Their cult could, in the course of time and even in the same community, be associated with the worship of various deities and with a diversity of magico-religious conceptions. It may, further,

---

[119]) For the interesting enumeration see Bharata NS. 1, 58 ff. (Ghosh, p. 9 f.).

[120]) For the sake of brevity I refer to Meyer, o.c., III, p. 17.

[121]) As soon as the opportunity presents itself I propose to make some remarks on Indian flags and banners in a special paper.

[122]) The reader might consult W. Mannhardt, Wald- und Feldkulte², Berlin 1904-05, esp. I, p. 312; H. Bergema, De boom des levens in Schrift en historie, Thesis Vrije Univ. Amsterdam 1938 (with abundant bibliographical references); M. Eliade, Traité d'histoire des religions, I, Paris 1949, ch. VIII (with a bibliography), and part of the materials collected by Sir James Frazer, The Golden Bough³, 1911-18.

[123]) Remember, to mention only this, the εἰρεσιώνη of the ancient Greeks: a branch of laurel or olive wound round with wool and hung with fruits, cakes, honey, wine etc.; it was, at the Πυανόψια (originally a harvest festival), dedicated to Apollo, but also borne about at the Θαργήλια, a festival for the ripening corn, which was sacred to Helios and the Hours. See e.g. M. P. Nilsson, Gesch. d. griech. Rel., Müchen 1941, p. 112 ff.

be taken for granted that both the Indo-European and the autochthonous ancestors of the Indians were familiar with the idea of sacred trees and branches or with the worship of a tree which has been cut down or re-erected [124]). It does, therefore, not seem to be a hazardous assumption that the Indians associated this cult with the worship of the god of power in nature, the possessor par excellence of that vital energy to which they gave the name ojas, that is: Indra. Or, if it would be more correct to express ourselves otherwise: that they called the divine power believed to be present in the tree and to display his power in the force of nature, Indra. We also see quite clearly that other divinities concerned with prosperity and influences for good have a share in this cult: the ornaments of Indra's banner were given by Śiva, Kubera, Varuṇa, the Sun, the Moon, and other powerful beings; Nandā and Upanandā "Invigoration, Delight, Felicity" [125]), Jayā and Vijayā "Victory", Vasundharā "tne Earth" were represented by minor flagstaffs (see e.g. Varāh. BS. 43, 39 f.), etc. That Viṣṇu's share could be so important that he was considered the originator of this 'tree-cult', and that the banner festival as celebrated by the Vaikhānasas could be his, can in my opinion only be accounted for by realizing his old and intensive relations with prosperity in general and fertility in particular. In the mythical account of the origin of the Indra banner Viṣṇu is, again, the divine power in the background who assists Indra in conquering the demons by introducing the standard festival. And although this cult remained, in general, associated with the ancient representative of the vital energy in nature, Viṣṇu even here succeeded in incidentally taking over his function, or playing his part

The next point to be considered is the *aṅkurārpaṇa-* mention of which is made by the Atri- and Kāśyapa-Saṃhitās in describing the great festival and other rites and ceremonies. In general, a rite addressed to Viṣṇu must be preceded by an offering of shoots [126]). The highly

---

[124]) See, e.g., O. Schrader-A. Nehring, Reallexikon der indogermanischen Altertumskunde, II², Berlin-Leipsic 1929, p. 182 ff.; 518; A. Bertholet und E. Lehmann, Lehrbuch der Religionsgeschichte (begründet von Chantepie de la Saussaye), Tübingen 1925, Register s.v. (II, p. 644 f.); Bergema, o.c., passim; Meyer, o.c., passim, and esp. III, p. 196 f.; Crooke, Pop. rel. II, p. 94 ff.; the same, in Hastings' Encycl. of Rel. and Ethics, IX, 504 f.; Enthoven, Folklore of Bombay, p. 117 ff.

[125]) See Acta Orientalia, 21, p. 81 ff. — Cf. also VaikhSmS. 3, 19 in fine.

[126]) Without an *aṅkurārpaṇa-* a ritual act is resultless, by a mere offering of aṅkuras without other ceremonies the god is much pleased. *Aṅkura-* or germinating seeds of the nine varieties of pulses (*navadhānya-*) in a vessel is believed to represent, or to be beneficial to, growth and prosperity. The custom is also associated with marriages.

remarkable ritual related to it is dealt with in ch. 58 of the Kāś. and ch. 26 of the Atri-Saṃhitā. It resolves itself into this: The requisites are boilers, pierced jars, and shallow cups or platters [127]) of definite size and number, and rice, beans, barley, wheat or other cereals or seeds of leguminous plants which have to be dried in the heat of the sun. After having "thrown, in the morning, corn into nine vessels in water" the yajamāna and his guru must, in the evening, in the proximity of the temple, erect in the midst of a 'row' (*paṅkti-*) of rice of definite dimensions a pedestal and altars for Brahmā, and also a pedestal for Śeṣa (the serpent which is represented as forming the couch and canopy of Viṣṇu whilst sleeping during the intervals of creation), Vakratuṇḍa ("having an (elephant's) curved trunk", i.e. Gaṇeśa who may, in various connections, be regarded as a divinity of fertility), the Lord of the *paṅkti-*, Soma (the king of plants), Jayā and the other apsarās [128]). These divinities [129]) are worshipped. (The vessels) [130]) are filled with clay, cow-dung, or sandy earth, and placed, with the accompaniment of the recitation of the Viṣṇugāyatrī, in a special manner. Then the goddess Earth (Medinī) is worshipped in the boilers, Rākā [131]) in the leaky jars, and Sinīvālī [132]) in the platters. The next act is a benediction for an auspicious day [133]). Panic seed [134]), beans, barley, dolichos, wheat, chick-peas, sesame [135]), symplocos racemosa, lentils, and

---

127) For the ritual use of leaky or perforated pots see e.g. ÇB. 5, 5, 4, 27; 12, 7, 2, 13: 8, 1, 8. Allowing liquid to flow slowly through holes or fissures, splashing or squirting water, pouring out the contents of vessels, pouring out water over the foot of a tree, and similar acts are essential features of rain-making ceremonies; see e.g. H. Webster, Magic, Stanford Cal. 1948, p. 45; 49 ff.; 310 ff. (Compare also E. O. James, in Hastings' Encycl. of Rel. and Eth. X, p. 561 ff.).

128) It is remarkable that *Jayā* "Victory" should have entered the group of female genii concerned with vegetation and fertility going by the collective name of Apsarās. Her name is not among those mentioned by G. Borsani, Contributo allo studio sulla concezione e sullo sviluppo storico dell' apsaras, Milan 1938 (see esp. p. 36 ff.). Elsewhere (e.g. Mbh. 4, 6, 16) Jayā is identified with Durgā.

129) The AS. 26, 19 mentions also the Garuḍa and the discus.

130) The texts are not very explicit on this point.

131) Rākā is an ancient deity of fertility to whom in MānGS. 2, 10, 7 oblations are offered at the preparations of the implements for ploughing, at sowing, reaping, at the offering to the furrow and to the threshing-floor; see also Meyer, o.c., III, p. 158.

132) This "Zeugungsgenie", requested to give sons or offspring is often connected with Rākā.

133) Here the ASaṃh. 26, 25 is shorter, leaving out R. and S.: *cintayen medinīdevīṃ tāṃ sarveṣu samarcayet*...

134) *kaṅku-* = *kaṅgu-* and *priyaṅgu-*, varieties of the panicum italicum, used as food by the poor.

135) The sesame is often used in rites of this description, cf. also Meyer, o.c., III, p. 319 f.

mustard[136]), or just beans if the other seeds are not available, are laid in water until the young sprouts are visible. Next, after having put food-grain (*dhānyāni*) in a vessel of brass and worshipped, in it (i.e. the grain), Soma, touching them whilst pronouncing the mantra *somaṃ rājānam*[137]), having caused music to be made, taken these cereals again whilst muttering the Viṣṇusūkta[138]) and the formula *somaṃ rājānam*, one offers the sprouts[139]). Whilst muttering the mantra addressed to Varuṇa[140]) one finally sprinkles them with water, covers the vessels with pieces of clay and plates (or: plates of clay?) and has them preserved in a hidden place[141]).

There can, in my opinion, be no doubt that this ritual was intended to promote a prosperous growth of the seedlings of all sorts of cereals and leguminous plants and to forward the processes connected with it. The obligatory offering of these sprouts to the god before other ritual acts is a strong argument in favour of the thesis that the Vaikhānasas who relied on Viṣṇu as their highest deity felt themselves especially dependent upon him with regard to the growth of their crops, the fertility of the soil, and a sufficient supply of food. It may be suggested that the main purpose of the *aṅkurārpaṇa-* was to support the

---

136) Mustard was believed to ward off evil. See e.g. also H. Marzell, in Hdwtb. de. Abergl. VII, 1649.

137) Vaikh. Saṃh. 1, 27 this pratīka is stated to represent TS. 1, 7, 10 g. "Soma, the king, Varuṇa, Agni, we invoke, the Ādityas, Viṣṇu, Sūrya, and Bṛhaspati the brahman", which, apart from *Varuṇam* instead of *avase*, is ṚV. 10, 141, 3.

138) See above, p. 236.

139) Instead of the last lines AS. 26, 26 f. has: *uddhṛtya toyamagnāni kṣīraiḥ prakṣālya tāni vai | bījāni pūrayitvā tu somaṃ tatra samarcayet || tatkāle tūryaghoṣaṃ ca ghoṣayitvā samāhitaḥ*. It, moreover, enjoins the guru or the institutor of the rite to put the young shoots in the ground, having put on a new garment (see WZKM. 48, p. 275 ff.). It would appear to me that the offering as well as the putting in the ground should have been mentioned in a complete description of all the relevant acts.

140) As is well known, Varuṇa has the disposal of water. The mantra referred to is likewise often mentioned in these texts: AS. 3, 25 (*bījāvāpanavidhi-*); 5, 33 (*kumbhasthena jalenaiva vāruṇaṃ mantram uccaran | avaṭaṃ pūrayitvā* . . .); 12, 33.

141) AS. 26, 31 ff. adds some ominous phenomena to be observed in the shoots; st. 38 it has the vessels preserved after decorating them with the five colours (see above, n. 56) and flowers (among which the *padma-*), adding the remark that the Moon is the lord of all shoots (st. 39). (It may parenthetically be recalled that according to the belief of many English country people seeds grow better sown when the moon is waxing). — For comparable customs see Meyer, o.c., II, p. 91 and Crooke, Religion and folklore, p. 88. — For Viṣṇu and the moon (V. worshipped with the names of the moon) see Hohenberger, p. 138; 142 f.

god's potency as the supreme authority governing these highly important events [142]).

Other features in the above description of Viṣṇu's processional festival are hardly in need of comment. That clay or mud are, in rites connected with vegetation, a matter of great importance might be illustrated by an abundance of Indian data [143]). Let it suffice to quote TĀ. 10, 1, 8 where the clay is invoked to give *puṣṭi-* "a thriving condition": *tvayi sarvaṃ* (to wit: *puṣṭisādhanaṃ yavagodhūmādidravyam* Sāyaṇa) *pratiṣṭhitam.* — Jars, pitchers, especially jars full of water [144]) are likewise often used for ritual ends. In a series of ceremonies described in the AS., ch. 35 the guru and the officiating priests are given directions to throw about a handful of flowers (st. 21, the accompanying mantra is *bhūḥ prapadye* [145])), to bow to the god and to ask his permission whilst pronouncing the formula *kṣamasva devadeva* [146]) — in the meanwhile dances, songs, and instrumental music are executed, and the śākuna sūkta [147]) recited to the accompaniment of the murmur arising from the recital of holy words —, to carry a jar "with a stream of water and a rain of flowers" on the head, to take the image of the god and, after performing a circumambulation of the temple and entering, to place a full jar on the right side of the god, etc. and to give the deities in the temple a bath.

According to the texts these festivals bring about *śānti-* (annihilation of all evil influences) and *puṣṭi-* (prosperity). The due observance of the god's great festival leads to health and prosperity and causes rain to fall in the proper season (cf. e.f. AS. 54, 2; 55, 1).

---

142) Cf. also the contexts in which the *aṅkura-* turn up in these texts, e.g. AS. 28, 47 *aṅkuraiḥ pūrṇakumbhaiś cāpy alaṃkuryat* . . .; 49, 6 *mṛdaṃ ca* . . . *dhānyāny apy aṅkurās* . . .; 50, 15 f.

143) The reader may for the sake of brevity be referred to Meyer, o.c., III, p. 294 (s.v. Einschmieren), 295, 318. Cf. also AS. 49, 25; 50, 2; 4 ff.; KS. ch. 47 and 48.

144) I refer to F. D. K. Bosch, De gouden kiem, p. 121 ff. and passim.

145) TĀ. the formula forms part of the mantras for the adoration of the great Brahma when reflected upon as a porpoise; 4, 42, 2 it is one of a long series of benedictions on the completion of a ceremony.

146) "Be indulgent, God of gods!"

147) ṚV. 10, 165.

INDEX I

Names of deities, mythical persons etc.

INDEX II

Subjects

INDEX III

Technical terms and other words

INDEX IV

Scholars

N.B. In the notes and indices the capital ś is rendered by Ç because this type was not available.